THE CAMBRIDGE COMPANION TO
LIFE AND DEATH

GiftAid Donation

CW00701317

This volume meets the increasing
philosophical issues connected with ...
cance of life and death, and the ethics of killing. What is it
to be alive and to die? What is it to be a person? What must
time be like if we are to persist? What makes one life better
than another? May death or posthumous events harm the
dead? The chapters in this volume address these questions,
and also discuss topical issues such as abortion, euthanasia,
and suicide. They explore the interrelation between the
metaphysics, significance, and ethics of life and death, and
they discuss the moral significance of killing both people
and animals, and the extent to which death harms them.
The volume is for all those studying the philosophy of life
and death, for readers taking applied ethics courses, and for
those studying ethics and metaphysics more generally.

STEVEN LUPER is chair of the philosophy department at
Trinity University. He is author of several books, includ-
ing *A Guide to Ethics* (2001) and *The Philosophy of Death*
(Cambridge University Press, 2009), and most recently editor
of *The Skeptics: Contemporary Essays* (2003) and *Essential
Knowledge* (2004).

Continued at the back of the book

The Cambridge Companion to
LIFE AND DEATH

Edited by
Steven Luper
Trinity University

CAMBRIDGE
UNIVERSITY PRESS

CAMBRIDGE
UNIVERSITY PRESS

University Printing House, Cambridge CB2 8BS, United Kingdom

Cambridge University Press is part of the University of Cambridge.

It furthers the University's mission by disseminating knowledge in the pursuit of education, learning and research at the highest international levels of excellence.

www.cambridge.org
Information on this title: www.cambridge.org/9781107606760

© Steven Luper, 2014

This publication is in copyright. Subject to statutory exception and to the provisions of relevant collective licensing agreements, no reproduction of any part may take place without the written permission of Cambridge University Press.

First published 2014

A catalogue record for this publication is available from the British Library

Library of Congress Cataloguing in Publication data
The Cambridge companion to life and death / edited by Steven Luper.
    pages   cm. – (Cambridge companions)
Includes bibliographical references and index.
ISBN 978-1-107-02287-4 (hardback) – ISBN 978-1-107-60676-0 (pbk.)
1. Life.   2. Death.   I. Luper, Steven, editor of compilation.
BD431.C225 2014
128–dc23
2013036667

ISBN 978-1-107-02287-4 Hardback
ISBN 978-1-107-60676-0 Paperback

Cambridge University Press has no responsibility for the persistence or accuracy of URLs for external or third-party internet websites referred to in this publication, and does not guarantee that any content on such websites is, or will remain, accurate or appropriate.

CONTENTS

CONTRIBUTORS

NICHOLAS AGAR is Professor of Ethics at the Victoria University of Wellington. His latest book, *Truly Human Enhancement: A Philosophical Defense of Limits*, will be published in 2014.

DAVID ARCHARD is Professor of Philosophy at Queen's University Belfast. He was previously at the universities of Lancaster, St Andrews, and Ulster. He is co-editor of *Procreation and Parenthood: The Ethics of Bearing and Rearing Children* (2010; with David Benatar).

MARK A. BEDAU is Professor of Philosophy at Reed College. His books include *Emergence* (2008; edited with Paul Humphreys), *The Nature of Life* (2010; with Carol Cleland), *The Ethics of Protocells: Moral and Social Implications of Creating Life in the Laboratory* (2009; edited with Emily Parke), and *Living Technology: Five Questions* (2010; edited with Pelle Guldborg Hansen, Emily Parke, and Steen Rasmussen).

KRISTER BYKVIST is Professor of Practical Philosophy at the Department of Philosophy, Stockholm University. Before taking up this professorship he was a Fellow and Tutor in Philosophy at Jesus College, Oxford. In addition to numerous articles, he is the author of *Utilitarianism: A Guide for the Perplexed* (2009).

DAVID DEGRAZIA is Senior Research Fellow in the Department of Bioethics, National Institutes of Health and Professor of Philosophy at George Washington University. His books include *Taking Animals Seriously: Mental Life and Moral Status* (1996), *Human Identity and Bioethics* (2005), and *Creation Ethics: Reproduction, Genetics, and Quality of Life* (2012).

ix

EYJÓLFUR K. EMILSSON is Professor of Ancient Philosophy at the University of Oslo. He is the author of two books, *Plotinus on Sense-Perception* (1988) and *Plotinus on Intellect* (2007), in addition to numerous articles on ancient philosophy.

JOHN MARTIN FISCHER is Distinguished Professor in the Department of Philosophy, University of California, Riverside, where he has been Chair and held a University of California President's Chair. He is the editor of *The Metaphysics of Death* (1993) and the author of *Our Stories: Essays on Life, Death, and Free Will* (2009).

MATTHEW HANSER is Professor of Philosophy at the University of California, Santa Barbara. His papers on harm and harming include "Harming Future People" (*Philosophy & Public Affairs*, 1990), "Why Are Killing and Letting Die Wrong?" (*Philosophy & Public Affairs*, 1995), "The Metaphysics of Harm" (*Philosophy and Phenomenological Research*, 2008), and "The Wrongness of Killing and the Badness of Death" (*The Oxford Handbook of Philosophy of Death*, 2012).

KATHERINE HAWLEY is Professor of Philosophy at the University of St Andrews. She is the author of *How Things Persist* (2001) and *Trust: A Very Short Introduction* (2012).

THOMAS E. HILL, JR. is Kenan Professor of Philosophy at the University of North Carolina, Chapel Hill. His essays on moral and political philosophy are collected in *Autonomy and Self-Respect* (1991), *Dignity and Practical Reason in Kant's Moral Theory* (1992), *Respect, Pluralism, and Justice: Kantian Perspectives* (2000), and *Human Welfare and Moral Worth: Kantian Perspectives* (2002).

JENS JOHANSSON is Associate Professor of Philosophy at Uppsala University. He is the author of several articles on the philosophy of death and related issues, and co-edited *The Oxford Handbook of Philosophy of Death* (2012; with Ben Bradley and Fred Feldman).

SIMON KELLER is Associate Professor of Philosophy at the Victoria University of Wellington. He has published extensively on topics in moral and political philosophy and is the author of *The Limits of Loyalty* (2007) and *Partiality* (2013).

NOAH LEMOS is the Leslie and Naomi Legum Professor of Philosophy at the College of William and Mary. He works in ethics and epistemology and is the author of *Intrinsic Value* (1994), *Common Sense* (2004), and *An Introduction to the Theory of Knowledge* (2007).

STEVEN LUPER is Professor of Philosophy at Trinity University. His books include *The Possibility of Knowledge* (1987), *Invulnerability: On Securing Happiness* (1996), and *The Philosophy of Death* (2009).

ERIC T. OLSON is Professor of Philosophy at the University of Sheffield. He has written two books on the nature of people, *The Human Animal* (1997) and *What Are We?* (2007), as well as numerous articles.

MARYA SCHECHTMAN is Professor of Philosophy at the University of Illinois at Chicago. She is the author of *The Constitution of Selves* (1996) and many articles on personal identity and the philosophy of mind.

MICHAEL TOOLEY is Professor of Philosophy at Colorado University, Boulder. He is the author of *Time, Tense, and Causation* (1997), *Knowledge of God* (2008), and *Abortion: Three Perspectives* (2009).

KADRI VIHVELIN is Associate Professor of Philosophy at the University of Southern California. She is the author of *Causes, Laws, and Free Will: Why Determinism Doesn't Matter* (2013) and of many essays on topics in metaphysics and ethics, including free will, causation, counterfactuals, the doing/allowing distinction, moral responsibility, and the unfreedom of the time traveler.

JAMES WARREN is a Reader in Ancient Philosophy at the University of Cambridge and a Fellow of Corpus Christi College. He is the author of *Facing Death: Epicurus and his Critics* (2004).

ACKNOWLEDGMENTS

The idea for this book was formed back in 2007, when I was working on a book about the philosophy of death and it occurred to me that it would be worthwhile to bring together some sharp people to write about the full range of issues concerning death. I was soon reminded that these issues very often are related to puzzling issues concerning life. The most obvious example is that to understand what it is to die, it is crucial to understand what it is to be alive. Similarly, to get clear about what it is to cease to exist, it is crucial to know what sort of thing we are. So the scope of the book grew. Fortunately, Hilary Gaskin at Cambridge University Press supported the project, and has helped in numerous ways to get it done. The result is before the reader. I am grateful to her, and to all of the contributors to this book.

Introduction

This book is devoted to the metaphysics of life and death, the significance of life and death, and the ethics of life and death. As will become apparent, these three topics are interrelated. Work on the nature of death benefits from work on the nature of life, and bears on life's significance, while discussions of the moral significance of killing people and other animals draw on discussions of the nature of the interests of such creatures (at various stages of their development), the significance of their lives, and the extent to which death harms them.

The first of the three parts of the book (concerning the metaphysics of life and death) begins with a chapter on the nature of life by Mark Bedau. As he notes, many theorists attempt to illuminate life by setting out necessary and sufficient conditions for being an organism. Bedau calls this the Cartesian approach, and suggests that we abandon it in favor of the Aristotelian approach, by which we attempt to explain distinctive features of "living worlds," or actual complexes of mutually interacting organisms and micro-organisms. To that end, we can begin with the simplest forms of chemically based life (such as bacteria). On the model Bedau endorses, a minimal chemical system is alive just if it brings together three mutually supportive capacities. First, it controls itself using information stored within it. Second, it maintains, develops, and repairs itself using materials and energy it extracts from its environment. Third, it protects its constituent chemical operations from external threats by "localizing" them, giving them an identity over time. Bedau goes on to suggest that "there is no particular time at which life begins or ends. As new chemical interactions among components create more complex networks of capacities, the whole chemical system becomes more and more alive."

The second chapter, by Eric Olson, considers what it is to be one of *us*. We must answer this question if we are to know when our existence begins, when it ends, and what it entails. Many issues hang in the balance. For example, if our persistence conditions include psychological continuity, it is much easier to justify the collection of organs from donors. Olson defends animalism, the view that you and I are organisms – specifically, human beings. The toughest challenge to animalism is the contention that we would go with our brains if these were moved into fresh brainless bodies. A human being can be kept alive, at least for a time, after its liver is removed, and the same goes for its brain. If its liver or brain is moved, the human being stays behind. So if you are a human being, you stay behind when your brain is moved elsewhere. By contrast, if you go with your brain, you are not a human being, and animalism is false. But if you aren't a human being what are you? According to Olson, theorists who claim that we go with our brains have not given us a satisfactory answer to this question, and their view makes it hard to avoid the strange metaphysical contention that being alive is incompatible with the capacity for thought.

Chapter 3, written by Katherine Hawley, is devoted to the question of how different views of time bear on our nature and interests. Eternalism says that past and future things are as real as present things. Does it follow that our lives are fated to unfold in certain ways? According to presentism, neither past nor future things exist. A third view of time, the growing-block view, says that while past and present things exist, future things do not. Neither presentism nor the growing-block view seems to suggest fatalism, but do they imply that we do not exist in the future, and that, consequently, nothing that happens in the future can affect us? Hawley denies that eternalism supports fatalism, and she denies that presentism or the growing-block view implies that what we do now cannot affect the future, since, on all three views, what happens now has a causal effect on what *will* happen in the future. She goes on to explain how different views of time are related to different views about how people and other things persist over time.

Chapter 4, written by Marya Schechtman, discusses whether identity is malleable in some sense – that is, whether it is possible to control what our persistence conditions are, to some extent. If we can manipulate the conditions under which we survive, many intriguing issues arise. For example, perhaps death does not occur when people usually think; maybe we can survive events that are normally considered fatal. Also, many theorists say that what is in our interests depends on our identities; if that is true, and identity is malleable, our interests may also be. Schechtman distinguishes between literal and figurative ways of understanding a person's identity. Typically, we think that only the latter sort of identity is malleable, but she offers an account of numerical identity within which it, too, is literally malleable, at least to a degree. Her idea is that whether one survives a change depends, at least in part, on whether one *identifies* with that changed individual – whether one recognizes her as oneself. It also depends on whether others believe one has survived. Since, on her approach, whether we survive over time depends, in part, on the attitude we and others take about whether we survive, and that attitude is malleable, so is identity.

Chapter 5 concerns the question: what is it for a human being to die? David DeGrazia discusses the strengths and weaknesses of three standards for determining when death occurs: first, the whole-brain standard, which says that death occurs when the entire brain irreversibly ceases to function; second, the traditional cardiopulmonary standard, according to which death occurs when the heart and lungs irreversibly cease to function; and third, the higher-brain standard, which says that death is the irreversible loss of the capacity for consciousness. He criticizes the last, mostly on the grounds that it rests on an implausible account of personal identity, and while he defends an updated version of the cardiopulmonary standard, he eventually concludes that, for practical reasons, the best policy is much like the one that is already in place in the USA, namely the standard that consists in the disjunction of the (updated) cardiopulmonary standard and the whole-brain standard. At the end of his chapter he suggests that some of the things that are now done only posthumously should be done sooner: in some cases, people who are irreversibly unconscious should be allowed to die and vital organs should be removed for transplantation.

Part II of the book concerns the significance of life and death. The first chapter in this part of the book, Chapter 6, clarifies how lives may be assessed. What makes one life better than another?

According to Noah Lemos, author of this chapter, the judgment that a life is good might mean that it is choiceworthy because it is high in various values, such as moral goodness, or welfare. However, Lemos limits his investigation to what makes a life high in welfare. He discusses the three leading accounts of welfare (noting that one or other might also turn out to be relevant to the moral goodness of a life): preferentism (or the desire satisfaction theory), which says roughly that you are well-off to the extent that you satisfy your desires; hedonism, which says that only your states of pleasure and displeasure determine your level of welfare; and the objective list view, which says that various things are good or bad for you regardless of whether you want them and no matter whether you enjoy them. All three views come in competing versions and face difficulties. In particular, on the objective list view it is difficult to compare the value of one good as against another, and to assess the relative contributions of different goods to welfare.

In Chapter 7 Eyjólfur Emilsson discusses the view that a good life is not made better by lasting longer. While this idea is no longer taken very seriously, it was defended by Stoics, Epicureans, and Plotinus. Emilsson reviews some of the grounds they offered for it, focusing mainly on the Stoic approach, then offers further considerations in its favor. If true, this ancient position would be very important, as it suggests that we are not harmed by our mortality: dying shortens a life, but it has no power to make that life worse than it would have been if it had gone on forever. It also bears on whether it might be good to be immortal. If extending a good life does not make it better, immortality is of no benefit to us. Emilsson suggests that when the ancient theorists deny that happiness is cumulative, they mean that it "does not accumulate like monthly savings that gradually raise the sum in our bank accounts." They do not deny that our happiness *over a lifetime* will be greater than it otherwise would be if we add on more happy days; they deny that our happiness *at later times* will not be greater than at earlier times if we add on more happy days. According to Plotinus, the former – having more happiness over a lifetime – should not matter to us, however, since neither past nor future happiness is "there for us to enjoy now."

In Chapter 8 John Martin Fischer asks: in what sense death is harmful to those who die? Famously, Epicurus denied that death harms us if it is understood as the cessation of existence. On one interpretation, his denial is based on the following experience requirement: we are harmed by something only if we can have an unpleasant experience as a result of it. According to the experience requirement, being punched or having one's reputation destroyed might be harmful to us, as these can give us bad experiences. But death seems harmless precisely because it removes the possibility of experience. According to Fischer, however, we should reject the experience requirement, as there are serious counterexamples to it. One that he offers is a modification of the betrayal example: suppose that a powerful person named White can and will prevent you from ever experiencing anything bad as a result of being betrayed. In that case, even though you are betrayed, you cannot have any bad experiences as a result. Yet it still seems bad for you to be betrayed. Fischer concludes that death is bad insofar as it deprives a victim of life that would have been good for her.

Chapter 9 concerns when, if ever, we incur mortal harm, or harm for which death is responsible. It seems reasonable to assume that something harms a victim only if there is indeed a *subject* who receives the harm and a *time* when that subject incurs that harm. But if death harms us, either it does so while we are alive or later. If we opt for the second solution we appear to run head-on into the problem of the subject: assuming that we do not exist after we are alive, no one is left to incur harm. If we opt for the first solution – death harms its victims while they are alive – we have a ready solution to the problem of the subject, but it seems impossible for death to have any ill effect on us while we are living since it will not yet have occurred. Jens Johansson, author of Chapter 9, criticizes two possible views concerning when death's victims incur mortal harm: subsequentism, or the view that they incur harm after death occurs, and priorism, the view that they incur harm while they are alive. Johansson then argues in favor of a third view, atemporalism, which says that while death does indeed harm those who die, there is no time at which they incur mortal harm. In this respect, death is not alone, he says: many sorts of events are also atemporally harmful.

The focus of Chapter 10 is the symmetry problem, which arises from the following symmetry claim: the period of non-existence that precedes my birth seems saliently identical to the period of non-existence that will follow my death. Appealing to the symmetry claim, Epicureans argued that since prenatal non-existence is not bad for us, posthumous non-existence is not bad for us either. In Chapter 10 James Warren discusses the two main ways to respond to the Epicurean argument if we wish to insist that death may harm its victims. Asymmetrists deny the symmetry claim and say that while death is harmful prenatal non-existence is not, while Symmetrists accept the symmetry claim and deny that prenatal non-existence is harmless to us.

In Chapter 11 Simon Keller discusses whether we may be harmed by events that happen after we are dead. He notes that different sorts of thing may contribute directly to our welfare, to how well our lives go. Among these are experiences; good experiences seem to boost our welfare, while bad experiences lower it. If experiences were the only constituents of welfare, then clearly posthumous events could not affect it at all. But it is plausible to say that welfare includes other elements, such as achievements. If that is right, then there is a strong case for the possibility of posthumous harm after all, since things that happen after we are gone may well affect whether we achieve goals we set ourselves, such as the goal of having a lasting reputation. So maybe one component of welfare – involving achievement – can be lowered (or raised) by posthumous events even though another component – involving positive experiences – cannot be. Keller goes on to point out that the two components differ in interesting ways. In particular, it might be that positive experiences contribute more to welfare than do achievements, and in that case it might be best not to allow our efforts to help the dead achieve their goals get in the way of our efforts to help the living enjoy positive (and avoid awful) experiences.

Chapter 12 discusses life's meaning. Here Steven Luper suggests that a person's life has meaning if, and only if, she achieves the aims that she devotes her life to freely and competently. These achievements are themselves the meaning of her life. He discusses how life's meaning is related to its purpose and to a person's identity and welfare. Luper suggests that, like happiness, meaning is an element of welfare; one's life can have meaning even if one is quite unhappy, and one could be happy even though one's life lacks meaning. He criticizes reasoning that suggests that life is absurd and emphasizes that, with respect to meaning, immortals are no better off than mortals: long or short, one's life can have meaning in the fullest sense.

Part III of the book concerns the ethics of bringing living things into existence and the ethics of killing them. The first chapter in this part of the book, Chapter 13, discusses the ethics of enhancing life, especially when this means replacing human beings with creatures that are thought to be superior to us. Nicholas Agar equates the enhancement of a human capability with its improvement. One scenario he discusses involves the enhancement of some people to such an extent that they are able to dominate others who opt not to enhance themselves. Another is the possibility that people could be so altered that they become more morally sophisticated, morally better. Yet another scenario involves replacing bits of the brain with electronic chips, allowing human beings to take advantage of the speedy pace of technological improvement.

Chapter 14, written by David Archard, discusses several issues that arise in connection with procreation or bringing people into existence. The main issue is whether it is wrong to create people. One line of thought is this: suppose that if we create someone her life will be worth living but just barely so – that is, what is good in her life more than offsets the bad, but not by much. When we focus on how low such a person's prospects are, it might seem objectionable to bring her into the world. But is it? Were we not to bring her into being, she would not exist at all; for her, the only alternative to a marginally good existence is none at all. This suggests that it is rarely wrong to procreate, since most people would prefer even a marginally good existence to none at all. On another way of looking at things, however, procreation seems to be entirely unacceptable. David Benatar asks us to consider a merely possible person named Fred. We do not think that Fred is harmed by not being made actual, even if it means he will miss out on a very good life. However, we do think that Fred is harmed by being made actual if it means that he will endure a very bad life. Hence we should maintain Fred's status quo as merely possible, which is unobjectionable, for fear of subjecting him to a bad existence, which is objectionable, and the same goes for any possible person.

In Chapter 15 Michael Tooley asks why and when we may kill embryos and fetuses. The answer depends on the nature of persons and the nature of life; if we were never embryos or fetuses it seems more plausible to say that killing them carries far less significance than killing persons. The answer also depends on what an individual's interests are and on what sort of harm death may do to its victims. Tooley criticizes Don Marquis' widely discussed view concerning the ethics of abortion. According to Tooley, Marquis objects to abortion on the grounds that (typically) it violates the principle that it is wrong to deprive a human being of valuable states which it otherwise would have had – states that normal human beings, such as you and I, enjoy. Tooley says that this principle is flawed, and hence Marquis' case against abortion fails. According to Tooley, you and I are neo-Lockean persons, which are roughly continuing subjects of mental states, that form memories, and that have various other sorts of psychological features, and whatever it is that makes killing *us* wrong would also make it wrong to kill other neo-Lockean persons. Yet something need not be an organism to be a neo-Lockean person; these might include angels and sophisticated machines that are not even alive. In place of Marquis' account, Tooley offers a rights-based account, according to which all and only neo-Lockean persons have a right to continued existence. As for fetuses, they are organisms, but not persons, and organisms do not have the right to continued existence.

Chapter 16, written by Thomas E. Hill, Jr., concerns whether we may kill ourselves and if so, why and when. His topic obviously is closely related to the permissibility of assisted suicide and euthanasia, but Hill does not address these directly. Arguing from a broadly Kantian perspective, Hill assumes that we owe it to ourselves to live and die with dignity, and suggests that suicide is objectionable when a failure to respect ourselves leads us to give up the potential to live on as rational autonomous agents. Proper self-respect rules out suicide in some circumstances, but not in others. For example, it rules out suicide when self-contempt prompts us to abandon life even though we could have remained rational autonomous agents, but not when extreme and irremediable pain would have made it impossible to continue to function rationally.

In Chapter 17 the aim is to clarify when we may kill others in self-defense. Kadri Vihvelin discusses Judith Thomson's influential view on the matter, according to which defensive force may be used against those who have lost the right not to be killed. Some of Thomson's critics reject her account since it implies that innocent people may have lost the right not to be killed. For example, if a villain gives you a drug that makes you crazy, and, thus crazed, you are about to kill me, you have lost your right not to be killed, and it is permissible for me to use lethal force to stop you. Vihvelin shows that some of these criticisms of Thomson fail, then offers her own criticism. According to Vihvelin, the moral appropriateness of defensive force does not depend on the forfeiture of the right not to be killed.

Chapter 18 concerns the nature of the obligation not to let people die. More specifically, it concerns the reasons we have to aid those in distress. In this chapter Matthew Hanser explores the view that the duty to aid is imperfect, meaning roughly that "[i]t requires one to perform aiding actions from time to time, often enough, but it does not specify exactly when one must give aid, or whom one must aid, or how much aid one must give." To clarify the duty, Hanser distinguishes between reasons that have requiring force and reasons that have justificatory force. The duty to aid involves the latter; that some person is in need justifies us, and makes it permissible (but not obligatory) for us, to assist that person even though it means neglecting other responsibilities (such as a promise we made to meet a friend for dinner). However, if we encounter enough persons in need, the justificatory force of our reasons to assist increases, so "although these reasons are not individually requiring, we do have a duty to act in accordance with reasons of this *kind* from time to time."

In Chapter 19, the final chapter, Krister Bykvist discusses the leading reasons why it might be objectionable to end the existence of animals, then considers whether on the same sorts of grounds it would be objectionable to bring about the extinction of a species. It seems wrong to end the existence of animals for three main reasons: we owe it to individual animals not to kill them; killing them frustrates their preferences; and killing them is against their interests. Species extinction need not involve killing any animals; it might instead result from causing them to be infertile. Still, perhaps it is wrong to annihilate a species because we owe it to that species that we not bring about its extinction, or because doing so would frustrate its preferences or because it would be against its interests. However, it seems difficult to make a strong case against species extinction on such grounds. According to Bykvist, it may be more promising to explain the wrongness of species extinction on the grounds that preserving species has some sort of noninstrumental value.

Part I The metaphysics of life and death

1 The nature of life

INTRODUCTION

The nature of life has implications for a variety of big questions. When does life begin and end? What does death entail? What sorts of things can die or be killed? What exactly is the difference between living and nonliving matter? What kinds of value do life forms possess? Do all life forms have some kind of intrinsic value or inherent worth? What exactly are we asking about when we seek the nature of life? Does life even have a nature that is fixed and objective?

Let us start by clarifying what we seek when attempting to understand the nature of life. Imagine that we had a complete list of each and every individual organism that actually was alive or had ever been alive in the entire history of our planet (or, by the same token, in the entire history of the known universe). This list would not be an account of the nature of life. It is silent about all of the kinds of life that could exist but never do. We seek an understanding of life that encompasses all possible forms of life that could actually exist anywhere in the universe.

Here are some things that we do *not* seek. We are *not* interested merely in the meaning of the word "life" (or its translations in other languages). Everyone who is reading this knows the meaning of that word, and anyone who does not can consult a dictionary. We are asking a different question, and its answer is not in the dictionary.

We are also *not* interested in the analysis of our current conception of life. We want to know the true nature of life, not merely someone's current conception of life. Some philosophers and scientists think that an account of the nature of life must mesh with our intuitions about which things are alive (e.g. Boden 1999). But we should not place *too* much weight on our intuitions. A good theory of the nature of life might make us reconceptualize and recategorize life. It might change our intuitions about which things are alive. Our intuitions carry some weight, but the true nature of life need not fit them all.

STRATEGIES FOR EXPLAINING THE NATURE OF LIFE

The nature of life is notoriously controversial. The lack of consensus among the scientists and philosophers who are interested in the question is well known. The standard views about the nature of life are quite diverse, and most seem to have straightforward counterexamples (Sagan 1970; Farmer and Belin 1992; Luisi 1998; Bedau and Cleland 2010). This section will survey the main strategies used to characterize life, and briefly indicate their strengths and weaknesses.

The simplest strategy for characterizing life is to focus attention on one key property. This property is typically one of the following three. First is the ability to reproduce (e.g. Poundstone 1985). A multiplying population of spontaneously reproducing entities is one of life's central hallmarks, but it cannot by itself be used to define life. A counterexample is living entities that cannot reproduce, such as mules or sterile insect casts. A deeper problem comes from nonliving things that *can* reproduce, such as certain robots (Lipson and Pollack 2000; Pollack *et al.* 2001).

The ability to undergo Darwinian evolution is a second property often linked to the nature of life (Sagan 1970; Maynard Smith 1975; Cairns-Smith 1985; Joyce 1994; Maynard Smith and Szathmáry 1995; Bedau 1996; Ruiz-Mirazo *et al.* 2004). The Darwinian focus comes from evolution's ability to explain the adaptive traits exhibited by all forms of life. One of life's central hallmarks is the impressive functional traits that were produced by cumulative episodes of Darwinian evolution. Since Darwinian evolution involves a population of reproducing entities, any problems with reproduction-centered views (such as mules and sterile organisms) tend to be inherited by Darwinian views of life.

A third property often used to define life is metabolism, or the related property of being a self-maintaining and self-sustaining chemical system. Closely related are accounts of life that focus on organization, autonomy, autopoiesis, and closed causal loops (Maturana and Varela 1973; Rosen 1991; Escobar 2012; Ruiz-Mirazo and Moreno 2012). An early influential statement of the metabolism-centered view of life appears in Schrödinger's influential classic, *What is Life?* (1969: 74–76):

What is the characteristic feature of life? When is a piece of matter said to be alive? When it goes on "doing something", moving, exchanging material with its environment, and so forth, and that for a much longer period than we would expect an inanimate piece of matter to "keep going" under similar circumstances ... It is by avoiding the rapid decay into the inert state of "equilibrium" that an organism appears so enigmatic ... How does the living organism avoid decay? The obvious answer is: By eating, drinking, breathing and (in the case of plants) assimilating. The technical term is metabolism ... [T]he essential thing in metabolism is that the organism succeeds in freeing itself from all the entropy it cannot help producing while alive.

There is much to say in favor of the view that life centrally involves metabolism. The view nicely explains why a crystal is not alive: because there is no metabolic flux of molecules throughout it. Furthermore, a complex chemical system can remain in existence in the face of the second law of thermodynamics only if it has a metabolism that enables it to feed upon negative entropy, as Schrödinger puts it. The second law of thermodynamics (the law that entropy always increases in a closed system) makes metabolism at least a necessary condition of all physical forms of life. The main drawback with viewing metabolism as the key to the nature of life is that many things that are not alive at all still have something like a metabolism. Standard examples are a candle flame, a whirlpool, and a convection cell (Maynard Smith 1986; Bagley and Farmer 1992).

If no single property defines life, perhaps we could still characterize life by a *list* of properties. For example, the so-called NASA definition of life as a self-sustaining chemical system capable of undergoing Darwinian evolution (Joyce 1994) is a list with two properties. Many lists are relatively short, and many contain the same or similar properties. Monod (1971) lists three properties: "teleonomic" or purposeful behavior, autonomous morphogenesis, and reproductive invariance. Crick (1981) focuses on self-reproduction, genetics and evolution, and metabolism. Almost identical is Küppers' list (1985): metabolism, self-reproduction, and mutability.

In *The Problems of Biology* Maynard Smith (1986) cites two properties: metabolism and parts with functions. Ray (1992) cites self-reproduction and the capacity for open-ended evolution. Farmer and Belin (1992: 818) list eight hallmarks of life: process, self-reproduction, information storage of self-representation, metabolism, functional interactions with the environment, interdependence of parts, stability under perturbations, and the ability to evolve. Koshland's list has seven properties: program, improvisation, compartmentalization, energy, regeneration, adaptability, and seclusion (Koshland 2002). Mayr (1982) once proposed a list with eight items.

Although different lists spotlight different properties, many of the same properties appear again and again. Below we will have occasion to use the list from Tibor Gánti (2003), which includes both criteria for life of an individual living organism and criteria for populations of organisms that populate a planet and sustain what Gánti calls a "living world."

- *Holism.* A living system must be an individual unit that cannot be subdivided without losing its properties. The system has properties that all of its parts lack.
- *Mortality.* Living systems must be mortal, so death is characteristic of life. Nonliving systems cannot die.
- *Active information.* A living system must have a subsystem carrying information that controls the whole system's origin, development (construction), and function.
- *Flexible control.* Processes in living systems must be regulated and controlled to achieve the system's continuous existence.
- *Metabolism.* A living system must have a metabolism that harvests material and energy from the environment and transforms them by chemical processes into the material and energy in the system. Dormant seeds and frozen bacteria have an inactive metabolism.
- *Robust stability.* A living system must be inherently stable, homeostatic, self-organizing, self-maintaining, robust, and adaptive. The system persists despite unpredictable changes in its environment.
- *Growth and reproduction.* Living systems in general must be capable of growth and reproduction if they are to form

a "living world." Some individual organisms cannot reproduce but are living; one example is old animals that can
no longer reproduce. So, the capacity to reproduce is neither necessary nor sufficient for an individual organism to
be alive.

- *Evolvability.* Living systems in a "living world" must have
the capacity for hereditary change and for evolution, which
can generate increasingly complex and differentiated forms
over successive generations. As with reproduction, an individual organism can be alive even if it cannot help produce
and shape future generations.

The properties in these lists of life's hallmarks are impressive
and interesting. They can deepen our sense of wonder that such a
striking collection of complex properties appear together in a wide
diversity of life forms. Of course, merely listing hallmarks does not
explain why some properties and not others belong on the list. And
there is always the looming threat of counterexamples: "Each property by itself, even when considered with others, is unable to clearly
delineate the living from the non-living" (C. Taylor 1992: 26).

If fixed lists of properties fail to capture the nature of life, perhaps a more loosely defined cluster of properties would do better.
Maybe the varieties of life are no more unified than the properties
studied in overlapping disciplines, such as population genetics,
molecular genetics, evolution, ecology, cytology, biochemistry, and
physiology (Sober 1992). We could represent the typical nature of
life with a *cluster* of properties. Individual living organisms would
typically have the properties in the cluster but the properties would
not be individually necessary or jointly sufficient for an individual
living entity to be alive. Instead, forms of life might share only a
Wittgensteinian family resemblance (e.g. Pennock 2012). Different
forms of life might share properties in the cluster, but properties
could be missing in some forms of life. The cluster of properties
associated with organisms are strictly neither necessary nor sufficient for an organism to be alive.

The cluster conception of life has a natural explanation for the
borderline cases, because clusters typically have vague boundaries. It also has a natural explanation for why life comes in degrees,
because the different regions of the cluster of all life forms exhibit

key properties to different degrees. The cluster conception also has a natural explanation for the meta-puzzle concerning why life is so controversial. Counterexamples to definitions of life are to be expected if forms of life are unified by only a Wittgensteinian family resemblance. The main weakness with the cluster conception is that explanations end too quickly. The view does not explain why certain properties in the cluster are significant and other properties are not. The dimensions of the cluster of properties associated with living organisms is simply accepted as a contingent empirical fact. The cluster conception cannot explain why life is characterized by one cluster of properties rather than another. Those who expect some further explanation for life's characteristic properties will find the cluster conception of life unsatisfying.

Various skeptics question whether there is anything interesting to learn about the nature of life. Sober (1992) suspects that the only interesting questions will focus on other more specific issues, such the nature of metabolism or Darwinian evolution. Machery (2012) finds it either impossible or pointless to identify the nature of life, and recommends that we no longer ask that question. Evelyn Fox Keller (2002) doubts that life is the sort of natural kind that has a scientific definition, and she concludes that life is instead merely a *human* kind. The view that life is a human kind easily explains the existence of borderline cases. As the concept of life changes with the interests of science and technology, one should expect boundaries of the concept to change, thus creating borderline cases. The view also provides some general ammunition for explaining life's puzzles, for it is unsurprising if a mutable human construct generates puzzles. New concepts generated by scientific and technological advances can be expected to violate older taxonomies, including the distinction between life and nonlife (Keller 2002).

An alternative to Keller is to figure out the biochemical universals that govern all forms of life in the known universe. Concerns from astrobiology sometimes motivate this kind of biochemical definition of life, when scientists attempt to specify the biochemical properties that any form of life must have (Pace 2001; Benner *et al.* 2004). The biochemical universals of life include limits from thermodynamics, energetics, materials, and even geography. A biochemical definition describes the physical, chemical, and biological possibilities open to any biochemical system that meets some prior account of life. This kind of "definition" describes the biochemical consequences and constraints that all actual examples of life must obey.

Another form of skepticism grows from our ignorance about life, and leads to doubts that we can formulate any good theories (Cleland 2012). Our ignorance is illustrated by the problem of the sample size of one. Generalizations about possible forms of life must rest on what we know about actual life forms. Biologists study a number of different model organisms, like *Escherichia coli* (a common bacterium), *Caenohabditis elegans* (a nematode), and *Drosophila melanogaster* (a fruit fly). The diversity of model organisms helps us generalize about all life. But all of the life forms we have studied are part of only *one* large, interconnected evolving network of organisms. So, generalizations about life now rest on a *sample size of one*. This problem can be overblown, though. Our one sample of life is a vast biosphere consisting of a vast number of species, many of which have millions (or more) of individual organisms. Furthermore, these individual organisms have many complex similarities and differences, because of the diversity of forms of life. Our one sample of life is much more than just one single organism. It is extremely heterogeneous, and it can suggest and support significant generalizations. Furthermore, progress in fields like artificial life and synthetic biology could easily increase the sample size beyond one. If we synthesize a new kind of system that exhibits life's characteristic properties, we have new opportunities to learn about the nature of life at its most general. Furthermore, even if we know that our current accounts of life have severe limitations, it can still be useful to formulate and defend provisional theories. These provisional theories would be acknowledged to be fallible and subject to revision, but the same holds for other scientific theories, and constructing and defending provisional theories helps improve our theories (Wimsatt 1987).

CARTESIAN AND ARISTOTELIAN APPROACHES
TOWARD THE NATURE OF LIFE

The diversity and lack of consensus about the nature of life is striking, and it frustrates progress on understanding life. In the rest of this chapter I will diagnose this controversy and propose a route to forward progress. The key to my diagnosis is the contrast between two approaches to understanding the nature of life, which with some historical license I dub *Cartesian* and *Aristotelian*.

Today, most discussions of the nature of life adopt the Cartesian approach. The Cartesian figures out the essential properties of life by collecting a large and diverse set of paradigm cases of individual living organisms and identifies the properties that are possessed by all and only those paradigm cases. The organisms are considered individually and in isolation from all other organisms, unlike the normal contexts in which they live their lives by continually interacting with many other kinds of organisms.

An Aristotelian asks a different question: what is the best way to explain the characteristic phenomena of life? Explaining the phenomena of life is a large and detailed job, which includes explaining life's familiar hallmarks, borderline cases, and puzzles. For the Aristotelian, the nature of life is revealed in the details of these explanations. The Aristotelian focuses on organisms in the natural context in which they carry out their lives, interact with their environment, cooperate with other forms of life (Dupré and O'Malley 2009), and ask what underlying processes and mechanisms generate and explain the characteristic phenomena of life.

We might debate exactly what is most characteristic of life but it is safe to include life's familiar hallmarks. A representative statement of life's hallmarks is Gánti's (2003) list, discussed above. The characteristic phenomena of life should also include its borderline cases, such as viruses and prions, which self-replicate and spread even though they lack a metabolism. Dormant seeds or spores are another kind of borderline case, as are frozen bacteria and frozen insects. Some nonliving things have some of the chemical characteristics of life. A candle flame preserves its form while its constituent molecules are constantly changing, so it has something like a metabolism (Maynard Smith 1986). Populations of microscopic clay crystallites growing, proliferating, and undergoing natural selection are another kind of borderline case; they seem to be nonliving but they evolve by natural selection (Bedau 1991). Any adequate account of the nature of life should explain these borderline cases.

The characteristic phenomena of life also include various puzzles about life. Any account of the nature of life should explain and resolve these puzzles. Let us look briefly at five puzzles that an account of life should help to illuminate.

Origin of life. How does life or biology arise from nonlife or pure chemistry? How does a system undergoing merely chemical evolution, in which chemical reactions are continually changing the concentrations of chemical species, differ from one that is alive?

Emergence of life. Life emerges from nonlife. The properties of life forms arise over time from the properties of various nonliving material components (molecules and the like). The puzzle of emergence is to explain what happens when life emerges from nonlife in a way that is consistent with the current state of science and the current philosophical approaches to emergence (Bedau and Humphreys 2008).

Degrees of life. Can something be more or less alive? Is the distinction between the living and the nonliving a dichotomy or a continuum with many shades of gray? Borderline cases like viruses, which are unable to replicate unless they infect a host, are one motivation for replacing a dichotomy with a continuum. Similarly for spores or frozen bacteria that remain indefinitely in a state of suspended animation but then come back to life given favorable conditions. Are viruses and spores alive, or only potentially revivable? Furthermore, the earliest life forms presumably differed very little from their recent nonliving predecessor. Maybe no sharp boundary separates life and nonlife, but rather things that are more or less alive, and life takes a continuum of values (e.g. Cairns-Smith 1985; Emmeche 1994; Dennett 1995).

Matter, form, and function. Each individual living organism is a material object, and it will remain in existence only if it is composed of the right material components. The individual molecules in the materials are inessential; they are transitory, continually recycling with material in the environment. What matters for life is the functional organization of those molecules. The nature of life concerns the form in which certain kinds of materials are arranged and organized.

Why so controversial? There is a meta-puzzle about why the nature of life is so puzzling. Life seems to be a basic and fundamental part of the natural world, but there is no consensus about the nature of life. Any account of the nature of life should clarify why it is so controversial.

In summary, the Aristotelian approach evaluates how well an account of life explains life's characteristic phenomena, including hallmarks of life like those from Gánti, borderline cases like the virus, and puzzles like the five just outlined. Later, this chapter illustrates an Aristotelian evaluation of an important account of minimal chemical life.

THE PMC MODEL OF MINIMAL CHEMICAL LIFE

We now focus on the nature of the simplest form of life: *minimal chemical life*. This focus serves two purposes. It provides a concrete illustration of the Aristotelian approach to the nature of life, explained above. In addition, the nature of minimal chemical life could eventually help illuminate certain aspects of the nature of more complex forms of life, including humans. The most familiar paradigm cases of minimal chemical life are bacteria and other simple single-celled organisms, such as archaea. Another paradigm case consists of the minimal chemical systems called "protocells" that are constructed out of nonliving materials by those who are trying to make new forms of life in the laboratory (Rasmussen *et al.* 2004; Rasmussen *et al.* 2009).

One might ask whether scientists need care about the nature of minimal chemical life. Most biologists can safely ignore the question and focus their attention on model organisms. However, those studying the origin of life on earth need some working hypothesis about what life is, so they can choose which chemical systems to study. Similarly, astrobiologists seeking signs of "weird" life on places like Mars or Titan (a moon of Saturn covered with lakes of liquid methane) need some working hypothesis about what life is (National Research Council 2007). Liquid water might be unnecessary for extraterrestrial life (Benner *et al.* 2004), which also might lack familiar molecular signatures, such as DNA, ribosomes, or proteins (Rasmussen *et al.* 2003). In addition, those attempting to create synthetic life in the laboratory need a working hypothesis about what life is (Szostak *et al.* 2001; Deamer 2005; Luisi 2006; Rasmussen *et al.* 2009). How can you create life from nonliving materials unless you are guided by some working hypothesis about the nature of life?

The PMC model abstracts away from chemical materials and concentrates on chemical functionalities, such as metabolism and spatial isolation. Most chemical functions can be chemically realized in many different materials. So, a functional account of life would cover all the chemical systems that share the right chemical functionalities. Physics and chemistry will constrain what kinds of materials can achieve which kinds of functional processes, but within those boundary conditions any material realization of the right functional details is an example of minimal life.

The PMC model is the rough consensus in the protocell community that is trying to make life from nonliving materials in the laboratory. According to the PMC model, a minimal chemical system is living just in case it integrates three chemical functionalities in such a way that they mutually support one another (Rasmussen *et al.* 2009). The first chemical functionality enables important chemical aspects of the system to be controlled by information stored in the system. This information is inherited when the system reproduces, and that can be modified and changed. The second functionality is the ability to extract materials and free energy from the environment and digest them to produce the chemical resources needed to maintain and repair the chemical system, and to enable it to grow and ultimately reproduce. The third functionality is for the system to maintain an identity over time by localizing all its material constituents, concentrating reagents and protecting their proper chemical operation from molecular parasites and poisons. These functions all exhibit an innocent kind of holistic autonomy, in the sense that they are created and sustained by the operation of the whole system itself, rather than by some external agency. For this reason, the system is responsible for its own continual functioning.

These three operational functionalities are embodied in three integrated chemical systems: a program that controls cellular processes with replicable and inheritable combinatorial information (the functional analog of genes), a metabolism that extracts usable energy and resources from the environment, and a container that keeps the whole system together. In this Program-Metabolism-Container (PMC) model, the terms "container", "metabolism", and "program" are to be understood functionally and with minimal constraints on their chemical realization. For example, the program might not use DNA, RNA, or any other familiar biopolymers (e.g. Sagre *et al.* 2000). Similarly, a metabolism might harvest redox energy or energy from light, and it might use complex material precursors or use ATP and complex enzymes. In many contexts the container will be an amphiphilic structure such as a vesicle or micelle, but the required spatial localization might be achieved in some other way.

The PMC model holds that the three functionalities of container, metabolism, and program must be chemically integrated so that they mutually support each other. The continual operation of each component functionality depends on the proper support from the other component functionalities. The integrated triad comes about because of chemical cooperation. A biopolymer sequence or structure can have catalytic properties. The production of the building blocks of containers and programs can feed on an external energy source provided by the metabolism. And a container can act as a catalyst in various ways, e.g. the thermodynamic conditions within a lipid aggregate or at the water–aggregate interface are different from those within bulk water, and the aggregate or interface conditions can be catalytic. These examples illustrate how one of the components of a PMC system can support the operation of the other components.

HOW THE PMC MODEL EXPLAINS THE
CHARACTERISTIC PHENOMENA OF LIFE

I have recommended an Aristotelian methodology for evaluating accounts of the nature of life. I have also proposed an account of minimal chemical life: the Program-Metabolism-Container (PMC) model. In this section I will show how the PMC model explains the eight hallmarks, borderline cases, and puzzles about life. The examples have two purposes. The first is to illustrate how an account of life could explain the phenomena of life, and thereby help clarify the Aristotelian approach. The second purpose is to illustrate the scientific support for the PMC model.

First, notice that the PMC model has, or fits with, natural and plausible explanations for each of Gánti's eight hallmarks of life:

- *Holism*. The PMC model depicts minimal chemical life as a specific kind of autonomous, self-sustaining holistic system of chemical interactions. This holistic system will not sustain itself if its parts cannot interact (if the catalytic and energetic interactions are dropped).
- *Mortality*. PMC systems are self-supporting functional systems, so the whole system will fall apart and "die" unless the parts remain correctly functionally connected.
- *Active information*. The P in PMC is precisely an active information system that programs and supports many of the living cell's important chemical processes. This information can mutate, and so natural selection can shape a population of PMC systems.
- *Metabolism*. The M in PMC is metabolism, signifying its central role in minimal chemical life.
- *Robust stability*. A properly functioning PMC system preserves its overall structure and organization in a changing environment, by adapting to environmental fluctuations. This robust stability is helped by a boundary (the C in PMC) that preserves the system's identity over time.
- *Flexible control*. The programs in PMC systems control many of the system's important holistic emergent properties, including those that enable the system to continue to exist and flourish. In general, the functional support provided by the PMC triad provides feedback loops that achieve a flexible self-regulation.
- *Growth and reproduction*. Individual PMC systems can grow until they are so large that they spontaneously divide in two by fission, and thereby reproduce. A population of PMC systems could survive and flourish if enough of them grow and divide quickly enough.
- *Evolvability*. A population of PMC systems could evolve, because the individual systems can reproduce, and pass on traits that affect the ability of the daughter systems to survive and reproduce. If there is a variety of possible forms of programs, metabolisms, and containers, and if information inheritance is somewhat imperfect, then the process of evolution by natural selection could improve the program,

metabolism, and containment functions, and it could improve the functions performed by component catalysts and structures. Thus, given the right conditions, a population of PMC systems could undergo evolution by natural selection.

So, the PMC model provides or fits with natural and unified explanations for many of life's heterogeneous hallmarks. This is one important piece of support for the PMC model.

A second important piece of support for the PMC model is its natural explanation for the virus borderline case. Viruses typically are biologically active only when they inhabit other cells as hosts. An isolated virus particle is not usually considered to be alive. But when a virus infects a cell it hijacks the cell's metabolism to generate copies of the virus, the cell containing the virus is itself alive. Some borderline cases are due merely to insufficient information; they are merely epistemic and reflect only our ignorance. The PMC model gives a *structural* rather than epistemological explanation of viruses. According to the PMC model, the relevant information about viruses is reflected in the different patterns of PMC interactions in the inert and infective phases of the viral life cycle. An isolated virus particle is an inert informational polymer (an inactive program, P), typically inside a protein coat (a container, C). This PMC model focuses on the way in which C functionally supports P. When this virus particle infects a host, it hijacks its host's metabolism and fills the host with copies of itself. The virus particle typically provides no support for its host's program, metabolism, or containment. Once we have sorted out these details of PMC interactions involving viruses, what further information could possible resolve whether viruses are alive? Some patterns of PMC interactions are so simple that they are clearly not alive, such as the inert virus particle. A fully connected and mutually supporting pattern of PMC interactions is the pattern of the minimal chemical life that protocell scientists aim to create in their laboratories.

The PMC model can account for life's hallmarks and its borderline cases. We will now see how it explains and resolves five puzzles about life. Explaining and resolving these puzzles is another important component of an Aristotelian evaluation of an account of life.

Origin of life. The PMC model is a natural framework for describing the stages by which a nonliving chemical system gradually becomes more and more alive. The process of adding more and more of the supporting interactions among the program, metabolism, and container is the process by which life originates. According to the PMC model, the origin of life was the process of adding supporting interactions until the PMC triad is fully mutually supporting.

Emergence of life. Minimal chemical life is the paradigm case of "weak" emergent properties, which are produced by causal webs that are so complex that they are incompressible (Bedau 2011). Weak emergence is consistent with many reasonable forms of reductionism (Bedau 1997, 2003). The PMC model reduces minimal chemical life to a network of functional connections among a program, metabolism, and container. Clearly, the causal webs in fully mutually supporting PMC networks are complex.

Matter, form, and function. Each individual life form is a complex chemical object. And being alive requires certain kinds of materials; it sets various constraints on the material components of life forms. But, in other ways, the materials are inessential. For one thing, they are transitory; the molecules in your body are continually cycling and recycling with material in the environment. What matters, in general, is the functional organization that is realized by combinations of those molecules. In other words, the defining feature of life is not the material out of which it is constituted, but the form in which that material is arranged and organized. The form of a living system is the functional network in which those materials interact. This formal, functional perspective on life supports all functional approaches to life. The PMC model is one example.

Degrees of life. The PMC model gives a natural explanation for how minimal chemical life is a matter of degree. Note that the PMC model concerns interactions among complex chemical capacities. The number and strength of interactions among the capacities introduces one natural scale for comparing chemical systems. Another natural scale reflects the degree to which the chemical capacities are operating properly. Yet another scale reflects the degree to which a PMC system is adapted to the contingencies of its current environment, thereby increasing the chance that the system will survive. All of these scales provide ample resources for explaining how minimal chemical life comes in various kinds of degrees.

28   MARK A. BEDAU

Why is life so puzzling? The PMC model itself can somewhat help explain why life is so puzzling, because the PMC model construes life as a certain kind of complex chemical system, and this complexity in itself will generate some puzzles. It helps to explain why someone could focus on metabolism or the ability to evolve as central to the nature of life. Another, independent explanation for why life is so puzzling is that many people give the question a Cartesian rather than Aristotelian interpretation. The Cartesian seeks necessary and sufficient conditions for being an individual living organism, independent of any particular environment. The Aristotelian seeks the most plausible, comprehensive, and unified underlying explanation for the characteristic phenomena associated with life, including its hallmarks, borderline cases, and puzzles.

What can we conclude from all this? First, the PMC model provides a concrete and detailed example of an Aristotelian evaluation of an account of the nature of life. Second, we learned that the PMC model either explains or fits with explanations for all of the characteristic phenomena of life. Given this the Aristotelian judges the PMC model to be a provisionally adequate account of minimal chemical life. Of course, there is nothing to stop a different account from also explaining the same characteristic phenomena. So, a second account may be equally adequate.

SUMMARY AND BROADER IMPLICATIONS

The nature of life is complex and controversial. There is a striking diversity among the main strategies for explaining the nature of life. At the same time, the core of the characteristic phenomena involving life is relatively uncontroversial, and it contains life's hallmarks, borderline cases, and puzzles.

Most investigations into the nature of life are Cartesian and seek necessary and sufficient conditions for being an individual living organism. This chapter instead recommends an Aristotelian strategy which seeks the best explanation for the characteristic phenomena exhibited by "living worlds" (to use Gánti's phrase). These worlds contain many interacting organisms and micro-organisms in some historically and geographically grounded environment.

We get an initial purchase on the nature of life if we focus on minimal chemical life. The PMC model is the view of minimal chemical life that is common in protocell science. The model emphasizes chemical supporting relations between three core capacities: program, metabolism, and container. The supporting relations are functional and can be achieved by many different materials. According to the PMC model, the paradigm case of minimal chemical life is a chemical network in which each core capacity supports each core capacity. If we evaluate the PMC model as an Aristotelian, the PMC model naturally explains or fits with explanations of the phenomena of life. The PMC model emerges as viable for an Aristotelian.

The PMC model specifically applies only to minimal chemical life such as bacteria. Nevertheless, the general form of the model does shed some tentative light on larger controversial questions, such as when life begins and when it ends. Humans and other organisms are much more complex than bacteria; they involve much more complex chemical and biological processes. But the life of an organism involves the functional integration of various complex capacities (including those in the brain and the immune system). Both living states of humans and bacteria involve the functional integration of complex biological and chemical capacities; although the details differ, there is a functional similarity. From the perspective of the PMC model, a minimal chemical system remains alive as long as it remains a self-sustaining, repairing, growing, and reproducing chemical network with complex production and feedback effects a program, metabolism, and container. The whole system remains alive as long as each of the components continues supporting the network and enabling it to function properly.

From this perspective, there is no particular time at which life begins or ends. As new chemical interactions among components create more complex networks of capacities, the whole chemical system becomes more and more alive. An analogous gradual decline in capacities happens at the end of life. As organisms age, capacities degrade and are lost. As more and more capacities decline, life lessens and eventually is gone altogether. When enough capacities fail to function properly, the organism dies. The loss of critical capacities can be either abrupt or gradual. As long as life's characteristic capacities continue functioning together properly, an organism remains alive and in general good health.

2   The nature of people

TWO QUESTIONS

What is a person? The question can mean two different things. One is what it is to be a person, as opposed to a nonperson – a some*one* and not merely a some*thing*. You and I are people (or persons); stones are not. Whether a chimpanzee is a person is disputed. What is this property – personhood – that we've got and stones haven't got, and which there is dispute about whether chimpanzees have? An answer would be a completion of the formula

> Necessarily, x is a person if and only if ... x ...

Or maybe the formula should be "Necessarily, x is a person at time t if and only if ... x ... t ...", so as not to prejudge the issue of whether something could be a person at one time and a nonperson at another.[1] Call this the *personhood question*.

The most common answer is that to be a person (at a time) is to have certain special mental properties (at that time). Locke, for instance, said that a person is "a thinking intelligent being, that has reason and reflection, and can consider itself as itself, the same thinking thing, in different times and places" (1975: 335). To be a person is roughly to be intelligent and self-conscious. Others say that a thing needn't actually *have* any special mental properties at a given time to count as a person then, as long as it can acquire them. A newborn infant is probably not self-conscious – not able to consider itself as itself, the same thinking thing in different times and places – but it might still count as a person because it has the capacity to develop to the point where it is.

I thank Steve Luper for comments on an earlier version.

These answers specify a sort of role or job. We call something a person because it fills, or has the potential to fill, that role. The personhood question asks what the person-role is and how a thing has to relate to it in order to be a person.

But to ask what a person is can also be to ask what sort of thing fills that role. Suppose Locke was right in saying that to be a person is to be intelligent and self-conscious. What sort of beings *are* intelligent and self-conscious? What are *we* – readers and authors of this book? What are our other fundamental properties, beyond those that make us people? And how do those other properties relate to our special mental properties? To put the question in the formal mode, what do we refer to when we say 'I'? We might call this the *question of personal ontology*.

An analogy will help distinguish these two questions. Suppose we ask what a star is. One sort of answer is easy enough: a star is a luminous object visible in the night sky. (Ignore the planets – "wandering stars" – and the moon.) The ancient Greeks knew this much. But they didn't know what those luminous objects *were*. They thought they did: they believed, naturally enough, that the stars were fires, and emitted light by combustion. But they were wrong. *We* know that stars are enormous balls of superheated gas that emit light by nuclear fusion. So in a way the ancients knew what stars were, and in a way they didn't. They knew the star-role, but not what sort of objects filled the role. In other words, they understood what it was to be a star, but not the nature of the stars.

This chapter is about personal ontology: about what sort of things stand to intelligence and self-consciousness as balls of superheated gas stand to the property of shining in the night sky. What is the fundamental nature of a human person? (I will say no more about the personhood question, which I don't find especially interesting or important.)

ANIMALISM AND ITS DISCONTENTS

You might think that modern science has answered this question, just as it has discovered the nature of the stars. The ancients (some of them) believed that intelligent, self-conscious beings were invisible, immaterial things, or at any rate things with an immaterial part – a part without which nothing could think at all. Neuroscience has proved them wrong on this point. *We* know that intelligent, self-conscious beings are biological organisms. We also know that organisms are made up entirely of atoms – tiny bits of matter – and that their being alive consists in a complex array of physical activities which impose a stable form on those atoms as they are constantly renewed by the processes of ingestion, excretion, and respiration. Some of those physical activities are mental phenomena: thought and conscious awareness. Or maybe the physical goings-on *produce* thought and consciousness but are not themselves mental. (How these physical goings-on relate to mental phenomena is the central topic of the philosophy of mind: the so-called "mind–body problem.") But whatever those details may be, the answer to the question of personal ontology is that we are organisms. There is an organism – a member of the primate species *homo sapiens* – that you see in the mirror. That animal is not merely "your body" (whatever exactly that means), or the material thing that somehow contains you. The person and the animal are one and the same being.

The view that we are organisms is nowadays called *animalism*. But despite its obvious appeal, few philosophers accept it.[2] Their main objection is that it has unattractive consequences about what it takes for us to persist from one time to another – what Locke called *personal identity*. Suppose your brain were put into my head. (These consequences do not arise only in science fiction, but that's where they are most forceful.) The being who ended up with your brain would remember your life, and not mine. He would have your beliefs, preferences, plans, and other mental properties, for the most part at least. Who would he be? Me with a new brain, or you with a new body? Or maybe neither, but someone else instead?

Animalism implies that he would be me with a new brain. He couldn't be you, because the operation does not move an organism from one head to another. It simply moves an organ from one animal to another, just as a liver transplant does.[3] One animal loses its brain and stays behind as an empty-headed vegetable or corpse; another has its brain removed and replaced with yours. According to animalism, you are the donor organism and I am the recipient. You get an empty head; I get your brain. So the operation would fill my head with false beliefs: I would become convinced that I lived in your house, worked at your job, and was the child of your mother.

I would think I was you. I would be systematically mistaken about who I am and how I fit into the world.

Many people reject this description. They say that the one who got your brain would be you, not me. A brain transplant is not like a liver transplant. It doesn't move an organ from one person to another. Rather, it moves a *person* from one organism to another. To transplant your brain is to transplant *you*. The surgeons remove you from your own head and put you into my head. More precisely, they cut away all your parts except your brain, move you across the room, then give you a new set of parts (previously mine) to replace the ones you lost. As for me: when my brain is removed to make way for yours, I go with that organ and leave the rest of my parts behind. So no one is mistaken about who he or she is.

Whatever the merits of this alternative description may be, however, it is incompatible with animalism. The animal you would be if you were any animal at all would stay behind with an empty head in the transplant operation. So the alternative description implies that you and that animal would go your separate ways: you would go with your brain and the animal would stay behind. But a thing and itself can never go their separate ways. Even though you are not actually going to have a brain transplant, you have a property that no animal has, that of *possibly* going with your transplanted brain and leaving your animal body behind. And if you have a property that no animal has, then you are not an animal. Not only are you not *essentially* an animal. You are not a biological organism at all, even contingently. Call the claim that animalism has false consequences about who would be who in a brain-transplant operation the *transplant objection*.

MIND–LIFE DUALISM

But if we're not biological organisms, what are we? On this point the transplant objection leaves us completely in the dark. It tells us as much about the nature of people as the ancient Greeks would know about the nature of the stars if the Oracle had told them that stars were not fires and then fallen silent.

In fact our position (if we accept the transplant objection) is even worse than that. Not only do we not know what we are, but we have to deny that a human organism could ever be intelligent and self-conscious. If a human organism *could* be intelligent and self-conscious, the animal now writing these words would be. But if I know anything, I know that *I* am intelligent and self-conscious. So if I were something other than the intelligent animal sitting here, I would be one of *two* intelligent beings writing these words and thinking these thoughts. In fact I would be one of two *people* here, since the animal would satisfy any plausible account of personhood (Locke's, for instance). What's more, some human people – perhaps half of them – would be organisms after all, and would stay behind with an empty head if their brains were transplanted. But the transplant objection was supposed to show that *any* person would go with her transplanted brain. If there really were two people now writing this, a nonanimal person who would go with his transplanted brain and an animal person who would stay behind, the animal person would have the same grounds for supposing that *he* would go with his transplanted brain as the nonanimal person has. They would both find the transplant objection equally convincing, since they would think in exactly the same way. But the animal person would be mistaken about what he was and what it takes for him to persist through time. So for all I could ever know, *I* might be the one making the mistake.

To avoid this problem of "too many thinkers," advocates of the transplant objection will want to say that the animal sitting here is not intelligent and self-conscious. I, the non-animal, am the only intelligent being here.[4] Yet that animal would be intelligent and self-conscious if any organism was. It has a normal adult human brain; it has just the right surroundings and the right education; it behaves exactly as an intelligent and self-conscious being does in both actual and counterfactual situations. If this doesn't suffice for it to be intelligent and self-conscious, that can only be because it is metaphysically impossible for *any* human organism to be intelligent and self-conscious. And in that case it is hard to see how any organism, human or otherwise, could have any mental property whatever.

So if we would go with our transplanted brains, then we are not organisms. And unless we share our thoughts with beings who *would* go with their transplanted brains, it follows that human animals have no thoughts at all and are not intelligent. That leads more or less inevitably to the conclusion that it is metaphysically impossible for any biological organism to have any mental property. This is a sort of mind–body dualism – in fact a form of substance dualism. It says that nothing could be both alive, in the biological sense, and thinking or conscious. What appears to be a single conscious, living being is in reality two beings, one conscious but nonliving and one living but nonconscious. A thing's physical properties would never suffice for it to have any mental properties.

This is not quite the Cartesian view that no material thing could think or be conscious. It is a dualism not of mind and matter, but of mind and *life*. If anything, it is even more baffling than Cartesian dualism. If we ask why it should be metaphysically impossible for an organism to think, the most natural answer is that this is because organisms are material things. The idea that no entirely material thing could think or be conscious – that mentality could not arise out of brute mechanics – has an undeniable attraction, and it is no surprise that great philosophers (Plato, Descartes, Leibniz, and Kant, for example) have found it compelling. But mind–life dualism allows that you and I are material things. In fact this is what most critics of animalism believe. It follows from their view that *some* material things can and do think, but no biological organism could be any more sentient than a stone. How could that be? If any material thing could think, would it not be some sort of animal?

THE BRAIN VIEW

Although the transplant objection rules out our being animals, it says nothing about what we might be instead. And it implies that no biological organism could ever think or be conscious, without saying anything about why. Can this double mystery be solved? Is there an account of what we are that would both make it possible for us to go with our transplanted brains and explain why it is impossible for organisms to think?

Few proposed accounts of what we are say or even suggest anything about animal thought.[5] Rather than go through these views and explain why they don't, I will devote the rest of this chapter to one that does: the odd-sounding view that we are *brains*.[6] Each of us is literally a three-pound chunk of soft, yellowish-pink tissue lodged within the cranium. Few of us have ever really seen ourselves, or any other person. (Most of us wouldn't want to.) We see only the organisms that we are hidden parts of.

Despite its faintly comical implications, the "brain view" has real virtues. The most obvious is that if you are your brain, then you go where your brain goes, answering the transplant objection. And it explains why organisms cannot think by implying (or at least suggesting) that a thinking organism is like a powerful car. Just as a car is powerful by having a powerful engine as a part, an organism thinks by having a thinking brain as part. Animals think only in the derivative sense of having a smaller part that thinks strictly speaking. So there are two thinking beings there, the organism and the person, only in the harmless sense in which there are two powerful things, the car and its engine, on the drive. There is only one true, nonderivative thinker. Those nonderivative thinkers – the brains – are ourselves.

The brain view may look even better supported by modern science than animalism, since it is informed by the knowledge that thought and consciousness are not distributed throughout the organism, but take place in the brain: the brain is the organ of thought, and not, as Aristotle believed, a device for cooling the blood. Here are two further advantages the brain view has over animalism.

THE REMNANT-PERSON PROBLEM

Suppose your brain is removed from your head as before, only this time it isn't transplanted, but kept alive in a vat. It may be possible for your brain in this condition to think more or less normally. (Countless philosophical thought experiments assume this.) That would make it a person. This "remnant person" would not be an organism. It would be "alive" only in the way that a kidney awaiting transplant is alive – in that its individual cells are kept alive. Nor was it previously an organism: there was only one organism there before your brain was removed, and the operation merely gave it an empty head.

That some people are not organisms is perfectly compatible with animalism. Animalism does not say that all people are organisms. It is consistent with the existence of a theistic god – an immaterial person. But it does say that all *human* people are organisms; and a remnant person would presumably be a human person. More seriously, it is difficult for animalists to explain where the remnant person could have come from. Did she exist before the operation? If so (and if she was a person then), animalism implies that there were then two people within your skin: the animal, who stayed behind with an empty head, and the remnant person, who went into the vat. It would be a mystery why they came out of the operation in such different states. And it's hard to see how you could have known which person *you* are: whether you were going to lose your brain or end up in the vat. If the remnant person did not exist before the operation, on the other hand, then the surgeons must have brought that person into being by removing your brain from your head. But how can you *create* a person just by cutting away sustaining tissues (Johnston 2007; Olson in press)?

It's hard to find a plausible account of the nature of remnant people and of what happens to them in the brain-removal operation that is compatible with animalism. But on the brain view there's no problem: the remnant person is just you. You were a brain all along. The operation merely changes your surroundings.

DOUBLE-BRAINED ORGANISMS

Another objection made against animalism is that it rules out the possibility of there being more than one person associated with a single organism at once (Campbell and McMahan 2010). There are real cases in which two heads grow from a single human torso, each supporting an independent mental life. There is every appearance of there being two intelligent, self-conscious beings here – beings as psychologically different as you are from me. In recorded cases of this sort there is always some duplication of vital organs – two hearts, for example – suggesting that there may be two organisms present, which simply overlap by sharing parts lower down. In that case each twin would be an organism. But this needn't always be so. It seems possible, at least, for a single organism to contain two independent brains or organs of thought. And here too there would appear to be two different people. If that appearance is correct, then at least one of them would not be an organism.

It is hard to say what sort of beings these "twin people" could be in a way that is compatible with animalism. If an organism with two independent organs of thought were to "contain" at least one human person who was not an organism, wouldn't an ordinary human animal also contain a nonanimal person – someone of the same metaphysical nature as the twin people? But in that case animalism itself would have the absurd consequence that there are two different people writing this chapter, one an animal and one a nonanimal. (The remnant-person case raises the same problem: since remnant people would not be animals, we should expect each human animal in normal circumstances to be associated with a person of the same nature as a remnant person.)

Perhaps animalists can say what sort of things the twin people would be and why there are no people of that sort in ordinary cases. Or maybe they can explain why there could never be a single organism with two independent organs of thought. Otherwise they will have to say that there would be just one intelligent, self-conscious being in such cases, namely the organism. Such a person would have two independent mental lives (van Inwagen 1990: 188–212). But friends of the brain view can accept that there would be two people in these cases, just as there appear to be. The two people would be the two brains.

THINKING-SUBJECT MINIMALISM

Let us now examine the brain view more critically. What makes it important as an alternative to animalism is its account of why an organism cannot think, namely because it has a smaller part that *really* thinks. This raises an obvious and pressing question: what determines which part of an animal is the thinking part? Why suppose that it's the brain? Why not the head, or the entire nervous system, or all of the animal except its feet? Why should having feet as parts prevent a thing from thinking (in the strict, nonderivative sense)? For that matter, why should *any* smaller part of the animal think nonderivatively? It may be true that an animal uses its brain to think, and not its liver or its heart. But why infer from this that the brain literally does the thinking? (I use my hands to tie my shoes. It doesn't follow that my hands tie my shoes.) If the brain view is true, this question must have an answer.

As far as I can see, the answer must be something like this: a being thinks in the strict, nonderivative sense only if all its parts

are somehow directly involved in its thinking (Hudson 2007: 218f.).
A human organism cannot think because it has superfluous parts –
feet, eyebrows, kidneys – that have no direct involvement in its
mental activities (or rather, those mental activities going on within
it). My feet may play a role in my sense-perception (one mode of
thinking) by enabling me to feel the ground, but that involvement is
indirect. Since I am a nonderivative thinker, it follows that my feet
are not parts of me. Neither is my liver, my heart, nor any other part
outside my brain. A true thinker must be made up of all and only
the objects directly involved in its thinking. Otherwise it would be
entirely arbitrary to say that each of us is a brain rather than some
other part of an animal, or indeed a whole animal.

Call this claim *thinking-subject minimalism* (Olson 2007:
87–90). Minimalism faces two serious objections. First, it implies
that every part of a human organism is either directly involved
in thinking or not directly involved (or neither definitely directly
involved nor definitely not directly involved – a borderline case).
But which parts are which? I couldn't think unless my brain had
a supply of oxygenated blood; so my heart and lungs are involved
in my thinking, but not, presumably, directly involved. Why not?
It's not generally true that for every activity an organism engages
in, there is a fact about which parts of the organism are directly
involved in it and which are only indirectly involved or not involved
at all. No one would say that every part of an organism is either directly involved or not directly involved in its *walking*. If anything
is directly involved in my walking, my feet are. Yet my feet have
parts – toenails, for instance – that make no contribution to my
walking. It seems to follow that only certain parts of my feet are
directly involved. But which ones? Suppose I have excess water in
my feet owing to poor circulation, which hinders my walking. The
"excess" water molecules could hardly be directly involved in my
walking. But which ones are the excess molecules and which ones,
so to speak, belong there? Yet *some* water molecules must be directly involved in my walking if anything is.

I doubt whether there is any principled way of saying which molecules are directly involved in my walking and which are not. The
reason is not that some are on the borderline between being directly
involved and not being directly involved, but that there is simply

no such distinction. The whole idea of "being directly involved in someone's walking" is a muddle. The same goes for such activities as eating and sleeping. And it looks no different for thinking or being conscious. Some atoms might be *more* directly involved in my thinking than others, but there is no saying which ones are "directly involved" without qualification. If so, minimalism implies that there is no saying which things are parts of me, and thus no saying which thing I am. That is not a coherent conclusion. Certainly it is incompatible with the brain view.

The second problem arises even if there really is an absolute division between the things directly involved in thinking and those not directly involved. If some things are directly involved in my thinking generally, some will be directly involved in specific mental activities. Some of my molecules will be directly involved when I imagine clouds; others – different ones – will be directly involved when I hope for rain. And any reason to suppose that a true thinker must be composed entirely of objects directly involved in its thinking looks like an even better reason to suppose that a true imaginer or hoper must be composed entirely of objects directly involved in its imagining or hoping, respectively. If that reasoning is correct, then each human being contains within it a nonderivative imaginer and a nonderivative hoper. On the likely assumption that these mental activities each involve different parts of the brain, the hoper and the thinker will be two different beings.

It follows that a human being hasn't got one nonderivative "general" thinker within it – the brain – but only a lot of specialist thinkers: one that imagines, another that hopes, one that thinks about metaphysics, and so on. It is unlikely that any part of the organism could have more than one sort of thought. The thing that imagines clouds, for instance, would be either too big to hope for rain – by having superfluous parts not directly involved in that hoping – or too small, by not including such parts (or both). What we take to be a person able to perform all sorts of mental operations would really be many beings, each able to perform only one. If a person is by definition both intelligent *and* self-conscious, there would be no people (or at least no human people). The reasoning behind the brain view leads almost ineluctably to this absurd conclusion.

THE BRAIN VIEW AND PERSONAL IDENTITY

A more obvious objection to the brain view has to do with its consequences for our identity over time. It implies that a human person could not survive without her original brain. Suppose the parts of your brain were all replaced with new parts just like them – gradually, so that your thought processes were not interrupted and there was someone psychologically continuous with you throughout the process. If these parts were large enough, the result would seem to be not your original brain with new parts, but a new and numerically different brain. Your original brain would have ceased to exist. But few would take this to imply that you had ceased to exist – that the resulting person would have to be someone else, mistakenly convinced that she was you (Unger 1990: 157f.). Likewise, it is tempting to suppose that you could become wholly inorganic, if your parts were gradually replaced with appropriate prostheses (e.g. Unger 1990: 122; Baker 2000: 123). Here too your original brain would cease to exist. The brain view rules out your surviving in these cases: if you are your brain and your brain ceases to exist, then you must cease to exist.

Or suppose that when I die my brain is fixed in a solution of formaldehyde and kept in a jar. It looks as if my brain would still exist in the jar: putting a brain in formaldehyde need not destroy it.[7] Otherwise we'd be left wondering what it *does* take for a human brain to persist (and whether your brain could continue to exist when removed from your head and transplanted or kept in a vat). But if my brain would exist in the jar, then according to the brain view *I* would exist in the jar. I could become a specimen in formaldehyde.

These consequences are not only implausible, but go against the thinking that led to the brain view in the first place. Its attraction lay in its compatibility with the thought that you would go with your brain if that organ were transplanted, rather than staying behind with an empty head as animalism implies. The reason *why* you would be the one who got your transplanted brain was supposed to be that she would be psychologically continuous with you. Everyone takes the moral of the transplant objection to be that our persistence through time consists in some sort of psychological continuity. But the brain view implies that psychological continuity is neither necessary for us to persist (as the formaldehyde case shows) nor sufficient (as the gradual-replacement cases show): as with animalism, our identity over time would consist in some sort of brute physical continuity.

THE FUNCTIONING-BRAIN VIEW

The brain view appears to have consequences about personal identity at least as surprising as those of animalism. This has led some of those attracted to the brain view to reject these consequences (Tye 2003: 143; Parfit 2012). They say that I couldn't literally become an anatomical specimen: if my brain permanently ceased to function, as it would if it were put in formaldehyde, I would no longer exist (though I would still exist if my brain were kept functioning in a vat). The thing in the jar would be my brain – or the thing that was once my brain – but it would not be me. They might also say that if the parts of my brain were gradually replaced with new ones in a way that preserved psychological continuity, I would still exist even though my original brain would not.

Either claim would imply that we are not brains. If I would not exist when my brain is fixed in formaldehyde, then my brain could outlive me. If I could exist after my brain has been destroyed and replaced with something new, then I could outlive my brain. But nothing can outlive itself. If my brain could exist in a jar of formaldehyde and I could not, or if I could become wholly inorganic and my brain could not, then my brain and I are two different things.

But if we're not brains, what are we? Merely saying that our identity over time consists in some sort of psychological continuity does not tell us what we are – not even if the sort is specified precisely. The claim that we are intelligent, self-conscious beings that persist by virtue of a certain kind of psychological continuity leaves entirely open what *sort* of intelligent beings we are. (Suppose the ancient Greeks had known not only that the stars were luminous objects visible in the night sky, but also the conditions under which stars persisted through time. They would still not have known what the stars were.)

Someone might say that we're just like brains, only with psychological persistence conditions: some sort of psychological continuity is necessary and sufficient for us to persist. So we survive as long as we continue to function psychologically, whereas a brain can exist in a nonfunctioning state. We are not brains, we might say, but *"functioning* brains."[8]

Of course, if there are things just like brains except that they persist by virtue of psychological continuity, then there are presumably things just like organisms except that *they* persist by virtue of psychological continuity. If we could be "functioning brains," we could just as easily be "functioning organisms."[9] And if our being functioning brains would answer the brain-part-replacement and brain-in-formaldehyde objections, our being functioning organisms ought to suggest analogous answers to the transplant and remnant-person objections – in which case those objections provide no reason to think that we're any smaller than whole organisms. But maybe the possibility of double-brained organisms is a reason to think that we're brain-sized.

SUBSTANCE DUALISM AGAIN

I find the "functioning-brain view" hard to understand: I don't really know what a functioning brain is supposed to be. But I will try to say something useful about it nonetheless.

One obvious question is whether there *are* such things as functioning brains. Maybe there are such things as brains. But why suppose that there are also things just like brains only with different modal properties? (What it takes for a thing to persist in a modal property in that it specifies what it is possible for that thing to survive.) Can you take the nonmodal properties of an ordinary object and combine them with an arbitrary set of new modal properties to get a description of a real object?

Consider the claim that there is such a thing as my *waking* brain: a thing just like my brain except that it can exist only as long as it is awake. When I fall asleep at night, my waking brain immediately vanishes (replaced, perhaps, by a "sleeping brain" – a thing just like my brain only essentially asleep); when I wake up in the morning it returns to being. I can see no reason to believe in the existence of functioning brains that is not equally a reason to believe in the existence of waking brains. And if there are waking brains, there are probably also things just like brains except that they are essentially reading, essentially thinking about philosophy, or essentially sober;

and likewise for each possible combination of such properties (sober and reading; sober, reading, and thinking about philosophy; and so on). That would be an extravagant piece of metaphysics to say the least. It would also raise a problem of too many thinkers infinitely worse than the one the brain view was supposed to avoid. If my skull contained not just a functioning brain but also a waking brain, a sober brain, and many more cerebral entities with arbitrary modal properties, all of them psychologically indistinguishable from me (by hypothesis they would differ from me only modally), how could I ever know which one was me?

Maybe there are functioning brains but no essentially waking brains and the like. That would leave us wondering why this would be so – how the cases differ. Nor would it solve the problem. If there are such things as functioning brains, there are surely such things as *brains* – anatomical organs that can exist even when they are unable to sustain intelligence or self-consciousness. And in that case there are two objects within my cranium – a brain and a functioning brain – physically identical and with the same surroundings. They differ only in their modal properties (and in their histories: my brain is older, since my functioning brain came into being only when my brain, in the normal course of its development, began to function in the relevant sense; and my brain is likely to outlive my functioning brain at the end of my life). That would make the two objects psychologically identical while they coincide. Being equally intelligent and self-conscious, both will count as people by any ordinary definition of the word. How, again, could I ever know which one I am – the brain that could exist in formaldehyde or the functioning brain that could not?

Friends of the functioning-brain view will want to say that ordinary brains cannot think or be conscious: brains and functioning brains differ not only modally but psychologically as well. The functioning brain is the only thinker of my thoughts. But why? It cannot be for the same reason that organisms were supposed to be unable to think, namely that they have parts not directly involved in the production of thought.

So the functioning-brain view implies that no physical properties are sufficient to give a thing any mental properties: my brain is physically identical to me (with the same surroundings and virtually the same history), yet has the psychology of granite. A thing's mental properties would not supervene in even the weakest possible sense on its physical properties. Having the right physical structure (and history and surroundings) may be necessary for a thing to be conscious or intelligent, but it could not be sufficient. What appears to be a conscious brain would really be two things: an unconscious brain and a conscious nonbrain. That is again a form of substance dualism. Until the friends of the functioning-brain view can explain why some things of the right physical sort are conscious and intelligent and others are not, their proposal will remain steeped in mystery.

CONCLUSION

The attractions of the brain view are superficial. It may seem to avoid the main objection to animalism – its surprising implications for personal identity over time – while avoiding the problem of too many thinkers. But it rests on the perilous metaphysical principle that nothing can think if it has parts not directly involved in its thinking. And its implications for personal identity are at least as counterintuitive as those of animalism. Attempts to amend the view so as to avoid those implications merely raise a new version of the too-many-thinkers problem, and end in a form of substance dualism.

If we have to be substance dualists, we might as well be Cartesians and say that we are immaterial beings whose nature is entirely psychological. That would at least tell us why human animals and other biological organisms are unable to think: because they are material things. It may not be easy to say why thinking is incompatible with being material. But it can't be any worse than explaining why thinking is compatible with being material but incompatible with being biologically alive. And if it *is* possible for an organism to think, it will be hard to avoid concluding that we are animals.

NOTES

1   Another alternative is that 'person' is a family-resemblance term for which there are no necessary and sufficient conditions. Wiggins' view (1980: 171) is something like this.

2   According to a recent survey (Bourget and Chalmers 2009), just 17 percent of professional philosophers lean towards a "biological view"

of personal identity, a thesis more or less equivalent to animalism. Defenders of animalism include van Inwagen (1990) and Olson (1997, 2007).

3   If an entire detached brain *would* be an organism (van Inwagen 1990: 169–81; Olson 1997: 44–46), let only the cerebrum be transplanted. This applies to the remnant-person problem discussed below as well.

4   For a different response to the problem, see Noonan 1998; Olson 2002.

5   For one that does, see Shoemaker 1999. Olson 2007 discusses all the main accounts of what we are.

6   Or maybe we would be certain parts of brains, since the brain has parts – blood vessels, for instance – that perform the same functions as parts of the organism outside the brain. Puccetti (1973), Tye (2003), Hudson (2007), Campbell and McMahan (2010), and Parfit (2012) all endorse this view or something like it.

7   Campbell and McMahan (2010: 289f.) disagree, as do Aristotelian hylomorphists. This is a thought worth exploring further. It may also solve the remnant-person problem by explaining how the operation creates a new intelligent being.

8   "Functioning brains" is not the best description of what we would be in this view. If a brain could be psychologically continuous with an inorganic machine, the view implies that we could become inorganic nonbrains. But I have no better description.

9   Shoemaker (1999) and Baker (2000) endorse views like this.

3 Persistence and time

Issues about life and death seem intertwined with issues about persistence and time: we live as long as we persist through time, and our deaths seem to mark the limits of our persistence. Metaphysicians have thought deeply about the nature of time, and about what it is for things in general to persist though time. In this chapter I outline some metaphysical views about time, and about persistence, and discuss how they can help us clarify our thinking about life and death.

TIME AND EXISTENCE

To understand time, let's start with space. Think of something which is not here, in the place where you are reading this chapter; for example Halley Research Station in Antarctica. Does Halley Research Station exist? It can be difficult for us to find out what exists far away, but we accept that many things do exist far away. From an ontological point of view, every spatial location is on a par with every other: things in all those places are real. Far-away things exist although they do not exist here.

Let's turn to possibilities. Think of something which is not actual; for example the 2010 Olympic games held in Timbuktu, Mali. Do these Olympics exist? Well, no. There were no Olympic games held in 2010, and the Olympics have never been held in Mali. From an ontological point of view, merely possible things and events are not

I presented parts of this chapter at the universities of Sheffield, St Andrews, and York, and I am very grateful for the discussions which followed. This work was supported by the European Community's Seventh Framework Programme FP7/2007–2013, under grant agreement no. FP7-238128.

on a par with actuality: they are not real. Merely possible things do not exist, because they do not exist in actuality. (Lewis 1986a is a famous exception to this ontological consensus.)

What about time? Think of something which is not present; for example the Tolpuddle Martyrs, pioneers of British trade unionism in the 1830s. Do the Tolpuddle Martyrs exist? According to some philosophers, other times are like other places: from an ontological point of view, every time is on a par with every other, and past and future things, the Tolpuddle Martyrs for example, exist although they do not exist now. For other philosophers, temporal distance is very different from spatial distance: from an ontological point of view, other times are not on a par with the present, and past and future things do not exist, because they do not exist now.

Presentism is the view that past and future things do not exist, whilst *eternalism* is the view that past and future things exist although they do not exist now. (For guidance into the literature about these matters, see Markosian 2010: section 6.) Presentists and eternalists disagree about whether the future is real. This sounds like a matter of pressing importance for all of us, since so much of what we do and feel is oriented towards the future.

Why should I bother preparing for that talk I'll be giving next month? Wouldn't a presentist advise me to seize the day, live for the moment, since the future does not exist? No. Presentists believe that my talk next month does not exist, but they also believe that next month my talk will exist, and that it will go better if I start preparing now: my choices and actions today will affect the future as it comes into existence. Moreover, presentists accept that the Tolpuddle Martyrs used to exist, and that their actions long ago have consequences for us today. But they deny that the Tolpuddle Martyrs have the same ontological status as Halley Research Station, just as most of us deny that the 2010 Timbuktu Olympics have the same ontological status as the 2012 London Olympics.

Eternalism, on the other hand, might seem to threaten my authorship of my own life. If my talk next month exists, then so does the audience reaction, for better or for worse. They like it, or they don't like it. This can prompt the fatalistic thought that there's no point in my preparing for the talk, since the future audience reaction is just as real as anything which exists right now. Wouldn't an eternalist advise me that it can make no difference how I decide to spend today? No. Eternalists believe that my talk next month exists, but they also believe that the talk is causally affected by my preparations between now and then.

Both presentism and eternalism treat past things and future things symmetrically: neither exists for presentists, whilst both exist for eternalists. An intermediate view – the 'growing-block' account – breaks this symmetry. According to the growing-block account of the metaphysics of time, past and present things exist, but future things do not: the universe grows larger with every moment which passes, as new things come into existence, and they remain in existence even as they move into the past.

PERSISTENCE THROUGH TIME

Just as there are rival metaphysical views of what time is, there are rival metaphysical views of how things persist through time. I will explain these rival views of persistence, before connecting them with the rival views of time. (For guidance into the literature about these matters, see Hawley 2010.)

Again, it is helpful to think about space. You currently occupy a modestly extended spatial region, and you have different features in different places, warm up here where you're holding your coffee, cold down there on the tiled floor. How do you do this? A natural explanation is that you have different parts in different places: warm hands here, cold feet there. You yourself vary across space as you are composed of your various spatial parts.

Now think about time. You persist through a lifetime, and have different features at different times, hungry when you woke up this morning, feeling full once you'd eaten breakfast. How do you do this? According to *perdurantism*, you persist through time much as you extend through space. You have an early-morning temporal part which is hungry, and a post-breakfast temporal part which feels full. You yourself vary across time by being composed of these various temporal parts.

According to *endurantism*, on the other hand, persistence through time is quite different from extension through space. You yourself, in your entirety, are first hungry and then full as you move through time, existing as a whole at each moment of your lifetime. Although you have spatial parts, you do not have temporal parts.

Both perdurantists and endurantists face further questions about what it takes for a single person to persist through time. Is this a matter of psychological continuity, or of biological development? When the teleportation device disperses Spock's molecules and creates a perfect duplicate of him from fresh matter down on the planet, is it Spock who steps out at the other end, or merely a simulacrum of Spock? If we hold out the hope of an afterlife, a spiritual or bodily resurrection, what exactly are we hoping for? What would it take for *me* to be resurrected?

Perdurantists and endurantists understand these questions in different ways. Perdurantists understand them as questions about what it takes for a sequence of temporal parts to compose one and the same person. Do the pre-teleportation temporal parts and the post-teleportation temporal parts together compose Spock, or do they compose, respectively, Spock and Spock's successor? Endurantists, on the other hand, understand them as questions about the identity or distinctness of entities wholly existing at different times. Is Spock, wholly present as he steps into the teleporter on the *Enterprise*, identical to the person who is wholly present moments later on the planet?

These are tough questions, but choosing between perdurantism and endurantism will not settle how to answer them. Perdurantists and endurantists alike can prioritize psychological continuity as the basis of personal persistence if that's what the arguments favor; alternatively, perdurantists and endurantists alike can prioritize our biological natures if the evidence points in that direction. The difference in underlying metaphysics will make some difference in how these views of personal persistence are articulated, but they do not dictate our choices.

Admittedly, there are more subtle ways in which the choice between perdurantism and endurantism, once embedded in a wider theoretical network, can make a difference to the relative attractiveness of different theories of personal persistence. For example, perdurantism is often held along with the view that any old collection of temporal parts, no matter how disparate, composes an object; on this view the world is jammed full of overlapping objects. Then questions about personal persistence become questions about what distinguishes individual people from the myriad of very similar people-like entities with which they mostly overlap; this in turn

makes a kind of conceptualism about personal persistence attractive, though not compulsory. Different theories of persistence cannot, in and of themselves, settle all the interesting questions about
what it is for us people to persist, though they can play a part in
more complex arguments about these matters. (See Sider 2001b: section 3 for related discussion.)

How do the rival views of persistence cohere or clash with the
rival views of time I reviewed in the preceding section? Eternalism –
which countenances the existence of past, present, and future – is
usually taken to be compatible both with endurantism and with
perdurantism (although Merricks [1994] argues that eternalism com-
mits us to perdurantism). Presentism might seem to rule out perdurantism, but if we squint a little perhaps we can combine the two:
on this view, first one part of you exists, and then another, never the
whole you at once, though by the end of your life each part of you
will have existed in turn. Growing-block perdurantism would have
it that more and more of you exists as time goes by.

In short, there are no direct paths between particular views of
persistence, particular views of time, or particular accounts of specifically personal persistence. Nevertheless, keeping these different positions clearly distinguished may help us avoid confusion as
we investigate issues surrounding life and death. To that end, we
should clarify some terminology. As we have seen, the view that
past, present and future things exist is known as 'eternalism'; it
is also sometimes known as 'four-dimensionalism'. But these two
terms also have other meanings in the literature on death, time,
and persistence. 'Eternalism' can refer to the view that death is bad
for us at all times, i.e. eternally (Luper 2009: 126). And 'four-dimensionalism' can refer to the view I have been calling 'perdurantism'
(strictly speaking, in this sense 'four-dimensionalism' refers both to
perdurantism and to the related stage theory of persistence) (Sider
2001a). I will stick with 'eternalism' for the view that past, present
and future exist, and I will not use 'four-dimensionalism' again in
this chapter.

TIME, EXISTENCE, AND DEATH

Is there life after death? Some of us believe that people continue after
their deaths in another realm or in another form, whether physical

reincarnation or spiritual presence. In contrast, some of us believe that death is the end: there was no Nelson Mandela in 1900, and likewise there will be no Nelson Mandela in 2100. An intermediate belief is that death is merely a transition from living human being to corpse, and that the end comes a little later once bodily remains decay or are cremated.

We could think of this as a debate about our existence after death, a dispute between those who believe we continue to exist long after our deaths, those who think that death marks the end of existence, and those who think that we exist just as long as our corpses still remain. But, in the context of the eternalism–presentism debate, this would cause confusion. After all, eternalists believe that past things, including Queen Cleopatra, exist in the same way as present things. Does this commit eternalists to thinking that Cleopatra survived her death?

No. Whilst eternalists might, perhaps for religious reasons, believe in 'life after death' they are not committed to this by their eternalism. Eternalists who believe that death marks the end believe that Cleopatra exists, but that she is not located at any times during the twenty-first century. This might seem puzzling, but again we can turn to the spatial analogy for clarification. Think of Halley Research Station in the Antarctic. Halley exists, and you can say truly, sitting here in the warmth at home, that Halley exists. But Halley is not located in your home. So Halley exists, but is not located *here* where you are. Likewise, say the eternalists who deny life after death, Cleopatra exists, but she is not located *now*. From the eternalist perspective, disputes about whether death marks the end of us are not disputes about existence, they are disputes about where our temporal boundaries lie.

EXISTENCE AND POSTHUMOUS HARMS AND BENEFITS

These points about existence and time may help us understand whether it is possible for us to be harmed or benefited by what happens after our deaths, if death is indeed the end. When someone dies, it matters whether we arrange a decent funeral for her, follow the directions in her will, and try to do "what she would have wanted." It matters partly because it's a consolation to those left behind, and a reassurance about what will happen after our own deaths. But in addition it seems important for the sake of the person who has died. How can this be? What difference could posthumous events make to how well someone's life has gone: surely it's too late by then?

In the face of this puzzle, we could try to explain away the intuition that posthumous harms and benefits are possible. We might try to understand the moral importance of our behavior with respect to the dead without reference to harming or benefiting the dead, either by taking morality beyond harms and benefits more generally, or by stressing the potential harms and benefits of post-death rituals for the living. Moreover, we might argue that belief in the possibility of posthumous harms and benefits is merely a cultural relic from a time in which almost everyone in our communities accepted that life continued in some form after death, and that the dead are aware of, or otherwise affected by, what the living do. Then those of us who now want to deny this should also now reject the possibility of posthumous harms and benefits. Or we might argue that the intuition that posthumous harms and benefits are possible is fuelled by a mistaken view of what well-being is. (Bradley [2009: 42–43] adopts some of these strategies.)

Alternatively, we can try to vindicate the thought that posthumous harms and benefits are indeed possible. We might pursue this by investigating the nature of harms and benefits more generally, attempting to understand what it is for us to have a good life, and trying thereby to understand whether the quality of our lives can be in part determined by what happens after our deaths. But in this chapter I will confine myself to the question of whether metaphysical accounts of time can help us understand the possibility of posthumous harms and benefits, prior to adopting any specific, substantive account of what our well-being consists of.

Harry Silverstein (1980, 2000, 2010) has argued that posthumous harms and benefits are impossible unless future things exist. He argues that an event can be good or bad for someone only if it is a possible object of that person's positive or negative feelings: as his slogan goes, "Values Connect with Feelings." Events which happen after your death can benefit or harm you only by being possible objects of your feelings now, whilst you are alive. And, argues Silverstein, if future things and events do not exist, then they are not the possible objects of your feelings now whilst you are alive. If, on the other hand, future things and events do exist, they can be the possible objects of your feelings now whilst you are alive. Thus what happens in the future, after your death, can be good or bad for you.

Let's suppose that Silverstein is right that posthumous events can benefit or harm us only by being the possible objects of our feelings whilst we are alive. Does this really generate a special problem for presentism, as Silverstein suggests, or, indeed, for the growing-block theory? No. If presentism could not account for the obvious fact that we sometimes think about the future, then nobody would be a presentist. (Likewise, we sometimes think about alternative possibilities, about what might have happened, without commitment to the existence of merely possible events such as the 2010 Timbuktu Olympics, or merely possible objects such as the older sibling I wish I'd had.)

Many presentists take it that there are, right now, truths about how the future will be: we have beliefs about the future, some of those beliefs are true, and some of them are false. Presentists owe us a story about what makes those beliefs true or false, given that future things do not exist. So, for example, Bourne (2006) argues that non-present times are abstract entities, which make our future-directed beliefs true or false. And Prior (1968) argues that present things exemplify all the future-directed and past-directed properties needed to provide truth values for our beliefs about the past and the future. (Merricks [2007] argues that presentists are entitled to truth and falsity about the past and the future, and that they need not provide any substantive story about what makes the relevant claims true or false.)

There are, admittedly, certain sorts of thoughts we are unable to have about the future: singular thoughts about wholly future objects. But this limitation is generated by our lack of causal contact with such objects, not their failure to exist: eternalists too must concede that we cannot have such thoughts. And in any case this doesn't restrict us too much: I can still hope that my great-great-grandchildren will have a liveable planet, even though I cannot have singular thoughts about those future people. So we can have feelings about the future, even if presentism is correct.

Bradley (2009) discusses a different challenge to presentists. His concern is not about our ability, whilst alive, to have feelings about the future beyond our deaths. His concern is that, once we are dead, we are not available to feature in singular propositions which say that a certain posthumous event is good or bad for us, or that we would have been enjoying good lives had we still been alive at that time (notice that this concern does not affect the growing-block theory). But, as he later concedes, this is just an instance of the general challenge to presentists, "a problem about how to ground truths about past things and people. The presentist must have some general story to tell about such truths; that story should just be applied to truths about dead people" (2009: 83). (Bradley 2004 and 2010 offer further reasons to think that presentists are worse-off than eternalists in dealing with these issues, but Bradley 2009 seems to retract these.)

Presentists must have some means of accounting for truths about the past and the future, and for our present ability to think those truths, even whilst they deny the existence of objects at those non-present times. So presentists and eternalists need not differ significantly in their treatment of posthumous harms and benefits: ontology isn't doing much work here. (Thoughts like this lead some philosophers to skepticism about the presentism–eternalism debate more generally; Sider (2012) sees in this an illustration of the gap between fundamental metaphysics and ordinary human concerns.)

Moreover, this is what we should have expected. If there is a genuine tension between the claim that death is the end of us, and the claim that posthumous events can harm or benefit us, this is rooted in the temporal separation between the person and the posthumous events. How can posthumous events "reach back in time" to affect us? *When* do they affect us: when we're still alive, or when the events occur? Even eternalists acknowledge that things and people are located at certain times and not at others. Given that Mandela is not located at the year 2100, how can he be harmed or benefited by events that occur then? When does the harm or benefit occur? Mere temporal separation seems to generate these concerns, without reference to non-existence.

How might we address these concerns or try to resolve the tension? As before, one good strategy would be to develop a substantive theory of well-being, of harm, and of benefit, then use that to understand whether, how, and when, posthumous events can contribute to our well-being by harming or benefiting us. For example, perhaps nothing can harm or benefit us except via our experiencing it, in which case posthumous harms and benefits are impossible. Alternatively, perhaps posthumous events can benefit or harm us by satisfying or frustrating the desires we had whilst alive.

I do not attempt to argue for any substantive theory of well-being in this chapter. Instead, I will suggest a role for the metaphysics of time in these debates, one which does not turn on issues about the ontology of temporal objects. Metaphysics can help us explore the nature of cross-time relations more generally, as we test our understanding of how these work for less controversial issues than harm-or-benefit. This improved understanding will then allow us to consider more carefully whether there is something distinctive about well-being, harm, and benefit which means that our usual understanding of cross-time relations cannot apply in this special case. The metaphysician of time can thus act as underlaborer, clearing the ground for discussions of well-being.

CROSS-SPACE RELATIONS AND NON-CAUSAL DETERMINATION

To understand cross-time relations, let's consider cross-space relations. Suppose that you and I live in the UK, that we have never met, and that I weigh significantly more than you do. Because of me, you are slightly below average (mean) weight for the UK. This is not because I have affected your weight, by cancelling your Chocolate Society subscription. It's because my weight has helped make it the case that the average weight for the UK is slightly above the level at which your weight is.

(We don't usually take an interest in where people stand with respect to average weight, but there are significant social science measures, concerning relative poverty for example, which work in relevantly similar ways.)

We can consider a range of questions about this obviously coherent hypothetical situation. For starters, what sort of property is *being below average weight for the UK*? Metaphysicians disagree about whether there is a property for almost every predicate: some say "yes," arguing that the properties are abundant, whilst others say "no," arguing that the properties are sparse, perhaps because only the predicates of fundamental physics correspond to genuine features of the world (Lewis 1983 is a classic discussion). But that's not important right now. We need focus only on the fact that you are below average weight for the UK, and that this is because of your weight and the weights of everyone else in the UK, including me. This is determined by a combination of your intrinsic features, the intrinsic features of other people including me, and our relations to the UK.

Second question: where are you below average weight for the UK? There are a number of possible answers to this peculiar question, but no single answer seems especially illuminating. We might say that you are below average weight for the UK right where you are. We might say that you have this property across the UK (either at each individual place in the UK, or somehow across the whole country). We might say that you are below average weight for the UK everywhere, including on the moon, insofar as it is true at every place that you are below average weight for the UK. But, in short, we'd be unlikely to ask this question in the first place.

Third question: do I affect you in any way? By stipulation, I do not causally influence you; moreover, I do not help determine your intrinsic features (that's part of what it is for them to be your *intrinsic* features). On the other hand, I do contribute to your being below average weight, this is partly due to me, I help make it the case that you are below average weight, I am amongst the truth-makers for the claim that you are below average weight, and so on. We might even say that it is my weight which pushes you below the average, or that I help to push you below the average.

Fourth question: does your being below average weight counter-factually depend upon my features? There is a relationship of determination, or grounding, or dependence, between my weight and residence, on the one hand, and your being below average weight for the UK, on the other. It's tempting to think of this in counterfactual terms: if I had been less heavy, or had emigrated, you would not have been below average weight. But for very familiar reasons, such counterfactual analyses of determination relations can easily go wrong. What is the nearest possible world in which I am less heavy? Perhaps it is one in which I cook calorie-rich meals for my family, and their consequent increase in weight more than compensates for my decrease. Perhaps it is one in which sugary soft drinks are taxed at 20 percent, with consequences for everyone's weight, including yours. And what about the nearest world in which I emigrate from the UK: is that closer or less close than the nearest world in which I weigh less?

By understanding the concept of an average weight, we understand a good sense in which I, my weight, and my residence in the UK help determine the fact that you are below average weight for the UK. We should not feel impelled to reduce this determination to a counterfactual dependence, especially once we realize the difficulties in coming up with a satisfactory analysis (Broome 2012: 225).

Fifth question: where, if anywhere, do I help make it the case that you are below average weight for the UK? Like the question about the location of your being below average weight, this question is peculiar. I have my location, you have your location, we each have our intrinsic features, there are relations between us, and moreover we stand in a complex web of relations with other people in the UK. Once these facts are specified, it is hard to see what further information could be requested by the question about *where* I help determine that you are below average weight for the UK.

CROSS-TIME RELATIONS AND NON-CAUSAL DETERMINATION

Let's say that a person's Height is the maximum height she has throughout her life (i.e. the height she reaches when first fully grown). Suppose we took each person whose lifetime includes at least some of the twenty-first century, and arranged them in Height order, starting with the shortest person. Then let's say that each person's Height Number is the number which indicates his/her place in that ordering. The taller the person, the greater the Height Number.

(We don't usually take an interest in Height, but in sports we often take an interest in, for example, the all-time fastest runners, or all-time highest scorers: Usain Bolt, for example, is the person out of all those who have lived so far who has the fastest maximum speed over 100m, whilst Maurice Greene will always be the fastest runner of the twentieth century over this distance.)

Suppose that your Height Number is 4 billion; suppose that Smallish Sam (b. 2079, d. 2154) has Height Number 4 billion minus one. (By the power of stipulation, I condemn you to die before 2079.)

In some sense, it's because of Sam that you have Height Number 4 billion, instead of 4 billion minus one. This is not because Sam affects your Height. It's because Sam's Height helps make it the case that your place in the Height line is the 4-billionth place.

As with my cross-space contribution to your being below average weight, we can ask a range of questions about Smallish Sam's contribution to your having Height Number 4 billion.

First, what sort of property is *having Height Number 4 billion*? Given that my stipulative definitions of Height and Height Number are coherent, and given the assumed facts about everyone's Heights, it is true of you that you have Height Number 4 billion. At the moment, we can't know this, not even if we have the Height information for everyone who has lived in the twenty-first century so far. Nevertheless, so long as there are truths about who will live in the twenty-first century, and about what their Heights will be (and recall that even presentists make room for such facts), then there is a truth about your Height Number. This is determined by a combination of your intrinsic features (your Height), the intrinsic features of others (their Heights), and their temporal locations (i.e. the fact that they live during the twenty-first century).

Second: when do you have Height number 4 billion? Superficially, this seems less peculiar than the question about where you are below average UK weight. But in fact it is problematic in the same ways. There are a number of possible answers, but no single answer seems especially illuminating. We might say that you have Height number 4 billion throughout your life, or perhaps during the portion of your life following the time when your height reaches your Height (i.e. once you have reached your maximum height). We might say that you have Height number 4 billion at all times in the twenty-first century, or only once everyone who has lived in the twenty-first century has reached their maximum height. We might say that you have Height number 4 billion at all times, past, present and future, insofar as it is always true that this is your Height Number, in the same way that it is always true that Maurice Greene is the fastest 100m-runner of the twentieth century. Each of these claims expresses some sort of information, and we can imagine a situation in which someone might be curious about this, but we should resist the thought that any one of these reveals a deeper truth than the others.

Third question: does Smallish Sam affect you in any way? Smallish Sam cannot causally affect you, since he is born after your death; moreover he cannot help determine your Height. But he contributes to your having the Height Number that you do, this is partly due to him, he helps make it the case that you have Height Number 4 billion, he is amongst the truth-makers for the claim that you have Height Number 4 billion, and so on. We might even say that Sam and his Height push you up the Height line from 4-billion-minus-one to 4 billion.

Fourth question: does your Height Number counterfactually depend upon Sam's Height? There is a relationship of determination, or grounding, or dependence, between Sam's Height and temporal location, on the one hand, and your having Height Number 4 billion, on the other. It's tempting to think of this in counterfactual terms: if Sam had not existed, or if he had been somewhat taller or somewhat shorter that would have meant changes for other people's Height Numbers. But, again, we should not treat such counterfactuals as analyses of determination relations. If Sam had not existed, perhaps his actual partner would have had kids with someone else and those kids would have affected the Height line in some way. If Sam had been taller than you actually are, perhaps that would have been due to improved general nutrition, and you also would have been taller than you actually are, retaining your actual Height Number. And so on.

By understanding the concepts of Height and Height Number, we understand a good sense in which Sam, Sam's Height, and his living during the twenty-first century help determine the fact that your Height Number is 4 billion. We should not feel impelled to reduce this determination to a counterfactual dependence, especially once we realize the difficulties in coming up with a satisfactory analysis.

Fifth question: when, if at any time, does Smallish Sam help determine your Height Number? You have your temporal location and your Height, and Sam has his temporal location and his Height. Once these facts are specified, it is hard to see what further information could be requested by the question about *when* Sam helps determine that you have a Height Number of 4 billion.

WELL-BEING AND CROSS-TIME RELATIONS

I have shown that we fully understand how certain features of a person can be partially determined by what goes on at places and times at which she is not located. There is no fundamental conceptual difficulty in understanding either average weight or Height Number, and no hint of problematic instantaneous-action-at-a-distance or backwards causation in either case. Eternalists can easily understand how cross-time relations are possible; presentists have more work to do in explaining this, but they will provide some explanation or other, on pain of giving up on vital cross-time relations such as causation.

We have various significant properties which fit this pattern. For example, your level of knowledgeability (how much you know) is partially determined by what goes on at places and times at which you are not located. In particular, how much you know is partially determined by events occurring after your death, given the plausible assumption that some of your current beliefs about the future are well grounded enough to constitute knowledge if they are true. (Don't be distracted by the worry that we can never be *certain* what the future holds: by this standard we are certain of very little about the past or present either, and we are headed for skepticism if we make such certainty a precondition for knowledge.) More controversially, semantic temporal externalists (Jackman 1999; Collins 2006) argue that the meanings of the words you use today are partially determined by facts about future linguistic developments (though see Brown 2000 for criticism).

What can this exercise tell us about the possibility of posthumous harms and benefits? Try thinking of it rather abstractly, as follows. Each of us has a level of lifetime well-being (just as each of us has a Height Number and a level of knowledgeability). Your level of lifetime well-being is determined by a combination of your intrinsic features, the intrinsic features of various events, and the relations between you and those events. Different substantive theories of well-being disagree about which intrinsic features and which relations are the relevant ones, and about how these combine to determine your lifetime well-being. So, for example, a simple hedonic theory of well-being says that an event can help determine your well-being only by standing in the *being-an-experience-belonging-to* relation to you. A preference-satisfaction theory of well-being says that an event can help determine your well-being only by satisfying or frustrating your preferences (it is a further issue whether the relations of *satisfying* and *frustrating* are reducible to intrinsic features of you and the events in question).

At this level of abstraction, an event's harming-or-benefiting someone is a matter of its contributing to the determination of her level of lifetime well-being. Intuitively, some such contributions are positive, pushing up the level of well-being, whilst others are negative, pushing it down. But, as with my contribution to your being below average weight for the UK, and as with Smallish Sam's contribution to your having Height Number 4 billion, it's possible for us to think of this 'pushing' as non-causal; moreover we should not try to reduce it to counterfactual dependence. Nor, finally, should we feel compelled to specify *when* a certain event contributes to someone's well-being by helping determine it: we have the temporal location of the person, the temporal location of the event, plus the relation between person and event. Nothing further needs to be said.

If this is a good way of thinking about well-being, harm, and benefit, then there is no general reason for thinking that posthumous harms and benefits are inherently problematic or mysterious, any more than is Height Number or your level of knowledgeability. Once we adopt some substantive theory of well-being, and accept what it says about which features and relations are relevant to the determination of well-being, we may then have good reasons to think that posthumous harms and benefits are problematic. But when posthumous harms and benefits are rejected on such grounds, this rejection cannot then provide a noncircular reason for adopting that very theory of well-being.

More optimistically, we might hope to establish some general claims about well-being, benefit, or harm which do not flow from any particular substantive theory of well-being, yet put constraints on the types of features and relations which can be relevant to the determination of well-being. We could then investigate whether those constraints permit posthumous harms and benefits. This would involve explicating the theoretical role of well-being, harm, and benefit, considering their connections to categories in moral theory for example, and also considering the relationship between well-being at a time and lifetime well-being.

This is an important, deep project which I am ill-qualified even to begin, so I return instead to my underlaboring task. We all have features which are partially determined by events occurring after our deaths, and there is no conceptual obstacle or consideration from the metaphysics of time which suggests that this is in general puzzling or problematic. If our lifetime well-being is not so determined, this is because of distinctive features of well-being, and if these distinctive features are established on the basis of some substantive theory of well-being, then the 'impossibility' of posthumous harm and benefit cannot function as a reason to adopt that substantive theory.

4   The malleability of identity

When someone undergoes a radical change it is common to say that she has "become a different person." This claim is usually meant figuratively and does not imply that the original person has actually gone out of existence. It is striking nevertheless that such cases are described in terms of identity, and although it is unwise to put too much weight on turns of phrase it is worth thinking about what talk of identity signifies here. Undoubtedly in some instances it is nothing more than a slightly exaggerated way of saying that the differences found within the life of a single person are of a kind or magnitude that usually occurs only between two distinct people. But sometimes it seems to imply more, suggesting a meaningful parallel between identity in this figurative sense and literal, numerical identity. This is an intriguing possibility, since we tend to think that identity in the more figurative sense is *malleable* – that it can be molded and changed by our actions and attitudes. We do not tend to think this about numerical identity, which is taken to be a metaphysical fact independent of what we think and do. If there are structural parallels between figurative and numerical identity, perhaps literal identity is more malleable than we think.

This chapter explores this possibility and sketches an account of literal identity on which it is malleable to at least some degree. The first section identifies a subgroup of figurative cases of identity change in which the notion of "identity" at issue seems especially closely related to literal identity and examines the kind of malleability "identity" in this sense possesses. The next section examines two major approaches to questions of numerical identity – biological views and psychological views – showing that on neither is identity malleable. The final section sketches an alternative account according to which literal identity is, to some degree, malleable.

FIGURATIVE IDENTITY AND SURVIVAL

There are many different kinds of cases in which we might say that someone has become a different person. We might say this, for instance, of an aimless friend who becomes energized and purposive after starting a new job, or of the shy classmate from high school who has dramatically changed his appearance and become outgoing and confident. We might also say it of someone who has been through a trauma and become fearful and edgy or of the free spirit who becomes conservative and careworn as she ages.

The heterogeneous group of circumstances that might be described in terms of a change in identity could be divided up in many different ways. One important division is between cases in which it is clear the locution is meant only to emphasize change and cases which, though still cases in which the person literally survives, are in some important sense akin to ceasing to exist. The first few cases described above are examples of the former kind. I am hardly going to say that a friend who has been invigorated and found new purpose has not survived the transition; it is much more natural to say that she has finally come into her own. And if the shy classmate gets contact lenses, goes to the gym, and takes classes to improve his interpersonal style I will more likely say that he has blossomed than that he did not make it through the transition from high school to adulthood. This kind of "becoming a new person," call it "survival-maintaining" change, is a kind of change one sticks around to enjoy or celebrate, not one that results in one's absence. This point is made (almost) explicit in Gloria Gaynor's 1978 disco hit in which she explains to her ex-lover that she is "not that chained-up little person still in love with [him]," while repeatedly asserting the continuation of that person with the title line: "I will survive."

The other cases (call them "survival-threatening" change) are quite different in this respect. Consider a famous fictional example from Derek Parfit's *Reasons and Persons*. Parfit imagines a nineteenth-century Russian who is deeply sympathetic to the peasants. He knows that he will inherit a great deal of land when he gets older, and fears that wealth will corrupt him. He therefore draws up a document transferring his inheritance, when he receives it, to the peasants. This document can be revoked only with his wife's permission, which he tells her never to give, explaining "I regard my ideals as essential to me. If I lose these ideals, I want you to think that I cease to exist. I want you to regard your husband then, not as me, the man who asks you for this promise, but only as his corrupted later self" (Parfit 1984: 327). A real and disturbing example of this kind of case is recounted in a recent article in the National Post which includes an interview with the family of a Canadian veteran who committed suicide. "Jamie never came home," the veteran's father says. "A different person came back from Afghanistan" (O'Connor 2011).

There are, of course, many other kinds of cases frequently described as changes of identity that fall at various points on a spectrum between these two. Here, however, we will focus just on the sorts of cases described above, asking what distinguishes them, making the language of failure to survive apply in one kind of case but not the other. In the abstract it might seem that the answer would lie in the degree or rapidity of change. Changes that are very extreme and happen quickly, we might think, seem like replacement of one person with another, while changes that are gradual and more modest seem to preserve the individual. This is not borne out by the examples. There is no reason to think, for instance, that the change in Parfit's Russian noble is any more rapid or extreme than that in the shy schoolmate; it might be less so.

The examples may seem to suggest another possibility. Perhaps the difference is nothing more than whether we perceive the change undergone as positive or negative. Becoming more confident and happy makes life better, and in changes of this kind we are unlikely to think about transformation in terms of someone ceasing to exist. Becoming greedy and corrupt or depressed and fearful are negative changes that make life worse, and it is here that observations about failing to survive seem more at home. This makes a good deal of sense. Where there is negative change there is a kind of mourning for a way of life that has been lost – something one values and cannot recover – while in the case of positive change there is something gained.

This analysis requires some refinement, however. As it happens, there are cases in which positive change can also be seen as survival-threatening. Psychiatrist Peter Kramer, for instance, reports a patient whose condition improved markedly on Prozac. While in some clear sense he undoubtedly felt better on the drug he did not wish to continue taking it because he "did not feel like himself" (Kramer 1993: 290–91). Similar concerns have been raised with respect to the use of Deep Brain Stimulation (DBS) as a treatment for depression. Some patients who respond very well and experience alleviation of symptoms also report that they find the changes unsettling and disturbing, as if they have been replaced by someone else (e.g. Economist 2005). In these cases there is obviously something more or different going on; these patients perceive the changes they undergo as survival-threatening even though they do not deny that they are in some sense positive. The life they lead to is better, but it is somehow not *their* lives which have improved.[1]

One diagnosis of these kinds of cases would point to differences concerning the degree of control a person has over the changes he undergoes. Radical change that results from one's own efforts, we might suggest, amounts to transformation of an existing self, while change that results from manipulations like medication or brain stimulation looks like replacement of the self. Again there is undoubtedly something right in this analysis, but we need to think more carefully about the relevant notion of "control." In some sense the person who takes an antidepressant, or gives informed consent for the placement of electrodes in DBS is just as much in control of change as someone who embarks on a course of self-improvement via behavioral therapy, and more in control than the person who falls into the job that changes her outlook on life. In fact, Kramer's patient who is made uncomfortable by his transformation on Prozac is in the minority. Many of his patients, even those who have been depressed for most of their lives, describe the changes brought on by the drug by saying that for the first time they are "truly themselves," and several report a feeling of being in control that was previously absent (e.g. Kramer 1993: 10).

Rather than a difference in degree of control per se the relevant difference between survival-maintaining and survival-threatening change seems to depend upon whether the individual who undergoes a transformation feels alienated from the change or identifies with it. It is alienation that makes a change feel like replacement, and identification that makes it feel instead like a kind of actualization. Of course, a person is more likely to feel alienated from a change of which she disapproves or which she feels she does not control. As we have seen, however, there are exceptions. A person can feel alienated from a change she played some role in bringing about or judges as objectively positive (e.g. the uncomfortable reactions to Prozac and DBS), or identify with one that is a matter of pure serendipity (e.g. falling into a life-changing job).

To develop this proposal fully it would of course be necessary to say something more about identification and alienation, which are notoriously difficult notions to pin down. This is a project well beyond the scope of the current discussion. As a rough approximation we can say that identification consists in being able to see how the person before and after the change can both be you. This is what is missing for Parfit's Russian, who states quite clearly that he cannot imagine that a person who wanted to hold on to aristocratic wealth and ways could be the same person as him. It is presumably also true for the traumatized soldier, who simply cannot recognize the carefree young man who used to enjoy watching sports with his father as himself. These are cases of alienation. The cases we have described as survival-maintaining are quite different in this regard. Here the fact that the person sees the intelligibility of being the same person on both sides of the change is demonstrated in the kind of satisfaction this kind of change often entails. This is what the language of actualization implies. The shy or timid person experiences the confidence he develops as having been dormant within him, and patients comfortable with the dramatic changes brought about by Prozac presumably see their newfound happy selves as the selves they were all along, selves whose expression was inhibited by depression.

It may seem that "identification" and "alienation" so described are merely new names for the distinction with which we started. What we really need to know, it might be argued, is what it is that makes identification possible in some cases but not others. This misses the point. The suggestion being made here is that attitudes of identification and alienation play a role in *constituting* the outcome of these changes, partly determining matters of identity and survival in this figurative sense. For this to be plausible, it is necessary to understand that identification and alienation should not be understood as isolated judgments about one's identity. Instead these terms refer to deeply held attitudes towards one's past or future with profound and far-reaching psychological and behavioral implications.

Whether someone understands herself as having survived some vicissitude will determine whether she experiences self-regarding emotions with respect to particular past actions. It will also affect her understanding of what she is responsible for, and of what she has reason to do, and condition her interaction with others. It is not just that a traumatized veteran, for instance, *feels* like a different person. Because he feels this way he is cut off from his past life in very tangible ways. He is no longer able to do the same things he did before, or relate to his parents and wife and friends as the son and husband and buddy who left them. He does not see any reason to take up the projects or pursue the goals that were central to life before deployment. The life lived by the carefree young man is not livable by him. And these facts in turn feed the feeling of alienation in a dynamic way that drives a real wedge between his past life and his present. The kind of survival to which this kind of identification contributes is thus not only, or even primarily, an internal state. It is an ongoing form of interaction with the world which is continuous over time where there is identification and which breaks radically where there is alienation. Alienation, as understood here, prevents the person who experiences it from picking up the thread of a life.[2]

This analysis reveals another important point. Up until now I have not discriminated between judgments of figurative identity and survival as they are made in the first-, second- or third-person. Identification and alienation are first-personal attitudes. The recognition that these attitudes are intrinsically connected with behavioral and interactive changes helps us to see how they can be the basis of judgments about identity and survival from the outside as well. The changes in the conduct of life that are a part of alienation in most cases will lead also to external judgments of identity change. It must be acknowledged, however, that internal and external perspectives do sometimes diverge. I may claim I haven't changed while my friend insists I've become a different person and vice versa, and we need to know what to say about identity in these circumstances. Here it is important to underscore that the relevant form of survival is interactive and not just internal. This means that the identity judgment of the individual who has changed is not privileged or incorrigible. It also means that there are methods for resolving disagreements about identity change – facts that can be marshaled in favor of one claim or another. If I say I am still the same person and my friend disagrees, I can point to the ways in which what I am doing now represents a continuation of what I did before and can be seen as an expression of dormant tendencies. My friend, meanwhile, can point to ways in which I have radically broken from my past. In *A Christmas Carol*, for instance, Scrooge's young fiancée tells him he is not the man who promised to marry her. When Scrooge denies he has changed toward her she points out the ways in which his ambition has in fact caused him to do so, and he comes to recognize that she is right (Dickens 1984: 71–72).[3] Conversely, Parfit's Russian may convince his wife to revoke the transfer of property by pointing to all the ways in which, although he has changed his mind on this, he remains the same person.

The details of these kinds of negotiations are extremely complicated, and we cannot explore them any further here. This brief discussion has, however, revealed that there is a meaningful sense in which, at least in these figurative cases, identity can be malleable. It is not merely the degree or nature of change that determines my identity and survival. My own attitudes of identification or alienation, in interaction with others' attitudes and actions, determine whether my life after some vicissitude is continuous with the earlier life in the relevant sense. Whether I survive this change thus depends on whether I and others believe that I have.

This conclusion may seem credible for figurative notions of identity and survival, but attitude, it would seem, cannot impact *literal* survival in this way. I turn next to an exploration of whether this is really so, beginning with a discussion of two approaches that have dominated much of the philosophical discussion – the psychological approach and the bodily or biological approach.

THEORIES OF NUMERICAL IDENTITY

As the names suggest, psychological accounts claim that personal identity should be defined in terms of psychological connections and biological accounts that it should be defined in physiological or biological terms.

Current psychological views are in many ways descendants of John Locke's account. Locke says that to find the identity criteria for any object we need first to know what kind of object it is. A person, he says, is "a thinking intelligent Being, that has reason and reflection, and can consider itself as itself, the same thinking thing in different times and places" (Locke 1975: 335). And also, famously, that "person" is "a Forensick Term appropriating Actions and their Merit; and so belongs only to intelligent Agents capable of a Law, and Happiness and Misery" (Locke 1975: 346). A person, for Locke, is a self-conscious subject who, in virtue of its self-consciousness, is capable of prudential reasoning and moral agency. In ordinary life, Locke acknowledges, sameness of person and of "man" (human) coincide. If they were to come apart, however, we would judge that the *person* goes where the psychological life goes, and does not stay with the body.

He offers a hypothetical case to make this point. We are to imagine that the consciousness of a prince comes to enter the body of a cobbler, replacing the cobbler's own consciousness. Everyone would judge, Locke says, that the person with the prince's consciousness and the cobbler's body would be responsible for what the prince had done before and not for what the cobbler had. We can add that anticipating the switch the prince would have reason to ensure that the individual with the cobbler's body and his consciousness would have access to the wealth and power of the kingdom. It would also be this individual who would be in a position to take up the prince's relationships with the king, queen, and princess. Locke therefore concludes that it is sameness of consciousness and not of substance, either material (the body) or immaterial (the soul), that constitutes personal identity. Similar stories are ubiquitous in popular culture – for instance the film *Freaky Friday* depicts the consciousness of a mother and daughter switching bodies for a day. We are clearly meant to understand this as a case where the mother and daughter themselves switch bodies, each following her consciousness to the body of the other, and this is how most people automatically interpret it.

Present-day psychological theorists offer similar forms of argument. Derek Parfit, for instance, presents us with the much-discussed case of Teletransportation, in which a person's brain and body are destroyed and a molecule-for-molecule replica built on another planet (Parfit 1984: 199–200). The assumption is that exact duplication of the brain will exactly duplicate psychological life. The person who steps out of the transporter station on the distant planet will thus experience a memory of stepping into the booth on earth and all that went before. This case, like those described above, is meant to support the psychological approach, and we are to conclude that Teletransportation is a way to travel quickly to distant places – that when I am teleported the person who emerges at the other end will be me. A fairly significant number of those sympathetic to the psychological approach actually do not have this intuition, however, and view Teletransportation as death followed by replacement with a replica. These theorists hold that psychological continuity constitutes personal identity only if it is generated by the continued functioning of the same brain.

The current major competitor to the psychological approach is the bodily or biological approach. The general idea here is that persons are fundamentally human animals, and personal identity must be defined in terms of the identity of an individual organism. This approach has always had adherents, and has enjoyed a recent resurgence of popularity due to the development of updated biological accounts, also known as "animalist" views.[4] Animalists argue that the Lockean notion of personhood does not really give us an account of what an entity *is*. To be a Lockean person is not to be a particular kind of thing, but rather to be a thing that possesses capacities for self-conscious reflection, prudential reasoning, and moral agency. We still need to answer the question of *what* it is that has those capacities, the animalist argues. Is it, for instance, a human? A chimp? A cyborg? The persons we know are *human* persons – humans that have the capacities of personhood. The human exists before gaining these capacities (as a fetus or infant) and can continue to exist after losing them (in, for instance, a vegetative state).

The key claim is that no entity literally comes into existence when a human (or other entity) gains the capacity for reflective self-consciousness, prudence, or agency, and no entity goes out of existence when a human (or other entity) loses these capacities. Moreover, when the capacities of personhood are present in human persons there are not two distinct entities, a person and a human animal, both thinking the same thoughts and taking the same actions at the same time. There is instead a single being that has the ability to think those kinds of thoughts and take those kinds of actions. The intuitions generated by cases like that of the prince and the cobbler are not intuitions about the numerical identity of an entity, animalists argue, but instead about which attributes of an entity we find especially salient or important.

The debate between psychological theorists and animalists is vigorous and ongoing and we will not resolve it here. We do, however, have enough information to see that each denies that one's self-understanding might play a role in determining facts about numerical identity or survival. Consider first the biological approach. On this view it is explicit that identity is a metaphysical/biological fact that is independent of what we think about it. It might seem that things are different with the psychological view, since our attitudes towards our survival are part of our overall psychological lives and so can contribute to psychological continuity or lack thereof. If we look at the view as it is usually presented, however, there is no room for a person's judgments or attitudes to play a role in determining her identity. To see this it is necessary to have a slightly more detailed picture of the psychological approach. According to this approach what makes a person at time t_2 the same person as someone at earlier time t_1 is that there is "psychological continuity" between the two times. The relevant kind of psychological continuity is typically defined in terms of overlapping chains of individual psychological connections.[5] The relevant connections are those that hold between a memory and the experience of which it is a memory, between an intention and the action that carries it out, and between the different moments of a continuing belief, value, or desire. When there is a large enough number of connections between each successive moment between t_1 and t_2 then, according to the psychological view, the person at t_2 is the same person as the person at t_1.[6]

Whether psychological connections of this sort are or are not present seems to be a fact that is independent of our judgments or attitudes. Of course, judgments and attitudes are *among* our psychological states, and so in that sense relevant to our continuation. If I am now an adherent of the biological account of identity, for instance, and become an adherent of the psychological approach, there is one fewer psychological connection over time than there would be if I had maintained my belief in the biological view. But views about my identity or survival have no special status, and do not count more toward creating identity-constituting psychological continuity than any other psychological state. Think, for instance, of Teletransportation as Parfit describes it. To determine whether the person who steps out of the teleporter is the same as the person who stepped in on earth we look at the psychological states and count how many are in common. By presumption they all are, including whatever attitudes I might have about whether Teletransportation will preserve my identity. This is all we need to know to determine that I am the same person. The question of *which* view I hold on this topic is unimportant.

On neither of these two major views of personal identity is it possible for our judgments or attitudes about whether someone survives some vicissitude to make a difference to whether she in fact does. This is not a very surprising result; few would expect a metaphysical fact of this sort to depend upon our judgments. In the next section, however, I will suggest that if we take seriously the idea that there are parallels between figurative claims of survival-threatening loss of identity and literal failures to survive we will find an account of our literal identity according to which something like identification does play a role.

LITERAL SURVIVAL AND SELF-UNDERSTANDING

In the first section we saw that identification played a role in figurative survival because of the way it impacts psychological life, behavior, and interactions with others. I suggest that there is a more basic kind of identification that impacts behavior and interactions at a more fundamental level and arguably plays a role in determining facts about literal survival. Both the proposal and the reasons for accepting it are complex and contentious, and I can do no more here than offer a brief overview.

The alienation involved in cases of survival-threatening change in the first section was profound but not complete. While those experiencing such alienation judged themselves to be "a different person" in terms of goals, dreams, aspirations, values, and temperament, they also acknowledged themselves to be the same person in many other respects. None of these individuals suggested that they

were in *no* sense continuous with their past selves, and their situations are so poignant precisely because of their acknowledgment
that in some sense they are. The veteran who "never came home"
recognized the parents of the person who went to war as *his* parents
and that person's wife as *his* wife. He was just unable to interact
with them as the person he had been. And Parfit's Russian knows
that that future landowner, however different politically, will be the
one to collect his inheritance. Moreover, he instructs his wife on
what to do because she will be the wife of that future person. There
is thus recognition of literal continuation in these cases, and this
has practical consequences.

My proposal is that there can be a more fundamental alienation
that involves a denial of literal identity as well, and that this has
implications sufficiently extreme that in the right circumstances
it can impact literal survival. The break in a human life is going to
be much more dramatic and much more complete when a person
believes that he is literally a different person from some earlier person than if he believes only that he differs in fundamental values,
desires, commitment, and temperament. I do not expect much disagreement with the claim that failure to recognize oneself as in any
sense the person who previously inhabited one's body would constitute a terrible disruption in the flow of a life. The claim that this
situation involves a change in literal or numerical identity brought
on by alienation is likely to be far more controversial, however. If
the man we know as John Smith suddenly insists that he is not John
Smith at all, but is instead Napoleon or Brad Pitt, and tries to live
Napoleon's or Brad Pitt's life, Smith's life will indeed be a mess.
We will not conclude, however, that John Smith has died and been
replaced, in his body, by Napoleon or Brad Pitt. We will conclude
that John Smith has had a psychotic break and needs treatment.

All this shows, however, is that this profound kind of alienation
does not *always* lead to change in literal identity; it does not show
that it cannot do so in the right circumstances. Understanding what
these circumstances are brings us back to the observations made
at the end of the first section; that it is not a person's own attitude
toward survival alone that is implicated in its malleability, but also
the attitudes of others, which interact dynamically with her own.
In our world it is simply taken for granted that the literal limits of
a single person coincide with the limits of a single human animal.

If we know that there is a single animal we assume that there is a single person; the question of whether this is the same person in a literal sense just does not arise. This is not an arbitrary choice about how to construct identity or a matter of mere convention. There are immense pressures, evolutionary, biological, and social, for thinking about persons in this way, and such thinking is therefore woven into the whole fabric of our lives. The psychotic who claims he is Brad Pitt and not John Smith is in fact John Smith with a shattered self-concept not simply because others think he is, but because the way our social infrastructure is set up he cannot live any life but John Smith's, and certainly cannot pick up the thread of Brad Pitt's life. He will thus live John Smith's fractured life and remain John Smith.

The fact that we never question the one body/one person principle in everyday life does not, however, imply that we cannot imagine circumstances in which it would be reasonable to do so. We have, in fact, already imagined such circumstances in the case of Teletransportation, where the principle is potentially violated not by the existence of more than one person in a single human body, but by the existence of a single person inhabiting different human bodies at different times. As we saw earlier, there is no consensus about whether the traveler who emerges from the Teletransportation booth on a distant planet is or is not the same person who entered on earth, and this makes the question of identity a real one. Let's explore this case a bit further. It is natural at first to presume that there is a fact of the matter about what happens in Teletransportation, even if we disagree about what it is. Either Teletransportation preserves identity or it does not. Parfit, however, suggests a third alternative; that the question of identity here is an "empty" one (Parfit 1984: 213). An empty question is one that we cannot answer because there is no determinate answer to be had. His example is the identity of a club. Suppose at some point in a club's history most members cease to attend but a few continue meeting. They convene in a different location, change the procedures a bit, add new members, and take up new topics. We might ask if the current club is the same as the original or whether the original club has disbanded and some of its members started a new and distinct club. We may not be able to give a definitive answer to this question – not because there is something we do not know, Parfit says, but because the question is an empty one. Affirming and denying that the current club is the same as the original are just two different ways of describing the same state of affairs. What we are arguing about is word choice, not a deep metaphysical fact. Ultimately, Parfit says, questions of personal identity are also empty in these tricky cases. We know everything that happens in Teletransportation, and it is just a matter of how we choose to describe it.

I am suggesting a fourth possibility, that the question of identity in this case is neither settled in advance nor necessarily indeterminate. Rather it is underdetermined by the details we have been given. Teletransportation might result in the survival of the traveler from earth or it might not, and the difference, on the view I am exploring, depends partly on how the traveler himself and others understand the impact of Teletransportation on survival. This is a complicated and counterintuitive claim, so let's unpack it a bit. Start by focusing on the traveler. I mentioned earlier that psychological theorists do not see a meaningful distinction between cases where travelers believe Teletransportation involves survival and cases where they do not. For the traveler, however, there will be a world of difference. If someone takes it for granted that Teletransportation is an efficient way of traveling the person who walks out of the terminus booth will have the same attitude toward the person who entered on earth as we have to our past selves in everyday life, and so will pick up the thread of the earlier life without a thought. Things will be quite different for someone who believes that Teletransportation is death (indeed it is hard to see why someone who thinks this would agree to be teleported). In this case the person who steps out of the booth will believe himself to be newly minted. He will view the beliefs, desires, and plans he experiences as someone else's and the traveler's friends and relations as people he has never met but for whom he has artificially been given strong emotions. We would not expect someone in this situation to simply pick up the thread of the old life, and it is somewhat difficult to imagine what he would do.

One reason it is difficult to fill in the details here is that we do not know how people more generally think about Teletransportation in the imagined world where it exists. If it is broadly taken for granted that this is a means of travel, an individual's protestations that he is a brand new person when he steps out of the transporter will be treated as a kind of psychosis, and he will be in the same situation as John Smith. But things will be quite different if everybody in this world takes it for granted that Teletransportation is death and replacement by a replica. In such a world no one would see the person stepping out the booth as the person who went in or treat him as the same person. In this case, I suggest, the social infrastructure would differ at a fundamental level and a whole new life would indeed begin for the person stepping out of the booth on the distant planet. In this society, a person who insisted that he was the same person as the earth traveler would be perceived as psychotic, misled by the fact that he has been created with memory implants.

The space of possibilities here is actually quite vast. To oversimplify a bit, however, the position is that in a world in which Teletransportation is viewed as a perfectly ordinary means of travel, the traveler whose attitudes are in synch with those of his society will survive the trip; in a world where Teletransportation is viewed as a form of replacement, a traveler whose views are in synch with those of his society will not survive. Cases where there is divergence of views, either within the society or between the society and the traveler, require detailed individual analysis.

To many, the fact that this view makes numerical identity dependent on our judgments will make it a nonstarter. What I have been discussing, they might argue, is a more fundamental figurative notion of identity, but the literal fact of whether a single object is involved in Teletransportation cannot be constituted by whether we think that it is. This kind of objection goes directly to foundational questions of metaphysics which will certainly not be resolved here. I conclude, however, with two thoughts which might make the idea more palatable. First, it is important to appreciate just how different it will really be for a traveler in a world where she and everyone else see Teletransportation as travel and a world in which they see it as death. The entire organization of human life will be different, and in a very robust way. This is not something that a society could simply decide to change its mind about on a whim; judgments of identity sit at the very core of almost everything we do. Second, lest it seem that literal identity cannot possibly consist in the continuity of a life because a continuous life requires that there first be a continuous entity to live it, we should remember that organisms provide an example of a case in which an entity and its life coincide, neither predating the other.

There are obviously many questions left to be answered and challenges to be met before this proposal can be fully understood, let alone defended. Among other tasks, we will need to answer some of the objections animalists raise to the psychological approach, which seem on the surface to apply also to this view, and speak to worries that the view presupposes an unacceptably conventionalist view of our survival, which are sure to arise. It does, however, offer the intriguing possibility that there are more parallels between figurative and literal identity claims than are immediately evident, and that identity may be more malleable than we thought.

NOTES

1   A slight variation on some of our own positive cases might give a similar result. The woman freed from a destructive relationship, for instance, might tell the ex-lover that the girl he knew before is gone.

2   Or, when experienced in anticipation (as with Parfit's Russian), leads to the anticipation of such a break.

3   The exchange here is a remarkable example of this phenomenon and well worth reading.

4   See, e.g., Snowdon 1990; van Inwagen 1990; Olson 1997.

5   With perhaps, as mentioned earlier, a requirement about how connections are caused, as well as a few other stipulations that we can safely ignore here.

6   Again, some views make additional stipulations.

5   The nature of human death

What is it for a human being to die? What, more generally, is it for any living thing to die? These questions, which are ontological or conceptual, seek a *definition* – a broad conceptualization – of death or human death in particular. Whatever human death is, how can we determine that it has occurred? A comprehensive answer to this epistemological question will include both a general *standard* of human death and *clinical tests* that indicate whether the standard has been met in particular cases. Because this chapter is primarily philosophical, it will focus on definitions and standards of human death, leaving it to clinicians to identify clinical tests.

Although the debate over the nature of human death typically refers to the locus of controversy as "the definition of death," most of this debate has focused on standards. Only the more philosophical contributions have engaged the issue of appropriate conceptualization. We will address both issues, but it will be convenient to organize the discussion around competing standards of human death.

The discussion begins with the currently mainstream *whole-brain standard*, according to which human death is the *irreversible cessation of functioning of the entire brain, including the brain-stem*. The whole-brain standard emerged as an alternative to the traditional *cardiopulmonary standard* – human death as the *irreversible cessation of heart and lung function* – in the context of advancing medical technology and interest in organ transplantation. After contending that the whole-brain standard has considerable strengths but also difficulties, I take up the progressive *higher-brain standard*, according to which human death is the *irreversible loss of the capacity for consciousness*. I argue that this standard is no more

irreversible :

resumes, it is presumably incorrect to say that the organism died before returning to life. It seems to be part of the concept of death that an individual's death is irreversible.[2] Suppose someone falls into a freezing lake and loses cardiopulmonary and brain function for an hour before being resuscitated. Even though this person might have appeared dead to observers prior to resuscitation, he did not actually die. Similarly, if technology permits people or other organisms to exist in "suspended animation" through cryo-preservation, it seems most cogent to say that they are not dead while frozen only to return to life upon successful thawing and resumption of life functions. Rather, I suggest, these individuals would avoid death through cryo-preservation. Although death, on this understanding, is irreversible, it does not follow that life and death exhaust all possible states of organisms. After all, the semi-frozen person in the lake and Woody Allen's character in *Sleeper* are devoid of integrated bodily functioning for significant stretches of time. Rather than abandoning the traditional assumption that death is irreversible, I suggest, we should abandon just the assumption that life and death are exhaustive. Between life and death, a state of *frozen, nonfatal inertness* is possible.

Returning to the conceptualization of death as loss of integrated bodily functioning, how is this definition supposed to favor the WB standard? According to the mainstream defense of this standard, the human brain *integrates* major bodily functions so that only death of the entire brain is necessary and sufficient for human death.[3] Life involves the integrated functioning of the whole organism. Circulation and respiration are centrally important, but so are hormonal regulation, maintenance of body temperature, and various other functions – as well as, in humans and other higher animals, consciousness. The integration of all these vital functions is made possible by a central integrator: the brain.

From this perspective, when cardiopulmonary function persists due to a respirator and perhaps other life-support technologies despite total brain failure, mechanical assistance presents a false appearance of life, masking the lack of integrated functioning in the organism as a whole. Before such life-supports existed, lack of cardiopulmonary function guaranteed total brain failure and the collapse of organismic functioning. With present technology, according the argument, we should not confuse the traditional marker of life – cardiopulmonary function – with the actual presence of life.

advantages: The WB approach – by which I mean the WB standard coupled with the organismic definition of death – has advantages. First, as suggested by its legal acceptance in recent decades, the standard 1) is largely continuous with traditional practices and thinking about human death. Current law in the United States incorporates *both* the CP standard and the WB standard in disjunctive form, most states adopting the Uniform Determination of Death Act (UDDA), while others have embraced similar language. As UDDA states it, "an individual who has sustained either (1) irreversible cessation of circulatory and respiratory functions, or (2) irreversible cessation of all functions of the entire brain, including the brainstem, is dead."[4] Relatedly, the WB standard is at least prima facie plausible as a specification of the organismic conception of human death.

The WB standard also offers practical advantages. Its acceptance 2) facilitates organ transplantation by allowing a declaration of death and retrieval of viable organs while cardiopulmonary function continues, with mechanical assistance, following total brain failure. 3) Another practical advantage is permitting discontinuation of costly life-support measures, even without an advance directive or proxy consent, for patients who have incurred total brain failure. Most proponents of the WB approach maintain that these advantages are fortunate consequences of an appreciation of the biological nature of death, but one might regard these advantages as an important component of the case for a standard whose justification cannot (as we will see) rest with appeals to biology alone.[5]

disadvantages: Let us now identify a few key challenges to the WB standard. 1) First, there are at least some members of the human species for whom total brain failure cannot possibly be *necessary* for their deaths for the simple reason that they do not have brains. Embryos and early fetuses, after all, are as capable as living and dying as you and I are. While a proponent of the WB standard might say that it applies only to those human beings who have brains, and advance a different standard for those human beings who lack brains, the ad hoc feel of this maneuver hints that biological considerations alone might not uniquely support the WB approach.

Perhaps more threatening to the present approach is empir-2) ical evidence that total brain failure is not *sufficient* for human death – that is, assuming the latter is conceptualized as the collapse of integrated bodily functioning mediated by the brain. Many of the human body's integrative functions, according to the challenge, are not mediated by the brain and can persist in individuals who satisfy WB criteria for death by standard clinical tests. These somatically integrating functions include homeostasis, assimilation of nutrients, detoxification and recycling of cellular waste, wound healing, fighting infections, and hormonal stress responses to unanesthetized incisions (for organ procurement); in a small number of cases, brain-dead bodies have even grown, matured sexually, or gestated a fetus.[6] These phenomena suggest that the WB approach should be either rejected or construed in some way that does not appeal to the brain's (dubious) role as indispensable integrator of somatic functioning.

According to an alternative rationale for the WB standard that has recently come into play, a human being dies upon *irreversibly losing the capacity to perform the fundamental work of an organism*, a loss that occurs with total brain failure.[7] The fundamental work of an organism is characterized as involving (1) receptivity to stimuli from the surrounding environment, (2) the ability to act upon the world to obtain, selectively, what the organism needs, and (3) the basic felt need that drives the organism to act as it must to obtain what it needs and what its receptivity reveals to be available.[8] The most sympathetic reading of the somewhat unclear discussion in which this argument is advanced is that satisfaction of any of these three criteria is sufficient for being alive. A patient with total brain failure meets none of the criteria. By contrast, a PVS patient meets at least the second criterion through spontaneous respiration. So far, so good. But present-day robots are capable of meeting at least the first criterion and, if they cannot yet meet the second, it is easy to imagine more advanced robots that could meet that criterion as well – without being alive. If one tried to exclude robots by insisting, contrary to what I call the sympathetic reading, that something must satisfy all three criteria to be alive, then one would thereby also absurdly exclude presentient fetuses and patients who are thoroughly paralyzed yet conscious. No matter how we understand its criteria, then, the "fundamental work" variant of the WB approach does not seem to improve upon the mainstream version.

best
reading of
WB:

What I find the most adequate formulation of the WB approach emerged in response to a challenge directed against a literal reading of the legally established WB standard, which requires irreversible cessation of *all* brain functions for a human being's death. It is now commonly acknowledged that some patients who are declared dead by standard tests for the WB standard continue to exhibit very minor brain functions. The consensus is that the residual functions are too trivial to count against a judgment of death. Thus, a leading proponent of the WB approach has revised both (1) the organismic definition of death to "the permanent cessation of the *critical* functions of the organism as a whole," and (2) the corresponding standard to permanent cessation of the *critical* functions of the whole brain.[9] According to this revised approach, the critical functions of the organism are (1) the vital functions of spontaneous breathing and autonomic circulation control, (2) the integrating functions that maintain the organism's homeostasis, and (3) consciousness. A human being dies upon losing all three.

I find the "critical functions" formulation of the WB standard relatively promising. It addresses the problem of trivial brain functions persisting in individuals who are regarded as dead by clinicians who apply the WB standard. Moreover, sympathetically construed, it can address the challenge that the brain does not mediate *all* somatically integrating functions. The brain doesn't need to do so, we might allow, so long as it plays a *major role in mediating critical functions*. And this it does, for it is impossible to maintain spontaneous breathing and circulation control and impossible to maintain consciousness if the brain isn't doing its job; and while some aspects of homeostasis can be maintained independently of the brain, the brain greatly enhances these processes.

What about those prenatal human beings who lack brains? Their deaths can't be defined in terms of brain dysfunction; and their immaturity and radical dependence on maternal bodies entail that these human beings do not yet participate in *any* of the "critical functions of the organism as a whole." Yet they are clearly alive and can clearly die. It is a disadvantage of the WB approach that it must offer a different standard of death for embryos and early fetuses than for those human beings whose brains are up and running. But two points put this disadvantage in perspective. First, to the extent that the traditional CP standard focuses on heartbeat and lung function,

I don't think
this is a disadvantage:
they aren't yet alive

bite bullet

it faces the parallel observation that embryos and very early fetuses don't have hearts or lungs. Second, we might reasonably understand the role of the brain in this way: before the brain has developed and begins its major functions, the life of the human organism consists in integration of its bodily functions (enabled in significant measure by its mother's body); once the brain is up and running, the life of the human being consists in the performance of some or all of the critical functions. For this reason, we may plausibly regard the death of a pre-brain human being as the total collapse of organismic functioning and the death of a biologically complete human being as loss of all of the critical functions.

This construal may leave a residual sense of conceptual fudging. After all, the conception of death shifts from total functional collapse, which is unobjectionable, to the total loss of *critical* functions, which incorporates a value judgment about which functions are crucially important. Any sense of fudging may derive from an austere philosophical principle that prohibits value judgments from playing a role in how we define life and death. Yet biology alone may not be able to vindicate a unique standard of death for human beings. I am open to an approach, like the present one, that allows reasonable value judgments to play a role in specifying the general concept of death into a useful standard. Let us now consider a quite different approach, which abandons the organismic definition of death and zeroes in on one very important brain function.

THE HIGHER-BRAIN STANDARD

The higher-brain (HB) approach, which has yet to be enshrined in law in any jurisdiction, makes a clean break with biology and conceptualizes human death in terms of the loss of our psychological lives. Accordingly, the proposed standard of death is the irreversible loss of the capacity for consciousness. "Consciousness" here is meant very broadly, to include any subjective experience, so that both waking and dreaming states count as instances. Not only humans but all sentient creatures, by definition, have the capacity for consciousness in this broad sense. Reference to the *capacity* for consciousness indicates that individuals in whom the neurological machinery needed for consciousness remains intact, including individuals in a dreamless sleep or a reversible vegetative state or coma,

fetuses would lack this capacity (I assume)

are alive. One dies, on this view, when one's brain becomes incapable of ever again returning to consciousness.

This implies, radically, that a patient in a PVS or irreversible coma is dead despite continuing brainstem function that permits spontaneous breathing and heartbeat. While many find this implication counterintuitive and jarring, proponents of the HB approach believe that the definition and standard of death that generate the implication enjoy the support of sound philosophical reflection. I maintain that in view of this counterintuitive implication and the availability of our ordinary (and widely accepted) biological conception of death, proponents of the HB approach bear a burden of justification and therefore need a very strong case to justify overturning the ordinary conception. I will argue that the strongest arguments for the HB standard are too questionable to make this case.

Proponents of the HB approach define death in different ways, but their definitions converge on the idea of the irreversible loss of some property for which the capacity for consciousness is necessary. The two strongest argumentative strategies for defending the higher-brain approach, I think, are (1) an appeal to the essence of human persons and (2) an appeal to prudential value.[10] Let's consider these in turn.

The appeal to the essence of human persons assumes that this essence requires the capacity for consciousness.[11] Employed in its strict ontological sense, "essence" here refers to the property or set of properties of an individual the loss of which would necessarily terminate the individual's existence. On this understanding, we human persons – more precisely, we individuals who are at any time human persons – are *essentially* beings with the capacity for consciousness so that we could not exist at any time without having this capacity at that time. We go out of existence, it is assumed, when we die, so death involves loss of what is essential to our continued existence.

Different authors who appeal to our essence advance different specific arguments and employ different terms to designate our essential kind. Nevertheless, we can boil down the collection of specific appeals to this argumentative core:

(1) For humans, irreversible loss of the capacity for consciousness entails (is sufficient for) loss of a property that is essential to their existence.

P (2)   For humans, loss of a property that is essential to their existence is (is necessary and sufficient for) death.

∴ Therefore:

C (3)   For humans, irreversible loss of the capacity for consciousness entails (is sufficient for) death.

The conclusion of this argument follows validly from its premises,
but premise (1) is highly debatable.

Some philosophers who advance this reasoning hold that we are
essentially *persons* in a sense of the term that implies the capacity
for relatively complex forms of consciousness such as those associated with self-awareness, reasoning, and linguistic thought. On this
view, losing the capacity for consciousness would entail loss of personhood and therefore the end of a person's existence. But this view
has incredible implications. It implies that people who undergo progressive dementia actually die – go out of existence – at some point
during the gradual slide to irreversible coma. Even if practical concerns recommend drawing a safe line at irreversible loss of the capacity for consciousness (to prevent errors and abuse), the implication
that, strictly speaking, we go out of existence *during* the course
of progressive dementia strains credibility. A second implication of
person essentialism along these lines is that because newborns lack
the capacities that constitute personhood, you came into existence
after what is ordinarily described as *your* birth. Although there is
nothing incoherent about these implications, or the essentialist
thesis that generates them, I find them too implausible to accept
without a very compelling philosophical justification – of which, I
think, there is none.[12]

A more promising view, which avoids these implications, is that
we are essentially beings with the capacity for consciousness – any
consciousness – who die upon losing this basic psychological capacity. Stated succinctly, we are essentially minded beings, or minds,
and we die when we literally lose our minds.[13] (Note that this view
need not be a version of substance dualism, because it leaves room
for the claim that we are also essentially embodied.)

A central challenge facing mind essentialism is to account
adequately for the human organism that is associated with one
of us: the mind. Consider first the human fetus that gradually

developed prior to the emergence of sentience or the capacity for consciousness – that is, prior to the emergence of a mind. Surely the presentient fetus was alive. On the other end of life, a PVS patient who is spontaneously breathing, circulating blood, and exhibiting brainstem reflexes is alive. The proponent of mind essentialism must hold that the human organism is a living thing distinguishable from one of us: while we are essentially minds, the associated organisms are essentially members of some biological category such as *homo sapiens*, *animal*, or *organism* – a claim that accommodates the plausible thesis that the presentient fetus and PVS patient are living things.

So what is the precise relationship between one of us and the associated organism? The relationship cannot be *identity*, because the mind has different persistence conditions or criteria of identity from the organism, which is why the latter can precede you in time and outlast you in the case of PVS or irreversible coma. Thus, you are not identical to any animal.[14] Perhaps this is a tolerable implication, but it is at least prima facie odd. Also odd, at least to my mind, is the implication that death should be conceptualized in one way for persons, or perhaps for all minded (i.e. sentient) beings, and in another way for all organisms, including the human organism. Different standards of death for different kinds of beings (e.g. those with and without functioning brains) is one thing; different *definitions* are something else altogether, a bifurcation of what appears to be a unitary concept: death.

If I, the mind, am not identical to the human organism associated with me, perhaps I am *part* of this organism – namely, the brain (or, more precisely, the portions of it associated with consciousness).[15] But I supposedly go out of existence at death, yet my brain seems capable of surviving in the corpse. So maybe I am a *functioning* brain, which ends its existence at the irreversible loss of consciousness. But how could I be some organ only when it functions? Presumably, I am a *substance*, something with properties, not a substance *only when it has certain properties*. If one claims that the functioning brain is itself a substance, one distinct from the brain, this seems implausible. Nor can we seriously claim that I, the mind, am simply the *conscious properties* of the brain. For that would imply that I am not a substance at all but just a bunch of properties. While it might be plausible to assert that what we call "the mind" is really

[margin note: CRIT]

[margin note: Just a bunch of identity theory]

just a set of properties, it is hardly plausible to claim that you and I
are just properties.

Another possible thesis about the mind/organism relationship is
that each of us is *constituted* by a human organism just as a statue
might be constituted by a hunk of marble.[16] This subtle thesis
encounters inter alia a challenge about counting conscious beings.
On the constitution view, I am essentially a being with the capacity
for consciousness. But the human animal that supposedly constitutes me has a functioning brain, so it too is a being with the capacity for consciousness. This suggests, strangely, that there are two
conscious beings sitting in my chair as I write these words.

As we have seen, the higher-brain definition of death can be motivated by the claim that we are essentially minded beings and by any
of several ways of understanding the mind/organism relationship.
All of the theoretical options encounter challenges. An alternative
view that does not support the higher-brain approach – namely, the
view that we are essentially human animals, organisms, or members of some other biological category – has a simple and unproblematic view of our relationship to the human organisms associated
with us. For on the biological approach, we *are* animals, as scientifically informed common sense generally assumes. This is not to say
that the biological approach to our essence faces no significant challenges (it does); this is just to note one of its advantages over essentialist views that motivate the HB approach. Rather than claiming
that mind essentialism is clearly indefensible, I claim that that it
encounters too many reasonable doubts for it to shoulder the HB
standard's burden of justification. Meanwhile, person essentialism,
as discussed earlier, is highly implausible. Although appeals to the
essence of human persons may not succeed in the ontological terms
in which they are couched, they helpfully direct our attention to a
thesis about *what matters in our existence.*

This brings us to the appeal to prudential value.[17] Conscious life,
the argument begins, is a precondition for nearly everything that
we value (prudentially) in our lives. We have an enormous stake
in continuing our lives as persons, or at least as sentient beings,
and little or no stake in continuing our lives as irreversibly unconscious biological blobs. The capacity for consciousness, therefore, is
essential not in an ontological sense, but in an evaluative sense of
indispensable to us. Although, for many people, consciousness is

prudential value

insufficient for what's prudentially important – insofar as they find certain capacities of normal persons indispensable (e.g. self-awareness, the ability to relate meaningfully to others) – it is necessary; and the basic capacity for consciousness is the only safe place to demarcate death for legal and social purposes. So, even if the HB standard is at odds with the original biological concept of death, the argument concludes, we should embrace it on the strength of these value-based considerations.

Despite having some sympathy for this argument, I do not think it carries the day. In proposing to overturn a biological understanding of human death on the basis of shared prudential values, it rests heavily on the principal value claims. I maintain that the appeal to prudential value founders on reasonable pluralism about this sort of value. While supporters of the HB approach and many other people (including me) are likely to have prudential values in line with this appeal, plenty of others will not. Some people believe that human life is inherently valuable to its possessor, even if the individual cannot appreciate its value at a given time. They are likely to favor the continuation of life-supports for patients in a PVS or irreversible coma (unless perhaps there is a countervailing advance directive).

A proponent of the HB approach might reply that it's *irrational to value the continuation of biological life* in the absence of any possibility of returning to consciousness, so we should ignore the aforementioned assertion of value. But this reply assumes the *experience requirement*: that only states of affairs that affect one's experience can affect one's well-being.[18] The experience requirement is debatable. Some people believe that they are worse off for being slandered or cheated even if they never learn of the wrong and its repercussions never affect their experience. It is surely coherent to hold that states of affairs that don't affect one's experience but do connect significantly with one's values can affect one's interests *at least while one still exists*. Preference-based accounts of well-being standardly accept this principle, for what is preferred or desired may occur without affecting one's experience. These points illuminate the possibility of one's prudential values extending (reasonably) to a portion of one's life when one is irreversibly unconscious. I do not believe such a value system is open to refutation. Thus, I doubt that the appeal to prudential value is any more successful than the appeal to the essence of human persons in carrying the burden of proof for the HB standard.

RESUSCITATING TRADITION: AN UPDATED CARDIOPULMONARY APPROACH

Prior to societal and legal acceptance of the WB standard, death was understood as the irreversible cessation of cardiopulmonary function. Several conceptualizations of death hovered in the supportive background of the traditional standard. Some were religious or spiritual – for example, death as the departure of the vital principle or soul. Another was the same conception that champions of the WB standard invoke: death as the irreversible cessation of functioning of the organism as a whole.[19] However death was defined, before the development of modern life-support technologies a functioning heart and lungs indicated continuing brainstem function. The WB and traditional CP standards came into competition only after it became possible to sustain cardiopulmonary function, artificially, without any brain function. Although the WB standard became widely accepted and codified in law, some traditionalists never accepted total brain failure as sufficient for death. Growing awareness of challenges that face the WB standard has contributed to renewed interest in something along the lines of the CP approach.

Those who champion the CP standard *alone* – that is, not alongside the WB standard as in current American law – believe that a breathing, heart-beating human body is alive irrespective of whether these functions require external support (e.g. life-supports, the mother's body in the case of a fetus).[20] At the same time, the usual formulation of the traditional approach problematically focuses on the state of two organs: heart and lungs. This picture is overly reductionistic, leaving room for an improved variant of the traditional standard.

A more realistic picture features integrative unity as existing diffusely throughout the organism. On this view, what is crucial is not the performance of a small number of organs, but rather "the anti-entropic mutual interaction of all the cells and tissues of the body, mediated in mammals by circulating oxygenated blood."[21] The brain's capacity to augment other systems presupposes their pre-existing capacity to function. With maintenance of body temperature, for example, the "thermostat" may be in the brain but the "furnace" is the energy metabolism diffused throughout the body. That is why brain-dead bodies may grow colder, but not as cold as corpses.[22]

According to this view, tradition's insight that respiration and circulation are especially important should be updated by de-emphasizing the organs and emphasizing a more holistic image: respiration and circulation as occurring throughout the body as oxygenated blood circulates to different organs and bodily systems. Unlike total brain failure, loss of respiration and circulation leads relentlessly to the break-down of cells, tissues, organs, bodily systems, and eventually the organism as a whole. This picture recommends an updated traditional standard, which we might call the *circulatory-respiratory (CR) standard*: death as the *irreversible cessation of circulatory-respiratory function*.[23]

This approach plausibly characterizes the difference between life and death – as understood in organismic terms – in a full range of cases, consistently with the clinical phenomena (discussed earlier) that challenge the WB standard. This is not to say that the CR standard is clearly superior to the WB standard – especially in its "critical functions" formulation. Rather, I claim, the CR standard is fairly plausible and is at least as consonant as the WB standard with an organismic understanding of death.

Not surprisingly, the traditional approach – under any formulation – faces challenges of its own. One challenge is the charge of overemphasizing our biological nature, as if we were merely organisms, while failing to appreciate our mental life and its control center, the brain.[24] As someone who has defended the updated traditional approach,[25] I cannot deny the intuitive power of this objection. In reply, I have urged that the ontological issues of our essence and the nature of death must be carefully distinguished from questions about what is most valuable in our existence. But as I now find the WB standard about as plausible as the CR standard – bearing in mind that both are motivated by an organismic conception of death – I am more open to values playing a role in arguments for particular standards of death. While this concession does not rescue the HB approach given its departure from the ordinary concept of death and its onus of justification, it keeps the competition open between the WB and CR standards.

Value considerations take us to another major challenge to any traditional approach: the specter of highly unpalatable practical consequences. If we changed our laws and adopted the CR standard while no longer accepting the WB standard, then a patient who had suffered total brain failure but maintained respiration and circulation via life supports would count as alive. Consequently, unless we abandoned the "dead-donor rule" – the legal requirement that a body must be dead before vital organs can be harvested – it would be illegal to procure organs from the patients in question. Yet the viability of these organs requires maintaining respiration and circulation with life-supports. So having to wait until CR criteria are met to harvest vital organs would constitute a great setback to organ transplantation. Moreover, physicians might feel that they could no longer unilaterally discontinue treatment – when a family requests its continuation – upon a determination of total brain failure despite what many would consider the futility of continued treatment. And, of course, laws for determining death would need to be changed as the medical profession acknowledged (what would now be considered) the error of having accepted the WB standard for several decades.

Importantly, these challenges confront those who champion the CR standard alone rather than disjunctively alongside the WB standard.

CONCLUDING REFLECTIONS

Let me conclude this investigation of the nature of human death with a few reflections.

First, both the WB standard (especially in its "critical functions" formulation) and the CR standard are plausible specifications of the organismic conceptualization of human death. Human death proves to be a somewhat vague concept, which is why there can be more than one plausible way to specify it with a standard.

Second, the organismic definition of human death is more defensible than the conceptions invoked in support of the HB standard, conceptions that assume either person essentialism or mind essentialism. Person essentialism is implausible. Mind essentialism is more plausible, but no more so than a biological conception of our essence, so mind essentialism does not carry the burden of justification shouldered by any view that would overturn the presumption favoring the everyday biological conception of death. Here I assume a sort of realism about life and death as biological phenomena. This realism does not preclude redefining death in the human case, but it imposes a burden of justification.

Third, the appeal to prudential value, like the appeal to our essence, fails to carry the burden of justification for the HB standard. This standard is not justified as a characterization of human death.

Fourth, the UDDA's disjunctive approach is optimal policy in view of the preceding conclusions. This approach accommodates reasonable pluralism about standards of death while neatly sidestepping the unpalatable practical consequences that would threaten the CR standard if it alone were implemented. It also permits taking advantage of the CR standard in what is called "donation after cardiac death" by permitting (with the patient's advance directive) the harvesting of organs just minutes after death is declared – and before total brain failure can be determined – on the basis of cardiac arrest.[26]

Finally, realism about death as a biological phenomenon does not entail acceptance of traditional assumptions about the moral significance of death. This is where the HB approach can make a significant contribution. Although unsuccessful in displacing the biological concept of death in the case of humans, this approach helpfully presses us to consider whether we must wait for death before engaging in "death behaviors." Along these lines, I make two suggestions. First, because the great majority of people do not value the prospects of surviving in an irreversible unconscious state, we should allow physicians and health-care institutions to terminate care unilaterally unless the patient had indicated in advance a preference to live in this condition and has the funds to pay for it. Second, we should seriously consider the possibility of vital organ transplantation, when authorized by a valid advance directive, in cases of PVS or irreversible coma even though such patients are clearly alive.

NOTES

1   See, e.g., Becker 1975 and Bernat *et al.* 1981.
2   This thesis does not conceptually preclude an "afterlife," because an individual in this state would remain biologically dead and would be "alive" only in some non-biological sense. Nor does it preclude a Frankenstein's monster: even though the monster is assembled from parts of corpses, after assembly *he* comes to life for the first time.
3   See Bernat *et al.* 1981.

4 President's Commission 1981: 119.

5 For reasons of space I will not discuss the closely related *brainstem standard*, according to which human death occurs at the irreversible cessation of brainstem function. This standard, which requires fewer clinical tests than the whole-brain standard while having largely equivalent implications for determining death, has been adopted in the United Kingdom and various other nations.

6 See Shewmon 2001.

7 President's Council on Bioethics 2008: chap. 4.

8 President's Council on Bioethics 2008: chap. 4.

9 Bernat 1998: 17.

10 Michael Green and Daniel Wikler influentially argued that appealing to our personal identity – more precisely, to the criteria for our numerical identity over time – represents a distinct argumentative strategy (Green and Wilder 1980). But this claim falsely assumes that we can know the criteria of our identity without assuming a particular account of our essence. See DeGrazia 1999.

11 See, e.g., Engelhardt 1975; Veatch 1975; Bartlett and Youngner 1988; and Baker 2000.

12 I develop this argument in DeGrazia 2005: chap. 2.

13 This view is developed in McMahan 2002: chap. 1.

14 This argument is developed in Olson 1997.

15 This is McMahan's view (2002: chap. 1).

16 See Baker 2000.

17 I present and evaluate this argument in DeGrazia 2005: 134–38.

18 For a discussion, see Griffin 1986: 16–19.

19 See, e.g., Becker 1975.

20 See Shewmon 2001 and Potts 2001.

21 Shewmon 2001: 473.

22 Shewmon 2001: 471.

23 Interestingly, the UDDA uses the more holistic language of "circulatory and respiratory" rather than "cardiopulmonary" even if tradition stressed heart and lung function.

24 Cf. Pallis 1999: 96.

25 DeGrazia 2005: chap. 4.

26 I believe that this practice involves a fudge, however, insofar as loss of CR functioning is only *permanent* – given a commitment not to resuscitate the patient – as opposed to *irreversible*. So I don't think these patients are dead (unless total brain failure has already occurred even if not yet confirmed by tests). At the same time, because I do not think we need to maintain the dead-donor rule, I approve of the practice. For a good discussion, see Truog and Miller 2008.

Part II   The significance of life and death

6   Assessing lives

There are many ways to evaluate lives. We might evaluate lives as being morally good or bad. We might think, for example, that St. Francis had a morally better life than Adolph Hitler or Joseph Stalin. Perhaps we think the life of St. Francis is morally better because of his moral virtues. Perhaps it is better because of the kinds of acts he performed. Perhaps it is morally better for both reasons.

Alternatively, we might evaluate lives aesthetically. We might think that one life would make a more interesting subject for a novel or movie than another. We might think that a life with interesting twists and adventures, where friends become enemies and enemies become friends, would be better aesthetically than one of comfortable, boring sameness.

Many philosophers focus, however, on another sort of evaluation, one that concerns *welfare* or *well-being* or how good the life is *for the person who lives it*. Evaluating lives in terms of welfare clearly differs from the aesthetic evaluation of a life. A life that is aesthetically good might be low in terms of welfare and vice versa. Consider the short unhappy life of Madame Bovary. Her life was aesthetically interesting. It made for a good novel. But it was not high in welfare. She suffered a lot and was unhappy much of the time. Similarly, we can imagine a life that is morally good, but not high in welfare. Some saintly or morally virtuous person might have a life high in moral goodness, but one filled with suffering, disappointment, and great sadness.

But what exactly is welfare or well-being? What is this kind of value? Fred Feldman suggests that we can understand welfare or well-being in relation to other concepts such as benevolence, altruism, and love. Welfare, he says, is

[t]he sort of value that is decreased when someone is harmed; the sort of value that we increase in a person when we benefit him. Additionally, when a person is selfishly trying to enhance his own self-interest, the sort of value he is trying to enhance is his own welfare. Contrariwise, it is the sort of value an altruistic or benevolent person tries to enhance in others. Welfare is the value we have in mind when we worry about the quality of someone's life, or we consider whether he has a life worth living. Welfare is the kind of value in another that we are concerned to enhance when we love, or care for, that person. Welfare is the value about which we are concerned when, at graveside, we reflect on the question whether the deceased "had a good life."[1]

Perhaps this is a helpful way to think about welfare. But is the question whether someone had a good life simply a question about his welfare or well-being?

As we noted, a life might be high in some kinds of value, e.g. aesthetic or moral goodness, and low in welfare. The reverse also seems possible. A life can be high in welfare and low in aesthetic or moral goodness. But if this is so, is there not yet *another* way to evaluate lives, one distinct from those considered so far? Consider three lives that one could have, A, B, and C. Lives A and B are equally morally good, but life C is not morally good at all. Suppose that lives A and C are high in welfare and equally high, but B is not very high in welfare at all. When we consider these three lives and note that life A is high in *both* moral goodness and welfare, could we not say that A is a *better* life than either B or C? In judging that A is better than the other two we are not evaluating them in terms of moral goodness since we assume that A is as morally good as B. We are also not claiming that A is better in terms of welfare since we assume that C is as high in welfare as A. The kind of evaluation of lives we are making here is distinct from one of well-being or moral goodness, although considerations of well-being or moral goodness might be relevant. The sort of evaluation we make here is akin to, or the same as, that which T. M. Scanlon calls "choiceworthiness."[2] Perhaps we might say that life A is more "choiceworthy." It is also, I think, the sort of evaluation that Thomas Hurka calls "moral in the broader sense," broader than one concerned only with choice and character.[3] Alternatively, we may say that A is "ethically better" than or "ethically preferable" to B or C. Perhaps we may say, roughly, that the contemplation of these three lives ethically requires that we prefer

Feldman's def. of welfare

life A for its own sake to either B or C. In any case, whether someone had a good life need not be taken to be simply a question about
welfare.

When philosophers discuss "the good life," some focus on one
sort of value, such as well-being or welfare, while others focus on
another value, such as choiceworthiness or ethical goodness. This
can create confusion. Sometimes it appears they are disagreeing
when in fact they are talking about different kinds of evaluations.
In what follows, I will discuss (i) preferentism, (ii) hedonism, and
(iii) objective lists theories. I will treat them as theories of welfare or
well-being, as theories about what makes a life high in welfare.

Of course, these three theories could also be construed as theories of choiceworthiness or ethical preferability and it is also worthwhile to consider them from that perspective. Indeed, one theory
might provide the best account of welfare and another theory provide the best account of choiceworthiness or ethical preferability.
Perhaps hedonism is the correct account of welfare and an objective list theory is the correct account of choiceworthiness or ethical
preferability. In any event, there are so many specific forms of these
three broad theories, we can only hope to mention some general
points and point to some of the main difficulties.

PREFERENTISM

Preferentism is very roughly the view that one's welfare or well-
being depends on the satisfaction of one's actual or ideal desires.
Roughly, it is the view that the more your desires are satisfied, the
better off you are in terms of welfare or well-being.[4]

Some desires and aversions are fairly stable and long lasting. These
include the desire that one's children be well, that one have a successful career, that one be healthy. Other desires and aversions are
more transitory, e.g. the desire that one's flight arrive on time, that
the waitress bring another cup of coffee soon, that the driver ahead
speed up. Which sorts of desires and aversions are relevant to well-
being? *Local preferentism* holds that one's level of welfare or well-
being at a time depends on the satisfaction of *both* sorts of desires
and aversions, those that are transitory and those that are stable.

Our desires and aversions come in different degrees of intensity.
We desire some things more than others and our aversions to some

things are greater than our aversions to others. Typically, preferentists hold that the satisfaction of a more intense desire contributes more to one's welfare. So, if you have a stronger desire for A than B, then the satisfaction of your desire for A will contribute more to your welfare than the satisfaction of your desire for B. Similarly, if you are more averse to C than D, then the "satisfaction" of your aversion to C will decrease your welfare more than the satisfaction of your aversion to D.

Preferentism says that welfare depends on the satisfaction of our desires. But what is the relevant notion of "desire satisfaction"? Let's say that one's desire (aversion) that p is *objectively satisfied* just in case one desires that p (is averse to p), and p. If, for example, you desire that your son is well and he is well, then your desire is objectively satisfied. It is more awkward to talk about the "satisfaction" of an aversion, nevertheless, let's say that if you are averse to your son missing his flight and he misses his flight, then your aversion is satisfied.

Objective local preferentism is the view that one's level of welfare or well-being at a time depends on, or is a function of, the objective satisfaction of one's desires at that time. We may take objective local preferentism to imply the following principle:

> (D1) If S desires that p (is averse to p), and p, then S's welfare is enhanced (decreased).

(D1) tells us that the objective satisfaction of any desire enhances or decreases welfare. Again, objective preferentism is not committed to the view that all satisfied desires contribute equally to one's welfare. It typically holds that the satisfaction of our stronger desires increases our welfare more that the satisfaction of a weaker desire.

CRIT   One objection to objective local preferentism is that it makes it "too easy" for one's welfare or well-being to be enhanced. Suppose one meets a young soldier on a train. He is heading off to a war zone. He is a pleasant young man. You desire that he will return home safely. You do not know that he will do so. You have no belief one way or the other. But suppose that it is true that he will return home safely. Since it is true at the time you form your desire that he will return home safely, your desire is objectively satisfied. According to (D1), your welfare or well-being is enhanced. Similarly, suppose you desire that there is intelligent life elsewhere in our galaxy. You do not believe or reject the proposition that there is. You have no opinion on the matter. But let us suppose it is true. Again, according to (D1), your desire is objectively satisfied and your welfare is enhanced. You are better off. To some, these implications are implausible. Even though your desire is objectively satisfied, it does not seem that you are better off, that your well-being has been increased.

Perhaps a more plausible form of preferentism would focus on *subjective desire satisfaction.* One's desire that *p* (aversion to *p*) is *subjectively satisfied* if and only if one desires that *p* (is averse to *p*) and one believes that *p*. So, if you desire that your son is well and you believe that he is well, then your desire is subjectively satisfied. One's desire that *p* can be subjectively satisfied whether or not *p* is true.

Subjective local preferentism is the view that one's level of well-being at a time depends on, or is a function of, the subjective satisfaction of one's desires at that time. It implies the following principle:

> (D2) If S desires that *p* (is averse to *p*) and S believes that *p*, then S's welfare is enhanced (decreased).

(D2) tells us that subjective desire satisfaction enhances welfare and subjective aversion satisfaction decreases welfare. In 1916, the Republican presidential candidate Charles Evans Hughes went to bed believing that he had won the presidential election. He was mistaken. The votes from California had not yet been counted. Still, that night his desire that he win the election was subjectively satisfied, and, according to (D2), his welfare level at that time was enhanced.

Like (D1), (D2) does not tell us how much subjective satisfaction of a desire or aversion enhances or decreases welfare. Again, it is plausible to think that the increase or decrease depends on the strength of one's desire or aversion. In addition, one might hold that it also depends on the degree of confidence or strength of one's belief that *p*. Thus, one might hold that if I desire that my son is well and believe strongly that he is well, this increases my welfare more than if I am less confident that he is well.

Subjectivism preferentism faces a variety of objections. One objection concerns cases of massive deception. Consider the victim of an "experience machine," a machine that produces vivid sensory experiences and a simulated reality. Imagine that Jones desires a successful

R: only if he finds out

CRIT

career, a loving wife, and wonderful children and friends. He believes that he has all of these things. In reality, he has none of them. They are all illusions created by the experience machine. Jones has no wife, no successful career, no friends, and no children. Still, Jones' level of subjective desire satisfaction is quite high. If (D2) were true, then Jones should have a high level of welfare. But, according to the objection, his level of welfare is not high. Therefore, (D2) is false.[5]

Another, perhaps more serious, objection to both (D1) and (D2) questions whether desire satisfaction actually enhances welfare at all. Derek Parfit asks us to consider a case where one is offered a drug such that if one takes the drug one will wake up every morning with an intense desire for the drug.[6] Taking the drug will not produce any pleasure but it will satisfy one's desire for the drug. If one does not get the drug, then one will experience pain and discomfort. However, one knows that there are ample supplies of the drug, one will never be without it, and it will cost nothing. In this case, one's desires for the drug would be satisfied, but would one's welfare or well-being be enhanced? Parfit holds that it would not be. Having one's desires for the drug satisfied does not enhance one's level of well-being or welfare.

A similar issue is raised in the following example from Feldman.[7] He asks us to imagine that Lois is visiting a museum with a group of schoolchildren. They see the fossilized skeleton and the sharp teeth of a *Tyrannosaurus rex*. One of the children exclaims that he wouldn't want to be eaten by a dinosaur. Lois realizes that she, too, desires not be eaten by a dinosaur. She also believes that she won't be. She knows that dinosaurs have been extinct for millions of years. Still, Lois is not relieved at this thought. She is not pleased or excited that she won't be eaten. Her emotional state is neutral. Feldman argues that while Lois' desire not to be eaten is satisfied, her happiness is not enhanced. Feldman uses this example to make a point about subjective desire satisfaction theories of happiness. But one can make a similar point about welfare or well-being. Lois' subjectively satisfied desire not to be eaten by a dinosaur does not enhance her welfare or well-being. More generally, one might object that we desire lots of things, e.g. that gravity continue, that there be oxygen, that we do not burst into flames, etc., and these desires are subjectively satisfied, but the mere subjective satisfaction of these desires does not enhance our welfare or well-being.

Finally, some critics object that welfare is surely not enhanced *CRIT* by the satisfaction of just any desire. Imagine someone with the strong desire to count blades of grass or to smash as many icicles as possible.[8] The critics argue that the satisfaction of such "crazy" desires does not make one better off or increase one's well-being. Similarly, imagine a jilted teenager who strongly desires to kill himself because his girlfriend has just left him. At the moment, he desires that more than anything else. But surely the satisfaction of that desire would not enhance the boy's welfare or well-being.

Sensitive to these criticisms, *ideal preferentism* holds that it is not *overcomes* the satisfaction of just any desire that increases well-being. Instead, *above* welfare is increased or decreased by the satisfaction of one's "ideal" *crits* desires and aversions. But what makes desires ideal? Ideal preferentists suggest a variety of different answers. Typically, they hold that ideal desires and aversions are those one would have if one (i) knew all relevant facts, (ii) had all relevant facts vividly before one's mind, and/or (iii) were rational.[9]

Consider the case of the jilted teenager. He desires to kill himself because he has a lot of false beliefs, e.g. that he will never get over his lost love, that no one else will ever love him, that he will never know joy again. Ideal preferentists would point out that if he knew all of the relevant facts he would not have these false beliefs and so he would not have the desire to kill himself. Therefore, the jilted teenager's desire to kill himself is not an ideal desire. Since it is not ideal, its satisfaction will not enhance his welfare.

Ideal preferentism faces a variety of objections. Suppose that John *CRIT* likes Mary and wants to ask her for a date. He summons the courage to ask her and she says yes. John is delighted. He is walking on air. It seems that his welfare or well-being has been increased. Still, unbeknownst to John, Mary's roommate, Jill, is in fact the ideal woman for John. She would be his perfect match. If John knew all the relevant facts about Mary and Jill and had them vividly before his mind, he would want to ask Jill for a date and he would not desire to ask Mary for a date. If this is so, then John's desire to ask Mary for a date is not an ideal desire and, according to ideal preferentism, its satisfaction does not enhance his welfare. But that just seems false. His welfare is enhanced when she agrees to go out with him. Again, suppose that you want to eat a steak. Plausibly, the satisfaction of this desire would enhance your well-being. But suppose that you were fully and vividly aware of all the facts surrounding the killing of the steer, its butchering, and the details of the digestion of the meat in your gastro-intestinal tract, you would not have that desire. If so, then your desire to eat the steak is not ideal, and its satisfaction does not, according to ideal preferentism, make you better off. But again, that seems false. The general problem here seems to be that there are often desires whose satisfaction makes us better off where those desires are *not* ideal, at least not in the sense that we would have them if we were fully informed and had all the relevant facts vividly before our minds.

CRIT   Furthermore, we mentioned above the problem of "crazy" desires, such as a desire to count blades of grass or smash as many icicles as possible. Suppose someone had a very strong desire for such an apparently worthless activity, that it became a central focus of his life, and he sacrificed his friends and his job to pursue its satisfaction. But suppose further that he would *still* have such a desire even if he knew all of the relevant facts, had all the relevant facts vividly before his mind, and was rational. Assume that such a desire met the criterion for being ideal. Would we think that the satisfaction of such a desire really enhanced his welfare? Even at the loss of his friends and his job? Would we not think, instead, that he is worse off for being in the grip of some terrible obsession? Critics of ideal preferentism hold that even the satisfaction of one's ideal desires does not necessarily enhance one's welfare.

HEDONISM

Hedonist accounts of welfare or well-being hold that one's level of well-being is determined solely by one's states of pleasure and displeasure. Roughly, states of pleasure increase one's welfare and states of displeasure decrease it.[10]

But what is the relevant notion of pleasure? Many hedonists distinguish between _sensory_ and _attitudinal_ pleasures and displeasures. We are all familiar with sensory pleasures and pains. Sensory pleasures include the pleasure we get from a good massage or a warm bath. Sensory pains include the pain of a toothache or the painful sensation that comes from touching a hot stove. Attitudinal pleasures and displeasures are intentional attitudes that take propositions or states of affairs as their objects. So, for example, one can be pleased that his son is doing well or pleased that he got a raise. One can be displeased that the negotiations failed or displeased that the price of bread has gone up. In this respect, attitudinal pleasure and displeasure are like other propositional attitudes such as fear, hope, belief, and desire.

Attitudinal pleasure and displeasure need not be accompanied by sensory pleasure or pain. If someone is pleased that his son is well, he need not be experiencing any sensory pleasure. Indeed, it is possible for someone to have attitudinal pleasure while experiencing sensory pain. Someone suffering tremendous physical pain from a car accident, for example, might be pleased that his son is unharmed.

Sensory pleasures and pains come in degrees. One sensory pleasure or pain can be more intense than another. Attitudinal pleasure and displeasure also come in degrees. One can be more or less pleased or displeased. One can be pleased, for example, that the weather is nice and be more pleased that one's son is doing well. If we assume that we can assign numerical values to the degree of pleasure or displeasure one takes in some state of affairs, then we might say, for example, that John is pleased to degree +9 that the weather is beautiful and Tom is displeased to degree −7 that there is no rain.

If we assume that sensory and attitudinal pleasure and pain come in degrees, then we can think of a person's level of welfare at a time as a sum of those degrees. More precisely, we can formulate a version of *simple hedonism* as:

> (SH) S's welfare level at *t* is the sum of the degrees of all the episodes of pleasure S has at *t* minus the sum of the degrees of the episodes of displeasure or pain that he has at *t*.

To illustrate, suppose for the sake of simplicity that at *t*, Smith has only two episodes of pleasure and one of displeasure: (i) Smith is pleased to degree +9 that his son is well, (ii) pleased to degree +8 that the sun is out, and (iii) displeased to degree −8 that he received no raise. According to (SH), Smith's welfare level at *t* is +9. One's welfare level over time will change as the degrees of pleasure and pain one is experiencing at those times change. Furthermore, the simple hedonist will typically hold that a person's welfare level over the course of his life is simply the sum of the welfare levels at each moment of his life.

Hedonists hold that only episodes of pleasure enhance one's welfare. Consider again subjective desire satisfaction. Hedonists would point out that the mere satisfaction of desire does not enhance one's welfare. Take, for example, Lois' satisfied desire that she not be eaten by a dinosaur. She does not take any pleasure in this fact. She does not enjoy it. Because she does not, her welfare or well-being is not increased. Similarly, in Parfit's example the addict's desire for the drug is satisfied, but it causes him no pleasure. Since it causes him no pleasure, his welfare is not increased.

Hedonists also reject ideal preferentism. According to ideal preferentism, it is only the satisfaction of one's ideal desires that enhance one's well-being. Recall John and Mary. John desires that Mary go out with him. His desire that Mary go out with him is not ideal, since if he had all the relevant information and had all the relevant facts vividly before his mind, he would desire to go out with Jill and not desire to go out with Mary. Therefore, according to the ideal preferentist, John's welfare is not enhanced when his desire that Mary go out with him is satisfied. The hedonist argues that this is mistaken. When Mary agrees to go out with him, John is very pleased. Since he is very pleased, his welfare at that time is enhanced. What matters to the hedonist is whether John is pleased or displeased, not whether his ideal desires are satisfied.

CRIT

Simple hedonism faces a variety of objections. One objection involves the experience machine scenario described above. Imagine two men, A and B. Both believe that they have successful careers, loving wives, wonderful children, and loyal friends. Imagine that both lives are equally pleasant. B, however, is a victim of the experience machine and his beliefs about his life are almost entirely false. He has no career, wife, children, or friends. According to this objection, if (SH) is true, their lives are equally high in terms of welfare. But they are not. Therefore, (SH) is false.

R

Hedonists have several responses to this objection. First, the simple hedonist might reply that the argument is simply mistaken in assuming that A's and B's lives *differ* in terms of welfare or well-being. As far as well-being is concerned, these two lives are equal. The simple hedonist might point out that B's life is worse in terms of other sorts of values. For example, it is worse *epistemically* since he fails to have much in the way of knowledge or true belief. It is also worse in terms of *accomplishment* or certain kinds of *excellence*.

But though it is worse in these ways, it does not follow that it is worse in terms of well-being or welfare. The hedonist might insist that we should not confuse these kinds of value with welfare value.

Alternatively, some hedonists suggest that simple hedonism does not get matters quite right. They say we should distinguish between "true" and "false" attitudinal pleasures. One's pleasure that p is true just in case one is pleased that p, and p. One's pleasure that p is false just in case one is pleased that p and p is false. So, if you are pleased that your son passed his exam, and he *did* pass his exam, then your pleasure is true. Given this distinction, the hedonist may hold that, other things being equal, the value of an episode of true pleasure is *greater* than the value of a false pleasure. The hedonist may thus hold that the value of an episode of pleasure can be "truth adjusted" and further that one's welfare depends on the sum of one's truth-adjusted pleasures.[11] If this is so, then "truth-adjusted" hedonism may hold that since A's life contains mostly true pleasures and B's life mostly false pleasures, A's welfare is greater than B's.

Yet another objection to simple hedonism and truth adjusted hedonism asks us to compare two lives:

SIMON: Simon is severely mentally challenged, but he has a very pleasant life. He enjoys many things such as trips to the zoo, watching Barney videos, and an extra cup of ice-cream. He has no worries or anxieties and he is very well cared for by friendly and loving caregivers.

FRED: Fred is a talented philosopher and a morally good and wise man. He performs virtuous actions. His life is very pleasant.

Let's suppose that these two lives are equal in term of the sum of the degrees of pleasures they contain. So, from the standpoint of simple hedonism they are equal in welfare. Let us suppose, too, they do not differ in terms of true and false pleasure and so are equal from the standpoint of "truth-adjusted" hedonism. But, the objection says, these two lives differ in terms of welfare and well-being. Fred's life is higher in welfare than Simon's. Consequently, simple hedonism and "truth-adjusted" hedonism are mistaken accounts of welfare.

Once again, the simple hedonist might claim that, as far as welfare goes, there simply is no difference between these two lives. Their lives might differ in some other value such as moral or epistemic value. They might differ in terms of excellence or achievement. But they do not differ in terms of welfare. According to the simple hedonist, we are simply confusing welfare or well-being with some other sort of value.

R2   In contrast, some hedonists will urge that the kinds of pleasures involved in Fred's life contribute more to his welfare than the sorts of pleasures had by Simon. John Stuart Mill famously held that intellectual pleasures were of higher quality than physical pleasures, and, other things being equal, they were of greater value.[12] *R3* Other hedonists suggest, along similar lines, that some things are more "pleasure-worthy" than others. For example, beautiful works of art, impressive intellectual achievements, or acts of virtue are more pleasure-worthy than what is ugly, banal, or wicked. On this view, if A is more pleasure-worthy than B, then one's taking a certain amount of pleasure in A enhances one's well-being more than taking the same amount of pleasure in B. Just as the value of pleasures might be truth-adjusted, so, too, their value can be adjusted for "pleasure-worthiness."[13] If the hedonist adopts such a "quality-adjusted" or qualitative hedonism, then he might hold that Fred's life is higher in welfare due to his higher quality pleasures.

CRIT   Finally, let us consider one further objection to hedonism. Imagine that Constance is reading a treatise in mathematics. She reads the proof of a theorem and takes much intellectual pleasure in the proof. She smiles in pleasure at the subtlety and soundness of the proof. Now, suppose that Constance is struck by a freakish blast of cosmic radiation. Her mental states become fixed. She is frozen in the pleasant contemplation of the proof. She is not upset or unhappy. She is not bored. She is unaware of her surroundings. Suppose that Constance spends the next fifty years in this pleasant, but unchanging state. Her life is filled with high-quality intellectual pleasure. Were we to sum up the amount of high-quality intellectual pleasure she enjoys at each moment, it seems that her life should be high in welfare. But, according to the objection, it is not very high in welfare. Since her life is filled with pleasure, but not high in welfare, hedonism as an account of welfare must be mistaken.

R   The hedonist might, of course, reject the assumption that Constance's life is low in welfare. They might hold that her life is remarkably high in welfare. From the standpoint of welfare, Constance is extremely lucky.

R2   Another response, however, would be to deny the summative assumption that the value of a whole is equal to the sum of the values of the parts of that whole. More specifically, one might deny that the welfare value of a life is equal to the sum of the welfare values at each moment of that life. Rejecting the summative view, G. E. Moore defended the principle of organic unities, which states "the value of a whole must not be assumed to be the same as the sum of the values of its parts."[14] The principle of organic unity seems quite plausible when applied to aesthetic value. It seems plausible, for example, that an ugly shade of color in one part of a painting might enhance the beauty of the whole, or that a rest or pause in a piece of music might enhance the beauty of the whole. But the principle applies to other kinds of value as well.

One form of organic unity involves a variety of goods. Roderick Chisholm writes, "[O]ther things being equal, it is better to combine two dissimilar goods than to combine two similar goods."[15] To illustrate this view, suppose that A is a beautiful painting, B is a beautiful painting exactly like A, and C is a beautiful piece of music. Assume that the aesthetic contemplation of A is the same in value as that of B and that of C. Chisholm suggests that the whole that consists of the aesthetic contemplation of A followed by the aesthetic contemplation of C is *better* than the aesthetic contemplation of A followed by the aesthetic contemplation of B. Along similar lines, it is open to the hedonist to hold that a life that has a rich variety of pleasures is better, other things being equal, than one that does not. Thus, the hedonist might hold that Constance's life is not high in welfare because of the lack of variety it involves. Her life would be better if she were to have a greater variety of pleasures.

"But if the value of a life," one might object, "depends on both pleasure and variety, doesn't that mean that hedonism is false, since the value of the life depends on something *other than* pleasure?" The hedonist may reply that the principle of variety concerns the variety of *basic* or *fundamental* goods and it is consistent with hedonism to maintain that the only basic goods are episodes of pleasure. Variety is not itself a fundamental value.

OBJECTIVE LIST THEORIES

Objective list theories of welfare or well-being hold that there are a variety of things that are good or bad for a person. In describing the view, Parfit writes:

The good things might include moral goodness, rational activity, the development of one's abilities, having children and being a good parent, knowledge and the awareness of true beauty. The bad things might include being betrayed, manipulated, slandered, deceived, being deprived of liberty or dignity, and enjoying either sadistic pleasure or pleasure in what is in fact ugly.[16]

According to the objective list view, such things are not good or bad because we desire them or because we take pleasure or displeasure in them.

Consider again the case of Constance. The proponent of the objective list theory would say that Constance's life is not high in welfare. He might concede that this is due in part to the lack of variety of pleasures in her life, but it is also because she lacks various other kinds of goods such as knowledge, acts of virtue, and friendship. The presence of such goods in her life would make her life better for her.

Proponents of objective list theories face a variety of problems. One problem concerns the relative value of the sorts of things they take to be good for a person. Consider, for example, episodes of pleasure and acts of moral virtue. Which of these is better and how much is it better? W. D. Ross once suggested that no amount of pleasure is better than a single act of virtue.[17] Such a view seems extreme, indeed, wildly implausible. Still, it is not clear what their relative value is, or which would contribute more to the welfare or well-being of a person's life. Perhaps there simply is no precise answer. Of course, the objective list theorist might note that other views face a similar problem. It is not clear, for example, that there is a precise answer concerning the relative value of true and false pleasures, or how pleasure-worthy are beautiful works of art, impressive intellectual achievements, or acts of virtue. Furthermore, it is not clear that there is any precise answer concerning how much a variety of goods enhances the value of a whole and to what degree.

More importantly, are acts of virtue, knowledge, or excellence in the arts intrinsically good *for* a person? While acts of virtue make a person's life morally better and instances of knowledge make a life epistemically better, do they also increase a person's welfare or well-being in and of themselves? Consider a life full of acts of moral virtue and knowledge, but devoid of any pleasure or enjoyment whatsoever. Imagine that no satisfaction of desire, no goal achieved, brought any amount of pleasure, that no pleasure was taken in the health or achievements of one's children or friends. Again, one might plausibly hold that such a life would be extremely low in welfare or even not good at all *for* the person whose life it was.

In reply, a proponent of the objective list theory might concede that a life of virtue and knowledge without pleasure is not very high in welfare, that it is not very good for a person. Still, he may say, it does not follow that acts of virtue and knowledge are not good for a person. Consider the life of Constance. Her life is not very high in welfare, but we are not forced to conclude that pleasure is not good for a person. If one accepts the principle of organic unities and holds that the value of a whole can be much greater than the sum of the parts, one might hold that a good life must be a mixed life that involves knowledge and acts of virtue as well as pleasure. One might consider the analogy to a piece of music in which no performance by any one instrument is especially beautiful, but the performance of them all taken together is very beautiful.

Still, even if one accepts the principle of organic unities and concedes that the best life is a mixed one, it does not follow that acts of virtue or knowledge are themselves good for a person, that they, in and of themselves, enhance one's well-being. It seems hard to maintain that all acts of virtue enhance one's well-being, especially if we consider those involving displeasure or "negative" emotions. Consider virtuous emotional attitudes such as sorrow at the suffering of an innocent child or righteous indignation at some serious injustice. While such attitudes are morally appropriate and fitting, is it plausible that they enhance one's welfare, that they are good for or benefit one? But further, consider instances of knowledge or acts of virtue unaccompanied by pleasure and not in the least bit enjoyed. Consider, for example, the mere having of a virtuous desire that a friend get well, or knowing that one's office light is on. Do such things in and of themselves enhance one's welfare or well-being? Could we not hold, plausibly, that they no more enhance one's welfare or well-being than Lois' subjectively satisfied desire that she not be eaten by a dinosaur?

In light of such objections, Parfit suggests that neither the objective list theory nor hedonism provides an adequate account of what is good for a person. He suggests that what is good for a person is a complex whole, involving both pleasure and such things as knowledge, rational activity, love, or the awareness of beauty. "Pleasure with many other kinds of object has no value. And, if they are devoid of pleasure, there is no value in knowledge, rational activity, love, or the awareness of beauty."[18] According to this view, the *only* states that are good for a person are states that involve pleasure. But further, some states that involve pleasure are *not* good for a person. They have no value.

Parfit suggests that this view is an alternative to both the objective list view and hedonism. But is it really an alternative to hedonism? Especially to a hedonism where the value of pleasures are adjusted to the "pleasure worthiness" of their objects? But, more importantly, one might wonder why some pleasures should have *no* welfare value. Suppose someone takes pleasure in, or enjoys, what is ugly or base or even disgusting. Why should we not think that such pleasures enhance his well-being or welfare? Why should we not think that such pleasures make him better off, at least in terms of welfare? Perhaps such pleasures are morally bad or lacking in some other sort of goodness, but we should not confuse these other kinds of values with welfare goodness.

Perhaps Parfit is right that the objective list theory is not a satisfactory account of what is good for a person. Perhaps the objective list theory is best understood as a theory about choiceworthiness or ethical preferability. It might be that such things as acts of virtue, virtuous emotions, love, and instances of knowledge make life good in this sense even when they involve no pleasure. One might hold that virtuous emotions and desires, noble sentiments and fine actions, contribute to the choiceworthiness or ethical preferability of a life, even when they involve no pleasure, and do not contribute to welfare or well-being.

NOTES

1   Feldman 2010: 168.
2   Scanlon 1998: 131.
3   Hurka 1993: 15.
4   For recent defenses of preferentism or desire satisfaction theories, see Heathwood 2005 and 2006.
5   Cf. Nozick 1974: 42–45.
6   Parfit 1984: 497.

7 Feldman 2010: 66.
8 See Kraut 1994.
9 Classic statements of this approach include Von Wright 1963: 86–113, and Brandt 1979.
10 Recent defenses of hedonism include Feldman 2004 and Crisp 2008.
11 Feldman 2004: 109–14.
12 Mill 1979: chap. 2.
13 Feldman 2004: 117–23.
14 Moore 1903: 28.
15 Chisholm 1986: 70–71.
16 Parfit 1984: 499. For an objective list view see also Ross 1930 and Griffin 1986.
17 Ross 1930: chap. 6, 150.
18 Parfit 1984: 502.

7   On the length of a good life

I

Epicureans, Stoics, and Plotinus all say that a happy life, if it is there at all, is there fully in the now. They also say that a life, once happy, does not become any happier by lasting longer. I shall be referring to this as 'our view' in what follows. This is remarkable considering that these were leading philosophical schools for at least 600 years or from roughly 300 BC onwards.[1] The ancients are presumably better known for a quite different idea, roughly the Aristotelian diachronic view that the goodness of a life hinges on its shape as a whole; for example, it hinges on whether the life generally improves or declines and how it ends.[2]

Even if prompted by specific ancient texts advocating such a view, my chapter is not conceived as a strictly scholarly interpretation of the ancient thinkers. I use them to explore an idea but I will enter into speculations that go beyond anything we find in these texts. My chapter is to be seen as an elucidation of and advocacy for a certain view. This does not mean that I myself have faith in our view. My role is comparable with that of the advocate of a popularly presumed guilty person who denies his guilt. The advocate doesn't necessarily share the standpoint of his client; his sole concern is to make the best of it and show his client to be innocent of the grave charges. The advocate may or may not believe in this himself, or he may be agnostic about it.

I will proceed as follows. First, in the following section – section II – I will discuss Plotinus' view of happiness and time. In section III I shall address some questions and objections, and respond to them primarily from a Stoic point of view. In section IV I briefly discuss diachronic alternatives to the view in question and in section V I present and critically discuss an alternative view that makes certain concessions to our view while combining it with elements of diachronic views. Finally, in section VI I very briefly consider objections against features of Stoic ethics on which our view, or at least the Stoic version of it, seems to depend. Plotinus and the Stoics are my main representatives of the unpopular view to be defended. For reasons of space, the Epicureans will be mostly left out. Some of the things said about Plotinus and Stoics will apply to them as well, others perhaps not.

II

Even if not particularly extensive or argumentatively complete, the fullest account of the ancient view in question is Plotinus' little treatise, *Ennead* I.5, "On whether happiness increases with time."[3] Here Plotinus replies to an imaginary opponent, who says:

> Well then, if one man has been happy from beginning to end, and another in the latter part of his life, and yet another has been well off at first and then changed his state, do they have equal shares? (I.5.5: 1–3)

The hypothetical opponent is suggesting that the one who has been happy throughout has a larger share of happiness than do the two others because he has been happy longer. Plotinus responds:

> Here the comparison is not being made between men who are all happy, but between a man who is not happy and a man who is happy. So if this latter has anything more, he has just what the man in a state of happiness has in comparison with those who are not; and that means that his advantage is by something that is present. (I.5.5: 4–8)

I take it that with this response Plotinus is saying: you may think that the person who has been happy his or her entire life has a larger share in happiness and, hence, is happier than those who have been happy only for a part of their lives. But note that when you compare the one who is always happy with the one who was happy only in, say, the first part of life but not in the latter half and come to the conclusion that the former is happier, you will agree that in the first part of their lives there was no difference between the two: they were both happy. When comparing the latter halves of their lives, you see that the one is happy, the other not happy, and of course you judge that the happy one is "happier" than one who is not happy at all. In any case, in so judging we are not comparing accumulated happiness over time but only judging on the basis of something that is present.

This response does not at all address the intuitions of someone like Aristotle who thinks one must consider a long period in order to judge someone's happiness and that happiness is contingent upon a certain temporal structure. Such intuitions suggest that happiness depends on a person's history; and successes and failures of intentions and wishes presumably enter crucially into the evaluation. Plotinus does not address such concerns at all. His response, however, reveals some interesting features of the position we are considering: (1) Plotinus asks his reader to consider the following question: would I rather be someone who is happy six years from now or someone who is not? Of course I would prefer to be the happy one. Accordingly, I don't think Plotinus would have had any qualms about admitting that a long happy life is preferable to a life with just a short period of happiness enclosed by the absence of happiness. When the Stoic Seneca says that "a short happy life does not become happier if it is prolonged" (Letter 132), he is indeed comparing a short and a long happy life and finding them equal; as we shall see, it does not follow that a person has no rational incentive to opt for a future happy life as opposed to an unhappy one or no life at all. (2) There is a crucial difference between our view, on the one hand, and Aristotle's and any contemporary view inspired by utilitarianism's ideas about accumulating happiness. Our latter-day ancients refuse to allow you to take credit for any past or future happiness: nobody is any happier now, or at any time, in virtue of the fact that they have been or will be happy.

Plotinus considers another objection against his own view: we divide time into past, present, and future, and we have no problem counting and measuring past time. The same can be said about things and events of the past, deceased people for instance: we have no problem counting them. So – and here comes the question – why is there not as much happiness as there is happy time gone by? Why not say that a person is happy in proportion to the amount of happy time lived, an amount which we can measure? To this Plotinus responds: "It would be absurd to say that happiness that no longer is present is greater than the happiness that is present. For being happy has to be occurring, but time over and above the present cannot any longer exist."[4] What are we to make of this answer?

Throughout this discussion Plotinus is presuming that the question is whether the past and the future matter for the evaluation of the happiness of a person at a particular time. We must assume that his imaginary objector shares this understanding. The objector is saying then that a person is happy now in proportion to the length of happy life so far. Happiness accumulates, so that the longer you have been happy the happier you are now.

Presumably, someone who thinks, as Plotinus' objector does, that one can count and measure past happiness and that this adds up, would not want to privilege the state at the moment of judgment. The objector's judgment is on a par with "Pelé is the greatest soccer player ever," even if Pelé no longer plays soccer and, e.g., Messi is much better than him at the time of judgment. For the objector, the judgment "the happiest" is a judgment concerning the achievement in a lifetime. This, however, has the consequence that a person who is not happy at all now by any sort of evaluation of his present state may turn out to be the happiest because of past achievements. This Plotinus finds absurd. That is the main point of his response: the happiness we credit someone with at a given time must be present, occurring happiness. Obviously, happiness does not accumulate like monthly savings that gradually raise the sum in our bank accounts. Past happiness is not there for us to enjoy now.

Plotinus' view on this need not depend on any metaphysical conviction about the unreality of times other than the present one. It may just as well be founded on the conviction that happiness that is gone or going to be cannot be relevant for my present state of happiness, no more than the good shoes I wore out as a child can bring me any warmth and comfort today.

Perhaps there is another sense in which happiness may be said to accumulate. Steven Luper (2012b: 102) proposes:

We might instead collect goods the way we gather glimpses of the setting sun. The glimpses are creatures of the moment; they are present to us only one at a time. We accrue memories of each glimpse in the way we gather gold, but we gain more and more glimpses only in the sense that they are all part of the life we live. We can accumulate goods in the same sense.

Might not the opponent's idea be that we accumulate happiness in the way Luper suggests we accumulate glimpses of the setting sun? That means that we collect happiness as an ingredient in our lives in proportion to the length of happy life lived. The longer happy, the happier the life, the opponent would contend.

Plotinus does not address this distinction between senses of accumulation. What the objector means, if this is his line of thought, is that the longer happy life, the happier the life. But Plotinus is concerned with the evaluation of the happiness of persons at a given time, not the happiness of lives. So he would presumably respond that the happiness of a life as a whole is no concern of his, unless it be contended that this has a bearing on the present state of happiness. Plotinus and his opponent may seem to be talking past each other.

We may however speculate what Plotinus would have said about Luper's kind of accumulation of happiness. He surely would have said that it is irrelevant for the question in which he is interested in this treatise: have as many happy days as you please, the past happy days are not constituents of present happiness. He presumably also would have questioned the relevance of the happiness of a life as a whole for any sort of rational concerns for an agent. This is speculation, however. In the following sections, I shall be relying on Stoic ideas rather than Plotinian. Hopefully, some reasons for a skeptical attitude towards the relevance of the notion of 'the happiness of life as a whole' will emerge from that discussion, even if I shan't resume the topic directly.

III

In what follows I shall proceed as if the Hellenistic philosophers and Plotinus are right, that if a person is happy now that must be in virtue of something present in the person now, not in virtue of something past and no longer existing or something still to come. Without being able to appeal to any kind of survey concerning this, I believe that many contemporaries would be tempted to agree with this assumption.

Assuming this, why would anyone still resist the idea our ancient thinkers insisted on that past and future happiness is irrelevant to our present happiness? In what follows I shall discuss this and some other questions prompted by the view under consideration. In doing this I will mostly be relying on Stoic thought. Hence, a brief sketch of the relevant parts of Stoic ethics is in order.

Stoics hold that virtue is the only absolute good. As Long and Sedley (1987 398–400) note, virtue and happiness are coextensive but clearly different concepts for the Stoics. Their exact relation is not particularly easy to determine. Virtue is mostly characterized as a disposition, as a kind of knowledge or expertise, i.e. art. It is evident from, e.g., Epictetus that this expertise is in constant application: it is after all the art of living and that is what we are doing all the time. The Stoic wise man even goes to bed and sleeps artfully (see Epictetus, *Discourses* III.2; 10). The original Stoic, Zeno of Citium, defined happiness as "the good flow of life" and others used the same or similar formulations.[5] Perhaps the reference to flow suggests that happiness is meant to be virtue in act: the art which is constantly being applied makes life flow smoothly and well.

As to other things than virtue, they are indifferent but some still to be preferred. Health is for instance to be preferred, even if it is not a good. That only means something like: yes, in general, go for health, other things being equal. Wisdom, the exercise of which is coextensive with happiness, consists in the artfulness of our selection among things with no intrinsic worth. This was found somewhat paradoxical already in antiquity but actually constitutes a coherent position. Stoics think that how we go about selecting these indifferent things and the attitudes we have in doing so is the stuff our virtue/happiness is made of: it is the quality of the aiming, not the success of the shot that matters. Thus, happiness has not to do with our successes or the extent to which our selections satisfy our desires.

It is commonly believed that the Stoics did not allow the wise person any emotions. It is true that the wise Stoic has what they called *apatheia*, emotionlessness. Still, the claim is misleading. Emotions that are vicious are or presuppose false judgments to the effect that some things other than virtue itself are intrinsically good. Fear and pleasure, as the Stoic understand these terms, are examples of this. This does not prevent the wise Stoic from having the kindred attitudes of joy or caution, which, however, do not involve a commitment to the intrinsic goodness of things other than wisdom itself.

With all this in mind, let us discuss how Stoics can reconcile the view that happiness is good (indeed, it is the greatest good) with their position that a longer life does not make for greater happiness. Any sane person, happy or not, would wish and choose happiness for herself tomorrow. Yet Stoics make it sound as if this wish and this choice are quite ungrounded: if a long happy life is no better than a short one why should I choose the longer one?

The answer is really quite simple: virtue is wisdom, i.e. the mastery of the art of living, the mastery of the art of choosing reasonably. One who has acquired this art has acquired it as a stable character trait. Therefore, such a person can be counted on to exercise wisdom in her choices also in the future. She knows that she is acting rightly and surely has no wish to be different. Hence, as long as she lives and does not lose her mind, she will make her choices (or selections as it often is called in relation to Stoicism) in a way that reconfirms her happiness. This is not because the things she selects actually bring her happiness – the Stoics deny that any external so-called goods can do that – but because of the internal good which consists in the wisdom and artistry of her selection.

So isn't the wise Stoic happy because of the assurance of happiness in the future that her mastery of the art of life guarantees? This is very far from the truth for several reasons. According to Stoicism, even the wise person might become ill or demented in such a way that it would be impossible for her to continue to exercise reason. The event of her ceasing to be virtuous could not be an act of her own doing, however, given what she is like. It would be some kind of misfortune of nature beyond her control. She will have the same attitude to this as she has to other so-called calamities of life. She will be concerned that this won't happen and avert it if she can but the prospect of it won't upset her. Similarly, our happy Stoic won't lament the fact that there once was a time when she wasn't happy. She won't think, for reasons already familiar, that she would be happier now if she had been happy then.

Secondly, even if Stoics sometimes say things like "happiness/ virtue is the only thing choiceworthy for its own sake" or "happiness is that for the sake of which everything is done,"[6] which makes it sound as if happiness is one of the things we choose, it cannot be the case that virtue/happiness is an option on par with

the morally indifferent things we constantly select. Happiness is
an end of action and choiceworthy somewhat in the same manner
as a karateka may regard the mastery of the art of karate: you can
work for it, aim at it; the only way towards it, however, is practice;
by practice, the karateka may eventually master the art, but its
mastery will never be one of the options she is faced with, one of
the things she can do or take in any situation. Once mastering the
art of karate, the master may, however, see and even be tempted
by the option of quitting karate. The virtuous/happy person will
never face any such choice: she is like a karateka whose situation
demands a constant exercise of her art and, moreover, in the case
of wisdom, the wise person's own reason demands and finds reasonable that she continue to exercise reason. The rationality of the
continuing exercise of reason is self-confirming in a way the art of
karate is not.

Even if we accept the Stoic claim that the choiceworthy things
we select are to be selected in due measure so that even if shoes
are good, 500 pairs are not necessarily to be preferred to 3 pairs, it
may strike us that virtue/happiness is different: there cannot be too
much of it. The Stoic (and Plotinian and Epicurean) reply is readily
predictable: longer is not more. If I am truly happy now, how could
more of the same tomorrow make me any happier? Surely, tomorrow's happiness is not mine now? In any case, the proper attitude
towards happiness is not to think: "Wow, I am happy! That's great!
How can I make sure I get more of this? It would be a terrible loss
if it went away!" Such exclamations are, by Stoic lights, a sure sign
that the person isn't happy to begin with.

Do Stoics, then, not care about the past or the future at all? Can
a Stoic consistently make plans? The Stoic is concerned but not
emotionally engaged. That is to say, the wise Stoic won't think
any past or future external event or state could matter for her happiness. That does not prevent her from planning rationally, that is
the sort of thing she is expert at. She won't be euphoric or all torn
up by any past event or state either – such reactions are or coincide with the false judgment that something other than wisdom is
intrinsically good or bad, a sure symptom of folly and unhappiness.
Nothing prevents the Stoic, however, from reflecting on the past
and future with joy or concern. She just does not get carried away
by this at all.

IV

I mentioned at the outset contemporary "Aristotelian," diachronic views that in one way or another seek to make happiness a function of a quality of life as whole. Taylor and MacIntyre have proposed "the narrative unity of a life" as such a quality.[7] Others have suggested that a kindred phenomenon, namely the successfulness of a life-plan, is a salient ingredient.[8] This is not the occasion to discuss such views in as detailed a manner as they no doubt deserve. They would have left our latter-day ancients unimpressed, however. This is so partly because of different intuitions we have seen that clash with any sort of diachronic account of happiness. So at some point, I think, we meet with a deep conflict of intuitions that may be difficult to settle by argument. Secondly, I believe the Stoics, Epicureans, and Plotinus would have had problems with the notions invoked or their relevance to the question of happiness.

The notion of a narrative unity is notoriously open to different determinations. Is it, e.g., sufficient that I perceive a narrative unity in my life or are there further constraints on the narrative? Does it have to be a good story? With a happy ending? Does it have to be true? Or is it perhaps not necessary that I, whose narrative unity is at stake, perceive and appreciate any of this; is it enough that the materials for the unified story are there? And so forth. With all this in the air it is hard even to begin a discussion.[9]

As to plans of life, we should first note that at least many quite normal people don't make any such plans. I for one have never had anything that I would describe as a life-plan. Admittedly, there are some long-lasting intentions and commitments, but a life-plan sounds too big and scary. We who are like that couldn't even start assessing our happiness in terms of success or failure of such plans. What should we make of such people? Force some sort of life-plan upon them willy-nilly or remove them singlehandedly from the group of contestants for happiness? It is not so much that they get classified as not-happy, they don't even come under consideration for happiness or lack thereof. It strikes me that the very notion of a life-plan must be something highly culturally contingent. Are the millions of people who sustain themselves from day to day, many of whom may indeed have a dream but not a plan, to be ruled out beforehand? Is it quite impossible that some of them are happy?

Moreover, even for a person who had such a plan, it is far from evident that her happiness depends essentially on its success. From a Stoic point of view, any position that essentially appeals to the *success* of a plan or success in satisfying desires, takes for granted the false view that happiness is essentially a matter of achieving something.

v

There is another reason why people may think that past and future happiness is relevant to their present happiness, even if they also believe that all the happiness we have got, we have got now. They may reasonably think that the quality of my present state is partly, perhaps even mostly, determined by my attitudes towards the past and the future. The present, past, and future are intertwined in a way our ancient thinkers fail or refuse to recognize. For instance, my well-being now has a lot to do with how I regard the past: how my day has gone, how recent months and years have been. The same holds of my prospects for the future: are there good things on my horizon? Am I looking forward to something or rather grudging the morrow? Thoughts and attitudes concerning the past and the future fill up our minds most of the time.

I am not thinking of purely causal effects of the past, although the past undoubtedly contributes causally to our present thoughts. As far as the future is concerned, surely its causal impact on the present is out of the question. Nor is the view I am sketching necessarily a simple hedonistic view according to which the past and the future matter insofar as we feel good or bad about them. We may also make further demands on the attitude so that not any old way of feeling good would count: one would have to feel about it in a certain way, e.g. a reflective way. It would still remain the case that the quality of the present essentially refers to the past and the future. We might also build an objectivity requirement into the view so that, e.g., a positive attitude towards something past or future counts as a sign of happiness only if the positive attitude is objectively justified. Yet another version of the view may even be devoid of any feelings: If I can now rightly consider a lot of the past and the future as good, this significantly contributes to my present happiness, with or without any accompanying good feeling about this.

So perhaps I should not talk about *the* view I am sketching. I am sketching a variety of views all of which say that what counts as happiness in the present depends on attitudes to the past and the future.

The kind of view I am sketching need not involve thinking that happiness accumulates over time. It is not that I can, e.g., count my past happiness as a present asset like the savings from last month that I still keep in my bank account. It is necessary, however, that I regard some significant past and/or future happenings, states, or things as good: if my present happiness essentially involves the past and the future in any of the ways I have sketched, I had better have some past and future to feel good about or consider as good. Thus, the present view in any of its varieties emphasizes the temporal connectedness of our lives: according to it, the past and the future are there in the present and contribute to its quality because of our ability to remember and conceive of the past and the time to come.

The proponents of the kind of view I have sketched would counter the ancient claims that happiness is "all there in the instant" (see Goldschmidt 1979: 168–86, and Hadot 1995) by insisting that the content of present happiness inevitably savors the past and the future; thus, good days gone and pleasant prospects are present resources that significantly contribute to the goodness of the moment. In a sense they are accumulated goods that we can use now. If any variety of this view is on the right track, it may seem that even if not strictly speaking accumulated, my present happiness nevertheless is at least in part constituted by the past, insofar as I have a positive attitude towards it, and similarly by my attitude towards the future. Many people may find some version of the present view palatable and reasonable.

At least initially, this view makes some sense. It would, however, have made the Stoics and Plotinus raise their brows. For one thing, the past and the future being there as present resources is of course metaphorical talk: the past and the future aren't really there. There is a danger that the view, insofar as it is plausible, collapses back into the Epicurean position about the utility of good memories and prospects. Secondly, assuming that the view amounts to something more than the Epicurean view that one can rejoice in memories and prospects, some things have to be considered good just by themselves if there are to be good memories or prospects about them, assuming that good memories and prospects are good because they are directed at something that at least is considered to be good. After giving a paper as a visiting speaker, a university professor may feel good about himself, thinking that the paper was rather clever and, moreover, well received; these thoughts may lead him to reflect that he is in fact a quite successful practitioner of his trade, that his private life too is going well, and he cherishes the prospect of soon finishing yet another brilliant paper and then going on a long vacation with his family up in the mountains. We need not suppose that these thoughts are any sort of self-glorification.

Yet, clearly, even such comfortable reflections from someone truly entitled to them hardly constitute the person's happiness, the person's doing well: the reflections are about how well he has been and will be doing; the goodness of these past or future states or events must be determinable independently of the subject's appreciation of them as good.[10] So they were or will be good independently of the appreciation. Why is the good life then not there when the goods were there or will occur? That again would lead us to the kind of success of life-plan accounts that we have rejected. We might try suggesting that the achievements and prospects become the sort of goods that are relevant to happiness only when appreciated as good things, so that the person's happiness now is, at least in part, a function of both: the goodness of the past or future things and the appreciation of them as such. That, however, also makes present happiness contingent on the achievement or obtaining of goods other than wisdom itself, and on goods that aren't available except as memories or hopes.

VI

As we have been taking the Stoics and Plotinus, who seems to be in essential agreement with the Stoics on ethical matters,[11] as the main proponents of the non-accumulation view on happiness, I shall end this chapter by briefly considering two common objections against Stoic ethics that bear on our topic. First, it is a mistake to identify happiness and virtue, as Stoics do, since some happy people are unethical and some ethical people are unhappy.[12] Second, Stoicism is wholly impractical, since no one can live up to its demands.

The objection that morally good people may fare badly is of course a powerful one and a commonplace since antiquity. In response, let me start by retreating a bit: perhaps the Stoics (and Plotinus) go too far in separating the question of happiness from any concerns about success or failure. Even so they have a point: people who lose their minds and claim their lives ruined because of mere nuisances are fools (as the Stoics would say). Even those who are devastated for a long time by not getting a job they hoped for or having their spouse leave them are a bit foolish too and clearly don't master the art of life. We may vary in where we set our limits for such judgments but we certainly think that people who are too easily victims of circumstances are not happy and do not know how to live. So, most of us go some way along with the Stoics but presumably not the whole way: their demands are too extreme. Perhaps, however, a weaker, more palatable form of Stoicism is conceivable. This form would avoid the extremes of making our happiness totally immune to external evils but incorporate the sound intuition of Stoicism that happiness has at least a lot to do with our skill in dealing with life, and far less with the success of our plans or the satisfaction of our desires.

The second objection is as powerful as the first: Stoicism may have an appeal as a theoretical set-up but the fact is that it is totally unrealistic. Even the Stoics themselves admit this in saying that virtue is extremely rare (see Alexander of Aphrodisias, *On Fate* 199.16–18 = Long and Sedley: section 61 N), which implies that happiness is also rare. Still, most of us are not sure how to answer questions like "Am I happy?" and "Is my life truly good?" We also find it difficult to identify anyone who is clearly happy. Is Obama happy? Paul McCartney? My spouse? So perhaps the Stoics were right to say that happiness is extremely rare. Perhaps that has to do with the fact that virtue, as the Stoics understood it, is extremely rare too.

NOTES

1   The Platonists of late antiquity continued as the dominating philosophical school for some 250 years after Plotinus; I am not aware of any clear pronouncements from these later Platonists on the issues of this chapter.

2   Aristotle's view here may not be as definitely "diachronic" as indicated here and generally held. See E. K. Emilsson, "Happiness and Time in Ancient Philosophy" (unpublished MS).

3 The account that follows of Plotinus' views is a significantly shortened
   and modified version of Emilsson 2011: 340–50.
4 The text is disputed here but this translation does not presuppose any
   emendation. For details, see Emilsson 2011: 345.
5 Stobaeus II.77 = Long and Sedley: section 63 A.
6 See Diogenes Laertius VII.127 = Long and Sedley: section 61 I; Stobaeus
   II.77.16–17 = Long and Sedley: section 63 A.
7 MacIntyre 1981: 203–4; C. Taylor 1989: 51–52; see also Velleman 1991.
8 Presumably the prevalence of this notion in current philosophical
   thought is due to Rawls 1971. It has even entered into the interpretation of ancient philosophers such as Aristotle, see, e.g., Cooper 1975:
   passim, even if Aristotle, so far as I can tell, never mentions or hints at
   such plans. For a recent subtle application of the notion of a life-plan
   directly relevant to the present issues, see Luper 2012b.
9 For a critique of narrativity as an ethically important notion, see
   Strawson 2004.
10 See Plotinus' criticism of, presumably, the Epicureans in *Ennead*
   I.4.2.
11 See Emilsson 2011: 348.
12 For an extensive discussion of the relationship between virtue and
   happiness in ancient ethical thought and Stoicism in particular, see
   Annas 1995: passim.

8   Mortal harm

Begin by distinguishing the process of dying, death, and being dead. Dying takes place during life, and death is typically construed as the transition from dying to being dead. Being dead takes place after both dying and death – it is the state or condition of being dead. Sometimes "death" is used simply to pick out the condition of being dead, and I will use the term in this way. The question I shall address in this chapter is this: in what way can death – the condition of being dead – be a harm or misfortune for the individual who dies? For some purposes it is important to distinguish the notions picked out by "bad thing," "misfortune," and "harm," but here I shall use the terms interchangeably.

Although there is of course considerable difficulty in giving an adequate definition or account of "death," I shall assume that death is the cessation (perhaps the *permanent* cessation, although this issue will not be relevant to the discussion here) of life. I shall accept, for the sake of the discussion, that the individual who dies goes out of existence.

It is obvious how dying could be a harm for the individual who undergoes this process insofar as it may involve pain and suffering, and it is relatively clear that pain and suffering are bad. But we are here considering whether death or the condition of being dead, rather than dying, can be a harm for the individual who is dead. It is perhaps also obvious how death could be harmful for the individual who is dead if there is an afterlife (construed in various ways, including existence in hell or reincarnation) insofar as the afterlife may involve something like pain and suffering. But here I shall

I am very grateful to Steve Luper for his detailed and helpful comments.

simply assume that death is an experiential blank. Thus, I am here adopting a secular conception, according to which death involves no consciousness or experiences. So our question is: how can death, construed as the (possibly permanent) cessation of life and experience, be a harm for the individual who dies?

SKEPTICISM ABOUT DEATH'S BADNESS

Death is perhaps not always a bad thing for the individual who dies. It may be that an individual is in such relentless pain that his continued life would not on balance be a good thing for him. Or it may be that he is so impaired or constrained either physically or psychologically that his continued existence would not on balance be a good thing. Of course, it is very difficult to specify the precise conditions in which an individual's continued existence would not on balance be a good thing for him, and thus it is challenging to specify the circumstances in which an individual's death would not be a bad thing or harm for him. Although reasonable persons can disagree about this point, it does seem to many that at least in *some* situations death would not be a bad thing for the individual who dies.

It also seems to most of us that in at least *some* cases – indeed, in many cases – the death of an individual is indeed a harm to the individual who dies. Perhaps it is the greatest harm that can happen to a person, but in any case it is often thought that death can be a bad thing for the individual who dies. But despite what might be described as the "common-sense" or "ordinary" view that death can be a bad thing or harm for the individual who dies, the ancient Greek philosopher Epicurus and his followers have taken the opposite view. On the Epicurean approach, death – as opposed to dying – cannot be a bad thing for the individual who dies, on the secular assumption to the effect that death is an experiential blank.

An important Epicurean assumption, as I wrote above, is that the individual who dies not only ceases to live, but goes out of existence. We can now formulate what is perhaps the most basic idea that drives Epicurean skepticism about the possible badness of death for the individual who dies: the "Existence Requirement":

> (ER) Something can be a bad thing or harm for an individual
> at a time only if that individual exists at that time.

Assuming (what is admittedly controversial, but not, in my view, implausible) that an individual's being dead cannot harm him while he is alive, (ER) implies that his death – his being dead – is not and cannot be a bad thing or harm for him.

But what is the reason why we should accept the Epicurean's (ER)? We might usefully distinguish between considerations that arise from the relationship between *experience* or *possible experience* and harm and those that are based in more abstract metaphysics, as it were. Because I believe that the fundamental reason for adopting (ER) stems from the relationship between harm and experience (or possible experience), I shall in this chapter focus on this approach to justifying (ER).

A natural and plausible thought about the basis for (ER) is that existence is required for experience, and that something can be a bad thing or harm for an individual only if the thing in question is connected in some way with unpleasant or negative experiences of the individual. So perhaps (ER) is rooted in something like the first version of the Experience Requirement:

> (ExpR1) Something can be a bad thing or harm for an
> individual at a time only if that individual experiences
> something unpleasant or "negative" (such as pain, suffer-
> ing, frustration, and so forth) as a result of the thing in
> question.

(ExpR1) would imply that death cannot be a bad thing for the individual who dies, on our secular assumptions about death. (ExpR1) explains (ER) by positing a strong link between harm and negative experience. But various philosophers have argued that the envisaged connection is *too strong*; they have presented examples in which it is alleged that an individual is harmed, although the individual in question experiences no unpleasant or negative consequences.

Consider, for example, the famous "betrayal" case suggested by Thomas Nagel (1979). In criticizing a view such as (ExpR1), Nagel writes:

It means that even if a man is betrayed by his friends, ridiculed behind his back, and despised by people who treat him politely to his face, none of it can be counted as a misfortune for him so long as he does not suffer as a result. (Nagel 1979: 4)

If a group of people who present themselves to you as your friends regularly get together behind your back and criticize you, accusing you of cheating on your spouse and plagiarizing others' work, and so forth – it would seem that you have been harmed, even if you never find out about these secret (to you!) "parties." Of course, it is uncontentious that your so-called "friends" have behaved wrongly and shoddily; but Nagel (and his followers on this point) wish to contend that it is *also* the case that a bad thing has happened to *you* – you have been harmed. If harm is to be conceptualized (roughly) as a setback of an interest (Feinberg 1984: 31–36), then you have been harmed insofar as your interest in a good reputation has been wrongfully set back. But no matter how one explains the harm, it has seemed to many philosophers that Nagel's example, and similar examples, show that an individual can indeed be harmed by something, even if he never experiences anything unpleasant as a result of the thing.

Some Epicureans, however, resist the conclusion of Nagel and like-minded philosophers, claiming that you are not indeed harmed in the example of the putative betrayal behind one's back. After all, you do not ever find out about the "get-togethers," and you do not ever experience anything unpleasant or negative as a result of these occasions. How can something that does not affect you psychologically in these ways be genuinely bad for you? Granted, the behavior under consideration is reprehensible; but that is a different issue from whether *you* have been harmed.

Other Epicureans will concede that the target of the scurrilous verbal attacks in Nagel's example has indeed been harmed, but only because the individual *could* (in some clear sense) find out about these activities and thus could have unpleasant experiences as a result. On this sort of view, the explanation of (ER) is still in terms of a connection between harm and unpleasant experience, but here the connection is envisaged as a bit looser. That is, the link between harm and unpleasant experience is forged in terms of *possible* experience, rather than actual experience:

> (ExpR2) Something can be a bad thing or harm for an
>   individual at a time only if the individual can experi-
>   ence something unpleasant or "negative" (such as pain,

suffering, frustration, and so forth) as a result of the thing in question.

Since we are assuming that individual who is no longer alive or in existence cannot experience anything, (ExpR2) is just as efficacious as (ExpR1) in supporting (ER).

Why should we accept (ExpR2)? I shall first consider an argument on behalf of (ExpR2) offered by Stephen Rosenbaum:

Suppose that a person P cannot hear and never will hear. Then the egregious performance of a Mozart symphony cannot causally affect P at any time, supposing that what makes the performance bad is merely awful sound, detectable only through normal hearing, and supposing further that the performance does not initiate uncommon causal sequences that can affect the person. It is clear that the person cannot experience the bad performance, auditorily or otherwise. Furthermore, it seems clear that the performance cannot be bad for the person in any way. It cannot affect the person in any way. The reason why it is not bad for him is that he is not able to experience it … Similarly, a person born without a sense of smell cannot be causally affect by, and thus cannot experience, the stench of a smoldering cheroot. The stench cannot be an olfactory negativity for her. We could imagine indefinitely many more such cases.

Since I see nothing eccentric about these cases, I believe that we are entitled to generalize and claim that our judgments about these cases are explained by the principle that if a person cannot experience a state of affairs at some time, then the state of affairs is not bad for the person. (Rosenbaum 1986: 219)

The problem with this argument is that it is a "hasty generalization"; Rosenbaum extrapolates from cases where the badness could only be (or be the result of) *sensory* unpleasantness to *other* cases – cases in which the putative bad would not be (or be the result of) unpleasant experiences. The class of putative harms can be divided into those which involve unpleasant sensory stimuli and those which do not. If there are indeed things that are bad for an individual, but whose badness does not involve or stem from unpleasant experiences, then in principle such things could be bad for an individual who could not experience anything unpleasant as a result of them. Thus, given the existence of this second sub-class of putative harms (or, alternatively, given the putative existence of such harms), it is inappropriate to extrapolate from a conclusion about the first sub-class to a more general conclusion that also applies to the second. Thus, one cannot decisively establish (ExpR2) or (ER) in the way sketched by Rosenbaum.

Consider also Nagel's thoughtful critical reflection on (ExpR2):

Loss, betrayal, deception, and ridicule are on this view bad because people suffer when they learn of them. But it should be asked how our ideas of human value would have to be constituted to accommodate these cases directly instead. One advantage of such an account might be that it would enable us to explain *why* the discovery of these misfortunes causes suffering – in a way that makes it reasonable. For the natural view is that the discovery of betrayal makes us unhappy because it is bad to be betrayed – not that betrayal is bad because its discovery makes us unhappy. (Nagel 1979: 5)

It seems to me that Nagel is correct here. But what if the Epicurean resists Nagel's Euthyphro-style point? What more can be offered in seeking to reject a principle such as (ExpR2)? The following examples purport to be cases in which an individual is harmed, even though he *cannot* experience anything unpleasant as a result of the putatively harmful event.

Nagel offers an example in which an intelligent adult receives a brain injury (perhaps as a result of an accident or stroke) which leaves him in the "mental condition of a contented infant, and that such desires as remain to him can be satisfied by a custodian, so that he is free from care" (Nagel 1979: 5). It is plausible that in this case the individual is indeed harmed by the brain injury, although we can assume that he does not and also *cannot* experience anything unpleasant as a result of it.

Here is another example that seeks to impugn (ExpR2). Suppose your daughter is trekking in the remote Himalayas and tragically dies in an accident (perhaps an avalanche). Before you can possibly find out about this tragedy – say, five minutes after the death of your daughter – you (independently) die of a sudden heart attack (McMahan 1988). The death of your daughter is clearly a bad thing for you – you are harmed by her death during the last five minutes of your life. But given the circumstances you *cannot* (in any relevant sense) experience anything unpleasant as a result of her death.

Nagel's brain-injury case and McMahan's trekking case (and similar cases) appear to show that an individual can be harmed, even though it is not possible for them to experience anything unpleasant as a result of the putatively harmful event. Thus, these examples seem to call (ExpR2) into question. I have provided another such case, building on the famous "Frankfurt-style" counterexamples to the Principle of Alternative Possibilities (according to which moral responsibility requires freedom to do otherwise or access to alternative possibilities) (Frankfurt 1969).

It will be helpful to begin with a version of a Frankfurt-style case:

Black is a stalwart defender of the democratic party. He has secretly inserted a chip in Jones' brain that enables Black to monitor and control Jones' activities. Black can exercise this control through a sophisticated computer that he has programmed so that, among other things, it monitors Jones' voting behavior. If Jones were to show any inclination to vote for a Republican (or, let us say, anyone other than the Democrat), then the computer, through the chip in Jones' brain, would intervene to assure that he actually decides to vote for the Democrat and does so vote. But if Jones decides on his own to vote for the Democrat (as Black, one of the only progressive neurosurgeons in the known world, would prefer), the computer does nothing but continue to monitor – without affecting – the goings-on in Jones' head.

Now suppose that Jones decides to vote for the Democrat on his own, just as he would have if Black had not inserted the chip in his head. It seems, upon first thinking about this case, that Jones can be held morally responsible for this choice and act of voting for the democrat, although he could not have chosen otherwise and he could not have done otherwise. (I originally presented a similar example in Fischer 1982.)

We can now return to Nagel's betrayal case, but adding a Frankfurt-style "counterfactual intervener," White (Fischer 1997). Call this the "modified betrayal case." White is similar to Frankfurt's Black in being a strictly counterfactual intervener – an untriggered ensurer of the relevant result. We suppose that White can effectively prevent you from ever finding out about the secret meetings and the activities that take place at those unfortunate gatherings. So, for instance, if someone were about to call you to inform you of these meetings, White can prevent him from making the connection by snipping the telephone line or temporarily paralyzing the person or whatever. Given that White has the power to prevent you from ever finding out anything about the meetings, you *cannot* have any unpleasant experiences as a result of those get-togethers. And yet it seems that you are harmed by the betrayals that take place at those meetings. And, again, if this is so, (ExpR2) is false and thus cannot provide support for (ER).

The Epicureans will resist the critiques of (ExpR2) and thus of (ER). I shall first explore their analysis of the modified betrayal case (and similar cases), after which I shall turn to a discussion of the brain injury case.

THE MODIFIED BETRAYAL CASE

In the modified betrayal case, in which White stands by ready to intercept any messages to the individual who is the target of the verbal "attacks," I contend that the individual is harmed, although it is impossible for him to have any unpleasant or negative experiences as a result of the activities at the secret meetings. There are two ways in which an Epicurean might respond. First, an Epicurean might contend that insofar as the individual really can't experience anything unpleasant as a result of the activities at the party, it follows that he is not harmed by those activities. Second, an Epicurean might admit that the individual is harmed, and thus concede that (ExpR2) is false, but still maintain (ER). The claim here could be that there is some other explanation of the harm in the modified betrayal case – an explanation that does not generalize to death. There are various ways of pursuing this second strategy, but they have in common the claim that it is inappropriate to extrapolate from examples such as the modified betrayal case, in which the individual in question *exists*, to death, which results in the non-existence of the individual.

David Suits provides a vigorous defense of the contention that the target of the verbal assaults in the modified betrayal case is not in fact harmed precisely because he *cannot* ever have a negative experience as a result of those assaults (Suits 2001). He points out that, typically, betrayals are risky; they are like "incautious firings of guns" in this respect. This is why, typically at least, betrayals are bad for the individual who is betrayed: it is possible that he find out about it and suffers as a result. But let us say that precautions are in place that absolutely guarantee that no one will be adversely affected by a particular incautious (from the perspective of the individual firing the gun) firing of a gun; in this case, what would typically be harmful to others is *not* in fact a harm to anyone, according to Suits. And, similarly, although betrayals would typically harm their target by exposing them to the risk of adverse psychological effects, what would typically be harmful to others would not in fact be harmful, if precautions are in place that guarantee that the target of the scurrilous verbal attacks never finds out about them.

Suits writes:

John Martin Fischer proposed an addition to Nagel's example of a secret betrayal; he adds a Frankfurt-style "counterfactual intervener" named White, who has the amazing power to intervene in case the secret betrayal starts to cause any bad consequences for the person betrayed ... The result is said to be a betrayal which not only does not, but, because of White, *could* not lead to any bad consequences for the "victim." Fischer claims that even so, the betrayal is bad, and the person is harmed. In a subsequent article, he responds to a criticism that a betrayal which is guaranteed to be effectless is not a bad thing any more than is firing a gun under strict conditions of safety: "I have no ... inclination to say that a mere firing of a gun, where there is no chance of hitting anyone, can harm anyone", whereas "I am inclined to say that the negative characterizations of you by your so-called 'friends' harm you, by the very nature of the behavior."

But why? What is this "very nature of the behavior" which Fischer is appealing to here? It has been named, but it has not been shown to be harmful. The counterfactual intervener ensures that the consequences are not harmful in any way, and so Fischer means to condemn "the very nature of the behavior," careless of any consequences. But my question is: What is condemnable about it? That is, why avoid such a thing, why try to prevent it, why deplore it, if all possible sources of aversion – that is to say, all the ill consequences – have been squeezed out of it, and there is nothing left but an old name? (Suits 2012: 225)

Suits emphasizes that in the usual case, something is a harm for an individual only if it is at least possible for the individual to have a negative experience as a result of it. To oversimplify his view a bit, Suits contends that when this presupposition fails, the status of what is typically deemed a bad, misfortune, or harm for an individual must be re-evaluated. He writes:

[Suppose X is a betrayal] ... if we know that because of a counterfactual intervener such as White (or indeed for any other reason) [the individual who is the target of the verbal attacks cannot ever experience anything negative as a result of them, among other special features of the situation], then either X has been mistakenly classified as a betrayal, or else we have learned – *perhaps to our surprise!* – that some cases of betrayal are quite unlike the usual sort. If the latter, then from then on, we would have to change some of our evaluations; we would have to say that we used to assume that all betrayals were bad, but now we know that some kinds of betrayal have no bad consequences after all. It would no longer be enough to say what Nagel *et al.* seem to be saying, namely, that if X is a case of betrayal, *it is therefore bad.* (Suits 2012: 227–28)

It is difficult to offer an *argument* against Suits here. (For a pre-liminary attempt, see Fischer 2006a.) I do indeed have the intuition that a White-monitored betrayal is nevertheless a harm to the indi-vidual who is being betrayed. Put somewhat more modestly, I have the intuition that a White-monitored verbal assault does indeed harm the target of the assault. But I do *not* have the intuition that an incautious firing of a gun, in a context in which it is impossible for (say) a particular individual to be affected by the gun-firing, is a harm to the individual in question. The incautious firing of a gun is wrongful behavior – it is either reckless or negligent. But it does not follow that it harms anyone.

Similarly drunk driving is wrongful behavior, and it is typically risky. But when it is absolutely impossible for an individual to be affected by a particular instance of drunk driving, I do not have the intuition that this behavior harms the individual. How exactly can I explain the asymmetry in the intuitions? Why do riskless gun-firings and riskless drunk-driving not count as harms to individuals who cannot be affected, whereas riskless betrayals do? This is an interesting challenge.

I'm inclined to say that the proper response might rely on a nor-mative theory of human interests. It is plausible that we have an interest in not having our reputations besmirched, even if we never find out about these besmirchings. Julian Lamont articulates this point nicely:

I have a preference for certain people not to think ill of me. Now I might never know if those people think ill of me, but I am worse off it that pref-erence of mine is not fulfilled.

...

I do not want people to slander me, *even if I suffer no other harm as a result.* Not having this preference fulfilled is *itself* a harm to me – if it is not fulfilled then I live a life where people slander me behind my back. I would much prefer that not to be true of my life. (Lamont 1998: 205)

Lamont puts the point in terms of preference-fulfillment, but the point could be put simply in terms of interests: it is normatively plausible that we have an interest in not having our reputations destroyed, even if we never find out about this. But I just do not think it is normatively plausible to suppose that we have an interest in other people not driving drunk or firing guns incautiously – where these activities are guaranteed not to pose *any* risk of untoward consequences for others.

Perhaps, then, the way to explain the asymmetry in our intuitive reactions to riskless incautious gun-firings and riskless drunk-driving, on the one hand, and riskless betrayals, on the other, is in terms of the implications of the most plausible normative theory. Such a theory would posit an asymmetry in the *interests* of human beings. Although I find this a promising way of seeking to address Suits' challenge, I also have the residual worry that the response is question-begging or perhaps simply pushes us back to the question of why we should suppose that the asymmetry in interests is normatively plausible.

Suits responds to the modified betrayal case by contending that the individual who is the target of the verbal assaults is not in fact harmed, despite the fact that betrayals are typically harms to the individuals being betrayed. As I pointed out above, another Epicurean strategy of response to the example is to contend that the targeted individual is indeed harmed, but that one cannot legitimately extrapolate from this case (in which the individual in question exists and has certain mental states) to death (in which the individual does not exist or have mental states). A particularly fascinating version of this approach is presented by Stephen Hetherington (2001).

Hetherington discusses the modified betrayal case, and he points out that in it "you are 'out of step' with the world, notably with some parts of the world that matter to you" (Hetherington 2001: 352). As he puts it, "Insofar as it matters to you to be right about what matters to you, therefore, your being mistaken about what matters to you harms you" (Hetherington 2001: 352). Hetherington continues, elaborating on a "further harm":

What is that further harm? It is the harm of human *absurdity* ... I am talking about an *objective* sort of absurdity. It is objective, in that it is not an *awareness*, either actual or even possible, of a discrepancy; instead, it is the *existence* of a basic discrepancy, one that can exist between a person and the world as a whole, and one that can exist without the person being aware of it, perhaps even with her being unable to be aware of it.

... To the extent that your belief in your friends' loyalty is also *important* to you, that absurdity is even tragic, no matter whether or not you are aware of this tragic dimension to your life. (Hetherington 2001: 355–56)

On this view, the badness of the betrayal is understood as a kind of *dissonance* or *discordance* between our mental states – certain beliefs – and external reality. If this is the *only* reason why the betrayal in a case such as the modified betrayal case is a harm to the targeted individual, then death could not be a harm or bad thing for anyone: there is no discordance insofar as there is just one "note," as it were.

I find Hetherington's critique of the modified betrayal case as it relates to death's purported badness fascinating and challenging. In seeking to address it, I would first note that there might well be more than one harm involved in a case such as the modified betrayal case. One sort of bad is precisely the kind identified by Hetherington – a kind of discordance between the targeted individual's perspective on the world – his mental states – and the relevant aspects of the world. This discordance or lack of "fit" issues is a kind of absurdity, and the absurdity is *tragic* insofar as the individual deems the matter important – that is, insofar as the loyalty of his "friends" is important to him. To the extent that these features are indeed present in the modified betrayal case (and similar cases), the extrapolation to a conclusion about death's badness is attenuated.

I still, however, think that the modified betrayal case provides resources that are useful in seeking to argue that death can be a bad thing for the individual who dies. Perhaps it is not the case that the *only* harm in a case like the modified betrayal case arises from the sort of discordance described by Hetherington; perhaps there is a badness that is not a kind of absurdity, and perhaps it doesn't (and need not) rise to the level of a tragedy. And yet the example still may be illuminating with respect to death's alleged badness.

Imagine that you are teaching a large lecture class, and you don't really know what your students think of the course. It briefly crosses your mind that it might be too difficult or "abstract" for them, as they are introductory students, but you don't pause to consider the question carefully and you form no belief about whether the students are enjoying the class or finding it rewarding or whether they like or respect you. Now imagine further that a group of your students meets regularly, as in the modified betrayal example, scurrilously attacking you verbally (for your lectures and mentorship and even personal matters), and that there is a suitably placed counterfactual intervener whose presence renders it impossible for you to find out about these gatherings. It seems to me that you are harmed by the verbal attacks, even though you do not and cannot experience anything unpleasant as a result of them. As above, I believe that you have an interest in not having your reputation besmirched – an interest in not being thought ill of in certain ways. The harm here is not a matter of a discordance between beliefs that you are well thought of by the relevant group and the nature of the corresponding part of reality; thus, the harm is not a kind of absurdity of the sort described by Suits. Rather, it seems to me that it is a matter of an interest of yours being set back wrongfully – your interest in having a good reputation. This example indicates that the wrongful setting back of this interest is in itself a harm to you, quite apart from any "absurdity" (of the sort specified by Hetherington) that might also be present in certain scenarios.

Suppose, also, that you apply for a job at a philosophy department and you give your "job talk" during an on-campus visit. The audience seems to like your talk and be impressed during the visit, but you really don't know what they think. When you return home, you simply refrain from forming any settled beliefs about how the visit went, and, in particular, what the members of the department thought of your talk and your visit in general. It turns out that at a meeting to discuss the candidates they excoriate you, ridiculing your lecture and your performance in general; various members of the department accuse you of plagiarism and even of making unwelcome sexual advances. Suppose, however, that the department is absolutely and sincerely committed to strict confidentiality about their deliberations, and it is thus impossible for you to find out anything about the content of their discussions. Further, the members of the department are absolutely committed to not causing you any pain or suffering in the future, apart from the specific decision about the job. (We could add a White-like counterfactual intervener to make it even clearer that you cannot have any unpleasant psychological consequences of the verbal attacks during the meeting. Let us suppose that White can absolutely "isolate" the goings-on at the meeting so that you can never find out about what happens and also the individuals present can never in the future cause you pain or suffering as a result of the discussions at the meetings.)

I think that you have been harmed by the verbal assaults at the meeting. And this is so, despite the fact that you cannot have any unpleasant experiences as a result. Further, you have been harmed, even though the harm does not consist in the sort of discordance and concomitant absurdity described by Hetherington. That is, you do not in fact believe that the members of the department in question think well of you; you simply withhold judgment about this matter, and you refrain from coming to any conclusions about their views of you. We cannot then tie the harm to a lack of fit between your beliefs and the relevant part of the external world. Again, this particular harm consists in the wrongful setback of your interest in a good reputation.

Of course, it is normatively plausible that we have *various* interests, including the interest not to have false beliefs about important features of our lives. Thus, in the modified betrayal case, this interest is indeed wrongfully set back, and one is thereby harmed. But it is not the *only* relevant interest: we also have an interest in being thought well of or not having our reputation besmirched; this interest is also wrongfully set back, and one is also thereby harmed. Perhaps it is a *tragedy* when an important belief around which one has structured one's life is false; perhaps then it is a tragedy that you are betrayed in the modified betrayal case. It does not seem similarly to be a tragedy that you are ridiculed in the two cases I have just presented: the lecture case and the job-talk case. But the critique of Epicureanism based on these sorts of cases does not require that these cases count as tragedies for the person who is harmed. It is enough that they are cases in which someone is harmed without the possibility of experiencing anything negative as a result of the harmful event or activity. It would then at least be possible that death is a harm for an individual, despite the impossibility of the individual's experiencing anything negative as a result of his own death. Because of the specific nature of death, it would then be plausible that it is the *kind* of harm that could count as a tragedy. The argument proceeds in steps, and it is not required that the initial step involves an example that is just like death in every respect, including its being a tragedy.

Obviously, *any* example that could be helpful in arguing that death could be a harm for an individual who dies cannot be *just like death*; if it were, then it would be question-begging to present the example as part of an argument for the conclusion that death can be bad for the individual who dies. This is why one must present examples in which the individual remains in existence but is nevertheless apparently harmed. One then seeks to *extrapolate* to the conclusion that death can be a harm for the individual who dies. If one sought to begin with an example in which the individual goes out of existence, it would be difficult to avoid the charge of begging the question, if one were to seek to invoke the example as part of an argument to the conclusion that death could be bad for the individual who dies. The fundamental point of the critic of Epicureanism based on the examples under consideration is this: *if* it is plausible that there can be cases of harm to an existing individual who cannot have a bad experience as a result of the harm, then it is also at least plausible (although it does not strictly follow) that an individual could be harmed by his own death.

THE BRAIN-INJURY CASE

Return to Nagel's "brain-injury case," which appears to be a case in which an individual is harmed and yet cannot experience anything unpleasant as a result of the apparently harmful event. Let's assume that the individual persists, that is, we assume that the brain injury does not make it the case that the original person goes out of existence and a new person now exists. (For discussions of the possibility that the original individual has gone out of existence, see Braddock 2000, and J. Taylor 2012: 78.) Given this assumption, Taylor has pointed out that the example is importantly different from death in precisely this respect:

If the intelligent man does not cease to exist as an experiencing being as a result of his brain injury, then his case is importantly disanalogous to that of a person who dies. As such, then, even though one might hold that his brain injury is a misfortune to him this cannot support the claim that death would therefore be a misfortune to the person who dies. (J. Taylor 2012: 78)

But, as above, it does *not* follow from the fact that the case is "importantly disanalogous" to a case of death that it "cannot support the claim" that death would, or at least could, be a misfortune for the person who dies. I would again emphasize that *any* argument from analogy must proceed from cases that are allegedly *similar to*, but *not identical to*, the cases or phenomena to which they are purportedly analogous. If they were in all respects identical, then we wouldn't have an argument by *analogy*, and the argument would presumably be question-begging (or at least not promising in terms of making intellectual progress). Again, Nagel's point is presumably this: *if* it is plausible that the individual who has had the brain injury has been harmed (where we assume that he *cannot* experience anything unpleasant as a result of the brain injury), then it is at least plausible that someone who has died can be harmed by death. We are invited by an argument by analogy to *extrapolate* from one kind of case to another, and this particular argument is no different.

Further, it seems to be a plausible extrapolation. Taylor writes:

If one holds that the intelligent man does continue to exist, then one could hold that his brain injury is a harm to him in that it adversely affects his experiences, even though he himself in his reduced condition is unaware of this. (J. Taylor 2012: 78)

It seems that Taylor is suggesting that, under the assumption of continued personal identity, the harm is to be understood as a diminution in the quality of the individual's experiences, where the quality (or quantity) is still non-zero, as it were. But why have the non-zero requirement? This just seems entirely arbitrary! Why not instead hold that the example suggests, at least, without (of course!) literally *requiring*, that an individual can be harmed when his experiences are "adversely affected" by reduction in quality or quantity to zero? The example at least invites this conclusion, and it might seem ad hoc to insist on the non-zero requirement, in any form.

DEATH'S BADNESS

Return to the question with which I began: how can death, construed as the (possibly permanent) cessation of life and experience, be a harm for the individual who dies? In this chapter I have discussed (and rejected) some of the most salient skeptical worries for the common-sense idea that death can indeed be a bad thing for the individual who dies. In my opinion, the main problem with these skeptical worries (stemming from Epicurus) is that they tie badness too closely with negative experience (either actual or possible). In contrast, I find it more plausible to suppose that death is bad insofar as it deprives the individual who dies of an on-balance good life. The deprivation theory of death's badness is defended by various philosophers, including Thomas Nagel (Nagel 1979) and Fred Feldman (Feldman 1994).

9   When do we incur mortal harm?

I

If there is no time at which my death fascinates me, then my death does not fascinate me. If there is no time at which my death scares me, then my death does not scare me. Is it also true that if there is no time at which my death is bad for me, then my death is not bad for me?

According to a well-known Epicurean line of thought, it is (Epicurus 1940; Hershenov 2007). Moreover, Epicureans add, there is no time at which my death is bad for me. Before it happens, I am still unharmed by it; and once I die, I am no longer there to be harmed. And so my death, Epicureans conclude, is not bad for me at all. It might fascinate me; it might scare me; but it does not harm me.

Most philosophers, however, reject this conclusion; more precisely, they espouse "anti-Epicureanism," the thesis that death, at least in many cases, is bad for the deceased. Most anti-Epicureans contend that, on closer inspection, my death *is* in fact bad for me at certain times. There are two main groups here: *priorists*, who locate these times before my death (Feinberg 1984; Pitcher 1984; Luper 2007, 2009: 134–36, 2012a), and *subsequentists*, who locate them after my death (Feit 2002; Bradley 2009: chap. 3).

Yet other writers agree with the Epicureans that there is no time at which my death is bad for me, but maintain that it is still bad for me (Broome 2012; Johansson 2012). These are the *atemporalists*.

Subsequentism is sometimes held to have an important advantage over priorism and atemporalism: it gives us a *uniform* account

Many thanks to Karl Ekendahl and Steve Luper for helpful comments.

of relevantly similar evils. When is it bad for me to miss my flight to Japan? To be drugged into unconsciousness? To have my home burgled? To lose my job? To lose my friends? In all these cases, the answer seems to be the same: the event harms me *after* it occurs. For that is when I would have received the benefits of which the event deprives me (the joys of Japan, for example). Subsequentists say exactly the same thing about death. Priorists and atemporalists, by contrast, have to treat death very differently from other harms. This seems unsatisfactory.

In this chapter, my focus is on this uniformity charge against priorism and atemporalism. It seems to me to constitute a more serious threat to the former than to the latter.

II

We need some relevant background.

First, the item we are evaluating is the particular event of a person's death – the brief event that marks the end of her life. We are not discussing the process of dying; even Epicureans agree that that may be bad. Nor are we discussing the fact that we are not going to live forever; even if this does not harm us, the particular event of death might still do, and vice versa.

Second, I shall assume that we go out of existence when we die. We do not exist after death as corpses, or as parts of corpses, or as anything else. In the present context, this assumption is innocuous. For instance, subsequentists believe that my death can harm me at a time t even if my corpse no longer exists at t.

Third, our issue concerns death's *badness*. Some might want to say that while my death is bad for me, it does not *harm* me (or that although my death is bad for me at a time, there is no time at which it harms me). In this chapter, however, I am using formulations like "my death harms me (at t)" merely as stylistic variations of formulations like "my death is bad for me (at t)."

Fourth, anti-Epicureans do not claim that my death is *intrinsically* bad – bad in itself – for me. Rather, they take it to be *overall* bad for me, a position they typically base on something along the lines of the "deprivation approach": an event is overall bad for a person if and only if, and to the extent that, she would have had an on-balance intrinsically better life if it hadn't occurred (e.g. Feldman 1991, 1994:

138; Bradley 2009: 50; Luper 2009: 86–87). The Epicurean, by contrast, denies that a person's death is bad for her in any way at all.[1]

Fifth, we need a firmer grip of the question to which priorism, subsequentism, atemporalism, and Epicureanism provide answers: "When is death bad for the one who dies?" As the kind of badness at issue here is overall badness, it is sensible to take the question to be, "When does death satisfy the criterion of overall badness?" Given the deprivation approach, this question should receive the same answer as, "At which times is the (entire) life that the person would have had, if she hadn't died, intrinsically better for her than the (entire) life she in fact has?" The answer to this latter question seems to be, "At all times"; for if the relevant value relation holds between the two whole lives at all, it holds between them at all times (Feldman 1994: 154). Or perhaps we should instead say that the relation holds between the two lives but not at any time. What we certainly should not say is that it obtains only before death, or only after death. Priorists and subsequentists are aware of this, however. The debate they are engaged in, together with atemporalists and Epicureans, presupposes another understanding of the question, namely this one: "At which times does the person have *a lower well-being level* than she would have had at those times if her death hadn't occurred?" (And of course, we shall assume the corresponding interpretation of questions of when events other than death are bad for a person.) The answer to the latter question is not, "At all times"; I wasn't worse off during the Battle of Hastings than I would have been if it weren't for my future death.[2]

III

But I will be worse off *after* my death, subsequentists say. This is admittedly a natural idea, in light of the fact that my death at t prevents me from enjoying myself at various times *after t*. And, to repeat, this is precisely how we tend to think about other events that are overall bad for me. Why not simply accept subsequentism, then? Life is short; do we really need to listen to priorists and atemporalists, and their predictably rather convoluted responses to the uniformity charge?

We do, for subsequentism faces a serious obstacle – to do, of course, with the Epicurean idea mentioned in section I of this chapter: "Once I die, I am no longer there to be harmed." If, as subsequentism says, I have a *lower* well-being level after my death than I would have had if I hadn't died, then I *have* a well-being level then. Naturally, this level need not be negative (or positive); Ben Bradley, a leading subsequentist, explicitly asserts that the dead occupy a well-being level of zero (2009: 99). But arguably, having well-being – even zero well-being – at *t* requires *being* at *t*; and the dead no longer exist. Once I am dead, I am, as it were, *too* off to be worse off.

Steven Luper has given a good argument for this verdict (Luper 2007, 2009: 132–33). Unlike me, my shoe seems to have no well-being level now at all, not even zero; no matter how happy I am, I am not better off than it. (Compare: no matter how much money you have, you're not richer than it.) Plausibly, the explanation of this difference is at least in part that I now have, whereas my shoe does not now have, the capacity to accrue intrinsic benefits and harms; on all reasonable theories of well-being, such a capacity requires a capacity to have mental states. When a person is dead, on the other hand, she lacks such a capacity even more radically than my shoe does; unlike a dead person, the shoe at least exists.

Bradley, however, offers an argument for the thesis that the dead do occupy a well-being level (2009: 108–9). I am prudentially required to be indifferent between a future in which I die instantly and one in which I instantly and permanently lose consciousness and die ten years later. According to Bradley, this suggests that I have the same well-being level in these two futures; hence, I have a well-being level in the first. But this argument is problematic. As David Hershenov has remarked (2007: 174), I am also prudentially required to be indifferent between two possible worlds in which I never exist. And if I had never existed, I would not have occupied any well-being level at all (no matter how happy you are, you're not better off than my non-existent little sister). Actually, however, Bradley has argued (in another context) that even those who never exist have a well-being level of zero (2013: 45–48). But this is a dubious view. Arguably, in the case of an existing individual, claims about her well-being levels are true by virtue of her exemplifying certain *properties* and *relations*. For instance, if an existing person has zero well-being, this is due to her exemplifying the property, *x has zero well-being*; similarly, if she is as well off as you are, this is due to her standing to you in the relation, *x is as well off as y*. But surely if an existing individual cannot have zero well-being, or be as well off as others, without exemplifying such properties and relations, nor can a non-existing individual. What work would the property or relation do, in the case of existing individuals, if the relevant value claims can be true without it? (Compare: if you are richer than I by virtue of standing to me in the relation, *x is richer than y*, then surely you stand in this relation to any individual you are richer than.) Crucially, moreover, on a plausible and widely endorsed view, in order for an object to exemplify properties and relations in a possible world *w*, it has to exist in *w*.

But even if there are reasons to be skeptical of subsequentism, it might still be true that a reason to prefer it to priorism and atemporalism is that it treats death like other, relevantly similar evils. So let us now turn to our main topic, the uniformity objection to priorism (sections IV–VI) and atemporalism (section VII).

IV

Again, if I miss my flight to Japan at *t*, and thereby a wonderful vacation, this is bad for me after *t* – for instance, at those times at which I would have enjoyed myself immensely in Tokyo and Kyoto had I not missed my plane. Analogous remarks apply to other harms, such as losing my friends or being drugged into unconsciousness. But not to death, priorism says. On priorism, if, in a variation of the case, I succeed in catching the flight but die en route, thus going to the Land of Non-Existence instead of the Land of the Rising Sun, this is bad for me *before* I die. This yields a suspicious lack of uniformity (Bradley 2009: 87–88; cf. Luper 2007: 242, 2009: 129). And it is evidently a non-starter to achieve uniformity by embracing priorism across the board: to hold, for instance, that losing my friends, too, harms me not after but before it happens.

This heterogeneity would have been less suspicious if death were bad for some significantly different reason than other harms. But that does not seem to be the case. Just like my death, missing my flight, losing my friends, and being drugged seem to harm me by depriving me of an intrinsically better life – they are overall harms in the way specified by the deprivation approach (section II).

Nonetheless, the mere fact that other overall harms are bad after they happen, whereas priorism takes death to be bad not after but before it happens, is far from enough to refute priorism. Maybe this heterogeneity lies only on the surface, and is an unproblematic consequence of a principled theory that, on a deeper level, treats death just like other evils. And maybe the priorist can supply such a theory.

Priorism has, however, no ally in *hedonism*: the view that a person's well-being consists in her receipt of pleasure and pain. For the conjunction of priorism and hedonism implies that if my death at t hadn't occurred, then my hedonic level at some point before t would have been different – and that seems clearly false. In my opinion, priorists worry less about this than they should; for hedonism may very well be true (Feldman 2004; Bradley 2009). But let this pass.

Priorists usually endorse instead some version or other of *desire satisfactionism*. According to this view, what makes my life intrinsically good (bad) is the satisfaction (frustration) of my desires; moreover, the stronger a desire is, the more its satisfaction (frustration) enhances (lowers) my well-being. Or at least this is so, desire satisfactionists add, provided that the desires fulfill certain requirements: for instance, maybe a desire does not count (or does not count as much) unless it is about the subject's own life; has an object that is desired for its own sake; has not been formed in dubious ways; or has a worthy object. For our purposes, though, it does not matter whether or not desire satisfactionism includes these requirements, for we can unproblematically assume that the desires needed by the priorist do not violate them.

Following Kris McDaniel and Ben Bradley (2008), we can say that a desire is satisfied if and only if its object (the desired state of affairs) obtains and the desire is not cancelled; similarly, it is frustrated if and only if its object fails to obtain and the desire is not cancelled. A desire is cancelled if and only if its "condition" – what it is conditional on – does not obtain. Suppose, for instance, that I want to drink coffee, on the condition that you do not prefer me not to. Then, if you *do* prefer me not to, my desire is cancelled, and thus – whether or not its object (my drinking coffee) obtains – neither satisfied nor frustrated.

How does desire satisfactionism help priorism? After all, just as my receipt of pleasure and pain before t would not have been any different if I hadn't died at t, so would my desires before t have been exactly the same. But priorists point out that my death at t makes a difference, not to which desires I have before t, but to their satisfaction. In particular, death prevents the satisfaction of many desires whose *objects* depend on what happens *after* t. Thus, on desire satisfactionism, if I now desire to be in Japan next week, but die en route tomorrow, and my desire would otherwise have been satisfied – that is, both its object and condition would have obtained – then my death affects my well-being negatively. It does this regardless of whether my desire is frustrated (which it is if its condition, in fact, obtains) or merely not satisfied (which it is if its condition does not, in fact, obtain). (There are also cases where death at t prevents the satisfaction of a desire by preventing its condition, though not its object, from obtaining: suppose, for instance, that I now desire that I now write this sentence, on the condition that I'm alive after t.) Of course, this still does not give us priorism. But priorists add that, since I have this desire *now*, it is plausible to say that my death affects negatively the well-being level I have *now* (e.g. Pitcher 1984: 162; Luper 2009: 135).[3]

What general principle underlies this crucial addition? Maybe this one: an event is bad for a person at a certain time just in case the desires she has then would have been satisfied to a greater extent if the event hadn't occurred. More precisely: an event, occurring in possible world w, is bad for a person at time t in w if and only if the balance of satisfaction over frustration of the desires she has at t in w is greater in the closest world to w in which the event does not occur, w^*, than in w. However, this principle should be rejected, even by priorists. Suppose I go for a walk. And suppose that, if I hadn't gone for a walk, the desires I actually have at a certain later time t would have been satisfied to a somewhat greater extent, and frustrated to a somewhat lesser extent. They thus fulfill the proposed condition. But suppose further that if I hadn't gone for a walk, I would also have had lots of strong desires at t which I do not in fact have at t – desires that, moreover, would all have been frustrated. Surely the priorist will not want to say that going for a walk is bad for me at t in this case – especially since, given our understanding of an event's being bad at a time (section II), this is equivalent to the untenable claim that my well-being level at t, in that other possible world, is higher than the well-being I have at t in the actual world.

Here is a more plausible view: an event, occurring in w, is bad for a person at t in w if and only if the balance in the closest world in which the event does not occur, w^*, of satisfaction over frustration of the desires she has at t in w^* is greater than the balance in w of satisfaction over frustration of the desires she has at t in w. Unlike the former view, this view avoids the implication that, in the case just described, going for a walk is bad for me at t. On the contrary, it implies that if I hadn't gone for a walk, my well-being level at t would have been lower than it actually is. For what this view, unlike the previous one, takes into account, in determining my well-being level at t in the closest possible world in which I don't go for a walk, are the desires I have at t in *that* world (whether or not I have them at t in the actual world).

In the particular case of death, this latter, better view has the same results as the former view. For as already indicated, if an event occurs at t, then the desires I would have had before t, had the event not occurred, are the same as those I actually have before t. Thus, the second view serves the priorist's needs equally as well as the former view.

Call the conjunction of desire satisfactionism and the second view "DS1."[4] DS1, the priorist might say, is the sought-after principled view that treats death like other evils. Granted, it has the result that whereas ordinary harms, like losing my friends or missing my flight, are bad after they occur (in realistic cases, at least), death is bad before it occurs. But it also has the result that ordinary harms are *also* bad *before* they occur: for instance, even before I lose my friends at t, I want them to be my friends after t. (This result is nowhere near as implausible as the one I deemed a non-starter at the outset of this section: that such harms are bad before *but not after* they occur.) In all these cases, the explanation is the same: the closest world in which the event in question does not occur is to a greater extent in accordance with the desires the person has at the relevant time in that world, than the actual world is with the desires she has at that time in the actual world. And, the priorist will add, the reason that death is not also bad after it occurs is simply that the person does not exist and thus occupies no well-being level then. This contention should meet no resistance, supposing the criticism of subsequentism was cogent (section III).

If DS1 is plausible, then, the priorist might be able to answer the uniformity objection. But *is* DS1 plausible?

v

One interesting objection to DS1 goes as follows.[5] Suppose I desired, strongly, yesterday to play tennis today, and that this desire was not conditional on my still having it today – or on anything else that fails to obtain. Today, I no longer desire this; I want to play soccer instead, although this desire is much weaker than my past desire for tennis. I must now decide what to do. Suppose there is no third alternative – I have to choose tennis or soccer – and that my decision makes no difference to the satisfaction or frustration of any other desires. If DS1 is true, I will maximize the intrinsic value of my life by playing tennis today – although this will be accomplished only by making yesterday, instead of today, better for me. Given DS1, then, prudence apparently requires me to play tennis today. But, the objection goes, this is the wrong result; surely I am prudentially permitted (if not required) to play soccer today.

It is hardly a promising response to reject this last claim. Nor is it promising to adopt a version of desire satisfactionism (and hence of DS1) that avoids the implication that I will maximize the intrinsic value of my life by playing tennis today – for instance, by claiming that the satisfaction of a desire for something to occur at t enhances the intrinsic value of the person's life only if the desire is not, at t, replaced by a conflicting desire. For compare our tennis/soccer case with one that is exactly similar except that, in the second case, I never have a desire to play tennis today. Suppose, in both cases, that I do play tennis today. Intuitively, my life seems intrinsically better in our original case than in the second case. This suggests that the satisfaction of a replaced desire does enhance the intrinsic value of the person's life. The proposed requirement, I suspect, will appear reasonable only if it is conflated with something like the following, more plausible claim: if a state of affairs is desired only on the condition that the desire is not replaced by a conflicting desire at t, but the desire is so replaced at t, then the obtaining of the state of affairs does not increase the intrinsic value of the person's life. By stipulation, however, my past desire for tennis today has no condition that fails to obtain.

In my view, friends of DS1 should instead dispute the connection presupposed in the objection between well-being and prudential obligation: that I am prudentially required to maximize the intrinsic value of my entire life (cf. Dorsey 2013: 163–64). Consider two versions of this line of response.

On the first, prudence is temporally biased, so that my past well-being matters less than my future well-being. In particular, it may be suggested, I am always prudentially permitted to maximize my future well-being, even if I thereby sacrifice my past well-being and fail to maximize the value of my life as a whole. Therefore, I am prudentially permitted to choose soccer now even on DS1. However, this response seems misguided, for the fact that DS1 places the greater benefit before the time of my act is not a crucial part of the tennis/soccer objection.[6] First, if that were the problem, we could just as well have objected to DS1 as follows: DS1 implies, implausibly, that if I could now somehow bring about the satisfaction of a desire I had yesterday to play tennis *yesterday* (using backwards causation, perhaps), and this act would not affect the satisfaction or frustration of any other desires, then this act would maximize the intrinsic value of my life, and thus be prudentially required.[7] But in fact, this implication does not seem nearly as implausible as the one ascribed to DS1 in the tennis/soccer objection. Second, suppose I had to make my choice about today's activity, not today, but at some earlier time t, when I hadn't yet acquired the desire to play tennis today. At t, that desire is in the future; and thus, so is the potential benefit given DS1. But it nonetheless seems that, at t, I am prudentially permitted (maybe even required) to see to it that I play soccer today. As these two remarks suggest, the proposed line of response does not seem to touch the core of the original objection to DS1. That core, it seems, does not appeal to what is past or future when I act. It is rather that I am not prudentially required, at any time at all, to bring about the satisfaction of my desire to play tennis today, since I lack this desire today and even have a desire that conflicts with it (and, again, the act doesn't affect the satisfaction and frustration of any other desires).

A second version of the reply seems preferable. The DS1 advocate could adopt a variant of Krister Bykvist's view of the moral relevance of past and future desires (Bykvist 2003).[8] According to Bykvist, just as I should have a special say over how I am to be treated, my person-stage I-at-t should have a special say over how *it* is to be treated. If you want me to play tennis, this matters less than what I want to do; similarly, what another person-stage of mine wants I-at-t to do matters less than what I-at-t wants to do.

Since I-today wants to play soccer, all my person-stages are permitted (indeed required, Bykvist thinks) to disregard the conflicting desire of I-yesterday that I play tennis today. This approach, Bykvist points out, has the advantage of taking seriously the fact that each person-stage has, as it were, a mind and will of its own: my current desires and other mental features differ substantially from those I have at other times – in much the way that they differ from those of other people.[9] Moreover, unlike the previous proposal, this proposal makes no appeal to whether a desire is past or future at the time of the act. Again, Bykvist's is a moral view, but as he suggests, analogous claims could be made about prudence (2003: 132). Fortunately for the DS1 proponent, a prudential view along these lines is fully compatible with the claim that I would maximize the intrinsic value of my life (as well as my yesterday well-being) by playing tennis today, not by playing soccer. Compare: it is not implausible to hold that even if I would maximize total well-being in the world (as well as your well-being) by playing tennis today, I am still morally permitted to act on my own desire to play soccer instead.

VI

Even though DS1 might survive the above objection from prudence, what it says about well-being at a time is rather counterintuitive.

Consider five examples. First, as David Velleman remarks, it seems wrong to say, "of a person who dies in harness, that he fared progressively worse toward the end, simply because he was acquiring more and more ambitions that would go unfulfilled" (1991: 339–40). Second, it also seems wrong to say, "of a person raised in adversity, that his youth was not so bad after all, simply because his youthful hopes were eventually fulfilled later in life" (1991: 340). Third, suppose my youth was an exact duplicate of this person's, but my hopes are *not* fulfilled later in life. While I may have reason to be envious, his *youth* would be a most inappropriate target of my envy. But it wouldn't be if his youth was better than mine (Johansson 2012: 263). Fourth, suppose I am ill on Monday but have no desires about the future. On Tuesday, I am just as ill, but also acquire the desire not to be ill on Wednesday. On Wednesday, I am not ill, and still desire not to be. Surely my well-being level begins to rise on Wednesday – not Tuesday. Fifth, suppose it is rational to be biased towards the near future: to prefer well-being in the near future to well-being in the more distant future, merely because the former is closer in time. Then, given DS1, if I will go to Japan in 2034, it is rational for me to prefer desiring next year (but not in 2024) that I will go to Japan in 2034 to desiring this in 2024 (but not next year). That doesn't ring any bells.

What these five points illustrate is the counterintuitiveness of DS1's implication that my well-being at t partly depends on what happens after t. They do not presuppose the hedonistic idea that my well-being at t can only depend on my *experiences* at t. For instance, I do not find it unappealing to say that my Wednesday well-being is boosted by the satisfaction of my Wednesday desire not to be ill on Wednesday, even if this desire satisfaction does not affect my experience on Wednesday.

Nor do the five judgments presuppose any particular view of when a desire *is satisfied*. For example, some writers argue that if I now desire a certain event to occur tomorrow, and it is *true* now that the event occurs tomorrow (and that the desire's condition obtains), then my desire is satisfied now (e.g. Luper 2012a: 327–30). This thesis is compatible with the five judgments, and thus does not rescue DS1. What's counterintuitive is that the *well-being level* I have now is enhanced by the satisfaction of such a desire – whether or not it is satisfied now.

It may be suggested that DS1 has a virtue that outweighs this counterintuitiveness. Many believe that the satisfaction of my desire for an event to occur at a later time t makes my life better, even if I lack this desire at t (and in section V I expressed some sympathy for this idea). Does not this belief require DS1? After all, if the desire satisfaction does not increase my well-being at the time of desire, when else? It seems wrong to say that it increases my well-being when the event in question occurs; for instance, that view seems to imply, implausibly, that I can have a positive well-being level tomorrow even if I die before then (Bradley 2009: 27; see also Dorsey 2013: 156–57). However, there is another option, which seems at least as plausible as DS1. On this view, call it "DS2," while such a desire satisfaction increases the intrinsic value of my life, it does not increase my well-being level at any time (Velleman 1991; Bykvist 2007: 76). We could still say, of course, that if the satisfaction of a desire, had at t, only depends on what happens at t, then it does enhance the person's well-being at t. Since there are plenty of such desires, this view leaves room for a lot of temporally located well-being.

DS2 may seem incoherent, though. Consider the duration that spans my entire lifetime. If a desire satisfaction enhances my well-being at this duration (regardless of whether it also enhances my well-being at any shorter time), then it does after all enhance my well-being at a time – for durations are times. This is true, but DS2 does not say that if a desire satisfaction enhances the intrinsic value of my life, then it enhances my well-being at this duration. We must distinguish how good my life is for me from how well off I am while it is going on. On DS2, something may affect the former without affecting the latter.

While DS1 is not indefensible, it is not particularly attractive. But something like DS1 is needed for the priorist to meet the uniformity objection. It is doubtful, then, whether the priorist has an attractive response to the uniformity objection.

VII

Consider now the uniformity objection to atemporalism. No one would say that whereas events other than my death fascinate me only if they fascinate me at times, my death fascinates me without fascinating me at any time. Similarly, since overall harms other than my death harm me at times, surely my death must do so as well. We should distrust any view that makes death the only exception to the rule, or one of a few exceptions (Feit 2002: 361; Bradley 2009: 74–78, 91–92; cf. Luper 2007: 242, 2009: 129). If nothing else, the idea that death is such a nonstandard harm provokes the Epicurean suspicion that it is not worth caring about (cf. Bradley 2009: 78).

Elsewhere I have responded in some detail to this and related arguments (Johansson 2012: 266–70). Here I shall focus on one point that I and others have frequently neglected. The atemporalist, I maintain, can plausibly deny that all, or nearly all, overall harms other than death harm us at times. While typical cases of missing my flight, losing my friends, and being drugged into unconsciousness aren't exceptions to the rule, plenty of other events are.

One view that gives us many such events is, of course, DS2 (section VI). On DS2, if you prevent the satisfaction of my present desire for some event to occur tomorrow, your action may deprive me of an intrinsically better life without making me worse off at any time.

But we can just as well appeal to hedonism, for example. For the main thing to note is that my death, occurring at t, is far from alone in being such that if it hadn't occurred, then I would have died much later than t. Assume, then, hedonism, and suppose that, as a result of waking up early, deciding to walk to work, and crossing a heavily trafficked street, I die in a car accident at t. Suppose that if I hadn't woken up early, a long and pleasurable future would have awaited me; the same goes for my decision to walk to work, and my crossing the street. Suppose also that none of these three events is such that, if it hadn't occurred, then I would have occupied a higher hedonic level at some point before t. Then, on the deprivation approach, each of these three events is overall bad for me; yet, the atemporalist will claim, none of them makes me worse off at any time. Obviously, moreover, none of them is the event of my death. (Indeed, they do not even owe their badness to my death's badness. Imagine that if my death hadn't occurred, then a sadist would have captured me as soon as I had crossed the street, and tortured me for fifty years. By contrast, if I hadn't decided to walk to work, for instance, I would have taken the bus and escaped him altogether. In this case, I am harmed by the decision, which deprives me of many happy years, but not by my death, which doesn't.)

These are just three examples. Myriad other events prevent me from living a long and pleasurable life after t, including many earlier ones – such as, presumably, my decision to move to my current neighborhood three years before t (had I not made this decision, I would be nowhere near the scene of the accident at t). Admittedly, for such a relatively early event, it is unrealistic to think that there is no time before t at which I am hedonically worse off because of it. However, this does not affect the main point, for it is still primarily by depriving me of many pleasurable years after t that the decision to move harms me; plausibly, even if it hadn't deprived me of any pleasures before t, it would still be true that my life as a whole contains much less pleasure than it would have done had I not made the decision.

Naturally, the above remarks have little force considered as an argument *for* atemporalism. The claim that choosing to walk to work, for instance, is an atemporal harm will probably be rejected by subsequentists and Epicureans, for precisely the same reasons that they reject the analogous claim about death. However, I am not here advancing an argument for atemporalism, but a response to the objection that the atemporalist is committed to the view that death is more or less the sole atemporal evil. She isn't, I suggest, for if atemporalism is true, there are lots of such evils. It does not matter whether opponents of atemporalists would, or should, accept the atemporalist's verdict on these other events – at least not so long as this verdict is intuitively appealing. And it is: the natural thing to say about my choosing to walk to work, for example, is precisely that it is an overall harm (considering how much pleasure it deprives me of) that does not harm me at any time (considering that it leaves my hedonic status until t unaffected, and I don't exist after t).

Perhaps it remains true that the subsequentist can say that *all* overall harms are bad for us after they occur (though see Johansson 2012: 269), whereas the atemporalist cannot: she can hardly deny that typical cases of missing a flight are bad after they occur. However, this should embarrass the atemporalist only if she cannot point to a crucial difference between, say, my death (or any of the three events in the above story) and missing my flight. But such a difference seems to be easily available: in the latter but not the former case, I exist at the times at which I am, because of the event, not experiencing pleasure (cf. Broome 2012: 221). Of course, this is a crucial difference only if – in contrast to what the subsequentist says – having well-being at a time requires existing at that time (section III). If that assumption is mistaken, we should reject atemporalism – but that would be simply because atemporalism relies on that mistaken assumption, and not because it is vulnerable to the uniformity charge.

NOTES

1   For an elaboration of this last claim, see Olson 2013.
2   Nor should we answer "At the time of death" (Johansson 2012: 261). For more on the different interpretations of the question, see Johansson (2012: 258–60) and Luper (2009: 122–26).
3   Luper notes (2009: 136) that this priorist strategy will not work in all cases. Suppose someone, who never has any desires about times later than t, dies at t, and would otherwise have acquired many new desires after t, which would have been satisfied. Such a person's death, Luper submits, is atemporally bad for her.

4   Dorsey (2013) defends DS1, or at least a very similar view, though not in connection to priorism or the evil of death.

5   The objection is a close variant of two arguments discussed in Dorsey (2013: 162).

6   For further problems for this sort of "tensed" approach, see Bradley (2011) and Bykvist (2003).

7   Dorsey (2013: 164) describes a similar case, in order to make a slightly different point.

8   Bykvist's view, as well as his defense of it, is much more sophisticated – and radical – than is indicated by my brief sketch (which is enough for my purposes here). Also, I'm not suggesting that he himself would endorse using it to defend DS1 against the present objection. For response to objections, and some reservations, see Bykvist (2007).

9   The suggestion does not require that expressions like "person-stage" and "I-at-t" be taken literally – as a commitment to four-dimensionalism about identity over time – rather than as just a handy way of referring to the person as she is at a certain time (Bykvist 2007: 74). By way of analogy, consider the "monistic" ontological thesis that there are no numerically distinct human people, only one super-individual with lots of distinct minds, and talk of "my desires" and "your desires" is just a handy way of referring to this individual as it is at different times and places. It seems to me that this thesis, even if true, gives us no reason to abandon the view that what I normally call "my desires about how I should be treated" matter more than what I normally call "your desires about how I should be treated." The distinctions between different sets of mental states seem important whether or not they correspond to distinctions between different individuals. See also Johansson (2007).

10 The symmetry problem

PRELIMINARIES

Grant that when a person dies, he or she ceases to exist. Why then should death in the sense of this period of inevitable and everlasting non-existence be a cause for concern? After all, non-existence is not confined to the period after a person's life; the person also did not exist before the first moment of that person's life. And it would be odd to claim that the person was even a potential subject of harm in that period before birth (although circumstances caused by events before that birth might well harm the person once he or she comes to be). It is similarly odd to say that anyone alive is much concerned, upset, or caused distress by the thought that there was an enormous stretch of time before he or she came to be. And yet our thoughts about the non-existence that follows our lives tend to be quite different.

The question of the symmetry of pre-natal and post-mortem non-existence was, as far as we can tell, first raised by ancient Greek thinkers concerned to minimize or eradicate the fear of death. The most famous exponents of this view were the Epicureans. They claimed that the two periods are relevantly symmetrical and that pre-natal non-existence is (or was) not a matter of concern for us. Hence the same should be true, *mutatis mutandis*, for post-mortem non-existence. Therefore, death cannot be a harm. The symmetry claim, taken on its own, holds only that whatever we say is true of the period post-mortem then we should say something relevantly similar about the period before birth. It can be coupled with the claim that post-mortem non-existence is a harm to show that pre-natal non-existence is similarly a harm. However, since many people think that death can be a harm but that the Epicureans are correct about pre-natal non-existence, their attention turns to the symmetry claim itself and they try to find grounds for rejecting it.

Given the relatively extensive literature on this topic, some taxonomy might be helpful. There are three significant camps in the debate:

	Symmetry of pre-natal and post-mortem non-existence?	Pre-natal non-existence a possible harm?	Post-mortem non-existence a possible harm?
Epicureans	Y	N	N
'Symmetrists'	Y	Y	Y
'Asymmetrists'	N	N	Y

The Epicurean view is clear. The other two camps agree with one another that death can be harmful and in this they disagree with Epicurus; but each of the two retains one of the two claims made by the Epicureans and denies the other. Their differing stances on the symmetry or otherwise of the two periods of non-existence accompany different conclusions about pre-natal non-existence. 'Asymmetrists' combine the claim that death can be harmful with the premise that pre-natal non-existence cannot be harmful. They therefore are committed to some relevant difference between the two periods of non-existence. 'Symmetrists', in response, reject the proposed distinction between these two periods.[1] Since they disagree with the Epicureans in thinking that post-mortem non-existence can be a harm, they conclude that it is possible also for pre-natal non-existence to be harmful.[2] Note that these two camps are here distinguished not in terms of whether or not we do take a symmetrical attitude to these two periods, but rather in terms of whether, irrespective of the attitudes we do or should take, the two periods are indeed alike in terms of their potential for harm. Symmetrists may accept that we have asymmetrical attitudes to the two periods while thinking that the two are in fact symmetrical in terms of their harmfulness.

There are in fact two distinct symmetry arguments, both of which are sometimes ascribed to the ancient Epicureans. In the first, the ① focus is on our attitudes. Its starting premise asserts that we are not presently concerned about the time before our existence, which combines with a symmetry principle to say that we should therefore not be concerned about the time after our existence. In the second ② version, the focus in on the fact that non-existence is not harmful since the putative subject of harm does not exist. The time before our birth was not harmful to us; it is not relevantly different from the time after our death; so that too will not be harmful to us.

The second version is the authentic ancient Epicurean argument and is by far the most prevalent form in all ancient discussions.[3] Some modern commentators find this disappointing since it seems not sufficiently different from the basic Epicurean argument that death cannot harm since there is no simultaneous subject of harm.[4] Epicurus nevertheless evidently thought that the conclusion that post-mortem non-existence will not be bad for us was somehow useful in preventing the living from fearing death and he therefore must have taken it to be the case that our present attitude towards our future non-existence should somehow follow the fact of the matter. An Epicurean might reason as follows. Since non-existence is not bad then we should not adopt any attitude towards either period of non-existence that holds falsely that non-existence is bad. As it happens, we get things half-right: we do not adopt a mistaken attitude to our past non-existence since pre-natal non-existence was not a harm. We are simply asked to recognize this and use it to reinforce what the Epicureans urge is the correct and symmetrical stance towards post-mortem non-existence. In part, Epicurus' confidence in the therapeutic use of this argument for a present state of mind is based on his commitment to the notion that if something is to be harmful then it must be able to cause harm to a subject contemporaneous with it. The question of the timing of the harm of death is dealt with elsewhere in this volume so we can leave it aside for now. Suffice it to say that here too plenty of people find reasons to depart from the Epicurean view.[5]

This discussion of the two forms of the symmetry argument is not merely of historical interest. The relationship between the fact of the matter of the harmfulness or otherwise of either or both periods of non-existence and the attitude we do or should adopt towards them is itself not straightforward. The attitudes we do have are sometimes used in support of the asymmetry between the two periods; and sometimes a conclusion about the two periods of non-existence is intended to have repercussions for how we should revise our attitudes. We can take different positions on the proper direction of fit between the attitudes we take to pre-natal non-existence and post-mortem non-existence respectively and their respective harmfulness.[6]

Asymmetrists have adopted various strategies in their attempts to retain the Epicurean view about pre-natal non-existence but deny the Epicurean conclusion about post-mortem non-existence. We can identify two general lines of argument. The first of these focuses on various asymmetries in our attitudes to the past and future respectively, picking out some sense in which we are concerned about the future that does not have a counterpart concern about the past. The second denies the symmetry of pre-natal and post-mortem non-existence by identifying some sense in which although it is true that a person might die later than he will – and thereby be harmed by being deprived of some good – he cannot have been born earlier than he was and thereby be harmed by being deprived of some good.

ATTITUDES TO THE PAST AND FUTURE

There are various possible asymmetries between our attitudes to the past and to the future. For example, various thought experiments suggest that we have a 'future bias' which involves our preferring experienced goods to be in the future and experienced bads to be in the past.[7] In short, these examples suggest we all are biased so as to prefer our own pains to be past but our pleasures to be yet to come. (Similar experiments suggest that we are not similarly biased in our assessment of the temporal location of other people's goods and bads; in that case temporal location matters little and we prefer only that their lives be better overall.) If this is true, then perhaps we should think similarly about our attitude to past and future non-existence: we prefer our non-existence to be behind us, as it were, and longer life to stretch ahead. In that case, there is an asymmetry in our attitudes to the two periods of non-existence.

Moving from the description or identification of a difference between attitudes that we usually adopt to past and future objects respectively to a fact about the harmfulness of the objects of these attitudes seems to require that the difference in the attitudes in question be rational or otherwise justified. For example, if it is agreed that we do seem to take asymmetrical attitudes towards future and past harms, being more concerned about those in the future than those in the past, then this perhaps points towards a similarly asymmetrical attitude to the respective harms of post-mortem and pre-natal non-existence. Yet any stronger conclusion about the fact of the matter concerning those two possible sources of harm must rely on a stronger thesis about the attitudes being used to justify the proposed conclusion; an Epicurean or symme-trist opponent will reasonably demand some reason why these atti-tudes should be given any justificatory weight. After all, they both can agree that we do tend to think differently about post-mortem and pre-natal non-existence while maintaining that we ought not to do so.

The Epicurean or symmetrist, on the other hand, starts from the assertion that, as a matter of fact and regardless of how it merely seems to us, post-mortem non-existence is no more harmful than pre-natal non-existence. They can then recommend a change of atti-tude. An Epicurean will recommend that we ought no more to fear death than we feel concern at pre-natal non-existence. And since we feel no concern at the latter we should feel no concern over post-mortem non-existence. The symmetrist will also argue that our attitudes should be symmetrical; we should acquire a concern over pre-natal non-existence since it too might be a deprivation of goods just as post-mortem non-existence is. (However, trying to recom-mend a change in our attitudes in this way may come up against the obstacles of apparently natural or necessary or otherwise irre-placeable attitudes. Perhaps we necessarily think in an asymmet-rical way about future and past harms respectively, regardless of the truth of the matter.)

If the asymmetrist points to the identification of a future bias towards experienced goods as grounds for denying the symmetry of the two periods of non-existence, there must be assumed in addition the following two points: (a) this future bias towards experienced goods is relevant in our thinking about attitudes towards experi-ential blanks such as the periods of non-existence; (b) the future bias towards experienced goods is justified in some way, perhaps because it is consistent with some objective relevant distinction between the past and future or because it is beneficial or because it is a necessary product of humanity's evolution. Otherwise, someone who endorses the symmetry of the two periods of non-existence can again simply say that we should revise our attitudes to them in the light of their symmetry. The claim that we do happen to think of them differently will cause no discomfort.

In support of (a), the asymmetrist might insist that the future bias shows not only why we care more about the possibility of experienced goods in the future than in the past but also why we care more about the possibility of being deprived of future goods than the possibility having been deprived of past goods. And if death is a possible harm because it is a deprivation of future goods then it may be reasonable to think that such attitudinal asymmetry is relevant. Those who agree with the Epicurean notion that harms ought to be at least possible objects of experience for the putative subject of harm will think (a) untenable.[8]

In support of (b), the asymmetrist must argue not from the presence of asymmetrical attitudes but rather in defense of those attitudes from some other basis not dependent on how we tend to view things. The choice is then between offering some objective criterion according to which post-mortem non-existence is more harmful than pre-natal non-existence of a kind that would make the asymmetrical attitudes rational and offering some other account of the benefit or necessity of our holding asymmetrical attitudes. If the former, then whether or not the proposed objective criterion is indeed the reason why we do tend in fact to hold these asymmetrical views, nevertheless some justification of those views is available. Post-mortem non-existence seems more harmful and it is more harmful. Perhaps it is better all round if it seems so *because* it is more harmful (that is, we adopt the asymmetrical views we do because of an understanding of its harmfulness), but either way there is no dissonance between our asymmetrical attitudes and the fact of the matter. The sought-after objective criterion is a matter of metaphysics. A popular approach is to look for some distinction between the two periods of non-existence based on an understanding of the conditions of the identity and persistence of a person such that post-mortem non-existence can be a deprivation of goods the person would have experienced had he or she died later, but pre-natal non-existence cannot be a deprivation of goods the person would have experienced had he or she been born earlier, because it is not possible for the same person to have been born significantly earlier. I address this suggestion in more detail below.

While much of the recent discussion of the symmetry problem has centered on the question of the impossibility of earlier birth, there are other approaches that deny symmetry by pointing to other objective features of post-mortem non-existence in contrast to pre-natal non-existence. For example, some asymmetrists argue that the directional nature of causation or the metaphysics of time give grounds for our holding asymmetrical attitudes to the past and future. Once again the argument can proceed in two directions: some argue that our attitudes give reasons for thinking in a certain way about time, while others think that a view about the nature of time ought to dictate and justify our attitudes to the past and future. In any case, it is open to debate whether the nature of time is indeed relevant to the question of asymmetrical attitudes in the manner needed for it to be used by our asymmetrists.[9]

Other attempts to locate objective differences between the two periods of non-existence are also difficult to sustain with much conviction. For example, Kamm suggests that one reason post-mortem non-existence is bad independently of brute concern for the future is 'the Insult factor': the fact that death happens to a person who has already existed and undoes him. This harm can befall a person regardless of that person's being aware of it. Contrast a person who has lost an arm with a person who only ever had one arm: "one has suffered an insult the other has not suffered, and in this sense, something worse has happened to him" (Kamm 1993: 42). This is supposed to be true whatever each of the two one-armed people may think about his own position and his position relative to the other; it should point to a property observable from a view 'outside the life' that does not rely on a comparison with some other life. It is undeniable that there is something true about the person who loses an arm that is not true of the person who has always had only one arm, namely the loss of an arm. But it is equally and for the same reason true that the person who loses an arm is the only one of the two who spends some of his life with two arms. And while any two-armed person would likely live a worse life if he loses an arm and therefore will be concerned at the prospect of losing an arm, regret having lost an arm, and so on, these all fail to provide the kind of harm that Kamm wants, namely one observable from 'outside the life'.[10]

In the absence of any other grounds for denying the symmetry between the two periods of non-existence, the asymmetry in attitudes is not defended on metaphysical grounds but either pragmatically or as a brute and non-negotiable fact about human psychology, perhaps in the latter case as being a necessary aspect of our lives generated by evolutionary forces. These are weak considerations. It is not obvious that an asymmetrical view is indeed better overall for us; and citing an evolutionary explanation for our holding such views is of itself neutral in terms of their justification.[11]

EARLIER BIRTH AND LATER DEATH

The second strategy focuses on the antecedent in the counterfactual hypothesis that grounds comparison between different possible personal pasts: "Had I been born earlier ..." For there to be any reasonable question whether it would have been better or worse to be born earlier or later then we must imagine that there is some genuine possibility being captured here that can indeed stand as a mirror-image of the hypothesis that grounds comparison between different possible personal futures: "Were I to die later ..." But if there is no genuine possibility that I might have been born other than when I was, although there is a genuine possibility that I might die other than when I will, then the two periods of non-existence are not symmetrical. I might die later than I will and thereby be deprived of goods my life would otherwise have contained. But I was not deprived of goods my life would otherwise have contained by being born later than I might have been. I could not have been born except when I was.

If the question is reduced to a mere quantitative analysis of either the amounts of goods and bads (perhaps pleasures and pains) in a life or simply the length of a life, then there seems much less ground for the asymmetry sought by those who want to defend the possibility that only death is a harm. Similarly, if the question is put in what might be called 'third-personal' terms then it is also harder to see how to maintain an asymmetry. For example, if we consider two lives which contain equal amounts of goods and are equally long then we might find it hard to decide that one of them is better than the other, even if one begins at a later date than the other. The earlier life does not contain the goods that the later life contains in the period between their respective end dates, but similarly the later life does not contain the goods that the earlier one contains in the period between their respective start dates. However, if you are now asked to say which of those two lives you would prefer now to be living – the one that starts earlier and ends earlier or the one that starts later and finishes later – it is likely that you will opt for the second. This shows only what we have already seen as our tendency to have a certain kind of biased attitude to the future: we prefer to have more of our goods ahead of us.[12]

Since it is not evident that we take a similarly asymmetrical view with regard to others' pleasures and pains (except insofar as we are adopting the other person's perspective and thinking that if we were they we would prefer pleasures to be yet to come and pains to be past) then if such thought experiments show anything then they point to some fact about the ways in which each of us views his or her own life from the inside, as it were, namely from the perspective of a particular agent considering his or her own past and future. In fact, in order to imagine a genuine choice between the two possibilities of my life having begun earlier or later it is necessary to build in a number of caveats and qualifications concerning the person making the choice. For example, I might not in fact welcome the news that I was born ten years later than I previously believed, even though this will presumably increase the number of goods I have yet to come, since I imagine it will make a significant difference to my conception of myself, my past, my memories, and so on.[13]

We need an account of the conditions under which it is correct to judge that two alternative possible lives are indeed two lives open for the same person to live and these conditions will in turn require a robust understanding of what the conditions are for us to identify the same person living different possible lives. In fact, some asymmetrists think that this is the place where they might find the required distinction between pre-natal and post-mortem non-existence because there might be something in the best available account of personal identity that will rule out the possibility of the same person having been born earlier than he or she in fact was but allow the possibility of the same person dying later than he or she in fact will. If this account is available then there will be an asymmetry between the potential deprivation caused by earlier death and the impossibility of any similar deprivation caused by later birth.

There are two popular ways of arguing for the necessary distinction. On the first view, it is held that our origins are an essential aspect of our personal identity: part of what it is to be person *P* rather than person *Q* is to have been born at the particular time person *P* was born with the same origins as person *P* and so on. Which aspects of a person's origins are relevant? We cannot simply say the time of their birth since this begs the questions, so perhaps a biological account is more helpful. We might say that it is impossible, for example, for the same person to come to be from a different sperm and egg than those from which they do in fact originate. But this will not help very much since it is nowadays of course practically possible for the same zygote to be allowed to develop at different times; we can delay the development of a particular individual. Even on this view of the necessity of origins, it seems that the same person might be born earlier or later and therefore reasonably be said to be deprived of goods by being born later.

The second tactic for defending an asymmetry based on the conditions of personal identity looks to a psychological account of personhood. On this view, to be the particular person I am, now looking back and wondering how my life might have been and looking ahead and wondering how it might turn out to be, it is necessary that I have lived the life I have up to this point. Put more precisely, if we adopt what is sometimes termed a thick notion of personal identity which makes reference not only to metaphysical or biological origins but to a biography – a developing psychological makeup which is in turn at least in part generated by a person's past experiences – then it is not possible for that same person (in this thick sense) to have lived any prior life that would have generated a relevantly different psychological result. And since the time of one's birth will have some effect, we assume, on the thick person who goes on to live a life from that point on, then we have a new account that denies the sense of the hypothesis "If I had been born earlier ..." Nevertheless, a thick person will go on to live one of a number of different possible lives. And some of the lives that person will not live involve a later death than he will in fact meet. So an earlier death can be a harm to a thick person while a later birth cannot.[14]

There is something undeniably true in the claim that in some sense the person I am now is the product of various events, circumstances, and experiences such that if this set of things were sufficiently different then I would now be different too. But it is another matter whether the difference here is enough to make us worry that the alternative past would have made such a difference as to prevent our reasonably taking this to be *my* alternative past. Asymmetrists claim that it does: the different past circumstances this will involve prevent reasonable regret that my past was not better than it was because the person who would have resulted from those different past circumstances cannot be said to be me. Symmetrists disagree. At this point the debate turns on the degree of tolerance that each side will allow in what is necessary for a person to be the particular thick person he now is and the importance placed on the identity of the thick person in contrast to some thin notion of personhood.

An extreme position holds that there are no relevant but contingent factors involved in thick personhood; nothing about a person's past could have been otherwise without resulting in a different present person. Most will think this intolerably strict. For the most part, both the asymmetrists and the symmetrists agree that there are some facts about my past that might have been otherwise and yet still the same 'I' would exist in the present. For example, an asymmetrist too should allow that we may want our past lives to have been better (perhaps contain more pleasure, less pain, even different birth), even if this allowance carries the qualifications that such wishes are limited so as not to be at the expense of what we think of value in our present lives. So a self is not so thick that it admits no contingencies whatsoever; there are ways a person's life could have been which, had they obtained, would not have jeopardized the identification of the person who would have resulted from that unactualized possibility with the person who did result from the actualized alternative.

For example, it is possible for me to consider what my life would be like were I not short-sighted and wonder if it would be better than my life now. (I do not mean that it is possible for me to imagine what it is like not to be short-sighted; I mean it is possible for me to imagine what it would be like *for me not to be short-sighted*.) I think about how much better it would be if I did not need to buy new glasses every two years, were able to see properly when I go swimming, and so on. True, were I not short-sighted perhaps I would have been more inclined to sport at school. Perhaps I would have been more outgoing, or less academic, and so on. But still, those possible differences are within the tolerable bounds of alternative ways that my own life might have unfolded.

The symmetrists might think that this allowance grants them all that they need. They think that we should also include within the bounds of what we can tolerate as alternative ways that a person's life could have been scenarios in which the person concerned was born earlier and experienced goods that he did not in fact experience given that in fact he was born later. Provided it is even possible for the same person (even conceived of in this thick fashion) to have come to be earlier, then this leaves room for a reasonable thought that we might have been deprived of goods we would have experienced had we been born earlier than we were. And while the deprivation of a late birth may be much less harmful than that threatened by an early death, the asymmetry of the two periods of non-existence is denied even with the acceptance of some role for thickness in our account of personhood.

The relationship between a thick person in this sense and thin personhood – which is some metaphysical essence of identity – is not clear. It is not obvious that there is in fact such a thing as thin personhood or distinct 'metaphysical essence' for each and every individual in the first place. Perhaps some kind of biological criterion is the most likely candidate to play the envisaged role, but even then there may be difficulties raised, for example, by cases of monozygotic twins. Nor is it clear whether thin personhood is a relevant issue for the current discussion. If we think about what matters to a person by considering his life and comparing different possible ways in which his life will unfold, it is likely that the level of concern and attachment a person will feel towards the various different possibilities is determined by the level of psychological connection between his present self and the envisaged person in the future. If that is right, then what is principally relevant in such concerns is surely the thick person he is and will be, whether or not there is also a thin person who persists in these various different possibilities. In other words, whatever the truth of the metaphysical question concerning whether the same person could indeed have been born much earlier, lived a radically different life, and so on, when it comes to questions about what we should be concerned about, it is the thick person that matters.

Of course, intuitions differ on this point. Some may well think that provided they have some reason to think that there is a meta-physical identity between an individual now and an individual at another time then, regardless of whether there is any psychological connection between them, these two just are in fact the same person. And that is what matters. So we can again imagine different possible lives this same person may have lived and may go on to live, some of which will be better than others, without insisting on the kind of psychological continuity or similarity that may incline us towards asymmetrism. Furthermore, consider the following: John is told he will develop a disease which will cause enormous psychological changes including complete loss of memory and various attendant alterations to personality and the like. People who are in this state require constant and expensive care. We can surely imagine that John may reasonably form the sincere wish that he be cared for properly should he develop that disease. If that is plausible, then this might incline us to the view that we can also care about a past or future individual who bears no psychological connection with our present self. On this view, thin persons matter too and an asymmetry reliant on thick personhood alone will not suffice to show a general asymmetry between pre-natal and post-mortem non-existence.

At a certain point, the discussion becomes a trade in intuitions, and different readers will have different intuitions about what they think matters to them in considering the range of alternative lives in question and therefore how to distinguish between those alternatives that should and those that should not be relevant to deciding the question of the symmetry or asymmetry of the times before life and after death. In fact, it seems to me important to think more about this range of different possible reactions and consider why it may occur since, evidently, different people are inclined to very different views on this. It is perhaps because we do not know precisely what in our past life is and is not necessary for our being the people we now are that we are inclined to be somewhat circumspect in our thinking about how our lives might previously have been, while we can have a free rein in considering various different paths our lives might take from this point on. We do recognize that we are to some extent the product of those experiences – however painful or harmful they were at the time and perhaps continue to be – and so if we do regret some past event it is with the qualification that the better alternative being envisaged is compatible with being the same person now. Of course, we are also capable of thinking about radically different alternatives: "If I had been adopted as a child and raised in an entirely different culture ..." But how much weight this imaginative possibility can bear is a matter of dispute because it is not perspicuous precisely what is involved in considering this kind of radical alternative.

For my own part, I can recognize that some people's lives are better than others, but when faced with thinking about alternative lives that I myself might have lived then after a certain point I simply have no idea whether my life would have been better under such very different circumstances than in fact it did turn out to be. True, it is possible to imagine various ways in which my life might be and might have been better than it is. But what is proposed by critics of 'thick-person asymmetry' is the possibility of comparing the life I have lived so far and an alternative possible life such as might be generated by my being born significantly earlier or later than was in fact the case. When I consider questions such as these radically alternative lives then it is no longer obvious that I am genuinely wondering about an alternative life that I might have lived.

Perhaps the point is clearest if we put the response in the form of a dilemma. In considering these radically different lives, I am doing one of two things, neither of which, on closer inspection, is a genuine contemplation of a radically different life that I could have lived. Either I am considering whether it would be better or worse for me as I am now suddenly to find myself living in an entirely different place, with an entirely different family, and other circumstances, or I am considering whether my life is better or worse than the life of some other person who may be in some respects like me but who lives in an entirely different place, with a different history, family, and other circumstances. But the symmetrist critic of 'thick-person asymmetrism' wants to insist on a third possibility between the two: the comparison between my life as it has turned out and my life had a very different set of circumstances obtained. It seems to me extremely difficult to grasp clearly and accurately the counterfactual involved in the radical alternative life story. To make the comparison, it would be necessary for a person to be able to think back to some point in his past, acquire a picture of the thick person he was at that time by paring away any psychological changes since then, and then extrapolate from that point on along an alternative life trajectory. This extrapolation would allow him to come to a picture of some alternative possible thick person that he might have developed into had his life taken a different path than in fact it did. Only then can this possible alternative life be usefully compared with his actual life.

CONCLUSIONS

For its application to the general understanding of the value of death, the symmetry problem is parasitic on the prior question whether any period of non-existence, and whether post-mortem non-existence in particular, can be harmful. For it to be of any positive argumentative use it will also need to be supplemented by at least some of the other controversial theses mentioned above, in "attitudes to the past and present" and "earlier birth and later death," namely those concerning our current attitudes to the past and future, the relevance of those attitudes to questions of the harmfulness or otherwise of the two periods of non-existence, and the relevant unactualised possibilities for a given person's life. The assertion of a symmetry between pre-natal and post-mortem non-existence is therefore likely to remain a controversial thesis. The Epicureans were sensible not to use the symmetry thesis as part of a stand-alone argument concerning the fear of death.

NOTES

1   Modern asymmetrism can probably be traced back to Nagel 1979. In fact, symmetrists too can trace their view to reactions to Nagel, who raised important doubts about asymmetrism in his report of a discussion between himself and Nozick and his reaction to work that later appeared in Parfit 1984. See Nagel 1979: 8 n.3.
2   Rosenbaum 1989: 368–73 considers the 'backfire problem'.
3   See Warren 2004.
4   For example Luper 2009: 61.
5   See Johansson, this volume.
6   Cf. Parfit 1984: 186; Kamm 1993: 28–9; Kaufman 1999: 6; Belshaw 2000b: 72–73; Pettigrove 2002: 417–19.

7   Parfit 1984: chap. 8, esp. 165–86. See also Persson 2005: part III.

8   See Brueckner and Fischer 1986. Their view is discussed critically by
    Haji 1991 and Belshaw 1993 and 2000a. Brueckner and Fischer 1993
    respond. Glannon 1994 argues against Brueckner and Fischer 1986, and
    Feldman 1994: 133–42. Similar criticisms can be found in Mitsis 1988:
    312–16, and cf. Belshaw 2009: 158–65.

9   Arguing from attitudes to metaphysics: see, e.g., Prior 1959; on argu-
    ments from metaphysics to attitudes: Parfit 1984: 168–70 and 177–81
    (with Moller 2002: 78–82); Persson 2005: 200–4; M. Burley 2007. On
    this general tactic see, e.g., Gallois 1994.

10 Kamm 1988, 1993: 25–71, esp. 39–55; her 1988 view is criticized in
    Feldman 1990 (criticisms echoed by Moller 2002: 81).

11 On whether it would be better not to have asymmetrical attitudes see
    Parfit 1984: 174–75 (and on the force of claiming an evolutionary basis,
    Parfit 1984: 186). Cf. Moller 2002 and Persson 2005: 222–34, who argues
    that the attitudes it is rational for us to hold diverge from those it is
    prudent for us to hold.

12 For an interesting discussion see Raz 2001: 88–99. I discuss his view in
    J. Warren 2004: 93–100.

13 See, e.g., Raz 2001: 94 n.11. Cf. Simon 2010.

14 For a defense of the thick self as a basis for asymmetrism: F. Kaufman
    1995, 1996, 1999, 2000. Belshaw 1993, 2000a, 2000b, and 2009: chap. 7
    offer a similar view, refining Kaufman's position. For criticisms of this
    position see Brueckner and Fischer 1993, 1998; Fischer and Speak 2000;
    Pettigrove 2002; Fischer 2006b; Johansson 2008.

11 Posthumous harm

THE IDEA OF POSTHUMOUS HARM

You probably do not want to die soon. One reason why you would prefer not to die is that there are so many good things about being alive. Dead people do not have leisurely lunches with friends, do not play with their grandchildren, do not read books, do not go hiking, and do not drink coffee. To enjoy the good things in life, you need to be alive.

Life contains bad things too, though, and one point to make in defense of death is that it puts an end to those bad things, even as it puts an end to the good. Dead people may not have much fun, but they do not get migraines or ear infections, do not have car accidents, do not get made redundant, and do not see their loved ones suffer. The thought of death can engender relief for what it allows you to avoid, as well as sadness for what it takes away.

We might then think of death as the event that marks the end of harms and benefits. Harms and benefits, on this way of thinking, are suffered or enjoyed by the living, and once you die, your ledger of harms and benefits is closed. If that is right, then we cannot be harmed or benefited by events that occur after our deaths; there is no such thing as a posthumous benefit or a posthumous harm.

The harms and benefits just listed, though, are not the only things we seek or hope to avoid for ourselves. You want to read good books and avoid ear infections, but you also want to achieve professional success, raise a happy family, have a good reputation, and

I am grateful for the helpful comments of Nicholas Agar, Steven Luper, and Dan Weijers.

make the world a better place. Whether you get *these* goods can depend on what happens after you die. After you die, your book might or might not get published, your children might or might not thrive, your reputation might grow or it might diminish, and your legacy might prove to be for the better or for the worse. Imagining such things happening after you die, it can feel as though you are imagining good and bad things that might happen to *you*. That suggests that what happens after you die can make a difference to how well things go for you – and hence that your ledger of harms and benefits is not closed at death, after all.

You are no longer around after you die; is it then impossible for you to be harmed or benefited after you die? But you are invested in projects that extend beyond your death; can events after your death then make your life go better or worse? The answer is not obvious, and this is the puzzle of posthumous harm.

THE QUESTION

To ask about posthumous harm is to ask about posthumous benefits, too; the possibility of posthumous harm goes along with the possibility of posthumous benefits. A discussion of harms and benefits is, for philosophers, a discussion about "welfare." A person's welfare is the measure of how well things go for her. Your welfare can be identified with your "well-being" and with your "best interests" – something that advances your welfare is something that serves your best interests – and we can also say that something that advances your welfare makes you better off rather than worse off, makes your life go better rather than worse, and is good for you, rather than bad for you. The question of posthumous harm, then, is the question of whether anything that happens after your death can advance or set back your welfare.

In asking whether you could be posthumously harmed, we are not necessarily asking whether you could be posthumously *wronged*. It is plausible to think that you can harm someone without doing her a wrong; perhaps I harm you, but do not do anything wrong, if I marry the person with whom you are secretly in love. It could conceivably be the case, then, that while it is possible to inflict posthumous harm, there is nothing wrong with doing so.

It is also plausible to think that you can do someone a wrong without harming her. Suppose that I break a promise to pick you up from a certain street corner at a certain time, and suppose that while you are stranded on the street corner, you meet someone who becomes your life partner and makes you the happiest person in the world. Then, by failing to pick you up when I said I would, I make you better off; I enable you to become the happiest person in the world. But still, plausibly, I do you a wrong; I make you a promise and I break it.

Another option in thinking about posthumous harm, then, is to say that a person may be posthumously wronged, but that there is no such thing as posthumous harm. Perhaps if I desecrate your grave or spread false rumors about you after your death, then I act wrongly towards you, but not in a way that involves harming you. Those who deny the possibility of posthumous harm may say that certain acts wrong the dead – and that that is why it is immoral to desecrate graves and spread false rumors about the dead – while maintaining that those acts are not harmful.[1]

The question of whether it is possible to be harmed after death is not the same as the question of whether death itself is harmful. That question raises different issues. You could believe that death itself is not harmful, but that events that happen after death can be. Or, you could believe that death is indeed harmful, but that it is the final harm that any person suffers, so that posthumous harm is still ruled out.[2]

It is natural to assume that our beliefs about posthumous harm will depend partly on our beliefs about what happens to us after our earthly deaths. It will matter, you might expect, whether we think that it is all over for us when we die here on earth, or instead that we live on, perhaps forever, in some other realm. In fact, however, that question does not have much relevance to the possibility of post-humous harm. If you survive your earthly death, then presumably you can be harmed in the afterlife. Those who believe in eternal life may believe that there is no posthumous harm, because they believe that there is no posthumous anything. But the important question is whether you can suffer harm once you are really, truly *dead*, not just when you are living elsewhere.

The question of posthumous harm has some theoretical interest, because of its connection with the debate about the nature of welfare. There is a long-standing philosophical debate over whether welfare consists in the enjoyment of pleasant experiences, or in the fulfillment of desires, or in the attainment of specified objective goods, or something else.³ The success of a theory of welfare may settle the question of posthumous harm; if welfare is just a matter of having pleasurable experiences, for example, then posthumous harm would be impossible. Conversely, a conclusion about posthumous harm may inform the debate over the nature of welfare; if we can show that posthumous harm is possible, for example, then we can rule out all theories of welfare that cannot account for it.

The main reason why the question of posthumous harm is significant, however, is more practical. It has to do with how we think of ourselves and our place in the world.

I can think of myself as a blip in the long history of universe: as something that exists for now but will soon be gone. My task, I could think, is to live as well as I can for my short time on earth, before I disappear and leave it to others. I can think of the dead as having had their time and vanished, so that the best thing for the living is to worry about the real flesh-and-blood people whose lives we can influence, not about the dead people whose lives are closed.

Alternatively, I can think of myself as someone capable of having a lasting influence on the world, able to leave a legacy for future generations. My task, perhaps, is to use my time on earth to create something that will stand: to ensure I will not fade into nothingness but will instead continue to influence the world for the better. I can think of the dead as still with us, in an important sense. I can think of them as people whose stories are yet to be concluded, and whose ultimate success or failure may be determined by what I do for them now.

The difference between these ways of thinking is difficult to describe precisely, but it is consequential. It matters for the questions of whether you should endure hardship while alive so as to work on a project that will come to fruition after your death, and whether you should commit yourself to redeeming the reputation of a dead relative, to give just two examples. Questions like these do not depend only on our conclusions about posthumous harm, but they are the kinds of questions that are at stake in the debate.

THE CASE AGAINST POSTHUMOUS HARM

Suppose that you and I are talking about your grandfather, and I ask, "How is he doing these days?" You respond, "Well, he died fifteen years ago," and I say, "Yes, I know, but how is he otherwise?" I would be talking nonsense. It is absurd to speak of harming and benefiting the dead in just the same terms in which we speak of harming and benefiting the living. For many, the idea that the dead could be harmed or benefited just seems ridiculous: no less ridiculous than the idea that the dead could be seen or tickled or surprised.

Two influential arguments set out to codify the conviction that the idea of posthumous harm leads to absurdity. The first concerns the "problem of the subject."[4] Something that happens now, we are told, may harm a dead person. But the dead person does not exist now, so there is no one, now, to whom the harm, now, can be done. What is absurd about the idea of posthumous harm, runs the argument, is the suggestion that harm can be done to someone at a time at which she does not exist. No one can be harmed when there is no one to harm.

The second argument expresses a worry about the kind of causation that posthumous harm appears to involve. An event now is supposed to make it the case that someone who no longer exists is in a harmed condition. So the person's being in a harmed condition is caused by an event that happens after her being in the harmed condition takes place. What we have here, it would seem, is backwards causation: an earlier event caused by a later event. And the idea of backwards causation – and certainly the idea that backwards causation can be shown to exist by a philosophical discovery about welfare – does seem ridiculous.[5]

Neither the problem of the subject nor the argument from backwards causation, as stated, is a knock-down argument against the possibility of posthumous harm, because there are other respects in which a person can be affected after her death without the involvement of any strange metaphysical phenomena. Imagine, for example, a person who makes reasoned but controversial predictions about what will happen in centuries to come. Is she a visionary? Only if her predictions are correct – and whether they are correct depends upon what happens after her death. Whether she has the property of being a visionary is determined by posthumous events. But that is not to imply that she must be around when those events happen, or that there is a causal link running backwards from the posthumous events to her condition while alive. So, there are at least some properties that a person can hold by virtue of events that occur after her death. If a person's being harmed by posthumous events is relevantly similar to a person's being a visionary by virtue of posthumous events, then the idea of posthumous harm need not lead to metaphysical strangeness after all.[6]

Still, there is *something* strange about the idea of posthumous harm. Perhaps being posthumously harmed is not really like becoming a visionary. The difference might be that harms and benefits are necessarily accrued at times, while properties like being a visionary are held, in some sense, timelessly; perhaps you become a visionary not at a time, but by virtue of the place you take in the overall story of the universe.[7] Perhaps being harmed or benefited is more like having a haircut than being a visionary. Further argument, in any case, is needed. Whether the problem of the subject or the argument from backwards causation succeeds depends on a broader question about the nature of harms and benefits.

THE CASE FOR POSTHUMOUS HARM

Suppose that you think of yourself as living a wonderful life, featuring professional success, good friends, and a healthy marriage. Suppose also that your colleagues do not really respect you, your apparent friends do not really like you, and your spouse does not really love you. Suppose that they all make fun of you behind your back; suppose that your own beliefs about your life are utterly misguided. But suppose also that the pretense carried out by your colleagues, friends, and spouse is immaculate, never making any difference to your subjective experience. Your life so imagined does not look like a life that goes well for you. It does not look like a life high in welfare – not because you have bad subjective experiences, but because your life, though you do not know it, is based on a lie.

Now imagine that your life is built around the project of preparing humanity for the end of the world, which you believe will occur on a particular date. Suppose that you die before that date. Whether your life is built upon a lie depends on whether the world indeed ends when you believed it would end. If it does not, then your life looks pathetic and misguided. Whether the world ends on the date specified makes no difference to your subjective experience, but that, as we saw in the previous example, need not mean that it cannot affect your welfare. Whether things go well for you, we may conclude, depends partly on whether your life is based upon a lie, which can in turn depend on what happens after your death.

A similar argument can be made with regard to your desires, your goals, and your cares. Whether your life goes well for you can plausibly be held to depend on whether you get what you want, whether you achieve your goals, and whether you get the things you care about. Living a good life, perhaps, is partly a matter of getting the things for which you strive, not just having it seem to you that you get the things for which you strive. And whether you get the things for which you strive can sometimes depend on events that occur after you die.

This is the thought that lies behind the best-known argument for the possibility of posthumous harm.[8] Once we acknowledge that something beyond your awareness can affect your welfare, runs the argument, it becomes arbitrary to claim that an event can affect your welfare only if it occurs while you are alive. If someone destroys your life's work, that is bad for you, even if it happens far from you. Whether it happens just before or just after your death would not seem to make the difference. Unless we are prepared to draw an arbitrary boundary at death, posthumous harm seems possible.

There are various ways in which the argument could be resisted. One is to deny its starting assumption, by saying that if something really does not in any way affect a person's experience, then it cannot affect her welfare. To make that claim is to accept an "experience requirement": a requirement that anything that affects a person's welfare affects her experiences.[9]

Another principled objection to the argument can be offered if we believe that something can only contribute to a person's welfare if it is viewed positively by that person: this is to accept an "endorsement constraint."[10] The endorsement constraint says that no event can enhance a person's welfare unless she has a positive attitude (of some specified kind) toward it, where it is possible to have that positive attitude toward an event without knowing about the event's occurrence, and without having your consciousness be affected by its occurrence. It makes sense to say, for example, that you have a positive attitude toward the thriving of your child – it is something you endorse, want, value, care about, strive for – even if you do not know whether your child is thriving. And the endorsement constraint, so construed, can still rule out the possibility of posthumous harm, if it implies that for an event to advance your welfare, you must view it positively *at the time of its occurrence*.

Why think that any welfare-affecting event must be endorsed at the time of its occurrence? Because – say the advocates of this view – people change, and as they change their sources of welfare change. Suppose that you once wanted a chocolate ice-cream, but now actively prefer not to have a chocolate ice-cream. Obviously the fact that you once wanted a chocolate ice-cream does not mean that it would be good for you to get a chocolate ice-cream now. What matters is what you want, not what you used to want. More broadly, we might then say, what matters is what you endorse now, not what you endorse or fail to endorse at other times. If that is right, then once a person is dead and unable to endorse anything, she cannot be benefited or harmed.[11]

The success or failure of the main argument for the possibility of posthumous harm, like the success or failure of the main arguments against it, then depends upon wider questions about the nature of welfare – questions about welfare and experience, and welfare and endorsement – which cannot be settled just by thinking about welfare and death.

LOCATING THE DISAGREEMENT

It is tempting to conclude that the disagreement about posthumous harm is simply a site at which larger disagreements about welfare are expressed. There are two deeply different attitudes to the possibility of posthumous harm, we might conclude, grounded in deeply different theoretical approaches to welfare. Before we can make progress on the question of posthumous harm, it might follow, we need to decide what kinds of things harms and benefits are, and to decide whether to accept an experience requirement or an endorsement constraint. The question of posthumous harm depends, perhaps, on what our larger theories of welfare imply.

Yet, stark as the disagreement over posthumous harm may seem, the domain over which it holds is quite limited. Everyone agrees that you cannot have experiences after you die; there is no posthumous pleasure or posthumous pain. Everyone agrees that you can have desires, beliefs, goals, values, and cares directed at posthumous events; posthumous events can determine whether your desires are fulfilled and whether your beliefs are true. Everyone agrees that whether your life is successful, on some measures, can depend on what happens after your death; posthumous events can determine whether you become famous, become a best-selling author, raise happy children, or change the world for the better.

At one level of detail, that is to say, the question of what can befall you after your death is not a matter of controversy. The disagreement only sets in when we ask whether any of the things that can befall you after death are relevant to your welfare. If we pay more attention to the extensive area of agreement within the debate, then perhaps we will find the resources for a self-standing view about posthumous harm, one we can defend without presupposing any controversial commitments in the wider debate about welfare.

POSTHUMOUS HARM AND THE NATURE OF WELFARE

When we think of the best and worst things that can happen to a person, we think mostly of harms and benefits that involve experiences. Excruciating pain, depression, and hunger; pleasure, joyfulness, and the rush of true love: only by having particular subjective mental states – particular beliefs, feelings, desires, and emotions – can you suffer any of these harms or enjoy any of these benefits.

Such essentially experiential harms and benefits are by nature temporally located. Any such harm or benefit lasts from one time to a later time, and exists by virtue of events that occur within those times. If you are in pain, for example, then the event of your being in pain has a beginning and an end, and is completely constituted by certain events that happen in the world – especially events that happen in your mind – during the time of your being in pain. You cannot be in pain, but at no particular time; and the fact that you are in pain at one time cannot be made true by events that occur at other, distant times. The same goes for depression, joyfulness, the rush of true love, and so on. There is a category of harms and benefits that are essentially experiential and temporally located, and this category includes many of the greatest of benefits and most horrible of harms.

Everyone should agree, then, that death marks a significant point of change in a person's ability to accrue harms and benefits. Once you are dead, you are no longer able to suffer harms or benefits of a certain central kind. If we focus on essentially experiential and temporally located harms and benefits, then the case against posthumous harm looks strong. The problem of the subject is a real problem, because harms like excruciating pain and humiliation can only befall a person while he is available to be pained or humiliated. The problem of backwards causation is a real problem, because an event that occurs now cannot make it the case that you are in pain or humiliated at a past time, unless some strange causal process is at work.

In ordinary life, in addition, the word "harm" is often used to cover only experiential harms. Suppose we both know that the wife of a mutual friend once had an affair. I ask, "Do you think it did him any harm?" You respond, "Well, he never found out about it, and neither did anyone who knew him, apart from his wife – and it never made any difference to her treatment of him. So he never knew about it, and never experienced any bad effects from it." Perhaps, under many conversational conditions at least, we can now take the question as settled. If his wife's having an affair made no difference to his experiences, then perhaps we can say that it never really *harmed* him.

That point established, however, we should also all agree that there are ways of evaluating a person's life that do not count only experiential and temporally located harms and benefits, and that can direct us toward events that happen after the person's death. When we ask, for example, whether a person lives a life of achievement, or a successful life, or a deluded life, we sometimes find our answer by seeing what happens after he dies. In thinking about the possibility of posthumous harm, the question is not whether evaluations like these are possible or sensible – of course they are – but whether they are of relevance to the person's welfare.

Imagine someone who spends his life trying to get a book published. He works hard at writing the book and marketing it to publishers, and if you ask him what he wants in life, he says that more than anything he wants to be a published author. His goal is self-directed; he wants to publish the book because he wants his life to include the writing of a published book. His goal does not change over time; even when his death is imminent, he works as hard as ever to get the book published, undeterred by his knowledge that the book will not appear during his lifetime. And his book, imagine, is published after his death, in just the way he wants.

There is a clear sense, we should all agree, in which the posthumous publication makes the man's life more successful that it would otherwise have been. By virtue of the posthumous event, the story of the man's life becomes a story of fruitful effort, of achievement, of work that pays off. To assess the man's life by asking whether his book is published is, furthermore, to assess his life as he assesses it. It is to accept a standard of evaluation that he, in a real sense, generates for himself.[12] The reason why the book's publication makes the man's life a success is that he invests himself so greatly in his project of becoming a published author. If he cared more about other things, then his success or failure would be assessed using other standards.

Does the man's success, owing to the posthumous publication of his book, make a difference to his welfare? Given all the uncontroversial facts of the case, it is difficult to see why it would not. Put it this way. If we say that the book's publication does *not* affect the man's welfare, then we need to accept that there exists a perfectly familiar and sensible way of evaluating the man's life, one that he generates himself and applies to himself, but that is nonetheless irrelevant to the man's best interests. That is an odd thing to say. If anything is relevant to how well the man's life goes for him, surely it should be a standard that he himself creates and accepts. In a case like this one, there is strong presumptive reason to accept that, somehow or other, a person's welfare is influenced by a posthumous event.

The case would not be so clear if the man's goal were not to publish a harmless book, but rather to do something stupid or evil. One response to the case is to deny that the man's publishing his book contributes to his welfare, for fear that we would otherwise need to accept that achieving stupid or evil goals (posthumously or not) contributes to welfare too.[13] But that would be to deny the most plausible judgment about *this* case, and besides, there are strategies by which that judgment could be preserved without the troubling implications. We could say that what matters is not the bare fact that the man achieved his goal, but rather the fact that he completed a rational life-plan, or that he did something worthwhile, or that he fully manifested a distinctive human skill, or something else. None of this need imply that he would also have had his welfare enhanced by the achievement of a stupid or evil goal.

The case would also fail to be so clear if the man's goal of publishing his book were one that came and went. As mentioned earlier, worries about changes in attitudes lead some to say that an event can only advance a person's welfare if she endorses it at the time of its occurrence. It is not unprincipled, however, to say that if a person's life *is* overwhelmingly characterized by pursuit of a certain good, then the attainment of that good advances her welfare; we can make that claim while holding back judgment about cases in which a person's goals do change over time. More positively, it can make sense to speak of the success of parts of lives. Suppose that the man spends twenty years trying to publish his book, then he spends five years concentrating on other pursuits, then he dies, and then his book is published. In that case, perhaps, the posthumous publication makes his twenty years of work on the book successful, and advances his welfare as regards those twenty years, without making a difference to his best interests as they are for the five years before his death.

Those, anyway, are the claims about welfare and death that emerge – according to me – from the points on which everyone can agree. Bringing them together, we ought to say, first, that there is an important, significant kind of harm – a kind of harm that under many conversational conditions is the only one that deserves the name "harm" – that cannot accrue to anyone posthumously; but, second, that a person's welfare can be affected by her success in achieving her own goals, and hence that there is another kind of welfare that can be influenced by posthumous events. Posthumous events can affect a person's welfare in one way, but not in others.

What does that tell us about the nature of welfare? In order to respect the most plausible view about welfare and death, it seems to me, we need to accept that welfare comes in different varieties. A theory of welfare should allow us to discriminate between kinds of welfare, and to say that while there is at least one kind of welfare that does not depend on posthumous events, there is at least one kind of welfare that does.

It is possible that the different kinds of welfare can all be drawn under one unified theory. Perhaps the harms and benefits we can only enjoy while alive are manifestations of the same basic good that can be affected by posthumous events. But perhaps we should accept that there are deeply different, perhaps mutually incommensurable, dimensions of welfare. That should not necessarily be surprising. There are different, mutually incommensurable, dimensions of intelligence; if you are a bit better than me at math, and I am a bit better than you at literary analysis, then we display very different skills, both of which nevertheless contribute to our respective levels of intelligence, and there need be no further fact about which of us is more intelligent overall. And there are different, mutually incommensurable dimensions of physical fitness, artistry, beauty, and all sorts of other things besides. The same could be true of welfare.[14]

SO WHAT DOES THIS MEAN FOR ME?

Theoretical questions aside, we can ask what insights about posthumous harm mean for our decisions about how to live our lives, and what they mean for our relationships with the dead.

Excruciating pain, humiliation, and depression are all bad for you, and you do not have much choice in the matter. You can try to avoid these harms, but you cannot make it the case that when they befall you they are not harmful. Similarly, it is in your interests to enjoy pleasure, joyfulness, and the rush of true love, and there is nothing you can do to change that fact – nothing you can do to make joyfulness harmful to you rather than beneficial. And this is indicative of a broad, if not exceptionless, truth. We do not have much control over the standards that determine what count as good and bad experiences for us. For as long as we are alive, we are vulnerable to certain particular experiential harms, and able to enjoy certain particular experiential benefits.

In contrast, it is largely for us to decide what would make our lives successful on our own terms. You can choose to aim to be a successful author, or to raise flourishing children, or to spend your life preparing for the end of the world, or just to have a good time. Insofar as our welfare is a matter of succeeding according to the standards we set for ourselves, we have some control over what kinds of events will make our lives go better or worse. And so we have some control over the extent to which our welfare can be influenced by what happens after our deaths.

If you spend your life trying to build a certain long-lasting reputation, then whether you live a successful life will depend partly on whether your reputation stays strong after you die; if, instead, you are genuinely indifferent to what other people think of you, then whether your reputation suffers after your death will not have such a bearing on whether your life succeeds or fails. If you aim to create a legacy, then someone who tarnishes your legacy after your death can prevent you from achieving your life's goals; if you never set out to create a legacy, then there is no legacy you care about that someone after your death can tarnish. If you aim to publish a book, then whether you achieve your aim can depend on whether someone publishes your book posthumously; if you instead aim simply to make every possible effort to get your book published, then nothing that happens after your death can make a difference to whether your aim is achieved.

Ask yourself how much influence you want posthumous events to have upon the story of your life. You have the option, in principle, of focusing solely on the time during which you live: of trying to make your time on earth as pleasant and productive as possible, and not worrying at all about what happens after you die. To make that choice is to inoculate yourself against posthumous harm, at least of the kind under discussion here, and also to retain for yourself greater control over whether your life goes well or badly. But it is also to close off the possibility of attaining certain kinds of success. Only if you have the goal of influencing the world for generations to come can you successfully achieve the goal of influencing the world for generations to come. If you focus only on what you do during your lifetime, then posthumous events cannot make you a failure, but they cannot make you a success, either.

How much influence you allow posthumous events to have on your welfare will depend largely on your own substantive values and commitments. It will depend on how much you care about the distant future, how much you value lasting fame, what constitutes true success in your chosen profession, and so on. But it can depend also on your temperament and your attitude toward your own life. Do you want your life to be spontaneous, or do you want to live out a specified life-plan? How much of your own success in life are you prepared to leave in the hands of others? Are you risk averse? Would you prefer to hold less ambitious goals over whose achievement you have more control, or more ambitious goals whose achievement is left largely to fortune? When it comes to the effect of posthumous events upon your welfare, these decisions are yours to make.

If I am right about the influence that posthumous events can have on welfare, then we all find ourselves able to do things that genuinely advance or set back the interests of the dead. You can still make a difference to the life stories of those you love but who are no longer alive. You can still damage a dead person by damaging her projects or her legacy or her reputation; in some cases, indeed, that might mean treating the dead person as she deserves. Any claims about our responsibilities regarding the dead, however, should be tempered by two points.

First, we cannot affect the welfare of the dead in all of the ways in which we can affect the welfare of the living, and how we weigh up the welfare of the dead against the welfare of the living will depend partly on which kinds of welfare we think to be more significant than others. In particular, there is a question about whether it is more or less important to ensure that (living) people enjoy experiential benefits and avoid experiential harm than to ensure that (living or dead) people achieve their goals or succeed in living their chosen life stories. It is a matter of judgment, case by case, and a matter for further argument. For what it is worth, though, my own sense is that we do someone a much more significant kind of harm by giving her horrible experiences than we do by tarnishing her reputation or failing to advance her goals after her death. Usually, I think, it would be a mistake to put the interests of the dead ahead of providing experiential goods to the living.

Second, what we can do for the dead depends largely on how they choose to live their own lives, and, especially, what goals they adopt for themselves. Perhaps your father invested himself entirely in your future career choice. Perhaps his life will have been a failure if you do not pursue the career he wanted for you. You may then have the ability to determine whether your father's life is a failure or a success – but perhaps that is his problem, not yours. We need to ask not only how we are positioned to affect the welfare of the dead, but also whether that is a position in which it is reasonable for the dead to leave us.

CONCLUSION

There are strong reasons to think that posthumous harm is impossible, but other strong reasons to think that we can make a difference to a person's welfare after she dies. To make progress in resolving the puzzle of posthumous harm, one strategy is to try first to resolve higher-level theoretical questions about welfare, with the verdict on posthumous harm to follow. Another strategy, and the one I have explored here, is to examine the points of agreement in the debate and see whether a stable self-standing view about posthumous harm can emerge. The crucial move, in my view, is to recognize a distinction between kinds of welfare. A dead person's welfare can be influenced in one respect, but not in others. There are various ways in which the relevant distinction between kinds of welfare could be drawn. I have concentrated on the difference between essentially experiential harms and benefits, on the one hand, and our investment in our own goals, on the other, and I have drawn out some of the consequences of making the distinction in that manner. If I am right, then it is possible to pay respect to the basic intuitions on both sides of the debate about posthumous harm, and to draw those intuitions within a single broad theoretical approach to welfare. The account of welfare that emerges will probably be disunified, but may be plausible nonetheless.

NOTES

1   For discussions of this possibility, see Partridge 1981: 254–64; Callahan 1987: 349–51; and J. Taylor 2005: 318–19.
2   This "intermediate thesis" is considered but rejected in Luper 2004; and it is defended in Bradley 2009: esp. 42–44 and chaps. 2–3. For more on whether death itself is harmful, see Luper 2009: chaps. 4–6.
3   For a survey of the major theories of welfare, see S. Keller 2009: 657–59.
4   Callahan 1987; J. Taylor 2005: 312. See also Bellioti 2012: esp. 21–22, on "the existence requirement."
5   Callahan 1987: 345; J. Taylor 2005: 312.
6   See Luper 2009: chap. 6. Pitcher 1984 gives a different response to the argument from backwards causation, see 186.
7   See Pitcher 1984: 188; J. Taylor 2005: 314–15.
8   For versions of the argument see Nagel 1979: 3–7; Feinberg 1984: 84–89; Parfit 1984: 495; Pitcher 1984: 185–86; Luper 2004: 69–71; Bellioti 2012: chaps. 3–4. There are other arguments for the possibility of posthumous harm. See, for example, Levenbook 1984: 412–19, and Grover 1989: 336–39.

9   This is the strategy of Partridge 1981: 251–52. The experience require-
    ment is endorsed, and connected with the denial of posthumous harm,
    in Sumner 1996: 126–28 and chap. 6, and Bradley 2009, chap. 1. See also
    the discussion in Bellioti 2012: 10–16.

10 See Sumner 1996: 160.

11 Portmore 2007 argues that the fulfillment of a person's desire can only
    count toward her welfare if the desire is "future-independent" – mean-
    ing that its fulfillment does not depend upon future events, including
    posthumous events; see 29–33. J. Taylor 2005 argues that a person can
    have an interest in distant events for as long as she is alive, but cannot
    have an interest in posthumous events: 316–17.

12 S. Keller 2004: 36.

13 On stupid and evil goals and their relevance to welfare, see S.
    Keller 2004.

14 See S. Keller 2009: 664–65.

12 Life's meaning

Your life has meaning just if, and to the extent that, you achieve the aims that you devote it to freely and competently. You adopt your goals and achieve them more or less through your own efforts, so meaning is something you bestow upon your own life. These achievements are *the* meaning of your life.

In what follows I develop this view.[1] Then I will discuss how life's meaning is related to its purpose and to an individual's welfare and identity. I also examine reasoning that suggests that life is absurd and show how it can be resisted.

MEANING

The achievementist view I am defending is an elaboration of two assumptions. First, the bearer of meaning is not, strictly speaking, a living subject, but rather that subject's *life*. Second, the meaning of one's life concerns what one devotes it *to*. While these assumptions are plausible, they are also strong; they imply, for example, that the lives of nonhuman animals (with some possible exceptions) lack meaning – which is not to say that they lack value, that they are not worthwhile; for reasons offered below, I reject the *value* account of meaning, which equates the meaning and value of a life. Animals may live well; however, animals cannot survey and take a stance on their lives as wholes, which is requisite for turning them to various ends. Nor are animals the only creatures with meaningless lives. Some people live in the moment, lost in *Alltäglichkeit*, and are oblivious to

I thank Stephan Blatti, Iddo Landau, and Steven Campbell for their helpful comments about this chapter.

their existence in its entirety. Such people may set themselves various tasks at various times, such as cooking a tasty meal or having a swim. However, they take no interest in their lives as wholes.

If it is indeed true that lives have meaning by virtue of the accomplishment of the things to which they are devoted, it follows that certain achievements supply the contents of meaning; they are what we are living *for*. They give life direction. Achievements are possible only for those who set themselves tasks, who adopt aims. In aiming, we want to bring about some state of affairs; accomplishing this state of affairs is the object of our aim. For example, if I aim to please you, the object of my aim is *my pleasing you*. To *achieve* is to do something we aim to do. Aims are desires, but not all desires are aims, and meaning cannot be attained through the fulfillment of just any desire. In desiring, we want some state of affairs to obtain, but we may or may not be interested in bringing it about ourselves. Because our survival and the success of our plans depend on it, we all want the sun to keep shining. However, it shines without our assistance; its illumination is no task, hence no aim, of ours. Because I want Seinfeld to amuse me, I might watch his comedy show, but in that case my amusement is the work of Seinfeld. The more passive I am in gaining something I desire, the less it is an achievement of mine. So sunshine and television give no one's life meaning. (Often when we desire something we do so because we think that thing has value: for example, some will say that pleasure's value is what makes us want it, not the other way around – not our wanting it that gives it value. So desire will have instrumental value to the extent that it helps us to acquire a detected good and in proportion to the value of that good. However, an aim is a special kind of desire. If my goal is to write a book, writing the book is prudentially desirable for me precisely because it is my goal. Writing a book has no importance in and of itself, but, for those who set out to do it, it is important to succeed.)

Devoting life to some task or tasks is a rather solemn matter that we undertake only after we are well on in our days. Even before then we probably will have begun to develop a life-plan, which is simply a plan, however inchoate and prospective, for how our life is to go. We find ourselves doing various things and planning to do other things. If we are prudent, we begin to think about the shape of our life. Our ideas are initially quite sketchy and incomplete; we revise our plan over time, taking into account our evolving grasp of our nature and place in the world. For a good while we regard the plan as a work under construction, whose components are subject to revision. At some point we may take a further step, and reach some decision about what we want our life as a whole to accomplish, about what we are to live for. These are the aims that constitute the meaning of life.

Not everyone will develop a life-plan; those who do plan their lives may not decide to devote them to anything. There is nothing inevitable about either sort of planning. I might add that while anyone who sets out to give her life meaning will have some sort of plan for doing so, her planning could end there – it might be more or less limited to achieving the aim that would confer meaning. Chances are, however, that people who care about meaning will not have such a truncated plan; they will have concerns other than the meaning-conferring tasks they set themselves, and much of their planning will concern these other matters. They might, for example, endeavor to spend their days agreeably, and take elaborate steps to preserve their health. They might also fret about advancing their careers, even if their work is devoid of meaning, and undertaken solely for the money they need to survive. Just about all of us do a great many things that do not contribute to the meaning of life, and can partition our plans for life into a component that bears on meaning, and another that does not. No doubt there also will be parts that are difficult to classify. Still, a plan to accomplish meaning-conferring aims is not identical to a plan for how a life is to go.

Because the bearer of meaning is a life, and meaning-conferring aims determine what that life is for, it is best to regard meaning as a global good: a good that, in the fullest sense, only entire lives admit of (Luper 2012b). However, the production of a global good can hinge on things we do at various points in life. Doubtless we will want to accomplish some aims that bear on meaning in accordance with a schedule of sorts. For example, an athlete will want to make his mark during early adulthood. The aims of some of us will be free-floating; we may want to do certain things before life ends, and find ourselves indifferent about when we get them done. In that case, during our middle years, we might find ourselves worried about the trajectory we are on, and whether we will be able to finish what we have taken on.

It may seem plausible to say that meaning is determined only by aims that are *outwardly* directed – not narrowly focused on the person who bears them – on the grounds that meaning relates a life to something outside it, something that transcends it (Nozick 1981: chap. 6). However, I see no compelling reason to take this view. Other things being equal (and with some qualifications), any aim we devote life to suffices, including the narcissistic desire to be a movie star.

I said that meaning concerns one's accomplishments but also what one is living for. These suggestions may appear to clash, since pursuits and accomplishments need not coincide: some people spend a great deal of time pursuing aims which they never achieve. Aims motivate them to accomplish things even if they never succeed. However, there is no conflict here. It is misleading to say that people's *pursuits* are what they are living for, and we should reject the teleological account of meaning (discussed in P. Quinn 1997) which equates meaning with the pursuit of aims. On the teleological account, it would not matter to people that their aims are unattainable, yet it plainly does. They *pursue* their aims in order to *achieve* them, and attain meaning only when they achieve, not merely pursue, their aims. Nevertheless, it is possible to take on a pursuit *as* an aim: one might opt to devote one's time to looking for a new species, for example, which does not require actually finding one. One's aim might be to learn about horticulture, which might keep one busy for a lifetime, yet does not require reaching any particular level of mastery.

To flesh out the achievementist view of meaning, we can relate meaning to other, closely related, notions. We can begin with the relationship between meaning and purpose.

PURPOSE

Having meaning entails having and achieving a purpose, but we should be cautious about how we understand such things. It can be tempting to assume that the point (purpose) of something must be another thing that has its own point. In that case having a purpose seems to require being part of an endless chain, each link of which gains its point from the next; otherwise, it ends with something pointless – something that is anchorless and incapable of supporting anything. It is hard to believe that such chains exist, so this reasoning suggests that nothing has a point, and hence nothing has meaning. However, this reasoning goes wrong from the start. One thing can be the point of another without having a point beyond itself (Luper 1992). I do many things because I love my wife; the latter has no point beyond itself.

It is best to say that ends (or aims) just *are* purposes, and that anything else acquires a purpose (possibly more than one) insofar as it is the means to someone's ends. That is true of small items, like pens, and it would also be true of the entire universe. On this view, one's life's meaning gives it a purpose: the accomplishment of the aims one sets oneself.

So we can give our own life a purpose, and do so when we give it meaning. Can we do the same for other lives as well? Can God do so? The answer is not straightforward.

When we use something, say a sled dog, to one of our ends, irrespective of its own ends if any, it is our tool. We use animals and mere objects, such as shovels, but these are not the only tools. It is possible for others to use *us* as the means to their ends or, in the extreme case, as slaves. However, this affronts us, because we are autonomous beings who set our own ends. We resist if others attempt to set ends for us. These reflections can seem to support the assumption that only self-given purposes are worth having and are consistent with meaning. Reasoning like this appears to have inspired Kurt Baier's (1957) well-known critique of Christianity. According to Baier, Christianity tells us that God gives life its purpose, but in that case Christians aspire to be tools – God's tools, but tools nonetheless.

Of course Baier's conclusion is easily challenged. When we use mere objects such as bananas solely as the means to our ends, we do not care about them for *their* sakes; it would make no sense to do so: only a lunatic cares about a banana for *its* sake. However, we should not overlook the possibility of being used by an agent, even a creator, who *does* care about us for our sake. Someone who is concerned about us might want something of us *for* our sake. This is incompatible with condemning us to spend eternity in an abortive attempt to roll a rock up a hill, as Zeus did to Sisyphus, but it is surely compatible with much that occurs in the context of loving relationships.

Others need not treat us as tools when they involve us in their plans, even though they are, in a sense, using us. It is not demeaning to be used by one who cares about us for our sakes; quite the contrary. Such people will want us to help them only in ways that we want to help. The importance of being valued for our own sake – by others we value for their sake – makes us want to be useful to those who take this same attitude towards us. Such people may plan their lives together, each creating a role for the other, because that is what both want.

What seems important about purpose is this: we create purpose when we set ourselves goals and devote our lives to some of these; the result is meaning. Relative to these goals, our acts take on importance; goals create significance for us. But these things need not be done in solitude. If you care about me for my sake and vice versa, together we can create and adopt plans that give purpose and meaning to the lives of both of us. Each one of us is the gatekeeper to his life's meaning, in that the aims of others will have no bearing on the meaning of his own life unless he so chooses. Nor can anyone else accomplish my aims. But together we can accomplish *our* aims.

IDENTITY

Many say that having meaning gives us an identity; however, this is to speak loosely about identity. As identity is understood by most philosophers, meaning has no bearing on it. Nevertheless, it is worth asking what we might mean by 'identity' to make us think that it is bound up intimately with meaning.

Many things persist over time, yet change in various ways; philosophers who ask about identity are looking for the conditions under which a thing existing at one time is *numerically* identical to a thing existing at another time. The answer presumably will vary depending on the sort of thing at hand. In my case, what is wanted are the conditions under which I, who exist now, am identical to someone existing at some other time.

Instead of associating the term 'identity' with properties that are necessary and sufficient for our continued existence, we might instead associate it with some of the properties that bear on whether we *want* to exist. Some features we want to retain; others we wish to acquire. Let us say that something is a *critical feature* just if the discovery that we have irretrievably lost it, or that we will never acquire it, would leave us indifferent about survival. We might say that a person's critical features constitute her *critical identity*, or *critical self*.

One of the ways in which we shape the critical self is by opting to live for something, assuming that success at this task will be one of our critical features. What individuals live for we might call their *conative* identities, or the *conative self*. To take on a conative self is to pursue meaning; it is in this way that identity is related to meaning. Yet the conative self is only one component of the critical self. Another may be the *moral self*, assuming that it is of critical importance to us that our conduct conform to certain principles. These components of the critical self must be shaped so that they are mutually compatible, or else its integrity may break down.

Critical identities differ greatly from numerical identities. First, I cannot possibly exist for a while then gain my numerical identity. Nothing can. Yet I might well exist for a time before I acquire a critical identity. Second, it is possible not to have a critical identity, or to lose and even replace the one I once had: I might, as it were, live for one thing, then be 'reborn' and live for something else. Yet I cannot lose my numerical identity and live on; I will exist only as long as I am numerically identical to someone in the future. Third, numerical identities cannot fail to be unique-making; no one else can share my numerical identity. However, while I might regard at least some of the features in my critical identity as unique-making, as setting me off from others, there is no special reason why I should take this view. Indeed, I might be happy in the thought that many people have a critical identity that is like the one I have adopted. Also, others might well be entangled with me, as their continued existence, or the continued existence of my relationship with them, might be implicated in my critical identity.

I said that we can survive the loss of our critical identity. However, this loss will *present* itself, phenomenologically, as tantamount to non-existence. Consider conative identity in particular. If we devote life to some aim, we may survive failure but the remaining person and her life will be of no concern to us. What is at stake is whether we continue to have a stake in life. Indeed, what I have said probably puts things too mildly; the catastrophic failure I have in mind may not leave us merely indifferent about life, it may lead us to deplore life, given the great evil that a failed quest for meaning constitutes. Something similar might result if we are unable to satisfy the demands we make on ourselves as moral beings.

WELFARE

Meaning is not the same thing as welfare (that is, well-being), and neither is the same thing as happiness as it is typically understood. Let us see whether we can clarify the relationship between the three.

What constitutes happiness is itself a disputed matter; instead of delving into that controversy, let us adopt a view that a great many theorists would accept, namely, that how happy we are, at a time or over a period of time, is determined by the amount of pleasure (or positive states of mind) we have then, which is a positive quantity, added to the amount of pain (or negative mental states) we have then, a negative quantity. Our *lifetime* happiness level is that sum over the entirety of life. By contrast, let us say that our lifetime *success* level is determined by the degree to which we achieve the aims to which we have devoted life. Achieving these aims boosts our success level while our failures lower it.

Happiness is one element of welfare: other things being equal, the happier, the better off we are. However, there is more to welfare than this. How well off we are is determined by our portion of *all* of the things which are intrinsically good or bad for us. While pleasure is one of the things that we value for its own sake, it is not the only thing. It is also plausible to count certain achievements among these goods, and certain failures among the evils. If that is so, then presumably the achievement of our meaning-conferring aims will count among the goods, and failure among the evils. Hence both happiness and success boost welfare. And there may well be other goods as well, such as loving relationships. How well off we are (over some time) is determined roughly by the sum of the goods and evils we incur (during that time).

So meaning is success, which is itself a species of welfare. But while meaning is an element of welfare, it is not the whole of it.

Meaning differs from other elements of welfare in an important respect: it is not summative. Contrast pleasure. Other things being equal, the more days a person spends pleasantly, the more pleasant her life is as a whole. Each boost in pleasure is a boost in her overall level of happiness. Meaning does not behave this way. It is true that meaning consists in achieving the aims we take on and these achievements are summative after a fashion: other things equal, it is better to achieve all of our aims than it is to achieve only some of them. However, we establish the entirety of what constitutes life's meaning by taking on the relevant aims; if we adopt only one aim, achieving only one aim gives life its full component of meaning. From the standpoint of life's meaning, achieving more things is not in itself better than achieving fewer things; if we take on only five tasks, only five achievements bear on life's meaning.

According to achievementism, meaning and well-being can easily diverge. At least in theory, a life might be good for us yet devoid of meaning, and a life might have meaning yet be, on the whole, quite bad.

The first point – a life may be good yet devoid of meaning – is in part a consequence of the fact that we might never feel the void that prompts people such as Tolstoy to yearn for meaning. We might instead focus on happiness – or on nothing. It is possible to accrue goods such as happiness even without seeking them out. The acquisition might be the result of dumb luck, or a benefactor's benign manipulation.

However, while it is conceivable for the lives of human beings to be good yet devoid of meaning, this possibility seems remote, because meaning is more important to us than other things that make for well-being, such as happiness, so we prioritize the quest for meaning, and because a fruitful source of happiness is meaning. Or at least this is true of most people, most of the time.

Consider the relative importance of meaning. To restate J. S. Mill's famous remark about pleasures, some goods are higher than others. To see that this is the case, consider Robert Nozick's (1974: 42–45) thought experiment in which we are offered the chance to spend our lives hooked up to an experience machine that will give us all the pleasure we can handle. It will also give us a high welfare level, because great happiness makes for high welfare. Yet no one (or very few) would accept the offer. This is best explained by two facts. First, life in the machine has (little or) no meaning, as we *accomplish* none or vanishingly few of the goals we have set ourselves. Of course, on one version of Nozick's fantasy we do not really even set goals for ourselves: even goal setting is part of the manipulation performed upon us, which makes meaning entirely impossible. Second, meaning is far and away more important to us than the happiness which the machine provides.

The experience machine suggests that happiness matters very little as compared to meaning. In fact, it suggests that except perhaps in extreme cases, meaning trumps happiness, in this sense: normally, if we must choose between the two, we will sacrifice happiness in order to give meaning to our lives, and it is best for us to do so. Unless we attain *some* minimal amount of enjoyment from time to time we might well fall into depression, and lose our interest in life altogether (Metz 2009: 5); that said, we will endure hardship indefinitely when meaning is at stake, and rightly so. The integrity of the conative self requires it. (One might argue that, from the moral point of view, it is the conative self, and its defining commitments, that matters, or matters most, but I will not pursue the matter here.)

Indeed, as Mill (1873) discovered, striving for happiness is largely self-defeating, while striving to accomplish things we regard as worth doing leads to happiness as a side-effect. (*Pace* Aristotle, it is best not to strive for *all* of the things that are worth having.) So it is impractical to plan life exclusively around achieving happiness or well-being via happiness. The better course is to put happiness aside and focus on the tasks to which we have devoted life. Typically, accomplishing these is a highly productive source of happiness.

Because meaning is usually a fertile source of happiness, it is unlikely that a life of meaning will be bad for us on the whole. Nevertheless, competent people can seriously neglect their own welfare. Suppose that, in laying out our aspirations for life, we do not seek loving relationships, so that, for us, the achievement of meaning does not require love. If loving relationships are good for us, missing out on them probably will mean that our welfare level will be lower than it might have been. The same goes for any good: a life that lacks goods is worse than it might have been but its meaning is not affected unless those goods are sought out. Similarly for evils: we worsen life by adding to the evils within it, but its meaning is not affected thereby unless we seek to avoid them.

Apparently, then, a plan that is capable of conferring meaning may nevertheless have serious defects. If I devote myself largely to dull or repetitive tasks, such as pushing rocks or counting blades of grass, I might well achieve meaning, yet live a greatly impoverished existence, and forgo goods which I would have attained as the result of a more ambitious, or better-designed, plan. At a minimum I will be less happy, assuming that success with richer and more robust aims brings greater happiness. I might also end up loveless. Consider, too, that if I ignore my obligations I will be immoral. Conceivably, even a morally neutral project, such as moving to Tahiti to paint, as Paul Gauguin did, can put me at odds with morality – by leading me to neglect my responsibilities (Williams 1979). So a life could have its full measure of meaning yet be barren and incomplete, even evil (cf. Edwards 1967: 125). To build a life with any of these defects – knowingly, and with full access to richer alternatives – would be madness.

ABSURDITY

The view that lives can have meaning is subject to grave challenges. If these cannot be met, we will have to conclude that life is meaningless or absurd. At that point we might attempt to make a virtue of life's absurdity, as Camus suggested (1955; cf. Thomas Nagel 1970), or reconcile ourselves to it, as Qoheleth advised. But I do not think we should accept such counsel, as the challenges can be met. Or so I will argue.

One concern confronts those of us who are struck by how precarious, how prone to failure, our plans are. If we live in a dangerous place and cannot escape, we might conclude that setting ourselves aims is futile, and that happiness is an unrealistic expectation, as we cannot be confident that death or some other peril will not destroy the things we care about, and abort our efforts to achieve our ends. Carried to an extreme, this line of thought may lead us to despair of giving life meaning. This, the problem of precariousness, is exacerbated by the problem of evil: the fact that, at some point in life, we almost certainly will face dire adversity that we simply do not deserve.

It is true that sufficiently grave misfortune will preclude our attaining happiness or meaning. The point is illustrated by the fate of the infants who were caught up in and entombed by the lava flow-ing from Mount Vesuvius in AD 79. However, as many theorists in the ancient world pointed out (Gautama, Epicurus, and Stoics, among others), even when confronted with adversity we are free to set our-selves tasks that fit the span of time we can expect and the powers nature has allotted us. Such plans will be modest as compared to what we might take on in more favorable times. If we are nomads roaming a desert wasteland, it may take all of our energy just to keep ourselves and our loved ones nourished and protected from the elements. Somewhat like Stoics, we may have to retreat to the inner citadel. Yet success, even at modest goals, gives life meaning, and happiness is likely to follow. Because meaning turns on the aims we actually set ourselves, the brevity of life and the paucity of our undertakings need not detract from the meaning we give to life.

So accepting achievementism helps us to respond to the problem of precariousness, as lower, more reasonable ambitions are consist-ent with meaning. But a worrisome question arises at this point: how low can we go before we miss out on meaning altogether? In his well-known essay "The Meaning of Life" Richard Taylor argued that triviality is consistent with meaning even though triviality features large in paradigm cases of absurdity or meaninglessness, such as that of Sisyphus (1970: chap. 18; but contrast 1987: 679, where Taylor says meaning results only from novel creations). What Sisyphus did amounted to nothing; it had no lasting value; in Taylor's version of the myth, what Sisyphus did was not even voluntary; nevertheless, Taylor said that if Zeus had made Sisyphus *want* to push his rock, he might have accrued meaning. Achievementists would reject that claim, but they would say that, in theory, a life may attain meaning by being *freely* devoted to something, even something as insignifi-cant as rock pushing. But is that plausible? Or does meaning accrue only to those whose achievements are, by some independent meas-ure, important? Plenty of people take the latter view; for example, John Cottingham (2003: 21) claims that accomplishments that suf-fice for meaning must be weighty, and Susan Wolf (2000) says that meaning-conferring accomplishments must have objective value, not the mere subjective value we bestow upon the things that we want (according to her).

I suggest that the achievementist claim – theoretically, people may achieve meaning by devoting life to trivial tasks – *is* plausible.

Those who deny it may have various grounds for doing so, but I suspect that the main source of doubt is the idea that something that is entirely independent of people's choices determines what their lives are for, what their purpose is. Assuming that a life's meaning is bound up with its purpose, this externalist picture implies that meaning is attained only by lives that serve their *actual*, independently given, purpose. Since serving this purpose is the one and only way lives can attain meaning, it sets the standard, including the standard for how important an achievement must be to confer meaning. However, externalism is difficult to defend, and if we reject it, it is hard to see why we should think that, to confer meaning, achievements must score well as assessed by some independent measure of importance. Certainly no such thing is true if one's life has just that purpose and meaning which one gives to it, as achievementism implies. The value to be had in meaning is prudential; accomplishing what we have devoted life to is good for us, good in and of itself, regardless of the contents of the goals we have set, and their value by any independent measure.

Nevertheless, meaning-conferring aims partly constitute the critical self. They are adopted as the very point of life, and not just any aims are fitting given the gravity of the role they are to play. While not impossible, it would be odd in the extreme to select something patently silly to fill this role. People who take themselves seriously enough to decide what to live for will not devote themselves to endeavors they consider to be ridiculous, any more than they would wear a clown suit to the funeral of a cherished parent, or construct marriage vows in the form of a bawdy limerick.

The view that life is absurd can arise in another, related way: as Socrates did, we might wish to live on endlessly, engaging ourselves in matters of eternal significance. We may also want to *have* lived forever – to exist without a beginning. We may not be satisfied unless non-existence is *impossible* for us. With limitless time at our disposal, our accomplishments might span eons. By contrast, the existence and deeds of a contingent, merely mortal being will seem ephemeral and inconsequential, perhaps even entirely devoid of meaning or any other sort of value. If we then come to have doubts about living forever, there is a good chance that we will retain some residue of our contempt for the all-too-brief lives of ordinary mortals. As William Craig (1994) wrote (paraphrasing Sartre's "The

Wall"), "several hours or several years make no difference once you have lost eternity." This is the problem of finitude. Some who find themselves in this predicament will attempt escape by cultivating the conviction that they will live forever. However, many will end up as Tolstoy (1884) and Unamuno (1954) did, vacillating between hope and despair: hope for a place in eternity, and despair at the thought that, since nothing transient has meaning, life is absurd.

It is true that immortals can do much, much more than mortals, and their lives can be immeasurably better (and also incalculably worse) than the lives of mortals. However, despair is unjustified, even for those who yearn for an endless life they do not expect to have. The brilliant vision of eternity should not blind us to the poignant beauty and charm of the transient things that make up the lives of mortals, and in one profound respect immortals may be no better off than mortals: the lives of both may have meaning in the fullest sense of the word. Because meaning consists in achieving what we are living for, and mortals and immortals alike can be fully successful with the plans they lay out for themselves, assuming that these are not overreaching, then mortality is no bar to meaning.

In this respect meaning is unlike happiness and well-being itself. If life is too brief, no plan can be conceived and achieved, but once that minimal lifespan is exceeded, we can accommodate a life of any duration without loss of meaning. Long or short, one's life can have meaning in the fullest sense (just as, large or small, one's house can be fully yellow). However, length of life greatly affects how much happiness one attains. Other things being equal, under favorable circumstances one will achieve far more happiness over the course of a very long life than one will during a brief life; the same goes for welfare, of which happiness is one component.

Mortality can foster despair for another reason: we might believe that the perspective we expect to end up with is authoritative in the assessment of life as a whole, and also that, looking back, our assessment will not be favorable. Once we have reached our final hours, when the indignities of aging have taken their toll, and death is no longer a distant abstraction, there is an excellent chance that we will be consumed by grief, and that we will be unable to affirm life, no matter how good it once seemed to us. But to think that our lives have precisely the meaning and value which we will attribute to them in *that* state of mind is a mistake. We are encouraged to make this error by the familiar fact that usually our most accurate assessments are done with the benefit of hindsight, which might lead us to think that life's most important features are those that will be important to us at its end; that, in turn, will shift our center of gravity and degrade life into "being-towards-death," to use Martin Heidegger's morose expression. (Worse: we might come to think, absurdly, that life's meaning and value just is the value *of* the brief segment of life which we spend on our deathbed – that no matter what life was like, it is no better than it is at its end.) It is true that hindsight often helps us to assess an accomplishment. Yet so does foresight, especially the ability to anticipate how things will strike us in the future. With time, our perspective on life will shift; we must use the best judgment we have at *each* stage, both to assess and to learn from what we have done in the past, to apply what we have learned when looking ahead, and to anticipate how we will see life when we are older, so that we do not have to alter our plan later. We defer to our future judgment, but we do so on the assumption that we will still be fully competent to assess life as a whole, and will heed what was important to us now.

If one wishes, one may choose for one's life a meaning that transcends its temporal limits. One might live, wholly or in part, for things that one leaves incomplete at death, such as the garden one is cultivating, or the research project one is advancing. This is possible because we can fulfill, while we are alive, aims whose achievement depends on events that occur only after we are dead (Luper 2012a). While alive, I can take on, achieve, and benefit from an aim whose fulfillment requires many things to happen after I am gone. But of course there is a tradeoff to consider: if we devote ourselves to something that transcends life, we have even less control over life's meaning, and that is something we might resist, given that meaning is more important to us than happiness, and perhaps even life, itself.

NOTES

1   It has its origins in the work of Jean-Paul Sartre and, as Andrea Staiti pointed out to me, Edmund Husserl (see Staiti 2013).

Part III The ethics of life and death

13 Enhancing humanity

According to a traditional view, the philosophical investigation of human enhancement leads to one of two straightforward conclusions. It's either right to enhance humans or wrong to do so. Enhancement's proponents defend it for a propensity to promote human well-being or because a ban would restrict liberty. Its most radical advocates hope for improvements of our physical and psychological capacities of such magnitude and variety that we will no longer be human. They think that we will come to view the traits that make us human as handicapping our development as a species. For the members of this group, human enhancement is good. Enhancement's opponents – sometimes labeled bioconservatives – seek to counter its appeal by pointing to values wedded to our humanity that are infringed by enhancement. According to them, societies that encourage or permit human enhancement will manifest dangerous inequalities. For these bioconservatives, human enhancement is bad.

This chapter surveys and selectively samples from contemporary moral debates about human enhancement. It seeks to reveal some of the philosophical complexity obscured by the traditional dialectic. Proposed human enhancements are hugely varied in the means by which they may be achieved, in the human capacities that are their targets, and in the degree to which they enhance. Four philosophically disparate cases of human enhancement are the disgraced Tour de France cyclist Lance Armstrong's use of synthetic erythropoietin (EPO) to enhance his sporting performances, the Hungarian educational psychologist László Polgár's program of extended deliberate practice that turned his three daughters into chess masters, the manipulation of genes that influence human intelligence, and a recent suggestion that we use selected pharmaceuticals to enhance our moral motivations and thereby avoid extinction by climate change.

There is no one-size-fits-all answer to questions about the morality of enhancing humans. We should acknowledge three dimensions along which human enhancements vary – the means of enhancement, the capacities that are targets of enhancement, and degrees of enhancement. I will argue that differences along these dimensions suggest different moral verdicts. I illustrate the varying moral significance of these considerations by discussing a selection of contemporary moral debates about enhancing humans. As I do so I indicate what I take to be the best way to navigate between values supportive of human enhancement, on the one hand, and values that tend to oppose it, on the other.

A SIMPLE DEFINITION OF ENHANCEMENT AND A REQUIREMENT FOR MORAL CONSISTENCY

Philosophers struggle to find a consensus on how enhancement should be defined. In this discussion I take as my starting point a very inclusive definition of human enhancement that identifies enhancement with improvement. According to this definition, one enhances a human capacity by improving it. If the acquisition of an additional ten IQ points counts as a cognitive improvement then a pill that produces this effect is a cognitive enhancer. The reference point here is the level of the given ability either before or without the administration of the putative enhancer.

Philosophers were initially drawn to the issue of enhancement by the unsettling possibilities suggested by the new genetics. We now know of many variations in human genes that make a difference to human attributes such as intelligence, athletic ability, and longevity. We may soon be able to alter human genomes in ways that predictably improve intelligence, athletic ability, or longevity. A definition of enhancement as improvement may seem a poor choice for those interested in exposing the dangers of genetic enhancement. It obscures what seem to be quite significant moral differences among ways of improving humans. Insulin injected by diabetics improves their health; it would, so long as we define enhancement as improvement, be a human enhancer. If human enhancement is human improvement then we enhance our children's intelligence by teaching them how to solve jigsaw puzzles. A definition of enhancement as improvement groups these ways of altering humans together with the modification of genes which influence intelligence and the implanting in human brains of electronic chips.

The ubiquity of human enhancement as improvement does not prevent us from morally distinguishing some ways of enhancing humans from others. But it does suggest a need for consistency among our moral assessments. We should draw similar moral conclusions about relevantly similar human enhancements. I propose that we subject our judgments about human enhancement to what I will call the enhancement consistency test.

> *The enhancement consistency test:* Suppose that we deem a given human enhancement to be morally good (or bad). We should say the same of similar enhancements. If not, we should make clear why the particular respects in which the enhancements differ justify differences in moral assessment.

In what follows I demonstrate three ways to apply the enhancement consistency test to human enhancements. These correspond to three ways in which enhancements can vary. I apply the test to suggestions that differences in the means of enhancement, differences in the capacities that are targets of enhancement, and different degrees of enhancement warrant different moral evaluations.

DIFFERENT MEANS OF HUMAN ENHANCEMENT

The means by which humans can be enhanced range from the traditional – the cognitive enhancements resulting from schooling and physical enhancements produced by exercise programs – through the somewhat futuristic – the genetic modification of genes that influence human capacities – to the truly outlandish – the attachment of cybernetic implants to our brains and bodies. Some may question whether attaching a cybernetic implant alters a human being rather than equipping her with a tool. The worry here is that if implants are tools rather than alterations, then they cannot be human enhancements. But if titanium hip replacements are properly seen as modifications of bodies then there should be no problem in accepting cybernetic implants as alterations of human brains or bodies. Viewed in this way, they can be human enhancements.

One way to apply the enhancement consistency test to these varied means of enhancement directs attention toward their consequences. According to this view, if different means produce the same results they should be morally evaluated similarly.

For example, John Harris (1998) compares educational and genetic enhancements. He imagines a school that "set out deliberately to improve the mental and physical capacities of its students ... its stated aims were to ensure that the pupils left the school not only more intelligent and more physically fit than when they arrived, but more intelligent and more physically fit than they would be at any other school" (Harris 1998: 171). This seems to be exactly what we would hope for from our schools. Harris then asks us to "entertain conjecture of a different sort of breakthrough with the same or comparable consequences and suppose the new biotechnological procedures could engineer into the human embryo characteristics which would make highly probable the expression of adult phenotypes like build, height, and even intelligence and could even reduce susceptibility to disease" (Harris 1998: 172). There seems, in terms of results, little to separate the two scenarios. Harris invites us to conclude that if the former is good then so should be the latter.

This kind of argument should endorse means of enhancement still more outlandish than genetic engineering. The traditional way to acquire an understanding of calculus is by study. Another way might be to attach to your brain a calculus neuroprosthesis – an electronic chip programmed to perform calculus. The neuroprosthesis would perform calculus and then convey its answers to the appropriate parts of your biological brain. A consequentialist presentation of consistency suggests that if these different means arrive at the same result – a capacity to perform calculus – then we should evaluate them similarly.

As with many claims for similar moral evaluation on the basis of similar consequences, this challenges common sense. Common sense finds a difference between *natural* ways of acquiring mathematical understanding – for example, those involving education – and *unnatural* ways including the modification of genes and the implanting of neuroprostheses. It endorses the former but treats the latter as sinister or at least suspicious.

Philosophical appeals to nature are notoriously problematic. First, the distinction between the natural and the artificial is vexed. We take technological objects to be paradigm cases of unnatural things. But they are really just different arrangements of nature from the arrangements that constitute paradigmatically natural rivers, mountains, or biological human brains. Second, many unnatural things are both good and indispensable parts of human lives. If you're reading this passage with the aid of spectacles you should not be bullied by allegations of unnaturalness into removing them.

We cannot make sense of appeals to nature as supporting a general rejection of human enhancement. But this does not prevent more philosophically modest appeals to nature as part of an argument against certain varieties of human enhancement. I think that such appeals can make sense in the context of elite sports.

Many who marveled at Lance Armstrong's performances in the Tour de France were deeply disappointed when it was revealed that he had frequently injected synthetic EPO to boost his body's supply of red blood cells. One way to express this popular disapproval is as a rejection of unnatural enhancers including synthetic EPO. Elite sports are venues for enhanced performances, but these performances must be achieved by measures focused on intensive physical and mental training, and healthy diets. We tend to view these as natural ways to achieve sporting success.

This reaction puzzles Julian Savulescu and his co-authors, who call for consistency about the consequences of the many ways in which athletes improve endurance. They say: "There is no difference between elevating your blood count by altitude training, by using a hypoxic air machine [a machine that boosts the percentage of red blood cells by simulating training at high altitudes], or by taking EPO. But the last is illegal. Some competitors have high HCTs [the HCT, or hematocrit, is a measure of blood's percentage, by volume, of red blood cells] and an advantage by luck. Some can afford hypoxic air machines" (Savulescu *et al.* 2004: 668). According to Savulescu *et al.*, we should consider both natural and unnatural performance enhancers in terms of their propensity to safely enhance athletic performance. If a performance enhancer poses an undue threat to health, it should be banned regardless of whether it is natural or unnatural. If it does not, then it should be endorsed without regard to its naturalness or unnaturalness.

One response to this application of the enhancement consistency test can be inferred from popular reaction to Armstrong's use of EPO. A belief in the naturalness of performances is a significant contributor to our interest in the Tour de France. We don't follow top-level cycling in the belief that there is something *objectively* superior about its performances. We know of many machines that could cover the Tour de France's 3,200 kilometers much faster than the fastest human cyclist, EPO-enhanced or not. Human spectators take an interest in the Tour because of a perceived relevance of its performances to them – a relevance lacked by planes, trains, and automobiles. When we watch elite sport, we have the opportunity to imagine ourselves as supremely fit athletes competing for glory. Unnatural means of athletic enhancement are barriers to this imaginative identification. The terms "natural" and "unnatural" in this context need carry no mystical or deep metaphysical significance. Natural means are those readily available to the audiences of elite sports. Unnatural means are either unavailable or unappealing. We accept that heroes of the Tour are more dedicated than casual weekend cyclists. We accept that they may have been born with various genetic advantages. We factor these traditional differences into our attempts at imaginative identification. But, these differences notwithstanding, when we turn on the TV to watch the Tour de France we expect to see people doing something that is, in essence, similar to what we do when we get on a bike. Weekend cyclists don't inject EPO. And, if he wants to retain the interest of weekend cyclists, neither should Lance Armstrong.

This distinction does, to a certain extent, depend on a naïvety about elite sport. There are a multitude of differences between Armstrong and amateur cyclists, many of which spectators choose to overlook. But a gap between the reality of the Tour de France and the naïve conception that deliberately obscures the difference between the professionals and the amateurs is no barrier to the naïve conception serving as an ideal that explains and justifies our interest in elite sport. Compare. We like to think of our political leaders as honest. The fact that this conception is at variance with reality does not prevent it from serving as an ideal against which to judge the behavior of politicians. We can judge politicians who approximate more closely to the ideal of honesty as better, at least in this respect, than others.

This is not to say that there is anything objectively wrong with elite performances produced by pharmaceutical, genetic, or cybernetic means. These performances should be very appealing and relevant to audiences whose members are pharmaceutically, genetically, or cybernetically enhanced. We are interested in natural performances simply because these are the conditions under which we run, cycle, or play tennis. We are entitled to place greater value on the performances whose conditions are similar to the conditions of our own. We have a bias toward natural forms of athletic enhancement simply because these are the modes of enhancement that we hope may improve our own sporting experiences – our own evening bicycle rides and weekend tennis matches. Even those who do not ride bikes or play tennis have some insight into the conditions that generate exceptional performances in these sports. This view would predict a greater interest in sports that emphasize activities with which many of us have some basic familiarity. Running, jumping, catching, and throwing are activities of which almost all of us have some awareness. It's not surprising that they are of central importance in the world's most popular sports.

Note the limited scope of this appeal to nature. It explains a preference for natural means of enhancement in elite sport. But it would not justify rejecting synthetic EPO as a means of enhancing the abilities of mountain rescuers, for example. Those sent to recover people in Everest's death zone do not perform their rescues for audiences who seek to imaginatively identify with them.

DIFFERENT TARGETS OF ENHANCEMENT

Many human capacities are candidates for enhancement. Metaphysicians have long given mental and physical properties of human beings separate philosophical treatment. Does the enhancement consistency test permit us to treat proposals to enhance mental characteristics of human beings differently from proposals to enhance physical characteristics? Or do all proposals to enhance human traits deserve similar treatment?

One way to respond to the enhancement consistency test in respect of the capacities that are the targets of enhancement, points to the differing social consequences of enhancing mental and physical capacities. In our age, cognitive differences have a greater

impact on success than do differences in physical ability. Many philosophers have expressed concerns about cognitive enhancement's
consequences for equality. If the rich are able to purchase cognitive enhancements unavailable to the poor then we should see a
widening of the gap that already exists as a result of educational
differences.

There are more and less extreme ways to object to cognitive
enhancement's propensity for polarization. Francis Fukuyama fears
a systematic exploitation of the unenhanced by the enhanced. He
cites Thomas Jefferson's assertion that "the mass of mankind has
not been born with saddles on their backs, nor a favored few booted
and spurred, ready to ride them legitimately, by the grace of God."
Fukuyama asks, "what will happen to political rights once we are
able to, in effect, breed some people with saddles on their backs, and
others with boots and spurs?" (Fukuyama 2002: 10). The deliberate
breeding of servant classes is a recurring feature of science fiction
accounts of the future made by advances in human genetics. For
example, in Aldous Huxley's *Brave New World* a deliberately bred
servant class of Epsilons caters to the needs of their Alpha cognitive
superiors.

The liberal context of some defenses of human genetic enhancement seems to preclude this scenario. The deliberate breeding of a
slave class of humans is incompatible with a morally mandatory
concern for children's welfare. Liberal approaches to education place
restrictions on how we can educate our children. We are not permitted to choose educational options that predictably harm them.
Similar restrictions should apply to plans to genetically enhance
children. It would be incompatible with a regard for a future child's
well-being to deliberately design into it the central characteristics
of a *Brave New World* Epsilon.

This liberal response leaves some legitimate concerns unad-
dressed. It may be morally impermissible to deliberately "breed
some people with saddles on their backs." But the enhancement of
some may leave the unenhanced with no truly viable option but to
accept the placement of saddles.

Allen Buchanan has explored implications of enhancements for
a society's dominant cooperative framework. A society's dominant
cooperative framework sets conditions for participation in important political processes and the mainstream economy. Basic literacy

and numeracy are conditions for meaningful participation in the political process and economies of early twenty-first-century liberal democracies. Buchanan fears for a future in which "the mainstream economy and the most important political processes are structured for enhanced cooperators. The result is that the unenhanced in effect become disabled: they are unable to participate, or unable to participate in a minimally competent way, in core economic and political processes that are designed for beings with quite different capacities" (Buchanan 2009: 372–73). The apparently self-regarding decision to enhance your own cognitive powers or the decision to enhance the cognitive powers of your children can have dire consequences for others.

Recently philosophers have become interested in the eligibility for enhancement of the human capacity for moral evaluation and action. This capacity has the potential to promote moral outcomes rather than acting against them. Thomas Douglas (2008) imagines biomedical interventions that give us morally better motives by modulating counter-moral emotions, those emotions that interfere with moral reasoning, sympathy, other morally good forms of thought. These counter-moral emotions include triggers of impulsive violent aggression and of racism. Douglas presents the evident goodness of interventions that make us less violent or racist as a counterexample to what he calls the bioconservative thesis according to which no biomedical enhancement is morally permissible. If moral bioenhancement is permissible then it follows that the bioconservative thesis must be false.

Ingmar Persson and Julian Savulescu offer a more emphatic endorsement of what they call moral bioenhancement. Moral bioenhancement makes use of "pharmacological and genetic methods, like genetic selection and engineering" (Persson and Savulescu 2012: 2) to improve moral motivation. They say: "Modern scientific technology provides us with many means that could cause our downfall. If we are to avoid causing catastrophe by misguided employment of these means, we need to be morally motivated to a higher degree" (Persson and Savulescu 2012: 8). They present moral bioenhancement as required to avoid Ultimate Harm, an event that would make "worthwhile life *forever* impossible on this planet" (Persson and Savulescu 2012: 46). The instrument of Ultimate Harm that features most prominently in their discussion is the climate crisis.

We have an urgent need for enhanced capacities for sympathy and justice to properly address climate change. Persson and Savulescu think that a solution to the climate crisis may lie in enhancing our capacity to cooperate. They describe some possible, first-generation moral enhancers including drugs that enhance empathy and a sense of justice.

John Harris, a philosopher who, in other contexts, is a vigorous advocate of human enhancement, proposes that there is a threat from moral bioenhancement to human freedom. Harris values the capacity to make bad moral choices. He suggests that without that capacity our good moral choices lose their value. Harris says that "sufficiency to stand is worthless, literally morally bankrupt, without freedom to fall. I, like so many others, would not wish to sacrifice freedom for survival" (Harris 2011: 110).

Harris may find it difficult to reply to an application of the enhancement consistency test suggested by his earlier described comparison of education and genetic enhancements. One purpose of education is to convey lessons about morality. In our history classes we learn about the evils of slavery. In biology classes we learn about our dependence on a fragile biosphere. It seems that education is not a particularly effective means of conveying certain kinds of moral lesson. Many people fully aware of the facts about climate change seem unable to muster the required levels of moral commitment to do what should be done. We would applaud a novel way to teach ecology to students that impressed upon them the seriousness of the climate crisis in a way that empowered them to take corrective action. Shouldn't we say similar of a biomedical means to this end? Brainwashing aims to change or shape moral views in ways that infringe learners' freedoms. But other forms of moral education do not involve such infringements. If the moral lessons can be taught in such a way as to preserve what is valuable about human freedom then there is no reason to suppose that interventions involving drugs or genetic modifications must necessarily be incompatible with freedom.

DIFFERENT DEGREES OF ENHANCEMENT

A different application of the enhancement consistency test concerns different degrees of human enhancement. Consider two cognitive enhancement scenarios.

> *Cognitive enhancement scenario 1:* It is thought that there
> are many genes that influence human intelligence.
> Variation in any given one of these genes may be respon-
> sible for a small fraction of the overall variation in intel-
> ligence. For example, one study, published in 2012, linked
> variation in the HMGA2 (High-mobility group AT-hook
> 2) gene with small variation in brain volume and an, on
> average, difference in tested IQ of 1.2 points. Suppose that
> it is possible to replace, in a developing human embryo,
> a version of the HMGA2 gene associated with a lower IQ
> with a version associated with a higher IQ.

We should expect a very modest gain in cognitive abilities from
substituting one version of HMGA2 by another in typical human
embryos. The genetic procedure would have to be very cheap and
safe to be worthwhile if all you sought was to increase the intelligence of your child.

> *Cognitive enhancement scenario 2:* The futurist and
> inventor Ray Kurzweil (2005) hopes to achieve quite dra-
> matic enhancement of human cognitive abilities by the
> progressive replacement of biological brain by electronic
> chips. We would, in the first instance, replace small parts
> of the brain with functionally identical electronic chips.
> The parts of the brain that have been replaced should then
> become more powerful at the same ever-accelerating pace
> that delivers improvements to other information tech-
> nologies such as cell phones and DNA sequencing. This
> schedule of cognitive improvements leads Kurzweil to pre-
> dict a human intelligence "about one billion times more
> powerful than all human intelligence today" (Kurzweil
> 2005: 9) by the year 2045.

According to Kurzweil this super-intelligence deserves the epi-
thet "human" because it emerges from the progressive improvement of biological human brains. Scenario 2 may seem vastly
improbable. This would certainly be a case in which science, or at
least Kurzweil's version of it, exceeds all but the very wildest fanta-
sies of science fiction. Kurzweil explains the apparent implausibil-
ity of billionfold cognitive enhancements by pointing to the great

difficulty our intuitions about technology have in tracking its exponential improvement.

I think that we should take scenario 2 seriously. Philosophers of human enhancement should adopt the motto of the scout movement. We should "be prepared." It is better to invest some effort worrying about a frightening technological development that never comes to pass than to be caught entirely unawares by one that, against all informed expectations, does come to pass. We should pay attention to what aspiring practitioners of human enhancement say that they may soon be able to do. Some scientists of human enhancement are now speaking with confidence about truly radical enhancements. There is Kurzweil's hypothesized intelligence "about one billion times more powerful than all human intelligence today" (Kurzweil 2005: 9), which should arrive, according to his calculations, in 2045. The unorthodox gerontologist Aubrey de Grey is currently seeking advances in medical know-how to extend human life expectancies not by 5 or 10 years, but to 1,000 years and beyond. Not altogether surprisingly, he wants to achieve these within his lifetime.

Do the differences in degree between scenarios 1 and 2 warrant a difference in moral evaluation? Should we treat scenario 2 as offering merely (a lot) more of the same? If scenario 1 is good, then scenario 2 would be extremely good. Alternatively, if scenario 1 is bad, then scenario 2 would be extremely bad. Or might the difference in degree of cognitive enhancement alter its moral polarity from good to bad?

Some philosophers invoke the concept of human nature to set limits on technologies of human enhancement. Kurzweil's reassurances notwithstanding, a series of cybernetic modifications that makes its recipients billions of times more intelligent does seem to take us to an endpoint not altogether human, at least in terms of criteria that we use to identify human beings. A future of human beings billions of times more intelligent than humans today does seem to have about as much in common with us as we have with our billions years past single-celled ancestors. It does not seem absurd to say that values linked to our human natures might have been sacrificed or suffered significant injury.

There is a widely shared intuition that we have human natures and these place some kind of limit on what can or should be done to

us. The difficulty lies in making claims about human nature sufficiently precise to support moral judgments about enhancement.

Consider the account of human nature presented by Francis
Fukuyama to demonstrate the wrongness of enhancement. He
identifies human nature with "the sum of the behavior and characteristics that are typical of the human species, arising from genetic rather than environmental factors" (Fukuyama 2002: 130).
Fukuyama understands that genes do not precisely fix human traits.
But he insists that they do set limits. Better diets add centimeters
not meters to genetically preprogrammed heights. Fukuyama links
our shared genetic endowment to a property of humans he calls
Factor X. Factor X justifies a shared human dignity by capturing
"something unique about the human race that entitles every member of the species to a higher moral status than the rest of the natural world" (Fukuyama 2002: 160). Fukuyama denies that Factor X
is constituted by "the possession of moral choice, or reason, or language, or sociability, or sentience, or emotions, or consciousness,
or any other quality that has been put forth as a ground for human
dignity." Rather, "it is all these qualities coming together to make
a human whole that makes up Factor X" (Fukuyama 2002: 171). Our
shared human genome plays a key role in combining these otherwise disparate traits. Would-be enhancers should show due defer-
ence to the shared human genome that gives us our shared human
natures and thereby entitles us to respect.

A problem for attempts to connect human nature with human
genes is that they do not support the assessments of those who
either oppose or want to place moral limits on enhancement. A
modification that substitutes one version of the HMGA2 gene for
another is an intrusion into our shared human genome. According
to Fukuyama it messes with the basis of human dignity. Yet the
recipients of this change should end up with IQs that are, on average, 1.2 points higher than they otherwise would have been. It's not
obvious how, should the procedure be safe, they might have suffered
some offence directed at their human natures. Consider Kurzweil's
series of cybernetic enhancements. These involve no modification
of human genes. The biological parts of Kurzweil's future super-
intelligence of 2045 may be genetically indistinguishable from
unenhanced humans of today. Yet this super-intelligence seems to
have taken a significant step away from humanity. There are many

science fiction cases that seem intuitively to starkly challenge our shared humanity and human natures without altering human genomes. Arnold Schwarzenegger's character in the *Terminator* movies is a robot encased by human skin. To the extent that the terminator is genetically anything it is genetically human. This fact notwithstanding, it does seem to be a fundamentally different kind of being from the humans that it hunts.

It's possible that the concept of human nature is not the right focus for many doubts about human enhancement. We seek restrictions on what can be done to individuals. Yet, according to Norman Daniels (2009), human nature is a property of collections of human beings rather than of individual humans considered in isolation. Even a significant change to an individual cannot, by itself, alter human nature. Rather, "it creates freaks" (Daniels 2009: 37). Certain, thankfully rare, genetic mutations cause significant malformations of human minds or bodies. They do so without altering human nature. Reasoning in an analogous way, so long as enhanced beings remain rare then there is no reason to suppose that enhancement must alter human nature. If our concern is about what might happen to individuals who undergo enhancement or miss out on it then the concept of human nature seems to be the wrong focus.

Nicholas Agar (2010, 2014) argues that different degrees of human enhancement can, in themselves, change its moral polarity. Agar distinguishes radical from moderate enhancement. Radical enhancement improves significant attributes and abilities to levels that *greatly exceed* what is currently possible for human beings. (Agar 2010: chap. 1) Moderate enhancement improves significant attributes and abilities to levels *within or close to* what is currently possible for human beings. Agar suggests that we acknowledge two distinct ideals that compete to direct the enhancement of human beings. There are *objective* and *anthropocentric* ideals of human enhancement. (Agar 2014: chap. 2) According to the objective ideal, human enhancements have value commensurate with the degree to which they objectively enhance our capacities. Greater degrees of human enhancement are better. The anthropocentric ideal assigns value to enhancements relative to human standards. It insists that some enhancements of greater objective magnitude are less valuable than enhancements of lesser magnitude.

We should not try to decide which of the objective or anthropocentric ideals embodies the correct way to value human enhancements. Rather, they describe two distinct, philosophically principled ways of valuing our capacities. We can view our capacities as instrumentally valuable. They have value in accordance with what they enable us to do. Stronger muscles enable heavier weights to be lifted. Cognitive enhancements of greater degrees increase the instrumental value of our cognitive faculties. They do so by enabling more difficult problems to be solved. This mode of valuing our capacities predominates in the discussions of the advocates of human enhancement. It is a perfectly legitimate way to assign value to human enhancements. But it is not the only thing that we value about our capacities. In addition, we find the exercise of our capacities intrinsically valuable.

Alasdair MacIntyre's (1981) category of internal goods points to the kinds of things that make exercises of our capacities intrinsically valuable. MacIntyre uses the example of chess to distinguish external from internal goods of exercises of our capacities. The external goods are contingently connected to playing the game of chess. World champion chess players achieve fame and fortune. But it's possible to play chess at a world standard and achieve none of these external goods. Many famous and rich people have never played chess. The internal goods of chess are, in contrast, inseparable from the activity of playing game. MacIntyre says "they cannot be had in any way but by playing chess or some other game of that specific kind." He adds that the internal goods of chess "can only be identified and recognized by the experience of participating in the practice in question" (MacIntyre 1981: 188). One partakes of the internal goods of chess by contemplating elaborate queen sacrifices or engaging with the more obscure details of the Ruy Lopez opening. It's clear how radical enhancement of our ability to play chess can boost the yield of external goods. Radical enhancement seems nevertheless to sever our connection with the distinctive collection of internal goods that characterize our playing of chess. The details of human engagement with chess are unlikely to present themselves to beings with superhuman intellects. When we express bewilderment about what we would do, want, or value with billionfold enhanced intellects we express a belief about reduced access to valuable internal goods.

Of course radically enhanced beings are likely to come to value their own internal goods. The fact that we could value them does not show that we do or should value them as we are now. We might come to value murder once some sadistic neuro-engineer had modified our psychologies to exactly resemble that of the Jack the Ripper. But this does not prevent us, as we are now, from expressing justified hostility at these transformations. In the case of radical cognitive enhancement we recognize increases in our capacities' instrumental value as entailing significant loses of intrinsic value.

CONCLUDING COMMENTS

As human enhancement moves from science fiction to science fact expect to see a proliferation in the variety of moral discussions about the rights and wrongs of enhancing human capacities. This discussion of the ethics of enhancing humans does not pretend to be exhaustive. Its main purpose has been to show how differences in the means, targets, and degrees of human enhancement have significant implications for moral evaluation.

14   Procreating

Procreating means nothing more than the creation of human beings. 'To procreate' can of course be loosely employed to mean 'to have sex'. However, strictly speaking, procreation is the generation of new lives. Heterosexual sexual activity can be procreative, but it need not be. Equally, and conversely, non-sexual acts and practices might be procreative, including those such as, most obviously, cloning and some forms of artificial mixed gamete reproduction.

This distinction is important because some ethical issues arise from the manner in which procreation is managed, or from a view as to what the proper function of sexual activity is. Thus we might object to cloning inasmuch as it is an ethically problematic technique for creating new lives, independently of the fact that new lives are created or that those lives are subsequently of a certain kind. Those of a conservative persuasion who see sex as having a natural end – namely procreation – will see all forms of non-procreative sex as morally objectionable.

In what follows I shall disregard these matters.

CAN PROCREATION BE WRONGFUL?

The case for thinking that it can only very rarely be wrong to procreate derives from, first, a belief that there is a fundamental right to choose whether or not to procreate, and, second, from a view about what would be involved in wrongfully creating another human being. I will consider the first belief in the section on "The right to procreate," below.

It helps to distinguish five elements of any evaluation of the putative wrongfulness of a procreative act. In what follows we should focus on procreative acts whose outcomes are known. There will, of course, be questions about what any procreator can reasonably know to be the outcome of any procreative act or omission. These must be set to one side.

The first element of the view is the principle that someone is wronged only if harmed. Call this the *wronging as harming condition*. The second element is a comparative construal of harm such that someone is harmed if and only if he or she is (unjustifiably) made worse off by an act or omission. The baseline by which the comparison of worse off is made is either temporal – before the putatively harmful act or omission – or counterfactual – what would have been the case had there been no act or omission. Call this the *comparative definition of harm*.

The third element of the view involves a characterization of the choice or choices open to the prospective procreator. This can be either one between two options – procreating or not procreating – or between three options – procreating in these or in other circumstances, or not procreating. Call these the *two- and three-option choices*.

The fourth element of the view concerns how we might evaluate non-existence. Either we can do so by comparing non-existence with existence or this is impossible inasmuch as non-existence cannot meaningfully be compared with existence. If a comparison can be made there is room for disagreement as to how non-existence fares in the comparison, and how we estimate the goodness or badness of existence. These disagreements derive from different views as to whether we see not coming into existence as exactly like ceasing to exist. Thus, for many, whilst death is a misfortune for someone who thereby no longer exists, failing to come into existence is not (Nagel 1979). This is for the simple reason that in the absence of existence there is no one for whom existing or not existing is good or bad.

Again, we need to be careful in how we evaluate the overall value of any actual life. We should thus acknowledge that persons, once they exist, might have strong preferences for staying alive, but judge that these preferences do not suffice to show that those who express them would have been mistaken, had they had the choice, to choose to come into existence given how their lives would turn out.

I shall assume that a life is worth living (and thus one that would rationally motivate someone to choose to come into existence) if it is better than non-existence. We might also say, a life is worth living if its goodness on balance and for the person whose life it is outweighs its badness. It is worth living even if the balance is only just on the side of goodness. Call this the *barely worth living condition*.

The fifth element of the view is the *non-identity condition*. Due to work by Derek Parfit (Parfit 1984) this affirms that persons created at different times or in different circumstances by the same pair of procreators are non-identical. This is a plausible claim given what we know about how genetic character is inherited and on any defensible theory of personal identity.

In order to see what the view constituted by these five elements licenses, we should consider what might be termed the difficult case: one in which individuals deliberately choose to procreate an individual whose life they know will be barely worth living. Such a life is better than non-existence but only just; it is preferable but by a very small margin to never existing. We can now show that on the view summarized the procreators do no wrong to the child they procreate in the difficult case.

If the procreators can only choose between procreating such a marginally worth-living life and having no child at all then the child they choose to create is not wronged since, had they not procreated, the child would not have existed. This is an instance of a two-option choice. According to the wronging as harming condition and the comparative definition of harm, either the child's existence cannot be compared with its non-existence, in which case the possibility of its being harmed and wronged does not arise, or such a comparison can be made in which case, *ex hypothesi*, life is preferable.

If the procreators face a three-option choice then, given the permissibility just established of choosing the child's existence over non-existence, the only remaining question is whether they do wrong in choosing to procreate this child rather than procreate at a different time or under different circumstances. Imagine that doing so would result in a child whose life was significantly better than that of the child in the difficult case. Nevertheless, the non-identity condition ensures that the comparison of lives is that of two distinct individuals. It is thus not worse for this child that she is procreated now; the happier child who might be procreated is a different one. The child whose life is barely worth living can only exist with that life, and so long as that life is (even if only barely) worth living its procreators do no wrong to her in bringing her into existence.

The outcome of the view summarized seems to be at odds with the ordinary common-sense moral judgment that individuals act wrongly in deliberately choosing to procreate a child whose life is only marginally worth living. This everyday judgment is reflected in legal provisions. Thus, those jurisdictions that regulate artificial reproduction normally proscribe selecting *for* disability, deliberately choosing to implant an embryo that is known to be at significant risk of inheriting a serious genetic abnormality. The resultant child may have a life that is marginally better than non-existence, but it is a life nevertheless that is known in advance will be burdened with considerable difficulties and be worse than the lives of most others. The common-sense judgment would also be that the individuals act wrongfully because they wrong the resultant child who is a victim of their reproductive choices.

Inasmuch as there is a prima facie conflict between the conclusions of the philosophical view summarized and ordinary moral judgments various moves are possible. The first is a simple 'bullet-biting' response that demands a revision of ordinary judgment in favor of the philosophical argument developed. Since most moral philosophers think that there should be full reflective equilibrium between any plausible moral theory and the developed intuitions of common-sense morality, and given, further, the significant gap between the two in this case, the bullet-biting response would be considered meta-ethically highly contentious.

A second response is to reject the non-identity condition, and claim that an actual person procreated at t_1 and a hypothetical person who would have been conceived at t_2 by the same two individuals are in fact identical. They are identical under some description such as 'the second child of this couple'. The problem with this response lies in seeing how we might specify the appropriate description that ensures the identity in a way that is neither question-begging nor such as to generate evident counterexamples.

A third response would be to accept all the elements of the view but maintain that nevertheless the procreators act wrongly in an impersonal sense. This is Parfit's own preferred response and amounts to what he terms the rejection of a *person-affecting* constraint on any judgment of moral wrongdoing. On this account no wrong is done to the resultant child yet the procreators act wrongly in choosing to procreate. In the case of a two-option choice this view seems to run afoul of the ordinary judgment in that it regards as permissible the procreation of a child whose life is (just barely) better than non-existence. In the case of a three-option choice the view conflicts with what ordinary common-sense morality may insist upon, namely that the wrong of the wrongful procreation does just consist of what is done to the child.

A fourth response rejects the comparative construal of harm. As McMahan suggests it may be possible to think that an act or omission can harm a person "'noncomparatively' – that is, it can affect him for good or ill even though the alternative would not have been worse or better for him" (McMahan 1981: 105).

However, in the absence of a baseline (non-existence) it is hard clearly to specify the badness of procreation. How exactly and to what degree does procreation affect the procreated person for good or ill? If the comparison is with other procreated human beings, then it is hostage to historical and social relativities. What would be a non-comparative harmful condition of existence in one society or epoch need not be so in another.

Moreover the response appears not to capture the specific wrong of bringing someone into existence such that her life is of a certain character. There is a morally significant difference between putting an already existent person into a harmed condition (for instance, blinding a child), and bringing it about that a person exists and is thereby in a harmed condition (for instance, creating a child without sight).

This is an important point. What is morally salient about procreation is that it puts a human being into a condition he or she did not choose to be put into, an uncertain and risky state. It is a 'predicament' (Velleman 2008), one in which the person is vulnerable to being harmed as well as open to having goods. That procreation is of this character – throwing the other without their consent into the perilous condition of existence – imposes stringent duties on the procreator. The scope of those obligations comprises both the kind of life the procreator must create in the first place, and the subsequent quality of life he or she must help to make possible once the child is born.

Finally, in response to the claim that harm might be construed without comparison to a baseline, it will be said that procreation can still affect a person non-comparatively for the better *on balance* if the ill of the resultant life is outweighed by its good. Those who respond that such goods cannot compensate for the harm involuntarily suffered (Harman 2004; Schiffrin 1999) are open to the further counter-response that their response appears ad hoc or is open to counterexamples. Moreover, a life with minimal harms but great compensating benefits is surely preferable to one without harms but no great benefits.

A fifth response to the conflict between the philosophical view on wrongful life and ordinary common-sense morality seeks to spell out the wrongfulness, and wronging of the child, in the difficult case other than by means of the causing of harm to the child. This response appeals to the more general thought that we may wrong someone by acting in a way that does not make worse and indeed may benefit the other overall (Woodward 1986). The wrong in question can variously be construed as the violation of a duty of responsible procreation (O'Neill 1979), the violation of legitimate expectations on the part of the prospective child (Kumar 2003), or the violation of a 'birthright' (Feinberg 1984).

The problems of a wrong- or rights-based account of wrongful procreation are at least fourfold. First, it is arguably still vulnerable to the non-identity problem. The child who is putatively wronged at being procreated would not complain since the only alternative is her non-existence and not complaining is equivalent to the waiving of the 'birthright'. Second, the response proves too much. Consider the case of those procreating in unfortunate parental circumstances who, through no fault of their own (such as extreme poverty in consequence of injustice), cannot but have a child whose life will be miserable. Third, inasmuch as we are committed to talk of parental rights to procreate, their exercise is straightforwardly inconsistent with the right of a child not to exist, and incoherence thereby threatens. Fourth, there is a threshold problem: what exactly is owed to the future child? By comparison with the relatively straightforward comparison of existence with non-existence, a rights- or wrongs-based account leaves it unclear at what point a future life is so miserable as to make its creation wrongful.

IS PROCREATION IMPERMISSIBLE?

On the view summarized above it is rarely wrong to procreate. On another view it is always wrong to procreate. This is inasmuch as existence is a harm for all of us, and it is the case, to use the familiar downbeat aphorism, that it would have been better never to have been born. Benatar defends such a view (Benatar 2006). Indeed he believes that life is so bad that there are overwhelmingly strong reasons not to procreate.

His defense appeals to a simple asymmetry, a distinction, and some further empirical facts about the extent of our miserable lives. First, there is a critical asymmetry. Whilst it seems wrong to create unhappy lives, it does not seem wrong not to create happy ones. We have an obligation to improve the lives of those who are born, but not an obligation to bring into existence people whose lives will be better than non-existence. Thus, it would appear that the absence of the benefits of existence cannot count in favor of procreation, whilst, nevertheless, the presence of the harms of existence do count against procreation. Consequently, when we balance the harms and benefits of existence against the harms and benefits of non-existence, we find that non-existence wins out. This is so even if the benefits of existence outweigh the harms of existence. This is because missing out on those benefits if one does not come into existence cannot count in favor of existing, whereas failing to suffer the harms of existence does count in favor of not existing.

The outweighing of the harms of existence by its benefits gives us reason to judge that life is worth continuing. However, it does not give us reason to start living. This is because we must make the distinction between what might warrant the commencement of existence and what might warrant its continuation. This is a distinction between a comparison *within* a life once started of its harms and benefits and a comparison of that life's benefits and harms with those of non-existence. In fact, and here Benatar appeals to various pieces of evidence, the sheer number and extent of harms that befall us as existent beings, and our tendency systematically to misjudge or misremember them, gives us overwhelmingly strong, and not just good reasons, not to come into existence.

The egregiously outrageous implications of Benatar's views do not of themselves provide sufficient reason to reject his view. The view itself can be neutral between different moral theoretical accounts of what should be construed as a benefit or an ill for human beings such that it is not vulnerable to criticisms that tell only against certain understandings of 'good' and 'bad'. He is careful to spell out what, if the view is correct, we are obligated to do. Thus, it does not follow that we can compel human beings not to procreate, even if the eventual disappearance of human beings would not be a matter for moral regret.

However, the view does rest on the critical asymmetry adumbrated above. Some at least will reject it. They might wonder, for instance, why the absence of good does not count in the balance of benefits and harms if there is no one for whom there can be such a lack, whilst the absence of ill does count in that balance even though, just the same, there is no one who suffers that absence (Overall 2012). Non-existence is neither a misfortune nor good fortune.

Others will insist that the asymmetry is so powerfully entrenched within common-sense morality that its abandonment is impossibly difficult or costly for the maintenance of our considered moral judgments.

THE RIGHT TO PROCREATE

So far the moral evaluation of procreation has been in terms of whether it is good or bad for those who are procreated. That leaves to be considered whether procreation is good for the procreators or is good in some distinct impersonal sense. Thus, in respect of the last possibility, it might be argued that even if procreation is bad for those procreated and even if procreation cannot be justified as good for those who choose to procreate, nevertheless it is good that there is procreation. Most obviously this would be the case if it is better that the human species survives than that it disappears. Indeed if it were good that humanity endures then individual human beings would be under an imperfect duty to procreate.

However, the question of whether the extinction of humanity is an evil will not be considered here (see Chapter 19 in this volume, on "Killing and extinction"). We should note only that there is, in

parallel with the case of individuals, a distinction that can be made
between the possible value of humanity ceasing to exist and that of
it never having existed.

Is it good for individual human beings that they can procreate?
Some will insist that there is a fundamental liberty right to procreate and that there is such a right because it engages a fundamental interest human beings possess in 'having children' (Robertson
1996). However, it is far from clear there is such a right once what
might be involved is carefully disambiguated.

In the first place, the negative liberty right *not* to procreate should
be distinguished from any positive liberty right *to* procreate. Thus
there are significant moral costs in denying individuals the freedom
to choose not to have children. Note that whilst this is normally
thought of as a woman's right to control her reproduction, men too
arguably have a right not to be a biological father. However, it is
less clear that there are moral costs of a similar weight in denying
individuals the right to procreate. Moreover, any such costs need
carefully to be weighed against any costs to the children of being
procreated.

Second, the phrase 'having children' to which there is the putative right is ambiguous. It could mean either being a parent in the
strict and limited sense of bringing children into existence; or it
could mean acting as a parent of any child brought into being. Of
course, adults procreate, normally, so that they can rear the children they bear. But this does not have to be the case. We can adopt
the children of others, and we can, conversely, grant to others the
custodianship of children we create.

Thus disambiguated the right to procreate seems to lack any evident or straightforward warrant. What could be the important interest for those who choose to do so that is served by bringing human
beings into existence? It is implausible to characterize procreation
as valuable inasmuch as it is creative, since, properly understood,
it is merely the transmission across generations of genes inherited
from one's own procreators. Moreover, the activity of parenting is,
by contrast, much more plausibly viewed as creative since it is the
molding of a child's identity throughout its minority.

Some will speak of procreation as valuable precisely because it
is the transmission of a genetic inheritance, or in old-fashioned
parlance, 'continuing the blood line'. However, construed in such

traditional terms it is unclear what is valuable to the one who procreates, rather than to others, in simply bringing it about that one set of genes is passed to the next generation.

Appeal to a basic desire to have children that it is impossible to resist is insufficient warrant for reproductive liberty inasmuch as such a desire may have critical social determinants, comprise several impulses some of which can be satisfied in non-reproductive ways, and because the idea that it is good or indeed obligatory to satisfy any felt desire is morally contentious (Chadwick 1987).

It is also worth being clear what the moral costs are in denying individuals a liberty to procreate. A classic American case, *Skinner* v. *Oklahoma* (Skinner 1942), found a State law allowing for the involuntary sterilization of criminals to be unconstitutional. The case is interesting for the various reasons it gives in support of its judgment. Sterilization is the *permanent* deprivation of a basic individual liberty. By contrast, we might think it permissible only to deny an individual the right to exercise that liberty on some occasions or in some circumstances, and to seek to do so by means (such as economic and other penalties) that do not entail an irreversible loss of a capacity. The judges also made reference to the improperly discriminatory eugenic functions of sterilization when it is performed in the service of eliminating a racial group or some putative characteristics of a race. Again, denial to one individual of a right to procreate need not have these moral costs.

In sum, it is not self-evident that there are essential human interests of such importance as to warrant the ascription of a basic right to procreate; nor is it clear that denial of the freedom to procreate must always cause egregious moral harms.

Two further clarifications of the idea of a basic liberty to procreate are in order. First, the freedom to procreate cannot be a freedom to create as many children as one might choose to do (Statman 2003; Conly 2005). Not only is it the case that the interest in having *a* child has a weight that having multiple offspring does not. There are countervailing reasons of ever-increasing strength not to permit unlimited procreation. These have to do both with the welfare of the children and with the public interest in limiting population size, especially in a context of scarce resources. In respect of the latter it is implausible to argue that there is an unconditional, absolute, and unrestricted individual right to procreate when the scale of the aggregate number of humans being brought into existence threatens the future sustainability of the world (Kates 2004).

Second, whilst a negative liberty right to procreate is correlative with a duty not to interfere with the exercise of reproductive capacities (such as, most obviously, by means of involuntary sterilization and abortion), a positive right to procreate would correlate with a duty to provide services that would assist those otherwise unable to have children. Put simply, there may be a basic liberty only of the fertile to procreate. This would not entail a right of the infertile to access provision for assistance with conception. There are opportunity costs in such provision. Hence, the warrant for such a positive right must be grounded in something other than the simple interest in having genetically related offspring, and cannot appeal to the moral costs of denying an exercise of powers to reproduce. Thus, for instance, one might ground it in a claim of justice made by those unlucky to be infertile that they are owed the means to reproduce (J. Burley 1998).

PROCREATIVE OBLIGATIONS

Do procreators have obligations, what is their scope, how are these acquired, and who must discharge them? The procreated are, to repeat, placed in a 'predicament'. They enter the world, without their consent, and into a state of vulnerability to harm and dependence upon others. That unsafe and uncertain state demands the devoted care of responsible adults who must care for, protect, and provide for children, at least during their minority. Who is responsible for providing this care? One might simply view moral responsibility as tracking causal responsibility, and thus identify those who caused the child to exist as being responsible for its care (Archard 2010). However, this view of moral responsibility is contentious. Moreover, it is certainly no easy matter to identify those whose causal role in the creation of a human being is sufficient or such as to burden them with a duty of guardianship. Some, for instance, are disposed to view even gamete donors as having a robust responsibility to ensure adequate care for those they helped, even at a considerable distance, to bring into being (Benatar 1999).

Others are inclined to favor an intentional or voluntarist account of the acquisition of parental responsibilities, wherein what matters is not the simple fact of causing a child to exist but the intention to procreate. Such an account may also take due account of how convention or social-role morality defines these procreative and consequent parental responsibilities (Brake 2010). Intentional accounts must ensure that those who do not manifest a will to care for their children are not thereby acquitted of the responsibility to care for them.

What exactly is owed to the procreated may be no more than the bare minimum of a life better than non-existence, or something more, namely the reasonable assurance of a decent or minimally adequate life. One's views on this matter are, of course, the corollary of one's understanding of how a child might be wronged by being brought into being.

CONCLUSION

Procreation is of course to be distinguished from parenthood, and the ethical issues specific to each need carefully to be separated, even if there are evident relations between them. Most obviously there is a morally salient difference between what is done to someone by bringing them into the world and what is done to someone once they are in the world. Procreation is also morally extremely weighty. It is at its simplest the creation of a brand-new human being and the exposure of that being to the unconsented predicament of existence. It is not to be undertaken lightly and should be done with a full and proper appreciation of what is involved. What is interesting is whether to that extent the ethics of procreation are *sui generis*; or no more than one part of any ethics of the proper treatment of our fellow humans.

15 Abortion

OVERVIEW

Main divisions

When, if ever, is it morally permissible to end the life of a human embryo or fetus, and why? As regards the first of these questions, there are extreme anti-abortion views, according to which abortion is prima facie seriously wrong from conception onwards – or at least shortly thereafter; there are extreme permissibility views, according to which abortion is always permissible in itself; and there are moderate views, according to which abortion is sometimes permissible, and sometimes not.

Moderate views appeal to a variety of considerations in support of the view that abortion is sometimes justified, but these fall into four main categories. First, there are cases where the developing human is seriously defective in some way – perhaps such that it will not have a life that is worth living. Secondly, there are cases where continuation of pregnancy would involve serious risks to the life or health of the woman. Thirdly, there are moderate positions according to which the developing human initially does not have serious moral status, or a right to life, but acquires such status at some point before birth. Finally, it is often held that abortion is justified in the case of rape.

With the exception of the last consideration, moderate views assume that the moral status of the developing human is crucial with respect to the permissibility of abortion. Moreover, this is a natural assumption that was shared by all sides until the publication in 1971 of Judith Jarvis Thomson's article "A Defense of Abortion," in which she argued that abortion is permissible even if one assumes, for the sake of argument, that human embryos and fetuses have a right to life. Thus we have one of the great divides in the philosophical discussion of abortion: is the moral status of the developing human generally decisive with regard to the moral permissibility of abortion or not?

The moral status of the developing human: Thomson and Boonin

Thomson's article evoked many critical responses, along with some defenses, which I have described elsewhere (Tooley 2013). Crucial, however, is David Boonin's defense (2003), which contains responses to all of the important objections directed against the attempt to show that one can defend abortion while granting that human embryos and fetuses have a right to life fully on a par with that of normal adult human beings.

Boonin's impressive efforts notwithstanding, I do not think that this way of defending an extreme permissibility view is successful. The crucial issue is whether it is morally permissible intentionally to bring into existence an entity with a right to life in a situation where one knows that it will not survive without one's assistance, and then to refrain from providing that assistance. An especially forceful way of arguing that this is not permissible is found in an article by Richard Langer (1993: 351–52), who argues that if this were permissible, it would follow not only that abortion was justified, but also that it is permissible to allow one's children to die, some years after birth, simply because one no longer wishes to care for them.

Moderate views

Moderate positions on abortion raise a number of issues that, for reasons of space, I cannot address here. Some of these depend on the issue of the moral status of the developing human, and defending a moderate view requires showing that both extreme anti-abortion and extreme moral permissibility views concerning the moral status of humans before birth are incorrect. I have argued elsewhere (Tooley 1983: 285–302, and 2009: 59–63) that the prospects of doing this are not promising.

As regards permissibility in the case of rape, everything depends upon whether, as Thomson contends (1971), there is no obligation to be a good Samaritan, rather than merely a minimally decent one, and so no obligation for a woman to remain pregnant to save the life of a being that she was not responsible for bringing into existence.

Finally, on the one hand, in cases where the woman will die if an abortion is not performed, virtually all moral philosophers, with the exception of those who embrace the moral view advanced by the Catholic Church in encyclicals by Pope Pius XI (1930: paragraphs 63–67; see paragraph 64) and Pope Paul VI (1968: paragraph 14), agree that abortion is morally permissible, while, on the other hand, if the situation is one where there is only *some* risk that the woman will die if an abortion is not performed, or where the threat is not to the woman's life, but only to her health, then the situation does seem clear-cut if one assumes that the embryo or fetus has a right to life.

Extreme anti-abortion views

Very different arguments are offered for the view that abortion is in itself never permissible. First of all, in popular discussions, appeal is frequently made to the mere fact of membership in the biologically defined species *homo sapiens*, but among those who are philosophically knowledgeable, this line of argument is almost invariably rejected, for reasons that I have set out elsewhere (Tooley 2009: 21–35).

Secondly, appeal is also made to the idea that humans have immaterial minds, or souls – for example, by Stephen Schwartz (1990), J. P. Moreland and Scott B. Rae (2000), Norman Ford (2002), and Francis J. Beckwith (2005). The postulation of immaterial minds or souls is, however, open to strong objections, since there is excellent evidence that human psychological powers have their categorical bases in neural structures, rather than in an immaterial substance (Tooley 2009: 15–19). In addition, the postulation of an immaterial soul, conceived of along Thomistic lines, is on a collision course with biology, since such an immaterial soul is held to govern a human's life processes and biological development.

Thirdly, there is the 'substantial identity' argument, advanced for example by Patrick Lee (2004), and which claims that an entity possesses a right to life by virtue of the type of substance it is. This view is exposed to a number of strong objections, however, among them the fact that it leads to the unacceptable consequence that a human that has suffered upper-brain death still has a right to life (Tooley 2009: 51–59).

The upshot is that most philosophers do not find any of the preceding three lines of argument for an extreme anti-abortion position promising. The focus, accordingly, has been elsewhere – namely, on arguments claiming that human embryos and fetuses have serious moral status, or a right to life, because they have the *potentiality* for developing those psychological capacities – for thought, self-consciousness, rationality, and so on – that seem clearly relevant to a being's moral status.

In what follows, then, I shall confine my discussion to what seems to me the most crucial issue bearing upon the moral status of abortion, namely, that between, on the one hand, a potentiality account of moral status, and, on the other, the type of approach most commonly appealed to in support of an extreme permissibility position on abortion, namely, a personhood account of the right to life.

One of the earliest defenders of the view that potentialities give something a right to life was Jim Stone in his article, "Why Potentiality Matters," where Stone argues for the conclusion, "we have a prima facie duty not to deprive them of the conscious goods which it is their nature to realize" (1987: 821). Stone's discussion, however, attracted much less attention than an article published two years later by Don Marquis, entitled "Why Abortion is Immoral" (1989). The latter is one of the most interesting articles on abortion, as well as one of the most discussed – and deservedly so. In what follows, then, I shall focus upon it.

My discussion is organized as follows. In the next section, I summarize Marquis' account of the wrongness of killing. Then, in the following section, I set out an alternative account, one in which the concept of a neo-Lockean person is central. Then come three sections devoted to criticisms of Marquis' approach, all of which also support the alternative, rights-based, neo-Lockean personhood account.

MARQUIS' ACCOUNT

The basic idea

In his article, Marquis (1989: 189–90) advances the following account of why killing an innocent, normal adult human being is morally wrong, and seriously so:

The loss of one's life is one of the greatest losses one can suffer. The loss of one's life deprives one of all the experiences, activities, projects, and enjoyments that would otherwise have constituted one's future. Therefore, killing someone is wrong, primarily because the killing inflicts (one of) the greatest possible losses on the victim ... When I am killed, I am deprived both of what I now value which would have been part of my personal life, but also what I would come to value. Therefore when I die, I am deprived of all of the value of my future. Inflicting this loss on me is ultimately what makes killing me wrong. This being the case, it would seem that what makes killing any adult human being prima facie seriously wrong is the loss of his or her future.

Marquis' proposal, then, is that when killing something is seriously wrong in itself, the reason is that it deprives the entity in question of the valuable states that it would have enjoyed in the future if it had not been killed.

What sort of entity suffers the deprivation?

When a normal adult human being is killed, what *type* of entity is deprived of a future that would contain valuable states of affairs? In the above passage, Marquis frequently uses the personal pronoun "I," and the expression "personal life," which suggests that what suffers the deprivation is a person. But his view is instead that it is *a biological organism* that suffers the loss, and this is crucial. For if it is a biological organism that is deprived of a certain sort of future, and if such deprivation is what makes killing a normal adult human being seriously wrong, then killing a normal human embryo or fetus is equally wrong, since the type of future that it will enjoy, if it survives, is the same sort of future that normal adult humans enjoy. Marquis has, then, an account of the wrongness of killing that, if sound, generates the conclusion that abortion is prima facie seriously wrong.

Marquis' concept of an organism

But while Marquis defends the view that abortion is wrong, he does not think that killing a developing human is prima facie wrong at absolutely every stage, since he holds it is not prima facie wrong to kill a normal human zygote, or what exists from the zygote stage up until "there is cellular differentiation within the inner cell mass and the embryo is implanted in the uterus" (2007: 200).

Why does Marquis think that killing is not wrong at these stages? His argument seems to be that until differentiation takes place, one has only a number of distinct cells, rather than any single thing with which the later organism can be identical. But given that different cells emerge, and must emerge in appropriate numbers and spatial arrangements, the earlier arrangement of the undifferentiated cells must be acting in concert. So what one has at the undifferentiated stages is not just a collection of unrelated, qualitatively indistinguishable cells: the relationship among the undifferentiated cells is crucial for the differentiation that follows. But given that this is so, how can it not be true that one has, throughout the process, a single organism? It seems to me, then, that Marquis is not justified in denying that a single organism is present from the zygote stage onwards.

A future like ours

Marquis' account of the wrongness of killing is formulated in terms of the idea of a future like ours, that is, a future like that of a normal adult human being. This raises the question of what it is about a future like ours that makes it significant. A natural answer – and one that is also suggested by the expression "personal life" that Marquis uses at one point, as we saw above – is that a future like ours is significant because it is the type of future enjoyed by persons.

As a result, a number of writers, including Peter McInerney (1990) and Gerald Paske (1994), argued that Marquis needs to employ the concept of a person in order to give an account of what the *intrinsic nature* of a future like ours is. Initially, Marquis (1994) rejected this contention, but in an important later article (2011), Marquis agreed that, in explaining the wrongness of killing, one did need to make use of the concept of a person.

This change does not, of course, undermine Marquis' basic account of the wrongness of killing, since it is perfectly compatible with the view that entities that are not persons – including, presumably, human fetuses – can have a future like ours.

A NEO-LOCKEAN PERSONHOOD ACCOUNT

Neo-Lockean persons

In this section I want to show that Marquis' account of the wrongness of killing is open to decisive objections, and that there is an alternative account that is very plausible indeed, namely, one formulated in terms of a neo-Lockean person.

But what is a neo-Lockean person? A neo-Lockean person is a *continuing* subject of experiences and other mental states, where a continuing subject is one whose experiences, beliefs, desires, intentions, values, and personality traits at different times are causally connected in certain ways, so that one has not only psychological continuity over time, but also *conscious psychological connections*, typically involving conscious memories of earlier experiences, and conscious intentions and desires that give rise to future actions.

But why not use the term 'person' here, given that that is a very natural way of referring to such a subject of experiences? The reason is that there is now a tendency among some who believe that abortion is morally wrong to use the term 'person' for entities, such as zygotes, that neither have had experiences of any kind, nor possess the capacities necessary if there are to be any conscious psychological connections between experiences at different times. Accordingly, I shall employ the expression 'neo-Lockean person' to avoid any confusion.

Why 'neo-Lockean'? John Locke (1632–1704), in Book 2, chapter 27, "Of Identity and Diversity," of his *Essay Concerning Human Understanding*, distinguished between the identity over time of a human organism and the identity of a person, and he argued that the latter was based not on bodily identity, but on psychological connections between experiences at different times, based in turn on memories of the earlier experiences. Later philosophers realized, however, that Locke's account was open to certain objections, and revised it in a variety of ways. Hence the expression 'neo-Lockean'.

The psychological connections required for the mental life of a neo-Lockean person involve certain capacities, such as the capacity to remember, to have desires, to form intentions, and so on. If such capacities, which enable mental states at different times to be connected via conscious psychological states, are *never* present in an organism, then no neo-Lockean person is associated with that organism. But notice that it is not the case that a neo-Lockean person exists only at times when such capacities are present. As long as some of the states that are relevant to personal identity are present – such as memories, certain desires, personality traits, and so on – it does not matter what general capacities are present. Even if an organism's brain were so damaged that the organism was no longer capable even of being conscious, let alone of having memories, or thoughts, or desires, and so on, a neo-Lockean person would continue to exist, since it would not be impossible for the general capacities for consciousness, thoughts, and so on to be restored, and if they were, there would then be memories of past experiences, along with beliefs, desires, personality traits, and so on that would be causally connected to, and continuous with, the beliefs, desires, and personality traits that were present at an earlier time.

An alternative account?

Given the concept of a neo-Lockean person, one could formulate an account of the wrongness of killing that paralleled Marquis' account, but where the subject of deprivation was a neo-Lockean person. Such an account may seem initially quite appealing; however, while it would escape most of the objections to which Marquis' account is exposed, it would not escape all of them. What is needed, as we shall see in the following subsection, is a rights-based account.

A right to life versus a right to continued existence

The final point that needs to be made about the rights-based, neo-Lockean account is that it is not formulated in terms of a right to *life*. The reason is that there could be neo-Lockean persons that did not involve biological organisms. First of all, many believe that there are minds that are either temporarily disembodied, or else permanently nonembodied. The first would include, on some Christian views, human souls that survive the deaths of human bodies, and, on Hindu views, transmigrating souls, while the second would include angels and some deities. Though possible, it does not seem to me at all likely that such beings actually exist. But if such beings did exist, not being biological organisms, they could not have a right to life, but they would have a right to continued existence.

Secondly, on certain accounts of the nature of mental states, our world could contain electronic persons, or mechanical persons, while on other accounts of the nature of mental states, electronic or mechanical persons would exist given appropriate laws of nature. Such persons could not have a right to life but would have a right to continued existence.

Here, then, is the account of the wrongness of killing that I shall be arguing is superior to Marquis' account:

(1) Only neo-Lockean persons have a right to continued existence.

(2) All neo-Lockean persons have a right to continued existence – unless it is possible to forfeit that right by doing certain immoral things.

AVOIDABLE OBJECTIONS

In this section, I shall mention two objections to Marquis' account as it stands, but that he could escape by reformulating his account.

Suicide

Suppose that it is true and reasonable for John to believe that if he went on living, he would enjoy a life that is full of things that he would value very much and that would contain very little pain or other negative states. If Mary were to kill John, Marquis' account would judge, quite correctly, that Mary had done something that was prima facie seriously wrong. But what if John views the human race as pitiful, and decides he does not wish to associate with grossly irrational and morally pathetic individuals, thereby choosing to end his life? Then just as Mary's killing John would deprive him of a future like ours, and one where the things he would value would greatly outweigh the negative things, so John's committing suicide would have the same result. On Marquis' deprivation account, then, John's killing himself is just as wrong as Mary's killing John. But this surely is not the case: John's killing himself, while foolish and irrational, is not seriously wrong, let alone on a par with murder.

The moral is that one needs a rights-based account of the wrongness of killing, such as is provided by the neo-Lockean personhood account just described, since given a reference to rights, one can appeal to a person's ability to waive his or her rights to explain why murder and suicide are not morally on a par.

Euthanasia

Consider now a case of two individuals who are suffering terribly, and where the suffering, by their own reckoning, grossly outweighs any positive things that are left in their lives, so that if either were to die, that person's life would be better than if he or she were to go on living. But suppose that while one of the people would like to undergo euthanasia, the other would not – perhaps because he or she thinks that doing so would be cowardly, or a sin. Would it not be wrong to kill the second person? But that individual would not suffer deprivation as a result of being killed, which means that Marquis' account is unable to explain why killing the second person would be wrong.

Such cases provide no problem, by contrast, for a rights-based approach, since one can appeal to the idea that one can waive a right. Killing the first person is morally permissible because, in asking to be killed, that person has waived the right to continued existence, whereas the second person has not.

While these objections to Marquis' account are sound, they do not cut deeply enough, since one could easily revise Marquis' account by embedding his idea of depriving something of a future like ours within a framework of rights. The basic claim would then be that anything with a future like ours has a right to continued existence, unless it has somehow forfeited that right.

Let us turn, then, to objections that cannot be avoided in this way.

THE SCOPE OF MARQUIS' ACCOUNT

If one is inclined to hold that abortion is not prima facie seriously wrong, it is tempting to argue that depriving an *organism*, as contrasted with a neo-Lockean person, of a certain sort of future is not sufficient to make such an action wrong. There is, however, a different sort of response that is virtually never made here, but which is important. It begins with the claim that even if Marquis were right that depriving any organism of a certain sort of future is prima facie seriously wrong, that principle could not be a *basic* moral principle.

Why? The answer is that there are logically possible actions that, intuitively, are prima facie wrong for the same reason that it is prima facie wrong to kill an innocent, normal adult human being, but that do not involve the destruction of an organism. Recall the possibilities of disembodied and nonembodied minds. If one had the power to destroy such entities, doing so would deprive those entities of a certain sort of future, just as much as, if humans are purely material beings, killing a human deprives that human of a certain sort of future. Consequently, the former action should be prima facie just as wrong as the latter. But destroying an immaterial mind or soul does not in itself deprive any biological *organism* of a future.

Moreover, such a case poses no problem for the alternative account according to which the relevant wrongmaking property is the destruction of a neo-Lockean person, since disembodied minds and nonembodied minds are neo-Lockean persons.

One might grant this point, but wonder whether it is important. I think it is, since it shows that the basic principle underlying the wrongness of killing cannot involve the concept of a biological organism, and this raises the question of *what concept* is to be put in its place. Marquis will be hard-pressed to find a satisfactory answer, for he needs an account that covers both biological organisms and immaterial minds, but that does not include combinations consisting of a human spermatozoon and an unfertilized human ovum, since he certainly does not want to hold that it is prima facie seriously wrong to destroy such a combination. Might he appeal to the idea of a substance, or to the idea of an individual? Perhaps, but there are at least two reasons for thinking that that will not work. First, if the notion of substance or individual is interpreted in a way that rules out spatially separated things from being substances, the reformulated principle will not cover the possibility of a person who is spatially scattered – something that I have argued elsewhere is logically possible (Tooley 1983: 179–83, 2009: 196). Secondly, one will have a principle that, although it rules out a combination of a spermatozoon and an ovum that are spatially separated, will not rule out a case where the two are in contact, or where the spermatozoon is in the process of entering the ovum.

In short, once one notices that one needs a basic principle that covers immaterial minds and souls as well as organisms, it is not even clear how a Marquis-style deprivation account, in contrast to a personhood-style deprivation account, is to be formulated.

The task becomes even more difficult if, like Marquis, one's concept of an organism is such that an organism is not present until differentiated cells are present, for then it is even less clear what concept will include embryos after differentiation has taken place, along with immaterial minds, while not including zygotes or the resulting entity prior to cell differentiation.

MARQUIS' ACCOUNT VERSUS A NEO-LOCKEAN PERSONHOOD ACCOUNT

Let us turn, in this final section, to objections that show conclusively that Marquis' account of the wrongness of killing is unsound and that also support the alternative, rights-based, neo-Lockean personhood account.

Animals that will never constitute neo-Lockean persons

This objection extends an objection advanced by Gerald Paske (1994) against Marquis' account. Paske argued that Marquis' idea of a future like ours presupposes the concept of a person, since otherwise Marquis would not be able to explain why, on the one hand, killing most non-human animals is not seriously wrong, while, on the other hand, killing intelligent, non-human, extraterrestrials would be seriously wrong.

As I noted above in the subsection on "A future like ours," Marquis initially (1994) rejected the contention that the concept of a person was needed to explain the idea of a future like ours, but then came to agree with Paske. Consequently, Paske's original objection does not tell against Marquis' revised view.

The response that is now open to Marquis merely leads, however, to the following variant on Paske's objection. The fundamental idea involved in Marquis' account is that the reason that killing is wrong in itself, when it is, is that the entity killed is thereby deprived of a future existence in which it would enjoy states either that it values now, or that it would value if it existed at the later times in question. Marquis, however, in revising his account in the way indicated, is shifting from a formulation based on the idea of a future of value to one based on the more limited idea of a future like ours, where the entity in question exists as a person and enjoys valuable states of the sort that persons can enjoy. But why should a future like ours – a personal future – be morally crucial? Why should that be the only sort of future that counts? An animal such as a deer or a cow does not have a future like ours, but it may very well have a future full of pleasures and almost entirely free of pain. If such an animal is killed, it is thereby deprived of those goods. Those goods may be inferior, of course, to the sorts of goods a neo-Lockean person can enjoy. But over the course of such an animal's life they may be very substantial indeed. Consequently, if the fundamental reason that killing is morally wrong, when it is, is that it deprives an entity of a future of value, then while it may not be as wrong to kill something that will never constitute a neo-Lockean person as it is to destroy something that either presently is, or will, if not killed, come to be a neo-Lockean person, the former action could still be very seriously wrong.

The objection, then, can be put as follows:

(1) No satisfactory defense exists for the view that while the property of depriving something of a future containing valuable states that only a neo-Lockean person can enjoy is a very serious wrongmaking property, the property of depriving something of a future of value that does not contain valuable states that only a neo-Lockean person can enjoy is not a significant wrongmaking property of an action.

Therefore, in view of (1):

(2) If the property of destroying something with a future like ours is a serious wrongmaking property, then the property of destroying a being that, if not destroyed, would enjoy a future of value, is also a significant wrongmaking property.
(3) Animals such as sheep typically enjoy futures that contain states whose total value is very significant.
(4) It is not typically prima facie wrong, and significantly so, to kill sheep, even though that deprives them of futures of value.

Therefore, from (4):

(5) The property of destroying a being that, if not destroyed, would enjoy a future of value, is not a significant wrongmaking property.

Therefore, from (2) and (5):

(6) The property of destroying a being with a future like ours is
     not itself a serious wrongmaking property.

Purely general potentialities versus 'same neo-Lockean person' potentialities

To say that an organism, such as a human fetus, has a future like
ours is not to say that it actually will enjoy such a future. It is to
say, rather, that it has a certain sort of potentiality for enjoying
such a future. That potentiality, moreover, is largely based upon the
intrinsic, physical makeup of the being in question, although the
realization of that potentiality also depends upon the entity's environment: a normal human fetus that is not in a uterus is not going to
enjoy a future like ours.

Marquis' argument for the view that abortion is morally wrong
is, then, a type of potentiality argument, and the dominant view
among philosophers who have thought seriously about abortion is
that the arguments against abortion that deserve serious consideration are potentiality arguments.

At the same time, the claim that an entity can have a right to
continued existence because it has a potentiality for developing in
such a way that it will constitute a person is open to objections.
Thus, in a book on the moral status of abortion (Tooley 1983: 175–
96), and in a later debate volume on abortion (Tooley 2009: 42–50),
I offered six arguments for the view that potentialities do not give
something a right to continued existence.

Most of those objections, moreover, have never been addressed,
let alone answered, by philosophers who hold that developing human
embryos and fetuses have a right to continued existence by virtue
of their potentialities, so any of those objections could be advanced
at this point against Marquis' view. Here, however, I shall focus on
only one argument, namely, a variant on an argument advanced by
Mary Anne Warren.

In her widely reprinted 1973 article "On the Moral and Legal
Status of Abortion," Warren argues that if potentialities gave something a right to life, then every cell in one's body would have that
right, since if the nucleus of such a cell were to be transferred to
an *unfertilized* human egg cell from which the nucleus had been
removed, the resulting cell would develop in exactly the same way

that a fertilized human egg cell develops. The possibility of cloning shows, therefore, that the potentiality for coming to constitute a person does not give something a right to life.

The standard response to Warren's argument appeals to a distinction between active and passive potentialities for neo-Lockean personhood, a distinction that can be set out roughly as follows:

(1) Entity X has an **active** potentiality for coming to constitute a neo-Lockean person means:
All of the positive causal factors that are required for a process that would result in X's coming to constitute a neo-Lockean person are present in X.

(2) Entity X has a **passive** potentiality for coming to constitute a neo-Lockean person means:
There is something that could be done to X that would initiate a process that would result in X's coming to constitute a neo-Lockean person.

The response to Warren's argument is then, first of all, that what Warren's argument shows is merely that a passive potentiality for neo-Lockean personhood – which is present in every cell in one's body – does not give something a right to continued existence: it does *not* show that an active potentiality for neo-Lockean personhood – something that is not present in any cells in one's body – does not give something a right to continued existence. But then, secondly, an active potentiality *does* in fact give an entity a right to continued existence.

The claim, in short, is that while active potentialities give something a right to continued existence, passive potentialities do not. But consider the case of a normal adult human being in a temporary coma. Here it does not matter whether the person will come out of the coma without assistance, or whether some medical intervention is needed for the person to recover. The fact, for example, that a person would emerge from a coma only if an operation were performed to relieve pressure on the person's brain would not make it permissible to kill the person. The case of a person in a temporary coma shows that, to the extent that potentialities are relevant to an entity's right to continued existence, *purely passive* potentialities are just as relevant as fully active ones.

The upshot is that if one asserts that an active potentiality for neo-Lockean personhood gives something a serious right to continued

existence, the same would have to be true for a purely passive potentiality. This generates, however, wildly implausible consequences,
such as the one pointed out by Warren, to the effect that every cell
in one's body has a right to continued existence.

Marquis has available, of course, a different sort of response to
Warren's argument, since, as we saw above in the subsection on
"Marquis' concept of an organism," he holds that until cell differentiation takes place, one does not have an organism, and so
one does not have the sort of being that can have moral status.
But that move would not enable Marquis to escape the underlying
point here, which is that passive potentialities possess whatever
moral significance the corresponding active potentialities possess.
The reason is that one can shift to a case that I have used before
(Tooley 1972: 60–61). Suppose a chemical is discovered that when
injected into a kitten's brain will change its brain so that it will
come to develop the capacities for thought and self-consciousness.
Any kitten, before it is injected, will then have a passive potentiality for coming to constitute a neo-Lockean person. It would then
follow, given that the relevant passive potentiality is morally significant if the corresponding active potentiality is, that if an active
potentiality for neo-Lockean personhood gave something a right
to continued existence, then kittens would, in the situation envisaged, have a right to continued existence. But that, surely, is not the
case. Consequently, an active potentiality for coming to constitute
a neo-Lockean person cannot give one a right to continued existence, and so having a future like ours cannot make the destruction
of such an entity wrong.

Compare this conclusion with the fact that potentialities, both
active and passive, are clearly significant in the case of a normal
adult human who is in a comatose state. What explains the difference? The answer is that in the case of the comatose individual,
the potentialities in question, both active and passive, are not
potentialities for something *to come* to constitute a neo-Lockean
person who does not yet exist, but potentialities for the continued
existence of an already existing neo-Lockean person. A rights-
based neo-Lockean personhood account of the wrongness of killing
can therefore explain why potentialities of the first type are not
morally significant, whereas potentialities of the second type are,
since killing in the former case does not violate any neo-Lockean

person's right to continued existence, whereas killing the comatose individual does.

There are, as I noted near the beginning of this section, many arguments for the view that the potential for coming to constitute a neo-Lockean person is not morally significant, and in the case of many potentiality-based arguments against abortion, the thing to do would be to develop those further arguments. But Marquis' approach is exposed to very different kinds of objections, and I think it is more important to set out two of those objections.

These two objections both turn upon the fact that an embodied, neo-Lockean person is *not identical with* the relevant organism. This is shown, as we shall see, by the existence, first of all, of cases where the organism survives the destruction of the neo-Lockean person in question, and, secondly, of cases where the neo-Lockean person survives the destruction of the relevant organism. Let us turn, then, to objections based upon those two types of cases.

The reprogramming objection

This first argument involves a case where a neo-Lockean person is destroyed, but no organism is killed. It is an argument that I first set out very briefly many years ago (Tooley 1972: 46), and then later developed at greater length (1983: 102–3, 2009: 31–32, 35, 56, and 64). The argument is as follows. First of all, as I have argued elsewhere (2009: 17–19), there are extremely strong reasons for holding that humans do not have immaterial minds or souls, and thus that there must be a neurophysiological basis at least for all of one's psychological abilities, and for all of one's 'non-occurrent' mental states – that is, mental states that can exist at times when one is not conscious – such as one's beliefs, memories, general desires, attitudes, and personality traits. Now suppose that it becomes possible to completely 'reprogram' an adult human's brain while the person is unconscious – that is, to act upon a person's brain in such a way as to destroy all of that person's memories, beliefs, attitudes, and personality traits and then to program in whatever new beliefs, attitudes, personality traits, and apparent memories one chooses.

Suppose that this happened to you. How would such an occurrence compare with your being painlessly killed? Which do you think would involve the greater harm?

One way of determining how you feel about the relative value of different outcomes is to consider how you would choose between lotteries involving those outcomes. So suppose that you could choose between the following two options:

OPTION 1: There is a 100 percent chance that your brain will be completely reprogrammed, modeled on a person who is radically different from you.

OPTION 2: There is an N percent chance that you will be painlessly killed, and a $(100 - N)$ percent chance that you will be released unharmed.

If you think that being painlessly killed would be a worse outcome than being reprogrammed, there should be some value of N – say, 95 – such that you would be indifferent between a 95 percent chance of being killed, together with a 5 percent chance of going free, and a 100 percent chance of being reprogrammed. But if that is so, then you should prefer being completely reprogrammed to a 96 percent chance of being killed, along with a 4 percent chance of going free.

Is this how one would choose? The vast majority of people to whom I have presented these options would not choose in that way: they almost always preferred the option where the chance of death is less than 100 percent to the option where one is reprogrammed 100 percent of the time. This shows that they do not think that being painlessly killed is worse than being completely reprogrammed. But neither do they believe that being completely reprogrammed is worse than being painlessly killed. The upshot, accordingly, is that most people view being painlessly killed and being completely reprogrammed as morally on a par. This is a striking fact that calls for explanation.

If, as I hold, the reason that it is wrong to kill normal innocent adult human beings is that it is wrong to destroy an innocent neo-Lockean person, an explanation is immediately available, since both painlessly killing someone and completely reprogramming a normal adult human being's brain destroys a neo-Lockean person. Marquis' account of the wrongness of killing, by contrast, cannot explain this relationship, since reprogramming a human organism does not kill that organism, nor deprive that organism of a future like ours.

Indeed, reprogramming could enable a human organism to have a better future. Perhaps the person is haunted by terrible memories. Perhaps the person believes that premarital sex, including masturbation, is a mortal sin, and, having strong sexual desires, upon which he or she acts, is in fear of spending eternity in hell. Or perhaps the person has desires, attitudes, habits, and beliefs that result in an unhealthy lifestyle that is likely to lead to illness and reduced life expectancy. Reprogramming could wipe all those negative states away, replacing them with ones that would maximize the organism's chance of a much happier and more productive life.

Transplantation, extreme amputation, and identity

The second argument involves a case where an organism is destroyed, but the relevant neo-Lockean person survives. Suppose that unless something is done to an adult human organism, A, that human will die. Two alternatives are available. One involves the destruction of the upper brain of A, with that upper brain being replaced by cells that will form a new, perfectly functioning upper brain, but where none of the memories, beliefs, desires, attitudes, values, personality traits, and so on previously associated with A are present, having been replaced by new, unrelated, psychological states, just as in the reprogramming case. The other alternative involves killing A, and then transplanting A's upper brain into another human organism – B – that lacks an upper brain. The result is that B now not only has a future like ours, but also all the memories, beliefs, desires, attitudes, values, personality traits, and so on, previously associated with the human organism that has been destroyed.

Which of these alternatives is morally preferable? On a rights-based neo-Lockean personhood view, since the first alternative involves the destruction of a person, whereas the second does not, the second alternative is preferable, and this moral ranking of the two alternatives is surely right. By contrast, it would seem that Marquis' view leads to the incorrect conclusion that the first alternative is preferable. For on that alternative, A, which had a future like ours, but one that was not going to last much longer, now has a much better future, whereas on the second alternative, A is destroyed, and another human organism B, that previously did not have a future like ours, is given such a future. Thus, the first alternative does not involve the destruction of any human organism with a future like ours, whereas the second does. The second also involves, of course, making it the case that there is a *different* human organism that acquires a future like ours, but it is surely not true that the destruction of something with serious moral status can be justified by creating something else with moral status.

Marquis, however, does not accept the description that I have just given of this sort of transplantation case. What he wants to say is that a case where an upper brain is removed from a human organism is just a case of amputation, albeit of an extreme sort. Accordingly, what I have described as making it the case that a human organism B, that is distinct from A, has a future like ours, Marquis wants to describe as a case where A survives.

Notice here that it need not be the upper brain that is transplanted. It could be that the only part of the upper brain that is transplanted is the part that contains the basis of the identity of a neo-Lockean person. Moreover, it could be that, rather than this being transplanted into a human body, it is transplanted into the body of an intelligent extraterrestrial cat that had had the corresponding part of its brain destroyed. On Marquis' suggested rejoinder, then, human organism A would be surviving as an extraterrestrial cat.

I suggest, then, that Marquis' 'extreme amputation' view of such a case involves shifting from the idea that it is organisms, including human fetuses, that have a future like ours, and thus that can be wronged by being deprived of such a future, to the idea that it is neo-Lockean persons who have such a future, for in the transplantation case, Marquis' claim that the original organism survives cannot be based on any plausible criterion for identity of an organism: no such criterion allows a human organism to be identical with an extraterrestrial cat. The identity criterion that Marquis is forced to use, if he is to avoid embracing the wrong moral view of the transplantation case, is precisely the criterion for the identity over time of a neo-Lockean person.

CONCLUSIONS

There are many important questions concerning abortion that I have not been able to address. But as I indicated at the outset, there are reasons for thinking that the crucial choice is between views that hold that general potentialities can give something a right to continued existence, and the view that only neo-Lockean persons have such a right. I therefore focused on one formulation of the

former sort of view, and argued that Marquis' account of the wrongness of killing is open to a number of decisive objections, and that
his defense of the view that abortion is wrong therefore fails. All of
those objections, moreover, provide support for a rights-based neo-
Lockean personhood account of the basis of the right to continued
existence. If my arguments are sound, then, there is good reason to
accept an extreme permissibility position on the moral status of
abortion.

16   Killing ourselves

Is it always morally wrong to kill oneself? If not, under what conditions is suicide justifiable? Even if not strictly wrong, does suicide fall short of what is morally ideal or what a virtuous person would do? If suicide is not morally wrong in certain cases, is there then any objection to *helping* a person to commit suicide? These questions are especially prominent now as liberal and traditional values conflict about both individual decisions and public policies.

My aim here is not to give definitive answers but to highlight certain central questions, briefly review several perspectives that philosophers have proposed for addressing them, and then describe two further considerations that draw from several different philosophical traditions. I focus primarily on the reasons for and against thinking that killing ourselves (unassisted suicide) is morally wrong or otherwise objectionable. Questions about assisted suicide and euthanasia raise special concerns about the enforcement of social and legal rules and so are considered here only briefly. Focusing first on the basic case of unassisted suicide makes sense because our conclusions about this basic case are highly relevant to the morality of assisted suicide and euthanasia.

My comments are divided as follows: **first**, I discuss briefly what I take suicide to be, distinguish different moral questions about it, and set limits on the scope of my discussion; **second**, I review briefly some different perspectives that philosophers proposed for assessing the morality of suicide; **third**, I describe a modified Kantian alternative that that emphasizes human *dignity*; **fourth**, I explain how a further ideal of *appreciation* goes beyond the Kantian value of functioning as a rational agent; **finally**, I add a few comments on the special concerns relevant to public policies permitting assisted suicide.

THE CONCEPT OF SUICIDE AND THE
CENTRAL MORAL QUESTIONS

"Suicide" is not just a descriptive term (like "swallowing a lethal amount of arsenic") but for many people it is a morally significant category (like "murder" and "torture") that is used primarily when they disapprove. To decide that a case counts as a suicide in this thick sense is already to make a moral judgment about it. Not surprisingly, then, debates about the definition of suicide are often not merely verbal disputes but disagreements about the wrongness of doing what one knows will lead to one's death. Even what counts as "killing oneself" can be influenced by prior judgments about responsibility. For example, most people would agree that the early Christian martyrs did not "commit suicide" or even "kill themselves" when they refused the Emperor's demand that they renounce their religion or else be eaten by lions.[1] They were killed by the lions in an obvious (nonmoral) sense but also by the Emperor whom we take to be responsible for their deaths. Both the order of the Emperor and the refusal by the martyrs were avoidable acts that everyone knew would lead to the martyrs' deaths, but because we judge their responsibility differently we usually say that although the lions were the immediate cause of death, the Emperor committed murder and the martyrs did not commit suicide. Similarly, insofar as we admire Socrates for drinking the poisonous hemlock rather than resisting the law that demanded his death, we simply say that he was (wrongfully) executed rather than that he committed suicide. Had he refused to escape and taken the hemlock in order to get back at his nagging wife, however, we would probably call his act a suicide. The upshot of these complications is just that to assess the morality of suicide without prejudging the issue it would be helpful if we could use a morally neutral descriptive concept of suicide that allows both opponents and advocates to be talking about the same thing.

Unfortunately finding a precise neutral definition is difficult if not impossible. Standard definitions, if taken as giving necessary and sufficient conditions, always seem open to counterexamples. For our purposes, however, a rough definition together with a range of examples should suffice. A common definition, for example, is that suicide is *the intentional taking of one's own life*. Some would add that suicide must be "voluntary" or non-coerced, thereby apparently ruling out Socrates' drinking the hemlock but unfortunately also excluding instances commonly regarded as suicides in which prisoners (for example, Joseph Goebbels and Adolf Hitler) shot or poisoned themselves to avoid the humiliation of execution. When we consider examples, there is a wide gray area about which there will be disagreement but, fortunately, there are also cases that obviously count as suicides and other cases that obviously do not. Since we disagree in our moral assessments even about the cases that are uncontroversially regarded as suicides, we should focus initially on these, setting aside for now the borderline cases. This is in accord with fairly standard methodology in moral and legal philosophy – first try to explain the clear cases and hope that our best explanation can be extended to hard cases. For example, in ethics first try to give an account of why murder, theft, and lying are generally wrong and then take up the more controversial cases such as assassinating oppressive leaders, stealing from the rich to share with the poor, and telling consoling lies to dying patients.

Once we have in view a range of cases that would be obvious instances of suicide, then there are different moral questions to consider. *First*, in contemplating or committing suicide, was the person mentally competent, and sufficiently rational to be self-governing and morally responsible? This raises extremely difficult conceptual and practical questions, important especially for medical consultants trying to decide when it is justified for them to intervene to prevent irrational acts of self-destruction. Most cases of tragic suicide may result from confused, unrealistic, irrational thinking, but this is not necessarily true of all suicides. In any case, my focus here will be on agents assumed to be mentally competent, rational, and morally responsible. *Second*, given this assumption, we can ask whether moral principles forbid, permit, or even at times call for suicide. In what circumstances, if ever, is suicide morally permissible? Do we have a moral right to end our lives whenever we choose, only in certain conditions, or never? And if we have the right, could it be wrong to exercise that right in certain contexts? Do circumstances sometimes make suicide the only right thing to do? *Third*, are there moral ideals, beyond strict rules of right and wrong, which could give us good reasons to prolong our lives – or to end them – in extremely hard conditions, for example, when suffering from an utterly debilitating terminal disease? If, as many people think, killing oneself is not strictly forbidden in some cases, is it better or morally admirable to hold on to life as long as possible – or to choose for oneself when to bring it to a close? *Fourth*, is *assisted suicide* morally permissible for individuals and as a part of medical practice? These are all hard and controversial issues. Here we consider mainly questions of the second and third type. In my view it is especially important to think about how at best we value our lives – about what makes continued living worthwhile.

DIFFERENT PERSPECTIVES ON SUICIDE: THEOLOGICAL, LIBERTARIAN, AND CONSEQUENTIALIST

Suicide has been condemned from *theological perspectives* for centuries. The explanation may vary but a common view is that because God created us and is infinitely good and wise, we are God's property and subject to God's authority. We were given our lives in trust and must not throw them away but wait for that time that God has willed for us to die by nature or external forces. Whether or not Scriptures explicitly support this view, it became the official doctrine of the Roman Catholic Church and was widely accepted by non-Catholics as well. The practical stance required by this view seems clear: voluntarily and intentionally killing oneself is always wrong, no matter how difficult the circumstances, even if it is intended as a means to a further good end. Our assisting the suicide of others is also wrong because their requests for aid in doing what it is intrinsically immoral for them to do cannot count as a valid consent that releases us from our duty not to kill them. If suicide is murder, albeit self-murder, the fact that a person consented, even requested, aid in carrying it out is neither justification nor excuse.

A crucial premise here that even religious critics may challenge is the claim that divine wisdom and authority demand an absolute prohibition on suicide. Scriptures have been interpreted in different ways, and critical philosophers regard neither Scripture nor Church authority as sufficient in itself to determine what is immoral. For theologians committed to the natural-law tradition the ultimate ethical question must be whether there are rational grounds for a moral prohibition. For others the question may rather be whether or not divine love and ideal human love would encourage a more nuanced attitude about end-of-life decisions, allowing possible exceptions to the traditional prohibition. Acceptance of a religious perspective, then, may still leave room for debate about whether suicide is always wrong.

Libertarianism takes a radically different view of suicide. The core idea is that individuals have fundamental rights to use their bodies, their labor, and (consequently) their legitimately acquired property as they see fit, unless and until they consent to the restriction of their natural liberty. Robert Nozick is commonly cited as a philosophical supporter of this point of view,[2] but contemporary libertarians may differ in more or less significant ways. A common theme is that government should interfere in the daily lives of individuals far less than others typically suppose. Regarding suicide, a libertarian perspective naturally encourages the conclusions that competent adults have the moral and legal right to end their lives whenever they choose, that others may assist them when they voluntarily request it, and there should be no governmental restrictions on active euthanasia of patients who have given genuine consent in a living will.

Libertarians may consider the quality of continued life to be relevant to an individuals' *personal decision* to exercise their right to end their lives or continue living, but insofar as they have a *moral right* to decide, either choice is morally permissible. A libertarian may take the position that in some contexts it may be morally *virtuous* to suffer irremediable pain rather than to exercise one's right to end one's life before it is taken by a terminal disease, but the only strict moral constraint is that the right of individuals to choose for themselves is limited by the rights of others. For example, one should not commit suicide in a way that endangers others (e.g. crashing a vehicle into on-coming traffic) or abandons one's responsibilities (e.g. primary care for a child). Critics challenge libertarianism, however, with regard to grounds and extent of moral rights, the pervasive status of consent to determine how we may be treated, and, specifically, whether one's consent to ending one's life makes it morally permissible for others to honor one's request for aid in the process.

Consequentialists hold that what is morally right for a person to do is ultimately determined by the consequences of that individual's action or by the consequences of general acceptance of the moral code for the relevant community to which he or she belongs.

An appealing feature of this perspective on suicide is that it acknowledges the importance of the effects that a suicide can have on family, friends, and the larger community. Rule-consequentialism especially takes seriously the overall effect of social and legal practices that permit or condemn suicide.[3] Consequentialism of all kinds requires us to reflect on the value of continued living to the person contemplating suicide and anyone else affected. Classic utilitarianism (e.g. in Bentham and Sidgwick) may see this as simply a matter of the balance of pleasures and pains, but contemporary consequentialists take a broader and more subtle view of the well-being that moral standards aim to promote. What is valuable to a person in a stretch of life may not be simply a balance of pleasure and pain or net satisfaction of desires but rather living in a way that satisfies an "objective list" of the aspects of well-being, including meaningful work, loving relationships, and worthwhile accomplishments.[4]

The main problem with consequentialist theories, critics insist, is that, although they reasonably acknowledge the moral significance of pleasure, pain avoidance, and individual well-being, they attempt to reduce all principles of moral right and wrong to the overarching aim to promote these values, even (according to many consequentialists) to bring about the maximum quantity of them. The problem, often repeated in contemporary literature, is that justice, fidelity, respect for persons, and other principles should constrain the aim to bring about the best consequences. Without constraints that are not themselves simply justified by consequences, critics argue, even the most idealistic consequentialism is subject to counterexamples – that is, consequentialism has implications for particular cases that most reflective people would find intuitively unacceptable. For example, executing a man for a crime that he did not commit seems wrong even if it would please a vast crowd and the executed person had little prospect of happiness or achievement. Similarly, whether it is wrong to commit suicide in a particular case arguably does not depend just on the extent to which it would please others or even enhance their well-being. Consequentialists often reply, however, that when the actual long-term consequences are taken into account they would not favor radically counterintuitive recommendations, such as executing the innocent or committing suicide just to please others. Whether this is so is an empirical question, which may be impossible to answer.

OBLIGATIONS TO OTHERS

When thinking about the morality of suicide, almost everyone will agree that one important consideration in most cases is how the suicide will affect others. Moral theorists generally agree with common sense that normally we have both general duties to take others' interests into account and special obligations to family, friends, co-workers, and those who have willingly made our lives better. Theists must consider what they owe to God, consequentialists must weigh the benefits and harms for everyone affected, and libertarians at least require us to respect the rights of others. What specifically these responsibilities to others are will no doubt vary with the context. For example, when a more or less healthy person is fully engaged in life, there are likely to be others who count on her and would be deeply distressed at losing her. Even libertarians can agree that to abandon one's children, dependent employees, or official duties without making adequate arrangements would be wrong, whether one abandons them by suicide or by simply running away. Killing oneself in vengeance to make an ex-lover suffer for ending a relationship may be not only foolish but also a malicious neglect of the general duty not to inflict unjustified harm on any other person. A highly educated, privileged person who has greatly benefited from the generous support of others may reasonably think he has a debt of gratitude that obliges him to "pay forward" by helping others rather than abandoning a productive life when personal losses make life temporarily miserable.

Other-regarding considerations, however, are not always decisive, and in some circumstances they may seem to speak in favor of suicide. When one is old, infirm, terminally ill, suffering uncontrollably, and utterly incapable of making others' lives go better, one no longer has the obligations to others that one had when young and healthy. Even if one has residual obligations and as well a general duty of due consideration for others, arguably these may be overridden by reasonable self-regarding concern. In some circumstances, many would say, suicide is a justifiable, even heroic, sacrifice for the sake of others. In war, for example, a prisoner facing torture may see suicide as the only way to avoid betraying his comrades and his just cause. When suffering from incurable and incapacitating illness, patients may see suicide as a justifiable way to relieve their families from prolonged emotional and financial burdens. Some Vietnam war protesters who burned themselves to death may have thought this to be their most effective means to save many others from the horrors of war. Again, although motives were no doubt mixed, Japanese kamikaze pilots and Al-Qaeda suicide bombers may have thought their sacrifices would help bring about a better world.

Without in the least denying the importance of other-regarding considerations, I want to concentrate for the rest of this chapter on what should matter morally to the person contemplating suicide *when responsibilities to others are set aside*. Arguably there are also self-regarding moral considerations that are relevant. Do we "owe it to ourselves," in some sense, to live and die with dignity? What would an ideal attitude about the value of one's life be and what would it imply about suicide?

RESPECTING ONE'S OWN DIGNITY AS A HUMAN BEING: A MODIFIED KANTIAN PERSPECTIVE

Here I will sketch a different way of thinking about suicide that emphasizes the value of continuing life as a free and rational agent – and the potential limits of this value. I draw from broadly Kantian ethics but let us focus here on the merits of the perspective rather than its origin.[5]

Immanuel Kant argued on several grounds that suicide is contrary to a "duty to oneself." For example, he argued that killing oneself "from self-love" could not be a universal law of nature because self-love has the natural purpose to preserve life.[6] He also argued that it presupposes the self-contradictory claim that that we have the moral authority "to withdraw from all obligation."[7] Even these arguments, he allowed, leave open "casuistical questions" about whether suicide would be wrong in extreme circumstances, for example, to save one's country, to anticipate an unjust death sentence, and to keep oneself from harming others when fatally bitten by a rabid dog.[8] Like many others, I am unconvinced by these arguments but will not dwell on them. The argument from which my modified Kantian view draws is the following.

First, as regards the concept of necessary duty to oneself, the man who contemplates suicide will ask himself whether his action could be compatible with the Idea of humanity as *an end in itself*. If he damages himself in order to escape from a painful situation, he is making use of a person *merely as a means* to maintain a tolerable state of affairs till the end of his life. But a human being is not a thing – not something to be used *merely* as a means: he must always in all his actions be regarded as an end in himself.[9]

The central point is that our "humanity," our nature as rational human beings, is a source of *dignity* – and unconditional and incomparable worth that should be respected by all persons, including oneself. Unlike consumer goods, human dignity does not depend on our being useful or liked by anyone. It is an irreplaceable and invariable value that must always be respected.[10] We cannot, for example, assess one person as having more dignity than another or think of equal dignity as a quantitative measure such that, for example, two people have twice as much as one. Human dignity is more like the status of equality under the law, which must be respected in every case, even though in particular, complex cases the law must try to balance the particular conflicting claims of citizens.

The idea of dignity, in my view, should not be understood as providing us with quick and easy solutions to all difficult moral decisions. It needs to be interpreted and applied systematically as we try to find the best coherent set of social rules and moral principles to guide us in particular cases.[11] Proper regard for human dignity is not only concerned with overt behavior but also with our attitudes and motivation. What matters is not just what we do but why we do it. This can be illustrated, I think, by distinguishing four different kinds of cases in which one might consider suicide.[12] For example, (1) some cases of suicide are **impulsive** in the sense that they are prompted by passing desires incompatible with one's deeper, more permanent concerns. They are acts one would have regretted, had one survived. (2) Other cases I call **apathetic** because they are the result of not caring about what one can do by continuing living – or even about one's capacity to act and develop an on-going life. Assuming the condition is not incurably pathological, there may still be a potential for an actively engaged future (perhaps with appropriate treatment), but suicide snuffs out this possibility in a final act that the apathetic person would have come to regret if she had survived. (3) Too often suicides are **self-abasing**, that is, resulting from contempt for oneself and a consequent desire to put oneself down. The self-abasing suicide does not necessarily see future life as devoid of enjoyment but as contemptible, like something one wants to swat or drive away in disgust. The problem, I imagine, is not merely a low assessment of one's merits compared to others, for unfortunately this assessment might be quite realistic in some cases. Rather, one sees oneself as a worthless person in a deeper sense, having no dignity just as a human being. (4) Finally, there are **hedonistic calculating** suicides where one sees the choice for life or death to be simply a matter of whether continued living promises more pleasure than pain. This seems to be the sort of case Kant had in mind in his famous example in the *Groundwork for the Metaphysics of Morals*.[13] Apart from his responsibilities to others, the hedonistic calculating person values his existence just for what he can expect to get, not for what he is and can do.

In Kantian ethics one's motives and attitudes in acting affect the moral quality of what one does. For example, Kantians join many others in regarding it as wrong to kill oneself with the attitudes expressed in the cases just considered (impulsive disregard for one's deeper concerns, apathy, self-contempt, and exclusive concern for pleasure and pain). Assuming that we are considering only persons who are rationally competent, from a Kantian perspective the choice to kill oneself from the motives characteristic of these cases is contrary to a proper self-regard – respect for one's dignity as a rational agent. The point here is not to blame others who, sadly, have made their final choices but rather to reflect for ourselves on future choices that we may face. My stories assumed that, despite their troubles, those contemplating suicide still had a potential for continued living as rational autonomous agents. Their failure of self-respect was to throw that away for the sake of things of lesser value; the object of impulsive desire, the ease of not trying to make a new life, escape from the shameful feeling of comparative worthlessness, and anticipation of a future with more pleasure than pain. The point of presenting these cases was not to propose new categories for therapists to use in diagnosis, but to highlight the Kantian theme that we "owe it to ourselves" to respect our own dignity as human beings with the capacities of a rational and moral agent.

Do these broadly Kantian considerations oppose suicide in all circumstances? Arguably they do not. In at least three kinds of cases suicide would apparently be permissible.[14] First, as one's body and mind degenerates from age and disease there may come a time when life as a rational autonomous agent is no longer possible. To end one's life just prior to that time for the sake of avoiding continuation on a sub-human level would not be condemned by the sort of considerations we have been considering.[15] Second, arguably suicide to end gross irremediable pain – pain that makes rational human functioning impossible – would be not only understandable but unobjectionable. Finally, if there is no other way to avoid a life that one sees as base, degrading, and contrary to one's deepest values, then arguably suicide is not incompatible with respect for one's dignity as a human being. Other arguments may be relevant as well, but my broadly Kantian considerations seem to permit, and even sometimes, to commend the choice for suicide in these extreme conditions.

APPRECIATION: FURTHER REFLECTIONS ON THE VALUE OF CONTINUED LIFE

Let us continue to focus on cases where the capacity for functioning as a rational autonomous agent is severely diminished, for example, elderly patients with Alzheimer's disease or dementia. Here the capacity to set oneself ends and rationally pursue them, which Kantians value so highly, becomes increasingly irrelevant except for past commitments expressed in living wills. Many people, including hedonistic utilitarians, will emphasize the value of the simple pleasures and enjoyment that are still available to those with diminished rational capacities. These do not rise to the level of "higher-quality" pleasures that John Stuart Mill so admired,[16] but they are not insignificant. Even Kantians may argue that before the onset of their diminished capacities the Alzheimer's and demented persons typically had a rational will that they live comfortably, enjoying the simple pleasures if and when they slip into a more childlike state. All too often, however, the pleasures available to these patients are offset by pain and suffering, and this prompts the question whether the value of continued living is entirely a matter of these two concerns – the exercise of rational agency and the expected ratio of pleasure and pain in one's remaining time.

A further value, not obviously reducible to these two, is what I call *appreciation*. In reflecting on the value to a person of a stretch of continued life we should consider not merely *what they can do* (physically and mentally) and *what gives them pleasure and pain*. It also matters what they can appreciate, find value in, see as worth attending to. Living with responsive awareness of some of the vast variety of good things that surround us can be enjoyable ("pleasant"), but focusing entirely on what it does for us (our pleasure/pain ratio) misses the point of the ideal of appreciation – it's just good, one might say, to live in responsive awareness of good things. Here I think of music, art, birds feeding outside one's window, contact with people one loves, watching children at play, being reminded of good times (even struggles) in the past, appreciating the good in people around one, and so on. The philosopher G. E. Moore emphasized the importance of appreciative awareness of a wide variety of "intrinsic values," but unfortunately he connected the thought with utilitarianism and a dubious metaphysics and epistemology.[17] If we drop those features of Moore's view there remains a core feature of the view, namely, that we can appreciate, take up, admire, attend and respond to intrinsically valuable things of all sorts – and we are living better, other things equal, to the extent that we do so. The capacity to appreciate intrinsic values tends to outlive the capacity to live as rational autonomous agents, and it adds a dimension of value to an ongoing stretch of life that arguably does not reduce simply to more pleasure or less pain.[18]

What are the implications of this line of thought when we consider ideal attitudes towards prolonging life – or deliberately ending it – when living is painful and provides little opportunity *to do* much of anything. Should caregivers do everything in their power to make their patients live longer? Should we, in anticipation of falling into the suffering patients' condition, cultivate the attitude that a longer life is always better and suicide should be unthinkable? If appreciation is generally an ideal attitude, how is it relevant here? In the earlier paper mentioned above, I described a contrast between three different perspectives on the value of one's life from now on, setting aside responsibilities to others.[19] One was the **consumer perspective** suggested by Kant's example of a man contemplating ending his life because "its continuance threatens more evil than it promises advantage."[20] Here the focus is on "what's in it for me, on balance, considering how much I will suffer and how little I can enjoy." It's if he is considering whether it is *beneficent* to himself to end his life or to prolong it. The second perspective I called the *obituary-writer's perspective*. Here one considers the narrative story-line of one's life, the achievements and failures, wanting to weave a narrative of the whole life that makes it admirable. Severe pains of the past matter relatively little as we look back, but good deeds and accomplishments stand out. From a Kantian point of view, I argued, both of these perspectives are flawed, the first because it treats one's life merely as a receptacle for pleasure and pain, and the second because it devalues one's existence as a rational agent at each present moment in favor of making a life that looks good at the end. Finally, I sketched an *author's perspective* which takes account of both the coherence of story-line(s) of one's life and the quality of one's existence as the author (a rational agent with autonomy) at each moment. A promising feature of this perspective, I thought, was that it acknowledges that we do often value "cross-time whole" stretches of past, present, and future in various paths we may take, and the value of the whole often has an organic unity, that is, it is often not the sum of the value of the parts. My reflections here about the value of appreciation, however, point to problems with taking this author metaphor too literally. The problem is that as patients gradually lose their capacity to be the "authors" of a life, the value of continued life for them seems inappropriately assessed by that standard. Painful continued life can be better or worse in ways other than the level of a person's ability to exercise rational agency and to experience more pleasure than pain.

Is the ideal of appreciation at least compatible with the broadly Kantian perspective sketched earlier? This depends primarily on whether we can understand "intrinsic values" without reifying them as metaphysical entities known by intuition and existing independently of any relation to human beings. In discussing the common idea that we can "find value in nature" I argued that a more plausible understanding of intrinsic values is available, but we cannot address that issue further here.[21]

CONCLUDING NOTE: ASSISTED SUICIDE

Recent controversies about whether assisted suicide should be legalized have renewed interest in many old and complex moral issues. When, if ever, may we help someone in their attempt to kill themselves? Cases vary. Consider, for example, a Roman soldier who

helps his defeated general to fall on his sword in order to avoid capture by the enemy, a kind-hearted care-taker who buys lethal drugs
for her patient to take, a doctor who secretly honors his patient's
request for a lethal injection, and a medical team that carries out
recently legalized procedures to end the life of a comatose patient as
requested in the patient's living will. These assisted suicide cases are
distinguishable from cases of *involuntary* euthanasia ("mercy killing"), where, for example, a care-taker intentionally kills a suffering
and totally incapacitated patient *without the patient's consent*. A
vast philosophical and empirical literature is developing about both
assisted suicide and involuntary euthanasia, but the issues there
extend far beyond the scope of this chapter. Nevertheless, I conclude
my discussion with three comments on the broader issues.

First, if unassisted suicide is not wrong in certain cases, then
a major ground for condemning assisted suicide is undermined for
those cases. It does not necessarily follow from the moral permissibility of a person's suicide that others are permitted to assist, but
a major argument against assisted suicide has been that one should
not be an accomplice in the immoral deeds of another person. Thus
if suicide is not immoral in certain cases, then it will be permissible
for others to assist *unless there are further arguments against this*.
If so, the default position is that assisting someone in a permissible
suicide is not wrong.

Second, there are in fact many further considerations that may
override this initial presumption. In particular, the general acceptance of assisted suicide may have social consequences that are
undesirable from many moral perspectives. For example, some
argue that acceptance of assisted suicide will diminish society's
respect for the dignity of human life and will undermine the primary commitments of medical professionals. There are also worries about *abuses* of any system that permits us to help others to
end their lives. For self-serving financial or personal reasons family
members may want to speed the end of a lingering relative, and
administrators of public facilities may prefer to get rid of their low-
paying residents with terminal illnesses. Trust in government and
the medical profession may erode further, which can have indirect
negative effects on the welfare and even liberty of citizens. On the
other side, however, it can be argued that the practice of assisted
suicide would not have these effects if it is carefully defined and

THOMAS E. HILL, JR.

regulated. Empirical studies are relevant here, and some apparently cast doubt that the dire consequences of assisted suicide predicted by its opponents would actually come about. From another perspective, Kantians and other advocates for human dignity may come to see that respect for the dignity of persons who are gradually losing all that makes life worth living is best served by facilitating their choice to end their lives before they fall into an animal-like condition. Some of these same controversies about undesirable consequences and dignity violations are raised when we move from a culture in which suicide is always strictly forbidden to a culture where suicide is sometimes permissible, but they arise most acutely when, beyond this, we contemplate the general acceptance of institutionalized assisted suicide. Obviously, the questions multiply when involuntary euthanasia is proposed.

Third, and finally, moral questions about assisted suicide are often entangled with the wider philosophical issue of whether it is worse to do something normally wrong (such as killing, lying, stealing, torturing) or to fail to prevent someone else from doing it when we could have. Is it worse, for example, for a mother to deliberately drown an unwanted child than to let it die when she finds that it has accidently slipped under the bathwater? In Bernard Williams' famous case of Jim and the Indians, would it be morally worse for Jim to kill one innocent Indian as the tyrannical Chief proposes or to let that Indian and many more die because he refuses?[22] With regard to the suicide of suffering and terminally ill patients, the questions are whether it is worse to kill oneself or to let oneself die naturally and whether it is worse to assist another's suicide (directly or indirectly) or to leave that person to die by disease or with the aid of someone else.

The debate on these matters may continue indefinitely, but I will venture one comment for now. If we review many cases that do or might arise in real life, I expect that we will discover a strong tendency to find it intuitively worse to do something normally wrong (like killing, lying, torturing) than merely to fail to prevent someone else from doing it (or something comparable) when we could. If so, this would help to explain the common generalizations that killing is worse than letting die, suicide is worse than waiting to die naturally, assisting in another person's suicide is worse than letting the person die without one's help. Intuitions about these cases, however, are not uniform. The context of particular cases matters. When particular details are provided to fill in the initially abstract descriptions, I find that many will agree that sometimes suicide is a better option than the alternative, for example, prolonged suffering with no remaining capacity for a human life. Of course, intuitions are not universal on either this qualified position or the strict prohibition of suicide and assisted suicide. In the end, intuitions cannot be the final court of appeal because they are so often shaped by unexamined current practices and cultural norms that are outmoded, irrational, and even oppressive. We need to look for the reasons why it is so commonly felt that killing a person, oneself or another, is worse that allowing that person to die in another way, but we should also look for the reasons why many feel that there are important exceptions.

To assess these reasons, we need to take seriously general facts about the human condition, such as our potential strengths as well as weaknesses and vulnerabilities, our aversion to premature death, devotion to family and friends, desire for quality of life and respect from others, limited altruism, liabilities to anger, malice, and indifference to others, need for rules, and tendencies to conform to what is familiar. Our ultimate aims may be different: for example, consequentialists will emphasize reasons to support norms and practices that tend to promote human well-being as they define it, and Kantians will give priority to reasons that support norms and practices that express respect for human dignity as they interpret this. In the end, one may hope, the various approaches will tend to converge in their specific conclusions, but in any case I would argue that a deep justification requires systematic thinking from a reasonably impartial and inclusive perspective that takes seriously the complexities of the human condition and the particular issues under debate. Intuitions regarding examples, especially unrealistic fictional examples, are not decisive. When we consider the usual priority of letting die over killing – and the possible exceptions – we are concerned with how a reasonable and fair system of moral norms can best respect, protect, and promote widely shared human values (life, liberty, welfare, mutual respect, etc.). In particular, the question is how the responsibility for preserving these values should be distributed. Given our naturally strong self-regard, limited altruism, and greater control over ourselves than others, it makes sense that the norms generally assign to each person the primary responsibility to prevent themselves from killing, lying, torturing, etc., and only secondarily and in special circumstances the responsibility to prevent others from doing these things. It seems natural to want to have a life of one's own without having the responsibility constantly to police the bad behavior of others. If so, the intuition that *in most cases* killing is worse than letting die would be backed by good reasons. This, however, only makes the case "for the most part," not absolutely. Special considerations apply when the person one proposes to kill is oneself. Normally the natural desire for self-preservation is strong enough to make this issue mute. It arises only when a person sees his or her present and future life as so bad that natural self-regard does not silence the question. Now the special questions we have been considering here become more prominent, in particular, what is the value of continued life when one's capacities to act and to appreciate are increasingly diminished? Neither this nor our other questions about the morality of suicide are easily resolved, but they are certainly not reasonably resolved by simple application of an absolute rule that it is worse to kill a person than to let the person die.

NOTES

1   Donagan 1977: 49–50, 76–79.
2   Nozick 1974.
3   Hooker 2000: 32–45. Here is Hooker's version of rule-consequentialism: "An act is wrong if it is forbidden by the code of rules whose internalization by the overwhelming majority of everyone everywhere in each generation has the maximum expected value in terms of well-being (with some priority for the worst off)" (32 and 43 n.13).
4   Hooker 2000: 42.
5   In this section I draw from Hill 1983 (reprinted in Hill 1991: 85–103). This essay was not entirely a response to philosophical debates but written from reflections on the hard decisions that my mother faced in the last stages of terminal colon cancer. Her explicit decisions were not directly for or against suicide but for or against surgeries that were expected to prolong her life briefly and with minimal quality.
6   Kant 2002: 223 [4: 422]. Bracketed numbers always refer to volume and page of the standard Prussian Academy edition.
7   Kant 1996: 177 [642–43].

8　Kant 1996: 177–78 [6: 423–24].

9　Kant 2002: 230 [4: 429].

10　Kant 2002: 235–36 [4: 435–36].

11　See Hill 2012a.

12　Hill 2012b: 86–89.

13　Kant 2002: 223 [4: 421–22] and 230 [4: 429].

14　Hill 1983: 90–91, 101.

15　Even Kant regarded it a "casuistic question" whether it would be wrong (before modern medicines were available) to kill oneself before the bite of a dog with rabies inevitably led to one's insanity and death. See note 7 above.

16　Mill 2001: 7–12.

17　Moore 1903 and 1912.

18　Some may argue that appreciating good things "makes one's life go better" and so belongs to an "objective list" of criteria for "well-being," but beyond this I suggest that it is an ideal (not a duty) for human beings, within their capacities, to appreciate many of the vast variety of ("intrinsically") good things that life can offer. The opposite – being negatively disposed and effectively closed off to possible appreciation – is far from a morally excellent ideal way for human beings to live and this is not just because it is not prudent to choose when aiming to "get the most" out of life.

19　Hill 1983: 98–99.

20　Kant 2002: 223 [4: 222].

21　Hill 2006. Reprinted in Hill 2012a: 95–106.

22　Williams 1973.

17 Killing in self-defense

I

Philosophical questions come in different shapes and sizes. Some are relatively small and well defined; others are big and unwieldy, spilling over into other philosophical questions and problems. My assigned question, for this volume – *when* and *why* may we kill others? – falls into the second category.

If we begin with the "when," we quickly find ourselves in the middle of a variety of hotly debated topics in applied ethics. Is the death penalty ever justified? Are we permitted to kill non-combatants in war, and if so, when? May we kill one person to save the lives of a greater number of others, and if so, when? May we kill to save our own life, and if so, when? And what we say in answer to each of these questions will depend on what we think about other things – punishment, desert, moral responsibility, just war theory, and so on. And this is just a subset of the "when" questions; for discussion of questions about abortion, assisted suicide and euthanasia, and the killing of nonhuman animals, see Chapters 15, 16, and 19 in this volume.

We could begin with the "why," and formulate the question in a different way: why and when is it prima facie wrong to kill others? This question puts the emphasis on *killing*, in contrast to *letting die*, and asks what makes it wrong, or especially wrong. But now the question is too big for a different kind of reason.

The question rests on a presupposition – that there is a difference between killing and letting die. Common sense assumes that there is a difference, and that the difference has moral significance, but both these claims are philosophically controversial. Consequentialists deny that there is any morally relevant difference between killing and letting die (or, more generally, between doing and allowing harm). Deontologists, or at least some deontologists, claim that there is a moral difference, but there is no consensus on the *nonmoral* difference that grounds the moral difference. And it's worse than that; the accounts that have been offered are subject to well-known difficulties.[1] Some deontologists say that this doesn't matter; that our intuitive understanding of the difference between paradigm cases of killing and letting die is good enough. I disagree.

I am a deontologist. I believe that our common-sense beliefs about the moral difference between killing and letting die are based on a coherent and defensible nonmoral distinction between causing an outcome and only allowing that outcome.[2] But I can't think of a plausible informative answer to the question of *why* causing a bad outcome is morally worse than allowing that outcome. So I'm not going to try to answer this question. On the other hand, I think there are plausible and informative things to be said about the permissibility and impermissibility of particular kinds of killing. I will narrow my topic by focusing on what is perhaps the least controversial kind of killing – killing in self-defense.

At first glance, killing in self-defense seems unproblematic. If someone is trying to kill you, you are not morally required to let yourself be killed; you have no "duty of martyrdom."[3] Of course you should run, or hide, or use lesser force, if you can. But if there is no way to save your life short of killing the person who would otherwise kill you, then you are morally permitted to kill that person. Killing in self-defense is, in other words, an exception to the general prohibition against killing. Call this "the Simple View."[4] The Simple View isn't quite this simple. There are complications having to do with situations in which your only means of preventing your attacker from killing you would cause the death of an innocent bystander. We will set these complications aside for now. Philosophers reject the Simple View for a more fundamental reason. They reject the Simple View because it fails to explain a certain *moral asymmetry* between an aggressor and his victim.

The problem is this: the Simple View says that you are morally permitted to kill, if need be, in self-defense. But when you fight back against your attacker, thereby putting his life at risk, he acts impermissibly if *he* fights back. You have the right of self-defense against him; he doesn't have the right of self-defense against you.

There appears to be a further asymmetry with respect to other-defense. It may be permissible for a third party to use force to defend *you* against someone who is attacking you, and even to kill, if need be. But when you fight back against your attacker, it isn't permissible for a third party to defend *him* against you.

Jeff McMahan sums up this objection to the Simple View as follows:

The mere fact that someone threatens your life is insufficient to ground a justification for killing him in self-defense. If, for example, you are morally liable to be killed, you have no right to self-defense. A rampaging murderer who sees that he is about to be killed by a police sniper will be guilty of one more murder if he kills the sniper in self-defense.⁵

McMahan concludes that the Simple View is wrong, and that an adequate philosophical account of self-defense will explain this moral asymmetry between a victim and his aggressor. And others have agreed. For a time, this was considered *the* problem of self-defense. Since it has now been displaced by a further problem, I will call it "the Asymmetry Problem."

II

In a highly influential paper,⁶ Judith Jarvis Thomson offered a solution to the Asymmetry Problem. I will call it "Rights Forfeit."⁷

Thomson said that we have the right not to be killed, and it is our right not to be killed that *explains* the permissibility of self- and other-defense. But rights are not inalienable. They can be forfeited or lost. In particular, they can be lost by *violating the rights of others*. In trying to kill you, the aggressor violates your right not to be killed, and in doing so he forfeits his own right not to be killed by you or by someone trying to defend you.

Thomson's view is appealing. It solves the Asymmetry Problem. And it does this by pointing to a plausible difference between an innocent victim and a villainous aggressor: the innocent victim has, and the villainous aggressor lacks, the right not to be killed.

Some philosophers are, rightly, suspicious of appeals to rights, but Thomson isn't doing any handwaving. In her book *The Realm of Rights*,⁸ Thomson defends a theory of rights with the following features: rights are objective features of reality with genuine

explanatory power – they *explain* facts about what it is permissible
and impermissible to do without being equivalent to permissibility facts. They are able to do this for two reasons. First, rights are
sparse – the realm of rights is not the realm of all of morality. You
may be morally required to do something – save a stranger's child
from drowning – even though no one has a right that you do that
thing. And the fact that someone has a right that you do or not do
something doesn't always entail that you are morally required to do
or not do that thing. If A needs to cross B's land and trample on B's
flower beds to get her sick child to the hospital, then A may be justified in infringing B's right that A not cross her land or trample on
her flower beds. Second, and related to the first point, rights leave
"moral traces." Even if A acts permissibly and with objective justification in crossing B's land and trampling B's flower beds, A still
owes B compensation for the damage done to her property. But some
rights – including the right not to be killed – are maximally stringent; they cannot be justifiably infringed.

Rights Forfeit seems to account for the facts about paradigm cases
of aggressors and victims. But, as Thomson noted, not all aggressors are villainous. She gave as an example *Innocent Aggressor*, who
has been made temporarily crazy by a drug injected into him by a
villain; he is now trying to kill you. She also gave the example of
Innocent Threat, a fat man pushed by a villain off the cliff above
your house; if you do nothing he will fall on you, squash you flat,
and kill you, while surviving the fall himself. Common sense says
that we are permitted to defend ourselves even in these kinds of
situations, and Thomson agreed. She acknowledged that it sounds
odd to say that someone can lose their rights by falling or going
crazy,[9] but she argued that to say otherwise is to make the unacceptable assumption that self-defense is justified only against those who
deserve punishment for their aggression. ("But who are you, private
person that you are, to be dishing out punishment to the villainous
for the things that they do?"[10])

Thomson defended her account partly by arguing that the morally significant difference between bystanders, on the one hand,
and threats and aggressors, on the other, is a *causal* distinction.
Bystanders, she said, are those who are "in no way causally involved"
in your being at a risk of death.[11] Aggressors and threats, by contrast,
are those who are "causally involved ... and not minimally so" in

your being at immediate risk of death.¹² On Thomson's view, we are not permitted to kill bystanders, even to prevent ourselves from being killed, because bystanders, unlike aggressors and threats, have the right not to be killed. There are, of course, alternative accounts of the impermissibility of killing bystanders, but these alternative accounts usually end up appealing, in one way or another, to the intentions with which we would be acting, if we killed a bystander. Thomson argued that intentions are irrelevant to questions of permissibility, and therefore rejected all versions of the Doctrine of Double Effect, as well as other intention-based principles.¹³ She didn't offer an analysis of the killing/letting die distinction, but she told us quite a bit about what we are *not* permitted to do in the course of self-defense. We are not permitted to do what will cause or otherwise result in the death of bystanders in any of the following ways: *Use-of-a-Bystander* (e.g. by grabbing a bystander and using him as a shield so that he is shot instead of you), *Substitution-of-a-Bystander* (e.g. by deflecting an out-of-control trolley so that it kills a bystander instead of you), or *Riding-Roughshod-over-a-Bystander* (e.g. by throwing a bomb at a trolley to stop it from killing you, causing the death of a bystander on the tracks, or by pushing a bystander off the one-person bridge that is your only means of escape from an Aggressor). Thomson noted that some of these categories overlap, and she acknowledged that her account was incomplete insofar as it is not intended to settle questions about self-defense in war.¹⁴ But she said enough to make it clear that on her view there are serious moral limits to the use of force in the course of self-defense.

III

Despite these appealing features, Thomson's account has come under severe criticism in recent years. The target of the criticism has been her claim that innocent aggressors and threats have lost their right not to be killed. I will formulate the argument in terms of Thomson's example of the falling man, but the argument is supposed to generalize to all cases of innocent threats and aggressors, including those who are not responsible for what they do because they are lunatics, children, sleepwalkers, or suffering from some other defect that renders them incapable of morally responsible agency.

The "You Can't Lose Rights by Falling" argument:

(1) You can't lose rights without exercising morally responsible agency (either by explicitly waiving your rights or by acting in a way that violates the rights of another person).
(2) The Falling Man does not exercise agency.
(3) Therefore, Falling Man has not lost any rights.
(4) Therefore, Falling Man has not lost the right not to be killed.

Therefore, Rights Forfeit doesn't explain why it's permissible to kill in self-defense.[15]

The falling man (madman, sleepwalker, etc.) cannot help what he does, so he is no more capable of wronging you than a rock is. But if he wouldn't wrong you, by landing on you and killing you, he doesn't violate your rights. And if he doesn't violate your rights, it can't be true that he has lost his own rights.

This argument has had an enormous impact on the recent literature. As Tyler Doggett notes, if the argument is sound, then we must choose between Thomson's why-thesis (her explanation of *why* we may kill in self-defense) and her which-thesis (her account of *who* we may kill and in *which* cases).[16]

If the first premise is true, the argument is sound. Is there anything to be said in favor of the claim that someone can either violate or lose rights simply by falling? Perhaps. Thomson cites Frances Kamm in support of the following "moral phenomenon": if Falling Man could alter the direction of his fall, then "morality would call for his doing so, even at considerable cost to himself."[17] Kamm stops short of saying that Falling Man's obligation extends as far as killing himself, but Thomson has recently suggested that the fault-free driver of a car whose brakes have failed might be morally required to kill himself rather than kill innocent people.[18] But this is inconclusive. The "moral phenomenon" might be a cousin of what Susan Wolf has called "the moral of moral luck" – the fact that we (rightly) feel worse when we have caused a harm than when we have only tried to cause it, or risked causing it.[19] What's needed is some argument that gives us reason to suppose that in the actual scenario, in which Falling Man *cannot* alter the direction of his fall, he nevertheless violates your maximally stringent right if he falls on you and kills you, and because he is *about* to do this, he loses his own maximally stringent right not to be killed. To many this seems unfair.

I suspect that the real reason Thomson defends this claim about Falling Man is that she is unwilling to give up common-sense verdicts about which-cases in the face of the implications of her theory of rights. The right not to be killed is a maximally stringent right, so if you are permitted to kill Falling Man this must be because he has – somehow – lost this right. But few have been willing to follow Thomson to this conclusion. Many have taken the lesson to be that Thomson's which-thesis is false and that the correct why-thesis must somehow appeal to the agency of those you may kill in self-defense.

The Falling Man argument is important because it highlights a conflict between two intuitions:

> Permission: You are not morally required to let yourself be killed; you may defend your life, by lethal force if need be.

> Limit: It is wrong to kill someone who isn't trying to kill you (or another innocent person).

If we focus our attention only on cases of aggressors (villainous or innocent), there is no conflict between the two intuitions. The first intuition says that we have the right to defend ourselves; the second intuition says that there are moral limits to this right. I may not save my life, or the life of another, at the expense of the life of an innocent person.

But the case of Falling Man shows that these two intuitions can come in conflict. Falling Man isn't trying to kill or even harm you, so it is wrong to kill him. But if you do nothing, he will kill you (albeit without intention or agency).

IV

Let's set aside the question of whether Rights Forfeit can explain your permission to defend yourself against Falling Man. Are we entitled to this common-sense belief? Michael Otsuka argues that we are not.

The Bystander Argument:

> (P1) It is impermissible to kill a Bystander to prevent oneself from being killed.

(P2) The killing of Falling Man[20] and the killing of a Bystander are, other things equal, on a par so far as permissibility is concerned. Therefore, it is impermissible to kill the Falling Man to prevent yourself from being killed.

Otsuka's defense of the second premise is based on a comparison between three cases:[21]

(1) Bystander is lying beside an empty runaway trolley that will kill you unless you throw a bomb at it that will stop the trolley but also kill Bystander.

(2) Bystander is the only person in the runaway trolley – the other details are the same.

(3) Falling Man will land on you, killing you, unless you vaporize him with your ray gun.

Otsuka says that it is clearly impermissible to kill the Bystander in the first case,[22] and the only difference between the first and second case is the location of Bystander. Since the location of Bystander is not morally relevant, it is impermissible to kill the Bystander in the second case. The only difference between the second and third case is that in the third case it is the person's *body* that will kill you, whereas in the second case it is "the *trolley* in which the person is encased" that will kill you. In putting it this way, Otsuka is vividly calling our attention to the fact that, so far as *control* over the outcome of your death is concerned, the Bystander inside the trolley and the Falling Man are equals. Bystander has no control over the movements of the trolley; Falling Man has no control over the movements of his falling body.

But we can agree that Falling Man resembles Bystander in this way while denying that this has any bearing on the *permissibility* of self-defense.[23] Control is relevant to the permissibility of self-defense only if a necessary condition of the permissibility of self-defense is that the target of our use of defensive force is culpable, or at least morally responsible, for what he does. But this isn't true. A grizzly bear is neither culpable nor morally responsible, but we are permitted to defend ourselves against it.

This shows that what we believe, concerning the moral limits of permissible killing in self-defense, is something weaker than:

Limit: It is wrong to kill someone who isn't trying to kill you.
It is:

Limit*: It is wrong to kill someone who would not otherwise kill you.

And Otsuka is wrong that there is no relevant difference between Falling Man and Bystander. If you do not use your ray gun, killing Falling Man, Falling Man will cause your death; more than that, he will *kill you*. But if you don't use your bomb, stopping the trolley and killing Bystander, he will neither kill you nor cause your death in some way that falls short of killing.[24]

Otsuka thinks that this difference is not morally relevant. But common sense says that it is,[25] and in the absence of some argument that common sense is confused about this, we are under no obligation to give up this belief.

Since the intuitive force of Otsuka's argument consists largely in his comparison of innocent threats to bystanders, it is worth taking a closer look at Otsuka's first premise – his *Inviolability of a Bystander* thesis. It turns out that Otsuka doesn't really mean what you might think he means, when he says that you may never kill a bystander to prevent yourself from being killed. He qualifies his claim thus:

For the purposes of this article, "killing" will refer only to the initiation or sustaining or the insertion of someone into a sequence of events that results in the death of a person ... It will not refer to instances of "ducking harm" that result in the death of a person. It is, I think, permissible to duck out of the way of an oncoming javelin even if you foresee that, by ducking, you will allow the javelin to impale a Bystander standing behind you.[26]

And he says:

Cases involving the redirection, as opposed to the initiation, of a lethal sequence of events (e.g. Philippa Foot's trolley problem) are a different matter.[27]

But now he is in trouble. For consider the following sequence of cases:

(1) Shoot: If you do nothing, Falling Man will land on you, killing you while surviving the fall himself thanks to the cushion of your body. You can prevent this only by shooting him with your vaporizing ray gun.

(2) Move Awning (Deflect Falling Man): As before, but this time you can prevent Falling Man from killing you only by shifting the position of your awning, so he is deflected away from you and lands on the road below, dying on impact.

(3) Duck (Deflect Yourself): As before, but this time you can prevent Falling Man from killing you only by quickly moving out of the way, so Falling Man misses you and lands on the ground, dying on impact.

(4) Deflect Trolley: You are trapped on a track facing an out-of-control trolley. You can prevent yourself from being killed only by pushing a button which will deflect the trolley on to another track. The story continues in two versions:

(4A) Bystander Inside: A bystander is trapped inside the trolley. If you push the button, the trolley will go off a cliff and Bystander will be killed.

(4B) Bystander Outside: The trolley is empty, but a bystander is trapped on the other track. If you push the button, Bystander will be killed.

The first three cases are cases where if you act, you directly and foreseeably cause the death of Falling Man. (If you doubt that you cause the death of Falling Man in the third case, consider the following, only slightly different scenario. You are a firefighter and your job is to hold the net for people jumping out of a burning building. Because you aren't paying attention, you move away, and Falling Man lands on hard ground and dies. If you had done your job and stayed in place, he would have lived. You caused his death, by removing the net that would have prevented his death. The third case is different from the firefighter case insofar as it is your body, rather than a safety net, that's needed to save Falling Man's life and insofar as it is not your job to save his life. But so far as the causal facts are concerned, the two cases are alike.[28]) The last two cases are cases where, if you act, you directly and foreseeably cause the death of Bystander.

In the first two cases, most people will agree that if you act, you don't just do something that causes the death of Falling Man, you *kill* Falling Man.[29] People disagree about whether you kill in the third case, so I won't assume this.[30] In the last two cases, if you act, you don't just cause the death of Bystander; you *kill* Bystander. This is uncontroversial.

Since four of these cases are cases in which preventing your death requires you to kill an innocent person (a bystander or a falling man), and the third is a case where preventing your death requires you to act in a way that directly and foreseeably causes the death of an innocent person, you might expect Otsuka to tell us that you are morally required to let yourself be killed in each case. But Otsuka gives us clear verdicts for only the first and third case. He says that you *must* refrain from Shooting, letting Falling Man kill you, and that you *may* Duck, saving your life at the expense of Falling Man.

The second case – Move Awning – is Thomson's version of the Falling Man case, so you might expect Otsuka to say that moving the awning is impermissible. (Perhaps on the grounds that moving the awning counts as "initiating," as opposed to merely redirecting, a "lethal sequence.")

But what's the difference between Move Awning and Duck? In both cases, you move something (the awning, yourself) and the causal upshot of this movement is that Falling Man lands on hard pavement, *rather than on you*, and dies, and you live. The only non-moral difference between the two cases is that in Move Awning, the movement alters the trajectory of Falling Man's fall, whereas in Duck the movement alters *your* trajectory. In Move Awning, you save your life by *altering the direction* of his fall; that is, by *deflecting* him. In Duck, you save your life by altering your position; that is, by *deflecting yourself* so that you are no longer on a collision course with him. But in both cases, the effect of one of these deflections is that the collision between Falling Man and you is avoided, with the upshot that he dies and you live.

But if it is permissible to do something that causes Falling Man to land on hard ground rather than you by deflecting *yourself*, how can it be wrong to do something that causes Falling Man to land on hard ground by deflecting *him*? Otsuka has no answer to this question, and I don't think any answer is available.

Suppose, then, that Otsuka says that it is permissible to proceed in Move Awning. But if he says this, then he must say the same about Deflect Trolley. For in Move Awning, you move something (the awning), with the causal upshot that Falling Man falls to his death on the hard ground. In Deflect Trolley (Bystander Inside), you move something (the button), with the causal upshot that the Trolley goes

off the cliff, killing Bystander. In Deflect Trolley (Bystander Outside),
you also move something (the button) with the causal upshot that
the Trolley switches tracks and kills Bystander. (The only difference
between these two cases is the location of Bystander.) People who
think that turning the trolley is permissible think this for reasons
having to do with the greater number of people who would be saved.
But in Deflect Trolley the numbers are equal. You save yourself,
and only yourself, by turning the trolley and killing Bystander.
Deflect Trolley is an instance of Thomson's *Riding-Roughshod-
over-a-Bystander*. If it is permissible, then Otsuka's Inviolability of
a Bystander Thesis is false.

v

Otsuka is on unstable ground. He criticizes Thomson's account for
having unacceptable implications concerning the killing of innocent persons, but since he lacks an account of the different ways in
which one may, or may not, cause the death of an innocent person,
he isn't entitled to say that his account respects the "inviolability" of innocent bystanders. And even if we set aside the problem of
bystanders, his account is problematic. He says that in order to lose
one's "moral immunity from being killed" one must have acted so
that one is morally responsible for this loss; you are permitted to kill
in self-defense only in situations in which "the action that endangers your life flows from an agent who identifies with the intention
from which she acts, is of sound mind when she acts, and could have
avoided endangering your life."[31] On Otsuka's account, neither the
falling man, nor a child, nor the insane have lost their immunity.
Yet he doesn't want to say that our permission to defend ourselves
against an aggressor turns on the difficult question of whether the
aggressor would be judged criminally insane. So he says that our
permission to kill the criminally insane has a *different basis* – the
fact that, like a grizzly bear, they are not persons and are therefore
worth less than we are.[32]

McMahan, who also defends a kind of moral responsibility
account of self-defense, takes a more nuanced view, but his account
has some surprising implications as well. In a recent paper, he
acknowledges this and makes a "partners in guilt" defense by arguing that all theories of self-defense have a problem with the Tactical

Bomber in a just war.[33] In the case that McMahan describes, the bomber drops bombs on a military facility located on the border of the enemy country; the explosion will kill innocent civilians living just across the border in a neutral country. The citizens cannot flee, but they have access to an anti-aircraft gun. McMahan says that intuitively the civilians are permitted to shoot down the bomber in self-defense, but neither Rights Forfeit nor his own account can say this because both accounts say that in a conflict between two parties, one party has, and the other lacks, the right to self-defense. Since the bomber acts with justification, he retains his right not to be killed, and this means that the civilians may not kill him. McMahan sums it up as follows:

> Yet intuitively it seems that, just as it is permissible for the civilians to kill the tactical bomber in self-defense, so it is also permissible for the tactical bomber to kill the civilians in self-defense. This apparent symmetry is, however, incompatible with the implications of the Rights-Based Account.[34]

This is a surprising point for McMahan to be making, but it is a good one. A simpler example is that of two soldiers on a battlefield. Regardless of the rights or wrongs of the conflict, it seems that each acts permissibly in defending his own life against the other. Some think that wartime situations are different. But similar situations can arise in private life, given any situations in which two persons (duelists, gladiators, slaves, the children in *The Hunger Games*, etc.) either freely or under conditions of coercion or duress must fight each other to the death. There need be no moral asymmetry, so far as rights and violations of rights goes, between the two parties. We *could* say that the party who strikes the first blow is the aggressor; he violates the right of the other and therefore has lost his own right not to be killed, and thus his own permission to defend himself, but this is not an appealing analysis of the situation. And we *could* say that both parties act impermissibly and are only excused, but this is also not an appealing view. (And would not explain the intuitive permissibility of other-defense.) Depending on the view we take about rights, we might say that each retains the right not to be killed, while retaining the right to defend himself, or we could say that each has, by choosing to engage in the battle with the other, given up his right not to be killed. But regardless of which we say, there seems no reason to think there is an asymmetry between the two. Either both retain their right not to be killed, or both lose this right. (Or, perhaps, never had it in the first place.) What seems clearest is that in these unfortunate situations, neither party to the conflict has a "duty of martyrdom"; each has a moral permission to defend himself against the other.

But now notice something. If the right to self-defense may be morally symmetric in this way, we don't need to suppose that *one person has*, while *the other lacks*, the *right not to be killed* (or an immunity against being killed, or some other more fundamental moral status) in order to *explain* the permissibility of self-defense. We can take the permissibility of self-defense for granted, as common sense does. We don't need to appeal to any deeper moral fact to explain *why* it is permissible – within limits of course – to use force to prevent ourselves from being killed. This leaves us free to do what really needs doing: to provide a systematic account of the limits of permissible self-defense. Who counts as a bystander, and is it really true that it is always wrong to kill or otherwise cause the death of a bystander? Why isn't ducking harm an instance of *Substitution-of-a-Bystander*, and why is ducking permissible when *Substitution-of-a-Bystander* and *Riding-Roughshod-over-a-Bystander* are not? The kind of account that's needed is a systematic account of the *nonmoral* differences between the cases in which it is permissible to act so that a bystander dies as a result (for everyone agrees that there are such cases) and the cases in which this is not permissible.

At this point you are no doubt wondering whether I have forgotten the problem with which we began. Why does the villainous aggressor lack the right of self-defense when his victim fights back? Even if self-defense isn't *necessarily* asymmetric, surely it is asymmetric in this paradigm case.

I haven't forgotten. I don't think there is any asymmetry, not even in this case. The Simple View was right all along.

VI

The right of self-defense is the right to use the *minimal* force necessary to defend yourself. A victim who fights back against an aggressor is not (or at least not typically) trying to kill; he is only trying to prevent the aggressor from killing him. So in the case of the aggressor, self-defense often requires no force at all. If Victim is waving a gun in his face, frantically shouting "Desist, or I will shoot you!" all that Aggressor needs to do is to drop his gun and raise his hands. We don't need to suppose that Aggressor has lost his right to use self-defense in order to say this.

There are, of course, different kinds of cases. Here is one, described by Thomson in an early paper on self-defense (a paper in which she worried about the account of forfeiture that she later adopted):

Suppose that as Victim raises his anti-tank gun to fire it, Aggressor's tank stalls. Aggressor gets out to examine the engine, but falls and breaks both ankles in the process. Victim (let us suppose) now has time to get away from Aggressor and is in no danger. I take it that you will not think that Victim may all the same go ahead and kill Aggressor. But why not? – if Aggressor really has forfeited his right to not be killed by virtue of his attack on Victim.[35]

Thomson described this case for the purpose of showing that the defender of an account like Rights Forfeit must say that the right not to be killed is a right that may come and go during the course of a conflict between an aggressor and victim. This is an odd thing to say, and Thomson agreed. (However, she thought that the alternatives were even worse.) But the Simple View can provide a much simpler explanation. According to the Simple View, Victim's permission to use minimal force to defend himself does not wax and wane as Aggressor loses, and then reacquires, his right not to be killed. Rather, Victim *always* has the right to use the minimal force needed to defend himself. After Aggressor breaks both ankles, the minimal force is none at all.

But what about McMahan's case of the murderer and the police sniper? The murderer has already killed some innocent people and the police sniper is preparing to shoot to prevent him from killing more. At this moment in time, it is too late for Murderer to drop his gun and raise his hands. If we say that Murderer still has the right of self-defense, don't we have to say that he is permitted to kill the police sniper to save his life?

No. To see why, consider a different scenario. I live in a dangerous neighborhood, so I own a variety of weapons. Today as I work in my home office, I have handy a ray gun and a stun gun. Villainous Aggressor walks in, holding a gun, and demands the contents of my safe. I quickly pick up both my guns and point them at Villainous Aggressor. He looks surprised, but stands his ground, holding his gun and repeating his demand. I toss away my stun gun, and say: "Put that gun down or I'll shoot." He continues to point the gun at me. I shoot with my ray gun, killing him.[36]

In this situation, my use of defensive force was not permissible. I did not use the minimal force required to stop Aggressor; I had a stun gun. It makes no difference that *at the moment* that I fired the ray gun, I no longer had the stun gun. Whether a person uses the minimal force needed to defend themselves is not a 'snapshot' fact about the person. Facts about their recent past conduct may be relevant.

In the case of the Murderer and the police sniper, the same kind of explanation applies. At the moment that the police sniper aims the gun at him, the only way Murderer can save his life is by shooting first. But that's not relevant. Murderer had a choice, only moments before, when the police sniper issued his last warning, to drop the gun and come out, hands in the air. Because of this wilfully lost opportunity, it isn't true that Murderer needed to shoot the police sniper to prevent himself from being killed.

There is a great deal more to be said, but I have no space to say it here. Hard questions remain about the relevant time frame for judging whether an instance of defensive force is the minimal force needed to preserve life. But suppose these questions can be answered. If so, there is no Asymmetry Problem and thus no need to invoke Rights Forfeit as the solution. Where does this leave us? That depends. If we are independently convinced that Thomson's theory of rights is basically right, we might conclude that Thomson's mistake was only to think that the right not to be killed is maximally stringent. Killing in self-defense is like trampling someone's rosebushes to get a sick child to hospital – a case of justified rights-infringement. (If we say this, we must say that defensive killing leaves "moral traces" – the killer owes compensation to his innocent or villainous victim.) But we might also draw a more radical moral – that the right not to be killed does *no explanatory work*, in this or in other cases, because the right *is* the permission to use defensive force. More generally, we might abandon Thomson's appealing idea that rights somehow explain permissibility and impermissibility facts without being reducible to these facts. How might such a theory go?

For a novel and interesting proposal, see Tomkow's "Self Defense"
and "Retributive Ethics."[37]

NOTES

1   See, for instance, Bennett 1995 and Howard-Snyder 2002.
2   I defended an account of the nonmoral difference that grounds the
     moral difference in Vihvelin and Tomkow 2005.
3   W. Kaufman 2010.
4   McMahan 1994 describes a similar view, calling it "the Orthodox
     View." McMahan argues that the Orthodox View is mistaken and that
     many of our common-sense beliefs about self-defense are mistaken.
5   McMahan 2009: 386.
6   Thomson 1991.
7   It is more commonly called "the Rights View" or "the Rights-Based"
     account.
8   Thomson 1990.
9   "I spelled all this out in detail in order that it be clear exactly where
     the shoe pinches" (Thomson 1991: 300).
10   Thomson 1991: 285.
11   Thomson 1991: 298. Thomson said that this is a sufficient condition,
     and left it open whether it is also necessary.
12   Thomson 1991: 299. Thomson said that this is a sufficient condition,
     and left it open whether it is also necessary.
13   Thomson 1991: 292–96.
14   Thomson 1991: 296–98.
15   This argument was most prominently made by McMahan and Otsuka.
     I will be focusing on Otsuka's (1994) version of the argument
16   In his excellent survey of the recent literature (Doggett 2011).
17   Thomson 1991: 302; Kamm 1992: 47; Uniacke 1994.
18   Thomson 2008: 371.
19   Wolf 2000.
20   Otsuka 1994: 76. These are the exact words of Otsuka's argument
     except for his use of "Threat" in place of Falling Man. Otsuka uses
     "Threat" to refer to an Innocent Threat, and he defines an Innocent
     Threat as a person "whose mere movements qua physical object or
     mere presence constitutes a threat to our life" (75).
21   Otsuka 1994: 85.
22   He cites, with approval, Thomson's claim that it is impermissible to
     kill a Bystander in the way that she characterizes as "riding roughshod
     over a Bystander."

23 Remember, the Bystander Argument is supposed to be an argument for the claim that it is impermissible to kill Falling Man, not an argument for the conclusion that Falling Man doesn't violate any rights.

24 See McMahan 1994 and 2002 for attempts to bolster Otsuka's arguments. Frowe 2008 and Quong 2009 criticize the argument.

25 McMahan 2009 agrees. He defends his account of self-defense despite the fact that it conflicts with these common-sense verdicts.

26 Otsuka 1994: 76.

27 Otsuka 1994: 77. Otsuka doesn't provide details, but it's clear that he shares the intuition that many people have: that a bystander may deflect a trolley, killing an innocent person in order to prevent some larger number of innocent persons being killed. This is deeply problematic for a deontologist; hence the name "Trolley Problem." After making a number of attempts to solve the problem, Thomson has changed her mind; she now thinks it is impermissible for anyone other than the driver to turn the trolley (Thomson 2008).

28 See Schaffer 2004 for a defense of causation by disconnection and preventing a preventer.

29 For some reflections on the difference between doing something that causes death and killing, see Lewis 1986b.

30 For extended discussion of ducking, see Boorse and Sorensen 1988. Boorse and Sorensen noted that at least some instances of ducking are instances of killing on anyone's account, and they argued that an adequate solution to the act/omission problem must also solve what they called the Ducking/Sacrificing problem. To Duck is, roughly, to move yourself, causing what would otherwise have killed or harmed you to kill or harm someone else. To Sacrifice is, roughly, to move someone else, so that what would otherwise have killed or harmed you, instead kills or harm them. Ducking is usually, but not always, considered morally permissible; Sacrificing is not.

31 Otsuka 1994: 91.

32 Otsuka 1994: 92.

33 McMahan 2009: 389.

34 McMahan 2009: 390.

35 Thomson 1976: 34.

36 I owe this example to Terrance Tomkow.

37 Tomkow 2011 and 2012.

18 Imperfect aiding

I

This chapter concerns the nature of the moral reason (or reasons) we have to come to the aid of those in distress. By aiding a person in distress I mean saving him from current or imminent harm. Aiding can be either direct, as when one throws a life preserver to a drowning swimmer, or indirect, as when one contributes money to a charitable organization.

Views regarding the morality of aiding range widely. Some think we needn't ever aid others – unless, that is, aiding them is our job, or the person in distress is our child, or some such. This view attributes great significance to the distinction between doing harm and failing to prevent it. Each of us, it is acknowledged, has a general duty not to harm people, but, it is claimed, we have no parallel general duty to prevent people from suffering harm. Any positive duty to render aid must be grounded in some *special* relation between the agent and the potential recipient of his aid; in the absence of such a special relation, aiding is at best supererogatory. Others think that failing to aid a person is morally indistinguishable from actively harming him. On this view we have a general *pro tanto* duty to aid people, and it is just as strong as our *pro tanto* duty not to harm them. (A *pro tanto* duty is one that can in principle be overridden. An agent is sometimes justified in failing to do that which he is *pro tanto* required to do.)

I wish to thank Steven Luper for his helpful comments on an earlier version of the chapter.

300

Most views about the morality of aiding fall between these extremes. Some hold that although there is a general duty to aid, it is less expansive than the duty not to harm: we need aid only those who are in danger of suffering especially serious harm. Others hold that the duty to aid is weaker than the duty not to harm: it is more easily overridden, and we needn't risk or sacrifice as much in order to fulfill it. I wish to examine a view according to which the two duties differ *structurally*: while the duty not to harm people is *perfect*, the duty to aid them is *imperfect*. Roughly speaking, an imperfect duty is one that allows the agent considerable leeway in choosing the occasions on which he shall act to fulfill it. (I shall try to make this characterization more precise shortly.) A perfect duty allows the agent no such leeway. If the duty to render aid is imperfect, we needn't render aid every time we are in a position to do so. Rather, we must aid people *enough* of the time – where it is left somewhat vague what counts as enough. An agent who rarely if ever aids others fails to do his duty; an agent who frequently aids others probably does more than his duty requires; and somewhere in between lies a range of morally acceptable (but not supererogatory) patterns of aiding. The duty not to harm people, by contrast, is perfect. One cannot fulfill this duty by occasionally, or even by often, refraining from harming people. If one *ever* inflicts serious harm upon another person, without justification, one violates this duty.

On one traditional understanding, imperfect duties require agents to have certain ends. The duty to aid, on this understanding, requires each person to have the good of others among his ends. This needn't (and shouldn't) be his only end; that's why he needn't aid people on every occasion when he could do so. But an agent who rarely if ever aids people does not have their good as a sufficiently weighty end.

My aim in this chapter is not to argue that the duty to aid *is* imperfect. It is rather to determine more precisely what it would be for this, or for any, duty to be imperfect, and to explore some of the implications of the thesis that the duty to aid is imperfect. In the final section I shall consider the possibility that sometimes aiding a particular person (to whom one has no special obligations) is morally required, and I shall ask whether this possibility is consistent with the thesis that the duty to aid is merely imperfect.

II

Before turning to these tasks, it will be useful to introduce another way of divvying up duties. Some duties are *directed*, while others are *undirected*. A directed duty is one that corresponds to another person's claim right, and is owed to the holder of that right.[1] If I promised my son I would take him to Disneyland, I am not merely *pro tanto* obligated to take him there: I owe it to him to take him there. He has a right against me that I take him there. And if I should fail, without adequate justification, to do as I promised, I would not merely act wrongly: I would wrong *him*. Promissory duties are products of voluntary acts, but this is not true of all directed duties. My neighbor John has a right against me that I not kill him. Correspondingly, I owe it to him not to kill him. If I were to kill him, without justification, I would not merely do wrong: I would wrong *him*. John's right against me, and my directed duty towards him, are two aspects of a single, relational moral fact.[2] Looked at from one direction, this fact concerns my duty to John; looked as from another direction, it concerns John's right against me. Of course John also has a right not to be killed by people other than me. He has a right not to be killed by anyone. This last right – his right not to be killed *simpliciter* – can be thought of as a composite of his right against A that A not kill him, his right against B that B not kill him, and so on. Likewise, I have a duty not to kill anyone. And this duty – my duty not to kill *simpliciter* – can be thought of as a composite of my duty to A not to kill him, my duty to B not to kill him, and so on. There will of course be a common explanation why I owe this duty to every other person, and why every other person owes this duty to me. Part of what it is to be a moral person is to stand in such moral relations with other persons.

Although the matter is controversial, I think it is best to understand a claim right as a kind of normative power. If you have a right against me that I not enter your property, then I may not enter your property *unless you give me your permission*. You have a say over whether I will be acting permissibly should I enter your property. Not that your say always settles the matter. There might be circumstances under which it would be permissible for me to enter your property without your consent (e.g. if there were no other way I could save a certain person's life); and, conversely, there might be circumstances under which it would be wrong for me to enter your property even with your consent (e.g. if there were some other decisive moral objection to my doing so). But if you have a right against me that I not enter your property, then there is one potential *pro tanto* objection to my doing so whose existence is under your control. You can waive your right or not, as you see fit. Waiving a right is not a way of giving it up; it is a way of exercising it.[3]

Directed duties concern what we owe to others as a matter of right. They are duties of *justice*. They are to be contrasted with undirected duties, which are not owed to anyone in particular, and which are not duties of justice. If I have an undirected duty not to litter in the park, then although I will do wrong if I litter there without adequate justification, I will not wrong any particular person. No one has a right against me that I not litter in the park. (Of course this may be a poorly chosen example. If there are people who have a right against me that I not litter in the park, then I have a directed duty not to litter there after all.)

Earlier I mentioned the view that agents have positive duties to render aid only when they stand in special relations to the potential beneficiaries of their aid. It is possible that those attracted to this view mistakenly think that all duties must be directed. That is, it is possible that they believe (controversially but plausibly) that B has a *right* against A that A aid him only if A promised to aid him, or it is A's job to save him, or some such; and that they also believe (mistakenly) that A can have a duty to aid B only if B has a correlative right to be aided by A. But to assume the latter is to ignore the possibility that A has an undirected duty to aid B. This possibility cannot be rejected without argument. Not all duties are duties of justice.

In fact, agents often have both directed and undirected duties to do (or to refrain from doing) the very same thing. Ordinarily it is wrong to cut off a person's arms. And there are (at least) two reasons for this. First, the person has a right not to have his arms cut off. Suppose that his health, or his odds of survival, would be greatly improved if his arms were to be cut off, but that he has refused his consent. Then cutting off his arms would be at least *pro tanto*, and probably all things considered, wrong. One may not, as a rule, cut off a person's arms without his permission. But now suppose that having his arms cut off would *not* improve his health or odds of survival, but that he *has* for some reason (competently) consented to the procedure.[4] Cutting off his arms would still be at least *pro tanto* wrong – not because it would violate one of his rights, since we are assuming he has waived the relevant right, but simply because it would harm him so much. Cutting off a person's arms does not become morally unproblematic simply because he has given his permission.[5] There are thus two distinct *pro tanto* duties in play here, one directed (corresponding to the person's right not to have his arms cut off) and the other undirected. The latter duty is undirected not because it doesn't concern a particular person – clearly it does – but because it corresponds to no claim right on the victim's part. The former duty is a duty of justice, the latter a duty of beneficence.[6]

Harmful attacks upon people can violate either duties of justice or duties of beneficence. Should we say the same of failures to render aid? Do we have duties both of justice and of beneficence to aid others? Or is aiding required only by beneficence, and not (barring promises, contractual obligations, or other special relations) by justice? I shall come back to this question later.

III

Let us return now to the distinction between perfect and imperfect duties. It is surprisingly difficult to characterize this distinction precisely.

Here's a first try. A duty to φ is perfect if and only if any occasion on which an agent could φ but does not is, absent some special justification, an occasion on which he violates that duty. A duty to φ is imperfect if and only if an occasion on which an agent could φ but doesn't, and on which he has no special justification for not φing, needn't be an occasion on which he violates that duty. This test correctly classifies the duty not to kill people as perfect, since any occasion on which an agent fails to refrain from killing – that is, any occasion on which he kills someone – is, absent some special justification, an occasion on which he violates his duty not to kill people. An agent cannot shrug off a killing by saying "I refrained from killing people all last month! I've done enough, at least for now, in the refraining-from-killing-people department. I needn't also refrain from killing this person, here and now." But the duty to aid seems different. An agent needn't aid people whenever he is in a position to do so, and he needn't offer any special justification for failing to aid on those occasions when he chooses to do something else instead. He violates his duty to give aid only if he fails to give aid often enough. A violation of this duty will show up only in his pattern of aiding over time. Or so those who regard the duty to aid as imperfect think. And if this is indeed how the duty to aid works, the present account correctly classifies it as imperfect.

But this account will not do: it classifies *most* positive duties as imperfect, even when they ought to be classified as perfect. Positive duties rarely specify the precise moment at which the required act must be performed. Suppose I borrow your book on Monday and promise to return it by the end of the week. If I do not return it at precisely noon on Tuesday, it does not follow that I am at that time violating my duty to return your book. I violate my duty only if I fail to return the book at *any* time during the week. Yet my duty to return your book should intuitively be classified as perfect. True, I am free (within limits) to choose exactly when I shall return it, but this is not the sort of "leeway" that makes a duty imperfect. How, then, should the account be revised? How do genuinely imperfect duties differ from positive perfect duties that are unspecific with respect to time?

Perhaps imperfect duties require the performance of multiple acts over time, whereas positive perfect duties require the performance of single acts. But this is false. My duty is no less perfect if I promise to take my son to Disneyland at least once every summer for the rest of my life than it is if I promise to take him there once this summer.

Another suggestion is that imperfect duties are those that agents can never finish fulfilling. By contrast, it is possible to "dispatch" a perfect duty – an agent can, by doing what the duty requires, bring it about that he no longer has that duty. This proposal classifies some cases correctly. When I return the book I borrowed, I cease having a duty to return it, whereas I will always have a duty to aid people, no matter how many I have aided in the past. But if I promised to take my son to Disneyland at least once every summer until I die, no number of trips to Disneyland will ever relieve me of that duty. And clearly there are many negative perfect duties that cannot be dispatched. One is never through fulfilling one's duty not to kill people.

Here's yet another proposal: the defining feature of an imperfect duty is not that it is unspecific with respect to the time or times of performance (since the same is true of most positive perfect duties), but that it is unspecific with respect to the beneficiaries of the required acts. If the duty to aid is imperfect, I have leeway not only in choosing precisely when to render aid, but also in choosing *whom* to aid. Suppose that A is in need of aid today, and that I am capable of providing that aid. If the duty to aid is imperfect, then I needn't aid A at all, and I needn't justify my failure to aid him by demonstrating that what I chose to do instead was more important. So long as I help enough people over time, I fulfill my duty. I needn't aid everyone. But while this is indeed arguably a feature of the duty to aid, it is not a feature of all imperfect duties. I have a duty to assist my friend with his projects, and intuitively this duty of friendship is imperfect. I needn't (and probably shouldn't) assist him with all of his projects, but I will fail him as a friend if I never assist him with any of them. My obligation is to assist him some of the time, enough of the time. But while this duty is unspecific in many respects, it is completely specific with respect to the beneficiary of the required acts.

One possible response to these reflections is to conclude that no sharp distinction can be drawn between perfect and imperfect duties. Imperfection in a duty is a matter of a lack of specificity, but specificity is always a matter of degree, and no positive duty is ever wholly specific. Even a duty to return a particular book to a particular person at a particular time leaves open the exact manner in which the book shall be returned. Shall it be done with the right hand or with the left? And even if the duty specifies that the book be returned with the right hand, there will still be many equally permissible ways of returning it with the right hand. The important point about the duty to aid, then, is simply that it is a highly unspecific duty to exemplify a certain pattern in one's aiding behavior over time. It requires one to perform aiding actions from time to time, often enough, but it does not specify exactly when one must give aid, or whom one must aid, or how much aid one must give. This lack of specificity is what people are getting at when they say that the duty to aid is imperfect.

IV

I don't think this is all there is to the idea that the duty to aid is imperfect. And I think it *is* possible to draw a sharp distinction between perfect and imperfect duties. A clue to how the distinction should be drawn is provided by a certain difference between actions fulfilling positive perfect duties and actions fulfilling imperfect duties, a difference that the account sketched at the end of the previous section cannot explain.

Let us start with positive perfect duties. Suppose that I have promised to take my son to Disneyland some day this week, and that I have also promised to meet a student in my office today. Unless today is for some reason the best day for the trip to Disneyland, it would be wrong for me to take my son there today at the cost of missing my appointment. This is true even if my duty to take my son to Disneyland is stronger than my duty to keep my appointment. The former duty does not override the latter because the two do not conflict: I could easily fulfill both by keeping my appointment today and taking my son to Disneyland some other day. When duties are unspecific with respect to the time of performance, one can generally avoid hard choices by means of appropriate scheduling. And when the duties in question are perfect, one *ought* to avoid hard choices in this way, other things being equal.

But now suppose that on my way to keep my appointment I encounter someone in need of aid. Even if I were not on the way to an appointment, I would not be required to aid this person. My duty to aid people is, after all, imperfect – or so we are assuming. I consequently need no justification for failing to aid this person. But if his need is significant, it might well be *permissible* for me to aid him, even at the cost of missing my appointment. I would be justified in failing to keep my appointment if what I was doing instead was aiding someone in great need. But how can this be? There is, by hypothesis, no conflict of duties here. I could easily fulfill both my perfect duty to keep my appointment and my imperfect duty to aid others: I could do this by keeping my appointment today and aiding someone else some other day. So why am I not required to do this? If my imperfect duty to aid others does not require me to aid this particular person, how can I be justified in aiding him at the cost of failing to fulfill my perfect duty to keep my appointment?

The same phenomenon arises in connection with other imperfect duties. Suppose that while I'm on my way to my appointment I learn that my friend needs assistance with an important project. My duty to assist my friend with his projects is imperfect, so choosing not to assist him on this particular occasion requires no justification. Yet if today's project is sufficiently important to him, I might be justified in breaking my appointment in order to assist him. How can this be? I could easily fulfill both duties: I could keep my appointment today and assist my friend with some other project some other day. So why am I not required to do this?

The key to solving this puzzle is to see that in such cases it is not the imperfect duty that justifies breaking the appointment.

First, we should recognize that reasons have (at least) two different sorts of force. Some reasons have *requiring* force. When a reason to φ has requiring force, the person subject to it is *pro tanto* required to φ, and so he needs special justification for failing to φ. Other reasons have *justifying* force. When a reason to φ has (sufficient) justifying force, it is capable of overriding a *pro tanto* requirement to act in some other way. But a person needs no justification for failing to act in accordance with a reason that has merely justifying force. Since such reasons lack requiring force, acting in accordance with them is at best optional. Arguably many reasons have merely justifying force.[7]

Next, we should grant that we have justifying reasons to aid each particular person in need. If person A needs aid, I have a justifying reason to aid A; if person B needs aid, I have a justifying reason to aid B; and so on. But these reasons lack requiring force.[8] The reason in favor of aiding A is, if sufficiently forceful, capable of justifying me in aiding A even in the face of a *pro tanto* requirement to do something else, but it generates no *pro tanto* requirement to aid him. I consequently need no justification for failing to aid him. Aiding him is optional.

If the justifying reasons we have to aid particular people do not amount to *pro tanto* duties to aid them, where does a duty to aid enter the picture? Here's where. As we go through life, we frequently find ourselves able to aid others. We thus frequently find ourselves subject to justifying reasons for aiding particular people. And although these reasons are not individually requiring, we do have a duty to act in accordance with reasons of this general *kind* from time to time. That is, we have a *second-order* reason to act in accordance with first-order reasons of this kind from time to time, and this second-order reason *does* have requiring force.

A parallel story can be told about my duty to assist my friend with his projects. I have a first-order reason to help him with project

A, a first-order reason to help him with project B, and so on. Each of these reasons has merely justifying force. But I also have a second-order reason to act in accordance with such first-order reasons from time to time, and this second-order reason has requiring force. The second-order reason amounts to a *pro tanto* duty to assist my friend with his projects from time to time.

I thus suggest the following account of the difference between perfect and imperfect duties. A perfect duty is a first-order reason, with requiring force, to act in a certain way. Perfect duties can be more or less specific in content, and can concern individual actions or patterns of action over time. An imperfect duty is a second-order reason, with requiring force, to act in accordance with first-order reasons of a certain kind often enough. The defining feature of imperfect duties is that they concern how we respond to first-order reasons of certain kinds over time.

Let's now return to the puzzle with which I began this section. And let's start with the example involving two perfect duties. My duty to meet my student in my office is a first-order reason, with requiring force, to perform an action of that type sometime today. My duty to take my son to Disneyland is a first-order reason, with requiring force, to perform an action of that type some day this week. As far as the latter reason is concerned, it is all the same whether I take him there today or some other day later in the week. (If there is a reason to take him there today rather than another day, that reason is independent of my promissory duty to take him there some day this week. No reason for taking him there today rather than another day is implied or suggested by my description of the example, so I shall assume that no such reason exists.) Since I can arrange my schedule so as to satisfy all of the requiring reasons confronting me, that's what I ought to do, other things being equal. I am consequently not permitted to break my appointment in order to take my son to Disneyland.

But now consider the example in which I could aid someone in need if I were to break my appointment. I have an imperfect duty to aid people in need. That is, I have a second-order reason, with requiring force, to act from time to time in accordance with my first-order reasons for aiding people. As far as this second-order reason is concerned, it is all the same whether I aid this person today or some other person some other day. So far, then, the cases are parallel. But I also have a first-order reason to aid this particular person today, and from the point of view of this reason it is *not* all the same whether I aid him today or some other person some other day. And because this reason has considerable justifying force, I am permitted to aid this person today even at the cost of breaking my appointment. The crucial fact about this justifying reason is that it is not merely a reason to advance some general end, such as the increase of aggregate human happiness. Such a general end would be equally well advanced by aiding someone else tomorrow. Rather, the justifying reason is a reason to aid this particular person, here and now. Each person's need makes an independent claim on me. Each person is a source of reasons.[9]

Likewise with the example in which I could assist my friend with an important project if I were to break today's appointment. I could equally well fulfill my imperfect duty to assist him with his projects by assisting him with some other project on some other occasion. But I also have a first-order justifying reason to assist him with this particular project today, and *this* reason cannot be satisfied by assisting him with some other project on some other occasion. Because this reason has considerable justifying force, I am permitted to assist my friend with today's project even at the cost of breaking my appointment.

This phenomenon is quite general. Every imperfect duty is a second-order reason, with requiring force, to act in accordance with first-order justifying reasons of a certain kind often enough over time. It follows that every action that helps fulfill an imperfect duty also satisfies a first-order justifying reason for performing the action in question. So long as this justifying reason does not derive from a reason to promote a general end that could equally well be promoted by acting on another justifying reason of the same kind on some other occasion, it will have the potential to justify a failure to fulfill a conflicting duty.[10]

V

Earlier I asked whether the duty to aid is directed or undirected. How should we answer this question, given the assumption that the duty to aid is imperfect? It has sometimes been suggested that there cannot be claim rights correlative to imperfect duties, and that all imperfect duties must consequently be undirected. But why should we believe this? Consider my imperfect duty to assist my friend with his projects (i.e. my duty to act, from time to time, in accordance with my first-order reasons to assist him with particular projects). There is no reason in principle why this duty of friendship should not be regarded as directed, why my friend should not be taken to have a right against me that I assist him with his projects from time to time. We might aptly describe this right as an imperfect one. But the imperfect duty to aid people is different. There is no particular person whom I am required to aid from time to time, so no particular person has a right against me that I aid him from time to time. Nor does it seem plausible to say that the needy as a group have a right against me that I sometimes aid some of them. Perhaps certain groups have claim rights (e.g. clubs, corporations), but I doubt that "the needy" constitute such a group – they lack the right sort of unity. So if the duty to aid people is imperfect, it does seem that it must be undirected. It is a duty of beneficence, not of justice.

VI

I have proposed that an imperfect duty is a second-order reason, with requiring force, to act in accordance with first-order justifying reasons of a certain kind often enough over time. But an alternative account is available: we could instead say that an agent has an imperfect duty to act in a certain way whenever he has both (i) a first-order reason, with *requiring* force, to act in that way, and (ii) a second-order *permission* to ignore first-order requiring reasons of that kind from time to time.[11] On this alternative account, first-order requiring reasons (which would ordinarily constitute perfect duties) are transformed into imperfect duties by the existence of a second-order permission to ignore such duties from time to time. Both accounts yield the same overall result: that an agent does not automatically violate his duty whenever he fails to perform an action of the relevant type, yet can be justified in performing an action of that type even in the face of a contrary duty. Which account should we prefer?

The two accounts present us with very different explanatory tasks. On my account, what needs explaining is why we have a second-order *duty* sometimes to act in accordance with first-order reasons of a certain kind, given that these first-order reasons lack requiring force. On the alternative account, what needs explaining is why we have a second-order *permission* sometimes (perhaps often) to ignore first-order reasons of a certain kind, given that these first-order reasons possess requiring force.

I suspect that the former explanatory task will be easier to perform. In the case of the imperfect duty to aid, the basic idea would be that a proper concern for others requires that aiding people in distress be an important part of our lives. But there are many kinds of worthwhile activities, and a good life will involve a variety of them. Taken one by one, then, aiding actions are not required, but actions of that general type cannot be absent from the mix entirely. The alternative picture holds that taken one by one, aiding actions *are* required, but that we are permitted sometimes (perhaps often) to ignore such requirements. But why should it be morally permissible sometimes (perhaps often) to ignore *duties* of a certain kind? Wouldn't this tend to undermine the idea that they really are duties?

VII

I'd like to close by considering a possible objection to the thesis that the general duty to aid is imperfect, namely that in certain circumstances aiding a particular person (to whom one has no special obligations) seems to be required, not optional. A child hits his head on the side of a swimming pool and goes under; I could easily pull him out; surely I must do so, at least if no other potential rescuers are on the scene. If I do not save him, I'd better have a very good reason, and it will not do to point out that I have already aided several other people this month. It appears, then, that I have a *perfect* duty to save this child. And isn't that inconsistent with the thesis that the duty to aid is imperfect? In what follows I briefly sketch a few ways a proponent of that thesis might respond to this worry.

One possible response is to postulate two distinct general duties to aid: an imperfect duty of charity and a perfect duty of emergency rescue. Many of us are frequently able to aid others indirectly, by donating to charitable organizations. And we regularly encounter people in our communities whom we could directly aid. But in cases of both sorts other agents could equally well provide the necessary aid. The duty to aid in such cases is imperfect: it is enough if each of us occasionally donates to charitable organizations and directly aids only some of the needy people he regularly encounters. It sometimes happens, however, that an agent is uniquely positioned to help someone in great need, and on such occasions he has a perfect duty to provide aid. If someone is in imminent danger of suffering serious harm and I am the only person able to rescue him, I am required to do so, even at some significant cost to myself.

If we opt for this solution, we must explain why the first duty is imperfect and the second perfect. And this in turn requires explaining why the difference between the two sorts of aiding is morally significant. Why should my duty to save the life of someone whom only I can save be perfect, but my duty to aid someone whom others could (but probably won't) aid be merely imperfect?[12]

Alternatively, we could try to solve this puzzle without postulating any reasons beyond those already appealed to in my account of the imperfect duty to aid. There are at least two ways such an explanation might go. First, we could hold that our first-order reasons to aid particular people have both requiring and justifying force. The requiring force of these reasons is typically quite weak – we are required to aid only when we can do so with negligible effort, inconvenience, and cost. Since the effort, inconvenience, or cost involved in aiding a person typically exceeds this minimal threshold, we typically needn't provide aid. But when aiding is sufficiently easy, it is required. The problem with this solution is that it does not explain why in certain circumstances the duty to aid a particular person is (seemingly) very strong indeed.

The other option is to maintain our original assumption that first-order reasons to aid particular people have only justifying force (except when these reasons are grounded in promises or the like) and try to show that in certain circumstances the second-order duty to act from time to time in accordance with such first-order reasons leaves us with no choice but to save a particular person. The success of this solution will depend upon the precise content of the second-order duty and upon its rationale. Suppose, for example, that the second-order duty amounts to a duty to "do one's share" of responding to first-order reasons to give aid. Usually there will be many people equally well placed to donate to this or that charitable organization, or to aid this or that needy person, and with respect to such cases doing one's share of aiding requires only that one perform aiding actions often enough. But each of us is occasionally the unique person able to aid someone in great need, and in such cases aiding that person *is part of our share*. In such cases one cannot fulfill one's imperfect duty to do one's share of responding to first-order reasons to give aid without acting in accordance with the reason one has to aid that particular person.

NOTES

1   More formally: person A has a duty to φ which he owes to person B if and only if person B has a claim right against A that A φ. For a classic statement of the correlativity of directed duties and claim rights, see Hohfeld 1919: 38. For more on rights and directed duties, see Kramer *et al.* 1998 and Kamm 2007, chaps. 7–9.

2   Michael Thompson (2004) insightfully explores this moral relation's significance, and its connection to the notion of justice.

3   In some cases it may be possible for someone other than the right-holder to waive the right on the right-holder's behalf. We consequently cannot define the right-holder as the person possessing the power to waive the right.

4   In the 1927 film *The Unknown*, Lon Chaney's character loves a woman (played by the young Joan Crawford) who has a pathological fear of being touched by men. Hoping to marry her, he convinces a doctor to amputate his arms. Sadly, the woman overcomes her fear shortly thereafter and falls in love with the circus strongman.

5   It is sometimes claimed that certain rights (such as the right not to be killed and the right not to be enslaved) cannot be waived. This view might be a mistaken response to the observation that consent, even when freely and competently given, does not always make the consented-to action morally permissible. But another explanation is available: actions of these sorts are typically objectionable for multiple reasons, and consent neutralizes only one of the objections.

6   Likewise, killing a person is typically objectionable both because it violates his right not to be killed and because it harms him. These objections can come apart. Even if the person has given his consent, killing him is *pro tanto* wrong if his death would come to him as a harm; and even if his death would not come as a harm, killing him is *pro tanto* wrong if he has refused his consent. The idea that killing

can be wrong for more than one reason is not new. Philippa Foot (1977) argues that killing can be contrary either to justice or to charity (benevolence) and Warren Quinn (1984) argues that killing people is typically prohibited both by "the morality of respect" and by "the morality of humanity". Jeff McMahan (2004), using slightly different terminology, follows Quinn.

7 A single reason, however, could have both sorts of force. A number of philosophers have defended the idea that reasons can have more than one sort of force, or play different roles in practical reasoning. See, for example, Dancy 2004, Greenspan 2005, and Gert 2007.

8 Or perhaps they have only weak requiring force. I shall discuss this possibility later. For simplicity we may assume for now that reasons of this kind have no requiring force at all.

9 My second-order duty to act from time to time in accordance with my first-order reasons for aiding particular people amounts to a duty to have the good of others as an end. But this end should be understood distributively: I am required to regard each person's good as a distinct end, and thus as a distinct source of reasons.

10 Patricia Greenspan (2010) takes the imperfect duty to give aid to be a *first-order* requiring reason to give aid often enough. This is roughly the account I described at the end of section III, above. Greenspan proposes that we also have justifying first-order reasons to aid particular people, but on her account the imperfect duty to aid does not entail or presuppose the existence of such justifying reasons. (Greenspan does not herself use the terminology of "justifying" and "requiring" reasons.)

11 Joseph Raz (1999: 85–97) appeals to second-order (or "exclusionary") permissions in order to explain the possibility of supererogation. But this is not how he understands imperfect duties.

12 Peter Unger (1996) presses such questions forcefully.

19 Killing and extinction

INTRODUCTION

The mountain gorilla, the black rhino, the Amur leopard, and the leatherback turtle are some of the species on WWF's list of critically endangered species.[1] Many would agree that we would act wrongly if we failed to preserve these species. There is perhaps even more agreement that it would be wrong to kill individual members of these species, especially if nothing good comes out of it. This chapter provides a short overview of the main reasons why species extinction and animal killing can be wrong. The main focus is on the question whether the considerations that are typically invoked to explain the wrongness of killing animals can somehow be extended to explain the wrongness of species extinction. But we will also consider whether there can be some more distinctive reasons against species extinction.

I shall put aside one obvious reason why both species extinction and animal killing can be wrong, namely, the fact that they will often have harmful effects on humans. The focus is instead on *non-anthropocentric* reasons. This is not an especially controversial restriction. Imagine, for instance, that you were the last human being and you could kill a mountain gorilla or make the whole species extinct. Surely, there is still reason not to kill the gorilla or make its species extinct. This and other similar 'last human' scenarios seem to show that the fact that there will be no human beings around to experience the effects of animal killing and species extinction does not make these acts morally unproblematic.[2]

In fact, I shall narrow my focus even further by only discussing reasons against species extinction and animal killing that have to do with the fact that the species or the animal *ceases to exist*. I take it that it is not especially controversial that it can be wrong to kill animals or make species go extinct when the *process* of dying or extinction is extremely painful for the involved animals.

I shall start by discussing the main accounts of the wrongness of killing individual animals. One such account argues that we owe it to individual animals not to kill them. Another account explains the wrongness in terms of the preferences of the animal. Killing an animal is wrong because it frustrates its preferences for the future. A third account explains it in terms of the well-being of individual animals, and states that the killing is wrong when the animal is thereby robbed of a good future. I shall then consider whether there are analogous reasons against species extinction. Finally, I shall explore whether there are any more distinctive reasons why species extinction may be wrong. More specifically, I shall discuss different ways in which the non-instrumental badness of species extinction may explain the wrongness of species extinction.

THE WRONGNESS OF KILLING INDIVIDUAL ANIMALS

We owe it to them

Can it be wrong to kill animals because we owe it to them not to kill them? Those who think we cannot owe it to the animal that it not be killed often back this up by arguing that we cannot owe *anything* to animals, for animals lack some of the features that are necessary for being someone who we can owe things to. Animals would thus lack the kind of moral standing that we think many adult humans have. Some suggest that the missing feature is that of being a moral agent. Since animals cannot make moral judgments they cannot be fully fledged moral agents.

This account of what is required to be owed something is very demanding, however, and would result in the expulsion of many humans from the 'moral club' of beings that we can owe things to. For example, young infants and severely mentally challenged adults would be expelled since they cannot make moral judgments either. Are we really willing to accept that we do not owe anything to them?

A less demanding account would say that we can owe it to an animal not to kill it if it has the capacity to *consent* or *dissent* to being killed. To be able to consent or dissent in this way does not require that the animal is a fully fledged moral agent. However, it seems to presuppose an ability to grasp the concept of killing or at least the concept of one's own death. Now, even if many animals have desires, self-consciousness and the ability to perform basic reasoning, it is not plausible to think that they have a concept of their own death. Hence, on this account, we could not owe it to an animal that it not be killed.

Now, as it stands this account is too strong because it again rules out young infants and many mentally challenged people, since they too lack the capacity to consent or dissent to being killed. Perhaps this can be fixed by weakening the account so that it only requires that one is able to consent or dissent to being killed at some time, not necessarily at the time of the possible killing. This would work with many young infants since they will grow up and later be able to consent or dissent, retroactively, to *not* being killed.

This is only a partial fix, however, since many mentally challenged adults are not able at *any* time to grasp the concept of their own death. Furthermore, some young infants will, in fact, die prematurely and not grow up and thus will never be able to retrospectively consent or dissent.

An even weaker account would say that to be owed something requires only that one has desires and the capacity for self-consciousness. We would not owe anything to animals, if it was also true that no animal had both these features. At the same time, however, many young infants and many severally mentally challenged adults will pass the test, because they have some desires and the capacity for some basic kind of self-consciousness.

The assumption that no animal has both these psychological features is very questionable, however, especially in light of recent research on animal behavior. That many animals have desires is obvious. Furthermore, many experiments (e.g. mirror tests) provide strong evidence that many mammals, including higher apes, have some degree of self-consciousness.[3] What we can conclude at most is that there are *some* animals towards which we cannot owe anything. Perhaps we cannot owe anything to a slugs and spiders; but we can still owe things to chimpanzees, gorillas, elephants, and dolphins.

Frustrated preferences

Even if we do not owe it to animals not to kill them, it may be wrong to do so just because killing them frustrates some of their desires. One obvious way this could happen is when the animal has a preference for continued existence. However, to have such a preference seems to require the ability to grasp the notion of one's own future existence, and it is not clear that many animals have such an advanced conceptual ability. On the other hand, there are many other kinds of preferences that are frustrated by killing the animal. For example, a preference to eat, drink, seek shelter, and protect one's young would all be frustrated by killing an animal, for these preferences are often future-directed, in the sense that whether these preference are satisfied or frustrated depends on what will happen in the (immediate) future. Note that the fact that they are future-directed in this way does not mean that the animal itself must be able to conceptualize its own future; it only needs to somehow conceptualize the *activity* that in fact would take place in the future.

Now, even if preference frustration constitutes one important reason against killing animals; it can hardly be the whole story, since it would only apply in those cases in which the animal has some future-directed preference that can be frustrated. What shall we say about cases where the animal at the moment lacks such preferences, perhaps because it is unconscious or too young to have such preferences? One could of course say that killing the animal is permissible in this case, but then one is hard-pressed to explain why it is not equally permissible to kill unconscious humans or very young human infants.

It is bad for them

This problem can be avoided if one bears in mind that many animals have well-being. Things can be better or worse for them; they can be benefited or harmed. Even if we consider the painless killing of an animal which has no future-directed preference, it can be true that killing it deprives it of a good future. Had it been allowed to live, it would have had a longer life and enjoyed more good things.

In a straightforward sense, then, it can be bad to kill an animal because killing it is worse for the animal.

Velleman has an intriguing objection to this deprivation account of the badness of animal death.[4] Even if we can meaningfully talk about the momentary well-being of an animal and say, for instance, that it is good for them to eat or play momentarily, it does not follow, he argues, that it makes sense to say that a *whole future* could be good for them. For he assumes that, in general, to say that *x* is good for an individual requires a capacity of the individual to care about *x*. Even if an animal can care about momentary eating or playing, it does not follow that the animal can care about future sequences of such things. Many animals – the cow is Velleman's favorite example – lack this capacity to care about their own future, simply because they lack the concept of continued existence. If they lack the capacity to care about the future, their future cannot be good for them, and, consequently, they cannot be robbed of a good future. In contrast, human persons typically have the capacity to care about their own futures and thus we can talk about them being robbed of a future that is good for them.

This is an interesting argument, but, as has been pointed out by Ben Bradley, it has some bizarre implications.[5] For example, it entails that we cannot say that a future full of intense suffering is overall worse for a cow than a future full of intense pleasure. We can only say the former future contains moments that are bad for the cow and the latter future contains moments that are good for the cow. Furthermore, as Bradley points out, one could accept a weaker version of Velleman's constraint and yet avoid the radical conclusion that death cannot be bad for cows (and other animals that lack a concept of a continued existence). Instead of saying that *x* is good for an individual only if the individual can care about *x*, we could say that *x* cannot be *fundamentally* good for an individual only if the individual can care about *x*. For something to be good in a fundamental way is for it to be good in a sense that is not derived from the goodness of anything else. When a future is good *overall* for an individual its value is derived from the fundamental value of the parts of this future. Hence, since cows and many animals can care about the parts that make up their future lives, we need not deny that their futures are overall good for them. We only need to deny that their futures are fundamentally good for them. It seems thus unwarranted to say without qualification that animals cannot be deprived of an overall good future.

THE WRONGNESS OF SPECIES EXTINCTION

The question is now whether the wrongness of species extinction can be explained by reasons analogous to the ones that count against killing individual animals. This could be done straightforwardly, if the wrongness of species extinction were fully explained by the very same factors that make it wrong to kill individual animals. Since species extinction is often done by the direct or indirect killing of individual members of the species, it is true that the facts that count against killing individual animals often also count against species extinction. It is not clear, however, that species extinction is wrong *only* when and because it involves the killing or harming of individual animals. After all, a species can become extinct because the members become infertile. Imagine, for example, that the mountain gorilla became extinct because we made individual members infertile by exposing them to some chemicals, which did not kill or harm any of them (except for making them infertile). Would this not still be wrong?

Concern for future members of species

It may seem that in order to give an affirmative answer to this question, we would need to adopt a holistic approach and ascribe some moral relevance to a species that goes beyond the moral relevance we ascribe to its individual members. But this is not so. If we can owe it to an animal that *it exists* (at least if it would have a good life), then preserving the species when no current member would be killed or harmed by the extinction still means that we do something we owe to the future members of the species. Similarly, if we can make it *better for an animal by creating it*, we could claim that it is right to preserve a species even if no currently existing individual member would be negatively affected by extinction, because preservation will make it better for those future individual members of the species who will have good lives.

Now, this reply is similar to some of the recent moves in human population ethics and it is in many respects equally problematic.

Even if we agree that we can say about an *existing* animal, a happy mountain gorilla say, that we owe it its existence or that its existence is better for it than its non-existence, what shall we say if we *fail* to create the gorilla? In that case, the gorilla does not exist and we cannot say that we owe it anything or that it is better for it not to exist. The conclusion seems to be that we ought to create the animal only if we in fact will create it. Thus the normative status of our action of creating the animal depends on whether it is performed. This kind of normative variance seems troubling, at least if we want some moral guidance in our moral deliberations.[6] For how are we to rationally deliberate about what to do if we first need to know what we will do?

It also seems strange to say that existence can be better for an animal than its non-existence, at least if 'better for' entails 'better off'. For how can an animal be better off existing than not existing? To be better off in one state than in another requires that one exists in both states.

One could avoid these problems by saying that species preservation is right in cases in which no current member would be negatively affected by extinction, not because it makes future individual members better off than they otherwise would have been, but because it creates lives that are *good for* the animals. This approach would then say that species extinction can be wrong because it prevents the existence of future members of the species that would have had good lives.

It is still not clear, however, whether an individualist approach of this kind provides an exhaustive explanation of why species extinction is wrong. To use Sober's famous '$n + m$ question', in a choice between a world with n sperm whales and m blue whales and a world with $n + m$ sperm whales and o blue whales, should we choose the former world, even if all the individual whales will enjoy exactly the same level of well-being?[7] If you are tempted to answer 'yes' to this question, which does not seem unreasonable, you need to consider more holistic approaches.

HOLISTIC APPROACHES

Holistic approaches argue that species extinction can be wrong because of certain facts about the species, which go beyond the facts about individual members of the species. One holistic idea is to try to apply the considerations that make killing animals wrong and say that by allowing a species to go extinct, we would wrong the species itself by failing to preserve it, frustrate its preferences, or harm it by robbing it of a good future. If this approach is successful, we would be able to explain why we should choose the world with n sperm whales and m blue whales over a world with $n + m$ sperm whales and o blue whales.

Owing things to species

It is fairly clear that we do not owe anything to species over and above what we owe to individual members of the species, if species are seen as properties, natural kinds, or sets of individual animals. Even though there is no agreement about what exactly passes the test for being something you can owe something to, it is clear that abstract entities like properties, natural kinds, and sets fail the test.

If a species is instead seen as a huge spatiotemporally continuous individual that evolves by evolution and that consist of the individual members of the species – a view that has gained popularity in recent times – it still seems questionable that we can owe things to species.[8] This is not to endorse the wholesale rejection of the idea that we can owe something to a group entity. Perhaps we can owe things to families, communes, and communities. But in these cases, the groups have certain unifying mental features not found in species. For example, families, communes, and communities can deliberate and make collective decisions.

Preferences of species

Now, some would argue that even if species do not make decisions, they can still be said to have some rudimentary preferences that would be frustrated if the species became extinct.[9] In order for this to qualify as a holistic account it is important that preferences of species are not reducible to preferences of individual members of species. If species are seen as individuals that have their members as parts, we can all agree that a species can have a preference for continued existence in virtue of having parts, individual animals, which have such preferences. For example, the species mountain gorilla has a preference for continued existence in virtue of individ-ual mountain gorillas' preferences for continued existence (or for some activities that in fact will take place in the future).

One way to argue that species have preferences in a non-deriv-ative way is to point out that species seem to have *interests*. For example, it might be said to be in the interest of a species to have enough resources so that its members can procreate. However, even if it makes sense to say that species have such interests, we need to be careful to distinguish between *having an interest* and *taking an interest*. Plants, trees, animals, and humans can all be said to have interests in the sense that they need certain things in order to func-tion well. But in order to have a preference one also needs to be able to take an interest in something and this requires a mind. Since species do not have minds of their own, they cannot take an interest in things, at least not in a non-derivative way, and thus we cannot ascribe them preferences. Of course, we can always talk metaphor-ically about species as having wants and preferences, just meaning that they have certain interests, but then, as I will argue in the next section, this account is better seen as version of the view that ascribes functional well-being to species.

The well-being of species

If by a species we mean a property, natural kind, or a set of individ-ual animals, then it seems clear that a species cannot be subject of well-being in its own right. Properties, natural kinds, or sets are not the kind of things that can have well-being. We can only talk about the well-being of these things as a shorthand for the well-being of the exemplifiers of the properties, the members of the natural kinds, and the members of the sets.

If by a species we mean a huge spatiotemporally continuous indi-vidual, then it seems more plausible to say that a species can be seen as a welfare subject in its own right. It is true that if we demand that welfare subjects have some sort of sentience or ability to have desires, then species, even if seen as individuals, cannot be said to have well-being, for it is only individual members of a species that can be sentient or have desires. Individual tigers feel pain and pleas-ure and desire things, but the species tiger feels nothing and has no desires over and above the feelings and desires of the parts of the species, the individual tigers.

On the other hand, each species does show some unity and continuity, especially in terms of genetic information, but it is unclear whether this is enough to make species count as proper well-being subjects. This is unclear in part because it is controversial how the notion of well-being should be understood. For example, in an extensive sense of 'good for' it is perfectly sensible to say that things can be good or bad for my lawnmower. Leaving it outside in the rain so that it rusts is bad for it, for example. I can say this without assuming, absurdly, that the lawnmower is sentient or has desires. What I mean is just that it will function less well if it is left outside. This extensive notion of well-being is thus applicable to not just sentient beings with desires but anything that can have a function. If species have functions that are not just derived from the functions of individual members, then we would be able to say that things can be good or bad for a species. What is good for a species is what makes it function well; what is worse, what makes it function badly.[10]

Even if species can be said to have well-being in this extensive sense it is not clear that this shows that we need to protect its well-being and that it is wrong to make things worse for them. Many things that have well-being in this extended sense seem to lack such a moral relevance. Think, for example, of torture instruments, such as thumbscrews. They have a function, and what is bad for them are things that make them function badly as torture instruments. But it is not true that we have a duty to protect their well-being or that it is wrong to make them function less well. On the contrary, we have an obligation to make them function less well. Natural species will not have man-made functions, of course, but it is still unclear why a natural function would automatically generate duties. For example, we could imagine a natural species whose members could reproduce only if they and the members of other species suffered immensely. Would it be morally important to protect the functional well-being of this kind of species?

THE NON-INSTRUMENTAL BADNESS OF SPECIES EXTINCTION

The prospects of finding holistic reasons analogous to the standard reason against killing individual animals look somewhat bleak. However, this does not show that holistic accounts are not to be taken seriously, for we might reject the assumption that there must be a close analogy between holistic reasons against species extinction and individualistic reasons against killing animals. Instead we could just to say that species extinction is *non-instrumentally bad*.

The most flat-footed version of this general idea states that *it is bad in itself that a species becomes extinct*. This is a coherent view, but it is difficult to find any supporters. It is not difficult to see why. Since it is overwhelmingly likely that every existing species will become extinct one day (at the very latest at the time when the sun explodes), this view would have no implications at all for what we should do. We cannot prevent this bad thing from happening. Also, one would have thought that the badness of species extinction has something to do with the goodness of species preservation. It is because it is good in itself that species are preserved that it is bad that they become extinct. The badness simply consists in the loss of something that is good in itself.

But what exactly is the good that is lost? One idea would be to say that it is good in itself that a species is ever instantiated. More specifically, the idea is that it is good in itself *that there are at some time some instances of a species*. But this is also a view that does not give us the whole truth. It would not have any implications for what you should do about currently endangered species since there are already some instances of such species around.

A view that would have more practical relevance is the one that says that *at any time* it is good in itself that there are some instances of a species. This good is something you can do something about, since you can decide whether there are going to be any *future* instances of a species. But it is not clear what this view amounts to. Exactly which species is it good to have future instances of? All possible species? This would make it difficult to give priority to preserving endangered species rather than making sure that new ones are created, perhaps by using some form of genetic engineering. But we seem to be much more concerned with preserving the currently existing species rather than creating new ones, or allowing new ones to be created. One could of course wonder why we should be so focused on the species that happen to be around today rather than those that could be around tomorrow.

One answer to this query is that the species that could be around tomorrow would be artificially created by genetic engineering, but it is only natural species that it is important to preserve. But the distinction between natural and non-natural is not very clear. Note, for instance, that since humans are a natural species too, whatever humans do is, in one perfectly respectable sense, natural.[11]

No matter how this issue is resolved, one could ask whether we really think that it is good in itself that existing species continues to have some instances. For example, do we want to say that it is sufficient that these species have instances no matter whether they will have them in zoos or in the wild? If we think it is crucial that they are preserved in their natural habitats, then what has value is not just future instances of a species, but *future instances of an existing species in its natural habitat*.[12]

But not even this seems to give us the whole story. Species preservation is often seen as especially important when it contributes to the *diversity* of species. This suggests that there is an additional value to take into account, diversity, which is not captured by the values of having instances of species. Exactly what this diversity amounts to is not at all clear. It is doubtful that people think that the mere presence of different species constitutes the right kind of diversity. After all, the members of two different species can be very similar in genetic makeup, behavior, and looks. More often diversity is praised when the relevant species show some distinctive features, for example, some distinctive colours and shapes, or some distinctive ways of adaptation to the environment.

Shall we then say that it is especially valuable in itself that there are instances of species in their natural habitats that together show a diversity of certain behaviors and looks? That is an option, but it is important to note that this would not give us a strong rationale for the preservation of individual species. After all, the extinction of a few but very similar species will not make much of a difference to overall diversity.

Another idea would be to say that species diversity is valuable not in itself but as a *constituent part* of something that is good in itself. We could, for instance, say that it is good in itself that we take pleasure in the beauty of the diversity of species and that we take intellectual interest in the complex and surprising ways different species adapt to the environment.[13] This is not to succumb to some narrow form of anthropocentrism, because the species and their features are crucial parts of what is good in itself. On the other hand, it is important that this idea is combined with the idea that species have value in themselves, for you might wonder why it is so crucial that species are constituents of these wholes if they themselves do not have any non-instrumental value. Would anyone consider the diversity of artworks in a museum aesthetically valuable if the artworks themselves lacked aesthetic value?

CONCLUDING REMARKS

We have seen that it is not easy to argue that there is a close analogy between animal killing and species extinction. It is not plausible to say that we owe it to species not to make them go extinct or that we should not frustrate their preference for continued existence, for species cannot be owed anything and have no preferences. It is true that by preventing the extinction of a species we prevent the existence of future members that would have had good lives. In a sense then, killing and extinction are similar in a morally relevant way: in both cases we prevent the existence of something good, a good future of a present animal, or a good life of a future animal. However, whereas killing an animal makes it worse off, it is much less clear that we can make a species worse off by preventing the existence of its future members, for it is unclear whether we should count a species as a well-being subject in its own right.

There seems to be some reason to think that species have non-instrumental value, but it is not clear exactly what this idea amounts to. It is doubtful that it is just the mere continuation of the species that matters. External factors of the species, such as its normal habitat and its role in making up a diversity of species, seem to matter too. Now, these evaluative questions are very hard, and we have to accept that we lack certainty about the non-instrumental value of species. Since the extinction of a species is something irrevocable and we have at least some reason to think that the preservation of species involves significant non-instrumental positive value, we need to be very cautious when deciding to allow some species to become extinct, even if no individual human or animal would be negatively affected in the process. Of course, this does not give us clear guidance in all cases. But we at least know the answer to Sober's intriguing 'n + m' question. In a choice between preserving n sperm whales and m blue whales and preserving n + m sperm whales and o blue whales, it is *rational* to preserve both sperm whales and the blue whales, if all the individual whales will enjoy exactly the same level of well-being. If we preserve both species, we know that we do not lose or gain anything in terms of future well-being, but we have some reason to think that we gain something in terms of the non-instrumental value of species. This means that we would risk doing wrong only if we did not preserve both species. So, it is rational to preserve both species, since it is rational to avoid the risk of doing wrong.

NOTES

1   WWF 2013.
2   For more on such 'last human' scenarios, see Routley and Routley 1973.
3   See, for instance, Gallup 1970.
4   Velleman 1991: 354–57.
5   Bradley 2009: 150–51.
6   Bykvist 2007.
7   Sober 1995: 228.
8   For more on species as individuals, see Hull 1978.
9   For a similar view, see C. Stone 1972: 24.
10 For more on this view, see Rolston 1985: 70.
11 Sober 1995: 234.
12 For this point, see, for instance, Rolston 1985: 72.
13 Regan 1986.

REFERENCES

Agar, Nicholas. 2010. *Humanity's End: Why We Should Reject Radical Enhancement*. Cambridge, MA: MIT Press.

2014. *Truly Human Enhancement: A Philosophical Defense of Limits*. Cambridge, MA: MIT Press.

Annas, Julia. 1995. *The Morality of Happiness*. Oxford University Press.

Archard, David. 2010. "The Obligations and Responsibilities of Parenthood," in Archard and Benatar (eds.), pp. 103–27.

Archard, David, and David Benatar (eds.). 2010. *Procreation and Parenthood: The Ethics of Bearing and Rearing Children*. Oxford University Press.

Bagley, R., and J. D. Farmer. 1992. "Spontaneous Emergence of a Metabolism," in C. Langton, C. E. Taylor, J. D. Farmer, and S. Rasmussen (eds.), *Artificial Life II*. Reading, CA: Addison-Wesley, pp. 93–140.

Baier, Kurt. 1957. "The Meaning of Life," inaugural lecture delivered at the Canberra University College.

Baker, L. R. 2000. *Persons and Bodies: A Constitution View*. Cambridge University Press.

Bartlett, Edward, and Stuart Youngner. 1988. "Human Death and the Destruction of the Neocortex," in Richard Zaner (ed.), *Death: Beyond Whole-Brain Criteria*. Dordrecht, the Netherlands: Kluwer, pp. 199–216.

Becker, Lawrence. 1975. "Human Being: The Boundaries of the Concept," *Philosophy & Public Affairs* 4: 334–59.

Beckwith, Francis J. 2005. "Of Souls, Selves, and Cerebrums: A Reply to Himma," *Journal of the Institute of Medical Ethics* 31(1): 56–60.

Bedau, Mark A. 1991. "Can Biological Teleology Be Naturalized?" *Journal of Philosophy* 88: 647–55.

1996. "The Nature of Life," in Margaret Boden (ed.), *The Philosophy of Artificial Life*. Oxford University Press, pp. 332–57.

1997. "Weak Emergence," *Noûs* 31 (supplement 11): 375–99.

2003. "Downward Causation and Autonomy in Weak Emergence," *Principia* 6: 5–50. Reprinted in Bedau and Humphreys (eds.), pp. 155–88.

2011. "Weak Emergence and Computer Simulation," in Paul Humphreys and Cyrille Imbert (eds.), *Models, Simulations, and Representations.* New York: Routledge, pp. 91–114.

2012. "A Functional Account of Degrees of Minimal Chemical Life," *Synthese* 185: 73–88.

Bedau, Mark A., and Carol Cleland (eds.). 2010. *The Nature of Life: Classical and Contemporary Perspectives from Philosophy and Science.* Cambridge University Press.

Bedau, Mark A., and Paul Humphreys (eds.). 2008. *Emergence: Contemporary Readings in Philosophy and Science.* Cambridge, MA: MIT Press.

Bellioti, Raymond Angelo. 2012. *Posthumous Harm: Why the Dead are Still Vulnerable.* Lanham, MD: Lexington Books.

Belshaw, C. 1993. "Asymmetry and Non-Existence," *Philosophical Studies* 70: 103–16.

2000a. "Death, Pain and Time," *Philosophical Studies* 97: 317–41.

2000b. "Later Death/Earlier Birth," *Midwest Studies in Philosophy* 24: 69–83.

2009. *Annihilation.* Stocksfield: Acumen.

Benatar, D. 1999. "The Unbearable Lightness of Bringing into Being," *Journal of Applied Philosophy* 16: 173–90.

2006. *Better Never to Have Been Born: The Harm of Coming into Existence.* Oxford: Clarendon Press.

Benner, Steven A., Alonso Ricardo, and Matthew A. Carrigan. 2004. "Is There a Common Chemical Model for Life in the Universe?" *Current Opinion in Chemical Biology* 8: 672–89. Reprinted in Bedau and Cleland (eds.), pp. 164–85.

Bennett, Jonathan. 1995. *The Act Itself.* Oxford: Clarendon Press.

Bernat, James. 1998. "A Defense of the Whole-Brain Concept of Death," *Hastings Center Report* 28(2): 14–23.

Bernat, James, Charles Culver, and Bernard Gert. 1981. "On the Definition and Criterion of Death," *Annals of Internal Medicine* 94: 389–94.

Boden, Margaret. 1999. "Alien Life: How Would We Know?" *International Journal of Astrobiology* 2: 121–29. Reprinted in Bedau and Cleland (eds.), pp. 249–59.

Boonin, David. 2003. *A Defense of Abortion.* Cambridge University Press.

Boorse, Christopher, and Roy Sorensen. 1988. "Ducking Harm," *Journal of Philosophy* 85: 115–34.

Bourget, D., and D. Chalmers. 2009. "The PhilPapers Surveys: Results," at http://philpapers.org/surveys/results.pl, accessed March 13, 2013.

Bourne, Craig. 2006. *A Future for Presentism*. Oxford University Press.

Braddock, G. 2000. "Epicureanism, Death, and the Good Life," *Philosophical Inquiry* 22: 47–66.

Bradley, Ben. 2004. "When is Death Bad for the One who Dies?" *Noûs* 38: 1–28.

2009. *Well-Being and Death*. Oxford University Press.

2010. "Eternalism and Death's Badness," in Campbell *et al.* (eds.), pp. 271–81.

2011. "Narrativity, Freedom, and Redeeming the Past," *Social Theory and Practice* 37: 47–62.

2013. "Asymmetries in Benefiting, Harming and Creating," *Journal of Ethics* 17: 37–49.

Bradley, Ben, Fred Feldman, and Jens Johansson (eds.). 2012. *The Oxford Handbook of Philosophy of Death*. Oxford University Press.

Brake, E. 2010. "Willing Parents: A Voluntarist Account of Parental Role Obligations," in Archard and Benatar (eds.), pp. 151–77.

Brandt, Richard. 1979. *A Theory of the Good and the Right*. Oxford University Press.

Broome, John. 2007. "Comments on Dennis McKerlie's 'Rational Choice, Changes in Values over Time, and Well-Being'," *Utilitas* 19: 73–77.

2012. "The Badness of Death and the Goodness of Life," in Bradley *et al.* (eds.), pp. 218–33.

Brown, Jessica. 2000. "Against Temporal Externalism," *Analysis* 60(2): 178–88.

Brueckner, A., and J. M. Fischer. 1986. "Why is Death Bad?" *Philosophical Studies* 50: 213–21.

1993. "The Asymmetry of Early Death and Later Birth," *Philosophical Studies* 71: 327–31.

1998. "Being Born Earlier," *Australasian Journal of Philosophy* 76: 37–45.

Buchanan, Allen. 2009. "Moral Status and Human Enhancement," *Philosophy & Public Affairs* 37: 346–81.

Burley, J. 1998. "The Price of Eggs: Who Should Bear the Costs of Fertility Treatment?" in J. Harris and S. Holm (eds.), *The Future of Human Reproduction: Ethics, Choice, and Regulation*. Oxford University Press, pp. 127–49.

Burley, M. 2007. "Lucretius' Symmetry Argument and the Determinacy of Death," *Philosophical Forum* 38: 327–41.

Bykvist, Krister. 2003. "The Moral Relevance of Past Preferences," in H. Dyke (ed.), *Time and Ethics*. Dordrecht, the Netherlands: Kluwer, pp. 115–36.

2007. "Violations of Normative Invariance: Some Thoughts on Shifty Oughts," *Theoria* 73(2): 98–120.

Cairns-Smith, A. G. 1985. *Seven Clues to the Origin of Life*. Cambridge University Press.

Callahan, Joan C. 1987. "On Harming the Dead," *Ethics* 97(2): 341–52.

Campbell, Joseph Keim, Michael O'Rourke, and Harry S. Silverstein (eds.). 2010. *Time and Identity*. Cambridge, MA: MIT Press.

Campbell, T., and J. McMahan. 2010. "Animalism and the Varieties of Conjoined Twinning," *Theoretical Medicine and Bioethics* 31: 285–301.

Camus, A. 1955. *The Myth of Sisyphus*, trans. J. O'Brian. London: Hamish Hamilton.

Chadwick, R. 1987. "Having Children: Introduction," in R. Chadwick (ed.), *Ethics, Reproduction, and Genetic Control*. London: Croom Helm, pp. 3–43.

Chisholm, Roderick. 1986. *Brentano and Intrinsic Value*. Cambridge University Press.

Cleland, Carol E. 2012. "Life without Definitions," *Synthese* 185: 125–44.

Cleland, Carol E., and C. Chyba. 2007. "Does 'Life' Have a Definition?" in W. T. Sullivan and J. A. Baross (eds.), *Planets and Life: The Emerging Science of Astrobiology*. Cambridge University Press, pp. 119–31. Reprinted in Bedau and Cleland (eds.), pp. 326–39.

Collins, John M. 2006. "Temporal Externalism, Natural Kind Terms, and Scientifically Ignorant Communities," *Philosophical Papers* 35(1): 55–68.

Conly, S. 2005. "The Right to Procreation: Merits and Limits," *American Philosophical Quarterly* 42(2): 105–15.

Cooper, John. 1975. *Reason and Human Good in Aristotle*. Cambridge, MA: Harvard University Press.

Cottingham, John. 2003. *On the Meaning of Life*. London: Routledge.

Craig, William. 1994. "The Absurdity of Life without God," in William Craig, *Reasonable Faith*. Wheaton, IL: Crossway Books, pp. 65–90.

Crick, F. 1981. *Life Itself: Its Origin and Nature*. New York: Simon & Schuster.

Crisp, Roger. 2008. *Reasons and the Good*. Oxford University Press.

Dancy, Jonathan. 2004. "Enticing Reasons," in Wallace *et al.* (eds.), pp. 91–118.

Daniels, Norman. 2009. "Why we Can't Really be Talking about Modifying Human Nature," in Julian Savulescu and Nick Bostrom (eds.), *Human Enhancement*. Oxford University Press, pp. 25–42.

Davis, Nancy. 1984. "Abortion and Self-Defense," *Philosophy & Public Affairs* 13: 175–207.

Deamer, D. 2005. "A Giant Step towards Artificial Life?" *Trends in Biotechnology* 23: 336–38. Reprinted in Bedau and Cleland (eds.), pp. 268–71.

DeGrazia, David. 1999. "Persons, Organisms, and the Definition of Death: A Philosophical Critique of the Higher-Brain Approach," *Southern Journal of Philosophy* 37: 419–40.

   2005. *Human Identity and Bioethics*. Cambridge University Press.

Dennett, Daniel C. 1995. *Darwin's Dangerous Idea: Evolution and the Meanings of Life*. New York: Simon & Schuster.

Dickens, Charles. 1984. *A Christmas Carol*. New York: Penguin.

Doggett, Tyler. 2011. "Recent Work on the Ethics of Self-Defense," *Philosophy Compass* 6: 220–33.

Donagan, Alan. 1977. *The Theory of Morality*. University of Chicago Press.

Dorsey, D. 2013. "Desire Satisfaction and Welfare as Temporal," *Ethical Theory and Moral Practice* 16: 151–71.

Douglas, Thomas. 2008. "Moral Enhancement," *Journal of Applied Philosophy* 25: 228–45.

Dupré, John, and Maureen O'Malley. 2009. "Varieties of Living Things: Life at the Intersection of Lineage and Metabolism," *Philosophy and Theory in Biology* 1: e003.

The Economist. 2005. "Deep Impact: Treating Depression," *The Economist* 374(8416), March 5.

Edwards, P. 1967. "The Meaning and Value of Life," in Klemke and Cahn (eds.), pp. 114–33.

Emilsson, E. K. 2011. "Plotinus on Happiness and Time," in J. Allen *et al.* (eds.), *Oxford Studies in Ancient Philosophy* 40. Oxford University Press, pp. 339–59.

Emmeche, C. 1994. *The Garden in the Machine: The Emerging Science of Artificial Life*. Princeton University Press.

Engelhardt, H. Tristam. 1975. "Defining Death: A Philosophical Problem for Medicine and Law," *Annual Review of Respiratory Disease* 112: 312–24.

Epicurus. 1940. "Letter to Menoeceus," in W. J. Oates (ed.), *The Stoic and Epicurean Philosophers*. New York: The Modern Library, pp. 30–34.

Escobar, Jorge M. 2012. "Autopoiesis and Darwinism," *Synthese* 185: 53–72.

Farmer, D., and A. Belin. 1992. "Artificial Life: The Coming Evolution," in C. Langton *et al.* (eds.), *Artificial Life II*. Reading, CA: Addison-Wesley, pp. 815–40.

Feinberg, Joel. 1984. *The Moral Limits of the Criminal Law*, vol. I, *Harm to Others*. New York: Oxford University Press.

Feit, Neil. 2002. "The Time of Death's Misfortune," *Noûs* 36: 359–83.

Feldman, Fred. 1990. "F. M. Kamm and the Mirror of Time," *Pacific Philosophical Quarterly* 71: 23–27.

1991. "Some Puzzles about the Evil of Death," in Fischer (ed.), pp. 305–36.

1994. *Confrontations with the Reaper.* New York: Oxford University Press.

2004. *Pleasure and the Good Life.* Oxford University Press.

2010. *What is This Thing Called Happiness?* Oxford University Press.

Fischer, John Martin. 1982. "Responsibility and Control," *Journal of Philosophy* 89: 24–40.

1993, ed. *The Metaphysics of Death.* Stanford University Press.

1997. "Death, Badness, and the Impossibility of Experience," *Journal of Ethics* 1: 341–53.

2006a. "Epicureanism about Death and Immortality," *Journal of Ethics* 10: 355–81.

2006b. "Earlier Birth and Later Death: Symmetry through Thick and Thin," in K. McDaniel *et al.* (eds.), *The Good, the Right, Life and Death.* Aldershot: Ashgate, pp. 189–202.

Fischer, John Martin, and Speak, D. 2000. "Death and the Psychological Conception of Personal Identity," *Midwest Studies in Philosophy* 24: 84–93.

Foot, Philippa. 1967. "The Problem of Abortion and the Doctrine of Double Effect," *Oxford Review* 5: 5–15.

1977. "Euthanasia," *Philosophy & Public Affairs* 6: 85–112.

Ford, Norman M. 2002. *The Prenatal Person: Ethics from Conception to Birth.* Oxford: Blackwell.

Frankfurt, Harry. 1969. "Alternate Possibilities and Moral Responsibility," *Journal of Philosophy* 66: 829–39.

Frowe, Helen. 2008. "Equating Innocent Threats and Bystanders," *Journal of Applied Philosophy* 25: 277–90.

Fukuyama, Francis. 2002. *Our Posthuman Future: Consequences of the Biotechnology Revolution.* New York: Farrar, Straus, & Giroux.

Gallois, A. 1994. "Asymmetry in Attitudes and the Nature of Time," *Philosophical Studies* 76: 51–69.

Gallup, G. G., Jr. 1970. "Chimpanzees: Self-Recognition," *Science* 167(3914): 86–87.

Gánti, Tibor. 2003. *The Principles of Life.* Oxford University Press (originally published in 1971). Selections reprinted in Bedau and Cleland (eds.), pp. 102–12.

Gert, Joshua. 2007. "Normative Strength and the Balance of Reasons," *Philosophical Review* 116: 533–62.

Glannon, Walter. 1994. "Temporal Asymmetry, Life, and Death," *American Philosophical Quarterly* 31: 235–44.

Goldschmidt, V. 1979. *Le système stoïcien et l'idée de temps.* Paris: J. Vrin.

Green, Michael, and Daniel Wikler. 1980. "Brain Death and Personal Identity," *Philosophy & Public Affairs* 9: 105–33.

Greenspan, Patricia. 2005. "Asymmetrical Practical Reasons," in M. E. Reicher and J. C. Marek (eds.), *Experience and Analysis*. Vienna: ÖBV and HPT, pp. 387–94.

2010. "Making Room for Options: Moral Reasons, Imperfect Duties, and Choice," *Social Philosophy & Policy* 27: 181–205.

Griffin, James. 1986. *Well-Being*. Oxford: Clarendon Press.

Grover, Dorothy. 1989. "Posthumous Harm," *Philosophical Quarterly* 39: 334–53.

Hadot, P. 1995. "'Only the Present is our Happiness': The Value of the Present Instant in Goethe and in Ancient Philosophy," in Pierre Hadot, *Philosophy as a Way of Life*. Oxford University Press, pp. 217–37.

Haji, I. 1991. "Pre-Vital and Post-Vital Times," *Pacific Philosophical Quarterly* 72: 171–80.

Harman, Elizabeth. 2004. "Can We Harm and Benefit in Creating?" *Philosophical Perspectives, Ethics* 18: 89–113.

2009. "Harming as Causing Harm," in Roberts and Wasserman (eds.), pp. 137–54.

Harris, John. 1998. *Clones, Genes, and Immortality: Ethics and the Genetic Revolution*. Oxford University Press.

2011. "Moral Enhancement and Freedom," *Bioethics* 25: 102–11.

Hawley, Katherine. 2010. "Temporal Parts," in Edward N. Zalta (ed.), *The Stanford Encyclopedia of Philosophy* (winter 2010 edition), http://plato.stanford.edu/archives/win2010/entries/temporal-parts/, accessed September 13, 2013.

Heathwood, Chris. 2005. "The Problem of Defective Desires," *Australasian Journal of Philosophy* 83: 487–504.

2006. "Desire Satisfaction and Hedonism," *Philosophical Studies* 128: 539–63.

Hershenov, David. 2007. "A More Palatable Epicureanism," *American Philosophical Quarterly* 44: 170–80.

Hetherington, Stephen. 2001. "Deathly Harm," *American Philosophical Quarterly* 38: 349–62.

Hill, Thomas E., Jr. 1983. "Self-Regarding Suicide: A Modified Kantian View," in *Suicide and Life Threatening Behavior* 13(4): 254–75.

1991. *Autonomy and Self-Respect*. Cambridge University Press.

2006. "Finding Value in Nature," *Environmental Values* 15: 331–41.

2012a. "Dignity, Problems, and a Proposal," in Thomas E. Hill Jr., *Virtue, Rules, and Justice: Kantian Aspirations*. Oxford University Press, pp. 185–202.

2012b. *Virtue, Rules, and Justice: Kantian Aspirations*. Oxford University Press.

Hohfeld, W. N. 1919. *Fundamental Legal Conceptions*. New Haven, CT: Yale University Press.

Hooker, Brad. 2000. *Ideal Code, Real World*. Oxford: Clarendon Press.

Howard-Snyder, Frances. 2002. "Doing vs. Allowing Harm," in Edward N. Zalta (ed.), *The Stanford Encyclopedia of Philosophy* (winter 2011 edition), http://plato.stanford.edu/archives/win2011/entries/doing-allowing/, accessed September 13, 2013.

Hudson, H. 2007. "I am Not an Animal!" in P. van Inwagen and D. Zimmerman (eds.), *Persons: Human and Divine*. Oxford University Press, pp. 216–34.

Hull, D. 1978. "A Matter of Individuality," *Philosophy of Science* 45: 335–60.

Hurka, Thomas. 1993. *Perfectionism*. Oxford University Press.

Jackman, Henry. 1999. "We Live Forwards but Understand Backwards: Linguistic Practices and Future Behaviour," *Pacific Philosophical Quarterly* 80: 157–77.

Johansson, Jens. 2007. "Non-Reductionism and Special Concern," *Australasian Journal of Philosophy* 85: 641–57.

  2008. "Kaufman's Response to Lucretius," *Pacific Philosophical Quarterly* 89: 470–85.

  2012. "The Timing Problem," in Bradley *et al.* (eds.), pp. 255–74.

Johnston, M. 2007. "'Human Beings' Revisited: My Body is not an Animal," in D. Zimmerman (ed.), *Oxford Studies in Metaphysics* 3. Oxford University Press, pp. 33–74.

Joyce, G. F. 1994. "Foreword," in D. W. Deamer and G. R. Fleischaker (eds.), *Origins of Life: The Central Concepts*. Boston: Jones and Bartlett, pp. xi–xii.

Kamm, F. M. 1988. "Why is Death Bad and Worse Than Pre-Natal Non-Existence?" *Pacific Philosophical Quarterly* 69: 161–64.

  1992. *Creation and Abortion*. Oxford University Press.

  1993. *Mortality, Morality*, vol. I, *Death and Whom to Save from It*. Oxford University Press.

  2007. *Intricate Ethics*. Oxford University Press.

Kant, Immanuel. 1996. *The Metaphysics of Morals*, ed. Mary Gregor. Cambridge University Press.

  2002. *Groundwork for the Metaphysics of Morals*, eds. Thomas E. Hill, Jr. and Arnulf Zweig. Oxford University Press.

Kates, C. A. 2004. "Reproductive Liberty and Overpopulation," *Environmental Values* 13: 51–79.

Kaufman, Fred. 1995. "An Answer to Lucretius' Symmetry Argument against the Fear of Death," *Journal of Value Inquiry* 29: 57–64.

  1996. "Death and Deprivation; or, Why Lucretius' Symmetry Argument Fails," *Australasian Journal of Philosophy* 74: 305–12.

1999. "Pre-Vital and Post-Mortem Non-Existence," *American Philosophical Quarterly* 36: 1–19.

2000. "Thick and Thin Selves: Reply to Fischer and Speak," *Midwest Studies in Philosophy* 24: 94–97.

Kaufman, Whitley. 2010. "Self-Defense, Innocent Aggressors, and the Duty of Martyrdom," *Pacific Philosophical Quarterly* 91: 78–96.

Keller, Evelyn Fox. 2002. "Creating 'Real Life'," in *Making Sense of Life: Explaining Biological Development with Models, Metaphors, and Machines.* Cambridge, MA: Harvard University Press, pp. 285–94. Reprinted in Bedau and Cleland (eds.), pp. 289–94.

Keller, Simon. 2004. "Welfare and the Achievement of Goals," *Philosophical Studies* 121(1): 27–41.

2009. "Welfare as Success," *Noûs* 43(4): 656–83.

Klemke, E. D., and S. Cahn (eds.). 2008. *The Meaning of Life.* Oxford University Press.

Koshland, D. E. 2002. "The Seven Pillars of Life," *Science* 295: 2215–216.

Kramer, M., N. E. Simmonds, and H. Steiner. 1998. *A Debate over Rights.* Oxford University Press.

Kramer, P. D. 1993. *Listening to Prozac.* New York: Viking.

Kraut, Richard. 1994. "Desire and the Human Good," *Proceedings and Addresses of the American Philosophical Association* 68: 39–54.

Kumar, R. 2003. "Who Can Be Wronged?" *Philosophy & Public Affairs* 31(2); 99–118.

Küppers, B. O. 1985. *Molecular Theory of Evolution: Outline of a Physico-Chemical Theory of the Origin of Life.* Berlin: Springer-Verlag.

Kurzweil, Ray. 2005. *The Singularity is Near: When Humans Transcend Biology.* London: Penguin.

Lamont, Julian. 1998. "A Solution to the Puzzle of When Death Harms its Victims," *Australasian Journal of Philosophy* 76: 198–212.

Langer, Richard. 1993. "Silverstein and the 'Responsibility Objection'," *Social Theory and Practice* 19(3): 345–58.

Lee, Patrick. 2004. "The Pro-Life Argument from Substantial Identity: A Defence," *Bioethics* 18(3): 249–63.

Levenbook, Barbara Baum. 1984. "Harming Someone after His Death," *Ethics* 94(3): 407–19.

Lewis, David. 1983. "New Work for a Theory of Universals," *Australasian Journal of Philosophy* 51: 343–77.

1986a. *On the Plurality of Worlds.* Oxford: Blackwell.

1986b. "Causation: Postscripts on Insensitive Causation and Causation by Omission," in *Philosophical Papers,* vol. II. Oxford University Press, pp. 184–212.

Lipson, H., and J. P. Pollack. 2000. "Automatic Design and Manufacture of Robotic Life Forms," *Nature* 406: 974–78. Reprinted in Bedau and Cleland (eds.), pp. 260–67.

Locke, John. 1975. *An Essay Concerning Human Understanding*, ed. P. Nidditch. Clarendon Press. (Original work, 2nd edn., first published 1694.)

Long, A. A., and D. N. Sedley. 1987. *The Hellenistic Philosophers*, vol. I. Cambridge University Press.

Luisi, Pier Luigi. 1998. "About Various Definitions of Life," *Origins of Life and Evolution of the Biosphere* 28: 613–22.

    2006. *The Emergence of Life: From Chemical Origins to Synthetic Biology*. Cambridge University Press.

Luper, Steven. 1992. "The Absurdity of Life," *Philosophy and Phenomenological Research* 52: 1–17.

    2004. "Posthumous Harm," *American Philosophical Quarterly* 41(1): 63–72.

    2007. "Mortal Harm," *Philosophical Quarterly* 57: 239–51.

    2009. *The Philosophy of Death*. Cambridge University Press.

    2012a. "Retroactive Harms and Wrongs," in Bradley *et al.* (eds.), pp. 317–35.

    2012b. "Exhausting Life," *Journal of Ethics: An International Philosophical Review* 16(3): 99–199.

McDaniel, K., and Ben Bradley. 2008. "Desires," *Mind* 117: 267–302.

Machery, Edouard. 2012. "Why I Stopped Worrying about the Definition of Life ... and Why You Should As Well," *Synthese* 185: 145–64.

McInerney, Peter K. 1990. "Does a Fetus Already Have a Future-Like-Ours?" *Journal of Philosophy* 87(5): 264–68.

MacIntyre, Alasdair. 1981. *After Virtue: A Study in Moral Theory*. University of Notre Dame Press.

McMahan, Jeff. 1981. "Problems of Population Theory," *Ethics* 92(1), Special Issue on Rights (October): 96–127.

    1988. "Death and the Value of Life," *Ethics* 99: 32–61.

    1994. "Self-Defense and the Problem of the Innocent Attacker," *Ethics* 104: 252–90.

    2002. *The Ethics of Killing: Problems at the Margins of Life*. Oxford University Press.

    2009. "Self-Defense against Morally Innocent Threats," in P. Robinson, S. Garvey, and K. Kessler (eds.), *Criminal Law Conversations*. New York: Oxford University Press, pp. 385–406.

Markosian, Ned. 2010. "Time," in Edward N. Zalta (ed.), *The Stanford Encyclopedia of Philosophy* (winter 2010 edition), http://plato.stanford.edu/archives/win2010/entries/time/, accessed September 13, 2013.

Marquis, Don. 1989. "Why Abortion is Immoral," *Journal of Philosophy* 86(4): 183–202.

1994. "A Future Like Ours and the Concept of a Person: A Reply to McInerney and Paske," in Louis Pojman and Francis J. Beckwith (eds.), *The Abortion Controversy: A Reader*. Boston, MA: Jones and Bartlett, pp. 354–69.

2007. "The Moral-Principle Objection to Human Embryonic Stem Cell Research," *Metaphilosophy* 38(2–3), Special Issue on Stem Cell Research: The Ethical Issues: 190–206.

2008. "Abortion and Human Nature," *Journal of Medical Ethics* 34(6): 422–26.

2011. "Strong's Objections to the Future of Value Account," *Journal of Medical Ethics: The Journal of the Institute of Medical Ethics* 37: 384–88.

Maturana, H., and F. Varela. 1973. *Autopoiesis: The Organization of the Living*. Dordrecht, the Netherlands: D. Reidel Publishing Company.

Maynard Smith, J. 1975. *The Theory of Evolution*, 3rd edn. New York: Penguin.

1986. *The Problems of Biology*. Oxford University Press.

Maynard Smith, J., and Szathmáry, E. 1995. *The Major Transitions in Evolution*. New York: Freeman.

Mayr, E. 1982. *The Growth of Biological Thought*. Cambridge, MA: Harvard University Press.

Merricks, Trenton. 1994. "Endurance and Indiscernibility," *Journal of Philosophy* 91(4): 165–84.

2007. *Truth and Ontology*. Oxford University Press.

Metz, Theodore. 2009. "Happiness and Meaningfulness: Some Key Differences," in Lisa Bortolotti (ed.), *Philosophy and Happiness*. New York: Palgrave Macmillan, pp. 3–20.

Mill, John Stuart. 1873. *Autobiography*, in J. M. Robson (ed.), *Collected Works of John Stuart Mill*. University of Toronto Press, 1963–, vol. I, pp. 1–290.

1979. *Utilitarianism*, ed. George Sher. Indianapolis: Hackett Publishing.

2001. *Utilitarianism*, 2nd edn., ed. George Sher. Indianapolis and Cambridge: Hackett Publishing.

Mitsis, Philip. 1988. "Epicurus on Death and the Duration of Life," *Proceedings of the Boston Area Colloquium in Ancient Philosophy* 5: 303–22.

Moller, D. 2002. "Parfit on Pains, Pleasures and the Time of Their Occurrence," *Canadian Journal of Philosophy* 32: 67–82.

Monod, J. 1971. *Chance and Necessity*. New York: Vintage Books.

Moore, G. E. 1903. *Principia Ethica*. Cambridge University Press.

1912. *Ethics*. Oxford University Press.

Moreland, J. P., and Scott B. Rae. 2000. *Body and Soul*, Downers Grove, IL: InterVarsity Press.

Nagel, Thomas. 1970. "The Absurd," *Journal of Philosophy* 68: 716–27.

1979. "Death," in *Mortal Questions*. Cambridge University Press, pp. 1–10.

National Research Council of the National Academies. 2007. *Introduction to the Limits of Organic Life in Planetary Systems*. Washington, DC: The National Academies Press. Available at www.nap.edu/category/11919.html.

Noonan, H. 1998. "Animalism versus Lockeanism: A Current Controversy," *Philosophical Quarterly* 48: 302–18.

Nozick, Robert. 1974. *Anarchy, State, and Utopia*. New York: Basic Books.

1981. *Philosophical Explanations*. Cambridge, MA: Belknap Press.

O'Connor, J. 2011. "A Different Person Came Back," National Post online, http://afghanistan.nationalpost.com/%E2%80%98a-different-person-came-back%E2%80%99/, posted July 9, accessed March 16, 2013.

Olson, Eric T. 1997. *The Human Animal*. Oxford University Press.

2002. "Thinking Animals and the Reference of 'I'," *Philosophical Topics* 30: 189–208.

2007. *What Are We? A Study in Personal Ontology*. New York: Oxford University Press.

2013. "The Epicurean View of Death," *Journal of Ethics* 17: 65–78.

In press. "The Remnant-Person Problem," in S. Blatti and P. Snowdon (eds.), *Essays on Animalism*. Oxford University Press.

O'Neill, Onora. 1979. "Begetting, Bearing and Rearing," in O. O'Neill and W. Ruddock (eds.), *Having Children: Philosophical and Legal Reflections on Parenthood*. Oxford University Press, pp. 25–38.

Otsuka, M. 1994. "Killing the Innocent in Self-Defense," *Philosophy & Public Affairs* 23: 74–94.

Overall, C. 2012. *Why Have Children? The Ethical Debate*. Cambridge, MA: MIT Press.

Pace, Norman. 2001. "The Universal Nature of Biochemistry," *Proceedings of the National Academy of Science USA* 98: 805–8. Reprinted in Bedau and Cleland (eds.), pp. 157–63.

Pallis, Christopher. 1999. "On the Brainstem Criterion of Death," in Stuart Younger, Robert Arnold, and Renie Shapiro (eds.), *The Definition of Death*. Baltimore: Johns Hopkins University Press, pp. 93–100.

Parfit, Derek. 1984. *Reasons and Persons*. Oxford University Press.

2012. "We Are Not Human Beings," *Philosophy* 87: 5–28.

Partridge, Ernest. 1981. "Posthumous Interests and Posthumous Respect," *Ethics* 91: 243–64.

Paske, Gerald. 1994. "Abortion and the Neo-Natal Right to Life: A Critique of Marquis's Futurist Argument," in Louis Pojman and Francis J. Beckwith (eds.), *The Abortion Controversy: A Reader*. Boston, MA: Jones and Bartlett, pp. 343–53.

Paul VI. 1968. *Humanae Vitae*, Encyclical on Human Life. Vatican City: The Holy See.

Pennock, Robert T. 2012. "Negotiating Boundaries in the Definition of Life: Wittgensteinian and Darwinian Insights on Resolving Conceptual Border Conflicts," *Synthese* 185: 5–20.

Persson, Ingmar. 2005. *The Retreat of Reason*. Oxford University Press.

Persson, Ingmar., and Julian Savulescu. 2012. *Unfit for the Future: The Need for Moral Enhancement*. Oxford University Press.

Pettigrove, G. 2002. "Death, Asymmetry and the Psychological Self," *Pacific Philosophical Quarterly* 83: 407–23.

Pitcher, George. 1984. "The Misfortunes of the Dead," *American Philosophical Quarterly* 21(2): 183–88.

Pius XI. 1930. *Casti Connubii*, Encyclical on Christian Marriage. Vatican City: The Holy See.

Pollack, J. B., H. Lipson, G. Hornby, and P. Funes. 2001. "Three Generations of Automatically Designed Robots," *Artificial Life* 7: 215–23.

Portmore, Douglas W. 2007. "Desire Fulfillment and Posthumous Harm," *American Philosophical Quarterly* 44(1): 27–38.

Potts, Michael. 2001. "A Requiem for Whole Brain Death," *Journal of Medicine and Philosophy* 26: 479–92.

Poundstone, W. 1985. *The Recursive Universe*. Chicago: Contemporary Books.

President's Commission for the Study of Ethical Problems in Medicine and Biomedical and Behavioral Research. 1981. *Defining Death*. Washington, DC: Government Printing Office.

President's Council on Bioethics. 2008. *Controversies in the Determination of Death*. Washington, DC: President's Council on Bioethics.

Prior, A. N. 1959. "Thank Goodness That's Over," *Philosophy* 34: 12–17.
    1968. "Changes in Events and Changes in Things," in *Papers on Time and Tense*. Oxford University Press, pp. 7–20.

Puccetti, R. 1973. "Brain Bisection and Personal Identity," *British Journal for the Philosophy of Science* 24: 339–55.

Quinn, P. 1997. "The Meaning of Life According to Christianity," in Klemke and Cahn (eds.), pp. 35–41.

Quinn, Warren. 1984. "Abortion: Identity and Loss," *Philosophy & Public Affairs* 13: 24–54.

Quong, Jonathan. 2009. "Killing in Self-Defense," *Ethics* 119: 507–37.

Rasmussen, S., L. Chen, M. Nilsson, and S. Abe. 2003. "Bridging Nonliving and Living Matter," *Artificial Life* 9: 269–316.

Rasmussen, S., L. Chen, D. Deamer, D. Krakauer, N. H. Packard, P. F. Stadler, and M. A. Bedau. 2004. "Transitions from Nonliving to Living Matter," *Science* 303: 963–65.

Rasmussen, S., M. A. Bedau, L. Chen, D. Deamer, D. Krakauer, N. H. Packard, and P. F. Stadler. 2009. *Protocells: Bridging Nonliving and Living Matter*. Cambridge, MA: MIT Press.

Rasmussen, S., Bedau, M. A., McCaskill, J. M., and Packard, N. H. 2009. "Roadmap to Protocells," in Rasmussen *et al.* (eds.), *Protocells*, pp. 71–100.

Rawls, John. 1971. *A Theory of Justice*. Cambridge, MA: Harvard University Press.

Ray, T. S. 1992. "An Approach to the Synthesis of Life," in C. Langton, C. E. Taylor, J. D. Farmer, and S. Rasmussen (eds.), *Artificial Life II*. Reading, CA: Addison-Wesley, pp. 371–408.

Raz, Joseph. 1999. *Practical Reason and Norms*. Oxford University Press (originally published by Hutchinson & Co., 1975).

   2001. *Value, Respect, and Attachment*. Cambridge University Press.

Regan, D. H. 1986. "Duties of Preservation," in B. G. Norton (ed.), *The Preservation of Species*. Princeton University Press, pp. 195–220.

Roberts, M. and D. Wasserman (eds.). 2009. *Harming Future Persons: Ethics, Genetics and the Nonidentity Problem*. Dordrecht, the Netherlands: Springer.

Robertson, John. 1996. *Children of Choice: Freedom and the New Reproductive Technologies*. Princeton University Press.

Rolston, Holmes, III. 1985. "Duties to Endangered Species," in R. Elliot (ed.), *Environmental Ethics*. Oxford University Press, 1995, pp. 60–75.

Rosen, R. 1991. *Life Itself: A Comprehensive Inquiry into the Nature, Origin, and Fabrication of Life*. New York: Columbia University Press.

Rosenbaum, Stephen. 1986. "How To Be Dead and Not Care," *American Philosophical Quarterly* 23: 217–25.

   1989. "The Symmetry Argument: Lucretius against the Fear of Death," *Philosophy and Phenomenological Research* 50: 353–73.

Ross, W. D. 1930. *The Right and the Good*. Oxford University Press.

Routley, R. and V. Routley. 1973. "Is There a Need for a New Environmental Ethics," in *Proceedings of the 15th World Congress of Philosophy*, vol. I, Sophia, Bulgaria: Sophia Press, pp. 205–10.

Ruiz-Mirazo, K., and Moreno, A. 2012. "Autonomy in Evolution: From Minimal to Complex Life," *Synthese* 185: 21–52.

Ruiz-Mirazo, K., J. Peretó, and A. Moreno. 2004. "A Universal Definition of Life: Autonomy and Open-Ended Evolution," *Origins of Life and Evolution of the Biosphere* 34: 323–46. Reprinted in Bedau and Cleland (eds.), pp. 310–25.

Sagan, Carl. 1970. "Life," in *Encyclopedia Britannica*, 15th edn., vol. X. New York: Macropaedia. Reprinted in Bedau and Cleland (eds.), pp. 303–6.

Sagre, D., D. Ben-Eli, and D. Lancet. 2000. "Compositional Genomes: Prebiotic Information Transfer in Mutually Catalytic Noncovalent Assemblies," *Proceedings of the National Academy of Sciences* 97: 4112–117.

Savulescu, Julian, Bennett Foddy, and Matthew Clayton. 2004. "Why We Should Allow Performance Enhancing Drugs in Sport," *British Journal of Sports Medicine* 38: 666–70.

Scanlon, T. M. 1998. *What We Owe Each Other*. Cambridge, MA: Harvard University Press.

Schaffer, Jonathan. 2004. "Causes Need Not Be Physically Connected to Their Effects: The Case for Negative Causation," in C. Hitchcock (ed.), *Contemporary Debates in Philosophy of Science*. Oxford: Blackwell, pp. 197–216.

Schiffrin, S. 1999. "Wrongful Life, Procreative Responsibility, and the Significance of Harm," *Legal Theory* 5(2): 117–48.

Schrödinger, E. 1969. *What is Life?* Cambridge University Press.

Schwartz, Stephen D. 1990. *The Moral Question of Abortion*. Chicago: Loyola University Press.

Shewmon, D. Alan. 2001. "The Brain and Somatic Integration: Insights into the Standard Biological Rationale for Equating 'Brain Death' with Death," *Journal of Medicine and Philosophy* 26: 457–78.

Shoemaker, S. 1999. "Self, Body, and Coincidence," *Proceedings of the Aristotelian Society, Supplementary Volumes* 73: 287–306.

Sider, Theodore. 2001a. *Four-Dimensionalism*. Oxford University Press.

2001b. "Criteria of Personal Identity and the Limits of Conceptual Analysis," *Philosophical Perspectives* 15: 189–209.

2012. "The Evil of Death: What Can Metaphysics Contribute?" in Bradley *et al.* (eds.), pp. 155–66.

Silverstein, Harry. 1980. "The Evil of Death," *Journal of Philosophy* 77: 401–24.

2000. "The Evil of Death Revisited," *Midwest Studies in Philosophy* 24: 116–34.

2010. "The Time of the Evil of Death," in Campbell *et al.* (eds.), pp. 283–95.

Simon, J. R. 2010. "Playing the Odds: A New Response to Lucretius's Symmetry Argument," *European Journal of Philosophy* 18: 414–24.

Skinner. 1942. *Skinner* v. *The State of Oklahoma, Ex. Rel. Williamson* (1942) 316 U.S. 535.

Snowdon, Paul. 1990. "Persons, Animals, and Ourselves," in C. Gill (ed.), *The Person and the Human Mind*. Oxford: Clarendon Press, pp. 83–107.

Sober, Elliot. 1992. "Learning from Functionalism: Prospects for Strong Artificial Life," in C. Langton, C. E. Taylor, J. D. Farmer, and S. Rasmussen (eds.), *Artificial Life II*. Reading, CA: Addison-Wesley, pp. 749–65. Reprinted in Bedau and Cleland (eds.), pp. 225–35.

1995. "Philosophical Problems for Environmentalism," in R. Elliot (ed.), *Environmental Ethics*. Oxford University Press, pp. 226–47.

Staiti, A. 2013. "A Grasp from Afar," *Continental Philosophy Review* 46: 21–36.

Statman, D. 2003. "The Right to Parenthood: An Argument for a Narrow Interpretation," *Ethical Perspectives* 10(3–4): 224–35.

Stone, Christopher. 1972. *Should Trees Have Standing?* Los Altos: William Kaufmann.

Stone, Jim. 1987. "Why Potentiality Matters," *Canadian Journal of Philosophy* 17(4): 815–30.

Strawson, Galen. 2004. "Against Narrativity," *Ratio* (n.s.) 17(4): 428–52.

Suits, David. 2001. "Why Death is Not Bad for the One Who Died," *American Philosophical Quarterly* 38: 69–84.

2012. "Death and Other Nothings," *Philosophical Forum* 43: 215–30.

Sumner, L. W. 1996. *Welfare, Happiness, and Ethics*. Oxford: Clarendon Press.

Szostak, J. W., D. P. Bartel, and P. L. Luisi. 2001. "Synthesizing Life," *Nature* 409: 387–90.

Taylor, Charles. 1989. *Sources of the Self: The Making of the Modern Identity*. Cambridge, MA: Harvard University Press.

1992. "Fleshing Out *Artificial Life II*," in C. Langton, C. E. Taylor, J. D. Farmer, and S. Rasmussen (eds.), *Artificial Life II*. Reading, CA: Addison-Wesley, pp. 25–38.

Taylor, James Stacey. 2005. "The Myth of Posthumous Harm," *American Philosophical Quarterly* 42(4): 311–22.

2012. *Death, Posthumous Harm, and Bioethics*. Abingdon: Routledge.

Taylor, Richard. 1970. *Good and Evil*. New York: Macmillan.

1987. "Time and Life's Meaning," *Review of Metaphysics* 40(4): 675–86.

Thompson, Michael. 2004. "What is it to Wrong Someone? A Puzzle about Justice," in Wallace *et al.* (eds.), pp. 333–84.

Thomson, Judith Jarvis. 1971. "A Defense of Abortion," *Philosophy & Public Affairs* 1: 47–66.

1976. "Self-Defense and Rights." Lindley Lecture at the University of Kansas. Reprinted in Judith Jarvis Thomson, *Rights, Restitution, and Risk*. Cambridge, MA: Harvard University Press, 1986, pp. 33–48.

1990. *The Realm of Rights*. Cambridge, MA: Harvard University Press.

1991. "Self-Defense," *Philosophy & Public Affairs* 20: 283–310.

2008. "Turning the Trolley," *Philosophy & Public Affairs* 36: 359–74.

Tolstoy, Leo. 1884. *Confession*.

Tomkow, Terrance. 2011. "Retributive Ethics," at www.tomkow.com, accessed September 13, 2013.

2012. "Self Defense," at www.tomkow.com, accessed September 13, 2013.

Tooley, Michael. 1972. "Abortion and Infanticide," *Philosophy & Public Affairs* 2(1): 37–65.

1983. *Abortion and Infanticide*. Oxford University Press.

2009. *Abortion: Three Perspectives*. With Alison Jaggar, Philip E. Devine, and Celia Wolf-Devine. Oxford University Press.

2013. *Abortion: Oxford Bibliographies Online Research Guide*. Oxford University Press.

Truog, Robert, and Franklin Miller. 2008. "The Dead Donor Rule and Organ Transplantation," *New England Journal of Medicine* 359: 674–75.

Tye, M. 2003. *Consciousness and Persons: Unity and Identity*. Cambridge, MA: MIT Press.

Unamuno, Miguel. 1954. *Tragic Sense of Life*. New York: Dover.

Unger, Peter. 1990. *Identity, Consciousness, and Value*. Oxford University Press.

1996. *Living High and Letting Die*. Oxford University Press.

Uniacke, Suzanne. 1994. *Permissible Killing: The Self-Defence Justification of Homicide*. Cambridge University Press.

van Inwagen, Peter. 1990. *Material Beings*. Ithaca, NY: Cornell University Press.

Veatch, Robert. 1975. "The Whole-Brain-Oriented Concept of Death: An Outmoded Philosophical Formulation," *Journal of Thanatology* 3: 13–30.

Velleman, David J. 1991. "Well-Being and Time," *Pacific Philosophical Quarterly* 72: 48–77. Reprinted in Fischer (ed.), pp. 329–57.

2008. "Persons in Prospect," *Philosophy & Public Affairs* 36(3): 221–88.

Vihvelin, Kadri, and Terrance Tomkow. 2005. "The Dif," *Journal of Philosophy* 102: 183–205.

Von Wright, G. H. 1963. *The Varieties of Goodness*. London: Routledge and Kegan Paul.

Wallace, R. J., P. Petit, S. Scheffler, and M. Smith (eds.). 2004. *Reason and Value: Themes from the Moral Philosophy of Joseph Raz*. Oxford University Press.

Warren, James. 2004. *Facing Death: Epicurus and his Critics*. Oxford University Press.

Warren, Mary Anne. 1973. "On the Moral and Legal Status of Abortion," *The Monist* 57(1): 43–61.

Wiggins, David. 1980. *Sameness and Substance*. Oxford: Blackwell.

Williams, Bernard. 1973. "A Critique of Utilitarianism," in J. J. C. Smart and Bernard Williams, *Utilitarianism: For and Against*. Cambridge University Press, pp. 77–150.

1979. "Moral Luck," in *Moral Luck*. Cambridge University Press, pp. 20–39.

Wimsatt, W. C. 1987. "False Models as Means to Truer Theories," in Matthew H. Nitecki and Antoni Hoffman (eds.), *Neutral Models in Biology*. Oxford University Press, pp. 23–55.

Wolf, Susan. 2000. "The Moral of Moral Luck," *Philosophical Exchange* 31: 5–19.

Woodward, J. 1986. "The Non-Identity Problem," *Ethics* 96:4: 804–31.

WWF. 2013. "List of Critically Endangered Species," at http://worldwildlife.org/species/directory?sort=extinction_status&direction=desc, accessed September 13, 2013.

INDEX

abortion, 8, 241, 243–63, 282
  and euthanasia, 251–52
  extreme views of, 245–46
  moderate views of, 244–45
  and neo-Lockean persons, 243–63
  and potentiality account, 246, 256–59
  and reprogramming objection,
    259–61
  and rights, 246, 250, 259
aiding others, 300–14
  and directed versus undirected
    duties, 302
  and duty of justice versus
    benevolence, 304
  and imperfect duties, 301–14
Alexander of Aphrodisias, 130
animalism, 2, 31–45, 72, 91
animals
  death not bad for, 320
  killing of not wrong, 254
  and meaninglessness, 198
  and species extinction, 316–29
  unable to think, 45
Annas, Julia, 131
Aristotle, 36, 120, 126, 130, 207
asymmetrists, 6, 166, 168, 169, 175, 179
atemporalism, 5, 149, 150, 151, 153–63

Bagley, R., 15
Baier, Kurt, 202
Baker, L. R., 41, 46, 97
Bartlett, Edward, 97
Becker, Lawrence, 96, 97
Beckwith, Francis, 245
Belliotti, Raymond, 196
Belshaw, Chris, 179, 180

Benatar, David, 7, 237, 241
Benner, Steven, 18
Bennett, Jonathan, 298
Bernat, James, 96
bioconservativism, 215, 223
Boden, Margaret, 13
Boonin, David, 244
Boorse, Christopher, 299
Bourne, Craig, 54
Braddock, G., 146
Bradley, Ben, 53, 54, 149, 152, 154, 160,
    164, 196, 320
brain view, 35, 37, 38, 40, 41
Brake, E., 242
Brandt, Richard, 117
Broome, John, 58, 163
Brown, Jessica, 61
Brueckner, Anthony, 180
Buchanan, Allen, 222
Burley, M., 180, 241
Bykvist, Krister, 158, 160, 164

Cairns-Smith, A. G., 14, 21
Callahan, Joan, 196
Campbell, T., 37, 46
Camus, Albert, 208
Chadwick, Ruth, 240
Chisholm, Roderick, 113
Cleland, Carol, 14, 19
Collins, John, 61
Conly, S., 240
Cottingham, J., 209
counterfactual intervener, 138–45
Craig, William, 210
Crick, Francis, 15
Crisp, Roger, 117

348

Lightning Source UK Ltd.
Milton Keynes UK
UKOW05f1822070517
300648UK00006B/58/P

9 781107 606760